INDIAN DEVELOPMENT

T0323387

UNU WORLD INSTITUTE FOR DEVELOPMENT ECONOMICS RESEARCH (UNU/WIDER) was established by the United Nations University as its first research and training centre and started work in Helsinki, Finland in 1985. The purpose of the Institute is to undertake applied research and policy analysis on structural changes affecting the developing and transitional economies, to provide a forum for the advocacy of policies leading to robust, equitable and environmentally sustainable growth, and to promote capacity strengthening and training in the field of economic and social policy-making. Its work is carried out by staff researchers and visiting scholars in Helsinki and through networks of collaborating scholars and institutions around the world.

INDIAN DEVELOPMENT
Selected Regional Perspectives

Editors

JEAN DRÈZE

and

AMARTYA SEN

A study prepared for the
World Institute for Development Economics Research
of the United Nations University (UNU/WIDER)

OXFORD
UNIVERSITY PRESS

Great Clarendon Street, Oxford, OX2 6DP,
United Kingdom

Oxford University Press is a department of the University of Oxford.
It furthers the University's objective of excellence in research, scholarship,
and education by publishing worldwide. Oxford is a registered trade mark of
Oxford University Press in the UK and in certain other countries

© United Nations University World Institute for
Development Economics Research (UNU-WIDER) 1997

The moral rights of the authors have been asserted

First published 1997
Reprinted 2006
First published in paperback 2020

Published in the United States of America by Oxford University Press
198 Madison Avenue, New York, NY 10016, United States of America

British Library Cataloguing in Publication Data
Data available

Library of Congress Cataloging in Publication Data
Data available

ISBN 978-0-19-829204-3 (Hbk.)
ISBN 978-0-19-886016-7 (Pbk.)

In memory of
T.N. Krishnan

PREFACE

The studies in this volume focus on the lessons that emerge from the diversity of regional experiences within India. They supplement what can be learned from international comparisons of successes and failures in economic development. The work is motivated by the general approach of looking for lessons for India from the diversity of its own experiences.

The experience of rapid economic development in many developing countries, especially those in east Asia, has recently engaged the attention of development economists in general and those concerned with the Indian economy in particular. In our monograph, published last year, *India: Economic Development and Social Opportunity* (Drèze and Sen, 1995), we have examined the lessons to be learned both from abroad and from the variety of experiences within India. This companion volume of essays scrutinizes the diverse experiences within India at greater depth. The studies include successes as well as failures, since there are lessons to be learned from each.

In chapter 1, 'Radical Needs and Moderate Reforms', Amartya Sen presents an analysis of the persistence of endemic deprivation in India, and of the role of public action in addressing that problem. This essay, which draws on the companion volume (Drèze and Sen, 1995), stresses the need to go beyond the narrow focus of current policy debates on the issue of market-oriented reforms aimed at accelerating the rate of economic growth. These reforms can contribute to the elimination of basic deprivations in India, but they need to be supported and supplemented by a far more active involvement in the provision of basic education, health care, social security, and related fields.

Chapters 2–4 present case studies of particular states in India, focusing on their respective experiences in improving living conditions. Chapter 2, by Jean Drèze and Haris Gazdar, discusses the problem of economic and social backwardness in Uttar Pradesh and its causal antecedents. Among these are the disastrous functioning of public services in rural areas, the persistence of widespread illiteracy, and the suppression of women's agency in society. The authors also discuss the social and political circumstances underlying these diverse failures.

Chapter 3, by Sunil Sengupta and Haris Gazdar, analyses recent attempts to address the challenge of rural poverty in West Bengal. One distinguishing feature of the recent history of that state is a significant change in the balance of political power in favour of disadvantaged groups, which took a concrete expression in 1977 when the Left Front coalition came to office at the state level. This change in the balance of power has made it possible to implement a number of far-reaching social programmes that are often considered 'politically infeasible' in many other states, notably including land reform and the revitalization of democratic institutions at the village level. At the same time, public policies concerned with health, education, and related matters have been comparatively neglected, and, correspondingly, the improvement of living conditions in West Bengal in recent years has remained relatively slow. These are serious failures of the West Bengal experience, but they do not detract from the value of that experience as an example of the possibility of radical political change in India today.

Chapter 4, by V.K. Ramachandran, provides a major historical account of Kerala's impressive record in eliminating basic deprivations at an early stage of economic development. Kerala stands out among Indian states in terms of a wide range of social indicators, including a life expectancy above 72 years and near-universal literacy in the younger age groups. The paper relates these social achievements to historical conditions and political action. The author draws particular attention to the role of early educational expansion, combined with a significant reduction of social and economic inequalities.

Chapter 5 examines inter-district patterns of fertility, child mortality, and gender bias in India using data from the 1981 census. The findings highlight the powerful effects of variables relating to women's agency (e.g. female literacy and female labour-force participation) on mortality and fertility. Further, higher levels of female literacy and female labour-force participation are associated with significantly lower levels of female disadvantage in child survival. In contrast, variables relating to the general level of development and modernization have relatively weak effects on demographic outcomes.

In this volume of essays, the primary focus of attention is on the direct role of public action in enhancing social opportunities. The case studies are not directly concerned with the relationship between social policies and economic growth, or with the recently launched economic reforms. These studies, however, do have considerable bearing on the broader question of the role and reach of the market mechanism, and on the diverse demands of responsible governance. These matters are discussed in greater detail in the companion volume (Drèze and Sen, 1995), where we have argued for putting the debate on economic reforms in a much broader perspective. The central issue is to expand the social opportunities open to the people. In so far as these opportunities are compromised by counterproductive regulations and bureaucratic controls, the removal of these hindrances must be seen to be extremely important. But the creation of social opportunities on a broad basis requires much more than the 'freeing' of markets. It calls, in particular, for expansion of educational facilities and health care for all (irrespective of incomes and means), and public provisions for nutritional support and social security. It also demands a general political, economic, and social programme for reducing the inequalities that blot out social opportunities from the lives of so many hundreds of millions of Indian citizens.

The inequalities build on each other. For instance, as discussed in the chapter on Uttar Pradesh, the education of children of poorer social groups and less privileged classes and castes can be fairly comprehensively neglected without this becoming a politically explosive social scandal, as it would have undoubtedly become had more powerful people been at the neglected end. The result is continued illiteracy, ill health, and other deprivations that keep the underdogs in a state of persistent weakness, making the remedying inequities that much more difficult. These deprivations are of direct importance to the nature of the lives that people can lead, and they can also have a crippling role in preventing the emergence of participatory economic expansion.

To remedy this situation, what is needed is not only more — and more focused — public action, but also general political interest in these deprivations. Public attention and activism may be the ultimate guarantee of governmental initiative and action, especially in a multi-party democracy. Hence the political parties — whether or not in office — have significant roles to play. In understanding and explaining the terrible overall record of India in the creation of social opportunities, not only the parties in office but also opposition parties have some considerable responsibility.

It is also important to take note of the fact that success in social policies need not automatically translate into great economic performance. The issue of economic incentives and the creation of an appropriate climate for production, investment, trade, and commerce has to be addressed, and while a favourable social background is important for this (as it has been in, say, South Korea or China), it is not in itself adequate. For example, despite its excellent social achievements, Kerala's record in domestic economic growth has not been impressive (on this see Drèze and Sen, 1995). The need for systematic institutional change that would favour economic expansion is at least as strong in Kerala as it is in the rest of India. The complementarity between economic incentives and social opportunities in generating fast and participatory growth operates both ways.

This study was prepared for the World Institute for Development Economics Research (WIDER) of the United Nations University, and was initiated under the Directorship of Dr. Lal Jayawardena. It draws particularly on the lessons that emerged from the 'India project' located at Santiniketan, directed by Professor Sunil Sengupta. We are grateful to WIDER for supporting this work, and to the Leverhulme Trust for supporting Haris Gazdar's contribution. At various stages of this project, the authors of the different chapters have also used the facilities of STICERD at the London School of Economics, the Centre for Development Economics at the Delhi School of Economics, the Indira Gandhi Institute of Development Research, the International Development Research Centre (IDRC, Canada), and Harvard University, and we take this opportunity of thanking them also. Finally, we are deeply grateful to Meera Samson for excellent editorial assistance, and to Jackie Jennings for ensuring smooth coordination of the activities undertaken under this project.

J.D.
A.S.

CONTRIBUTORS

JEAN DRÈZE
    Centre for Development Economics at the Delhi School of Economics, Delhi
HARIS GAZDAR
    STICERD, London School of Economics
ANNE-CATHERINE GUIO
    Centre de Recherche en Economie du Développement, Namur, Belgium
MAMTA MURTHI
    Department of Economics, University of Sussex, UK
V.K. RAMACHANDRAN
    Indira Gandhi Institute of Development Research, Bombay
AMARTYA SEN
    Department of Economics, Harvard University, Cambridge, MA
SUNIL SENGUPTA
    Department of Economics, Visva-Bharati, Santiniketan, West Bengal

CONTENTS

FIGURES

TABLES

1

RADICAL NEEDS AND
MODERATE REFORMS*

Amartya Sen

1. ENDS, MEANS AND PRACTICAL REASON

Economic policies in India have undergone much change over the
last few years, and more changes are in the process of being implemented. The central approach underlying these reforms, initiated
in 1991, involves a greater reliance on the market mechanism, and
this translates into a class of public policies including deregulation
and reduction of governmental controls, greater autonomy of private
investment, less use of the public sector, more opening of the
economy to international trade, less restrictions on the convertibility
of the rupee, and so on. While many critics had wanted faster
reforms (and a quicker change — basically in the same direction),
there can be little doubt about the gathering force and the growing
reach of the reforms, or about the break that has been initiated in
the established conventions of Indian planning and policy-making.
Nothing quite like this has happened earlier in the Indian economy,
since independence — or for that matter, before it.

Outside India the reforms have been fairly universally welcomed,
but they have been, since their inception, the subject of severe
debate within India. The controversies have been extensive, and
the arguments on each side quite forceful and firm. This collection
of essays is not — at least not directly — a contribution to those
debates. Rather, it is a part of an attempt to shift the concentration
of economic arguments away from the rather limited issues on

* This chapter draws extensively on a monograph jointly authored by Jean Drèze
and myself, *India: Economic Development and Social Opportunity* (Oxford University
Press, 1995). The research underlying that monograph (to be referred to occasionally
as the 'companion volume') has been closely connected with the studies included
in the present volume.

which these largely political debates have tended to focus. The object is not so much to search for authentic answers to familiar and well-rehearsed questions, but to ask and explore quite a different set of questions. These broader investigations, we argue, are needed right now, and they can *inter alia* alter even the way the more traditional queries are answered.

There are two elementary points of departure. First, there must be an attempt to link the strategies of development to something more fundamental, in particular, the *ends* of economic and social development. Why do we seek development? What can it achieve, if fruitful? How are the successes and failures of policies — including the 'reforms' of traditional policies — to be judged? It is only with an explicit recognition of the basic ends that debates on means and strategies can be adequately founded.

The second basic departure takes us beyond the scrutiny of ends, to the investigation of means. What are the means that have to be employed to achieve these ends felicitously? While the debates on the current reforms concentrate on a particular class of means related to the use or non-use of markets (such as incentives for private investment, reliance on international trade, and so on), there are many other means, especially dealing with the 'social' side of economic operations and successes, which typically tend not to figure in these debates. To the foundational lacuna of neglecting the scrutiny of the basic ends is, thus, added the more immediate gap of ignoring the examination of some powerful means that help us to achieve those ends. In fact, we argue that achievement of even the limited objectives of the current reforms will depend crucially on conscious and organized pursuit of the social means on which economic performance and results are frequently conditional.

This collection of essays presents and develops the arguments for taking a much broader view of the needed economic and social change in India. In this first chapter the reasoning is developed at the national level, looking at India as a whole. That reasoning has been developed more extensively in the companion volume (Drèze and Sen, 1995). While that is mainly a 'national' study, the argument draws, among other things, on the deep diversities that characterize the varied economy of India. The diversities are partly related to India's varied history before independence (for example, the bulk of modern Kerala is made up of what were so-called 'native states' — Travancore and Cochin — formally outside the British empire) and after the British left (for example, the relative strengths of political parties have been quite different in the different regions of India). But the diversity relates also to the nature of the Indian constitution, which identifies as 'state subject' many areas of governmental action that are crucial to economic and social development. Thus, the historical diversities have tended to be consolidated and reinforced by the legal structure of the Indian union. An understanding of the Indian economy has to be informed by an adequate recognition of deep-seated regional diversities and heterogeneities.

2. REGIONAL DIVERSITIES AND CONTRASTS

Given the extremely heterogeneous character of the Indian economy and society, India's achievements and failures cannot be understood in composite terms, and it is essential to examine the experiences in sufficiently disaggregative form — and in adequate detail. In the set of studies in this book, the regional perspective has been extensively explored, concentrating on three states in particular: Kerala, West Bengal, and Uttar Pradesh. Kerala's achievements in the social fields have been quite remarkable, including an achieved life expectancy of well over 72 years (69 for males and 74 for females by 1991) that compares well with China's (69 years) and South Korea's (71 years) achievements, despite the much greater economic advancement of these other countries. At the other end, Uttar Pradesh remains one of the most backward states in India, and had this state of 140 million people been an independent country, it would have been not only one of the largest, but also one of the most socially deprived countries in this world — giving its citizens less than some of the worst-performing economies in sub-Saharan Africa. We have to ask why — and to what extent — Kerala has succeeded, and why Uttar Pradesh has failed so badly in precisely those fields. West Bengal's experience is more mixed, including some remarkable achievements and some conspicuous failures. Again, we have to identify the successes and deficiencies there, and link them with the nature of policies pursued and the overall political economy of West Bengal.

The internal diversities in India offer a great opportunity to learn from each other. This is part of the objective of this set of studies. This must not, however, be taken to suggest that the lessons for India must come mostly from 'inside'. On the contrary, there is a great deal to be learnt from successes and failures of other countries as well. Even Kerala, successful as it is in many social fields, must learn more about how to generate and stimulate straightforward economic growth — an area in which it has been conspicuously unsuccessful.

Some 'lessons from abroad' have often been aired in the current economic debates, particularly in motivating the on-going reforms and deregulation. It is, however, important, in learning from other countries, to take an adequately comprehensive and discriminating view of their experiences. I shall argue, later on in this chapter, that some parts of the essential lessons — related in particular to the generation of social opportunities — have been particularly neglected in the typical readings of these experiences.[1] This collection of studies is aimed at scrutinizing the lessons from other countries as well as from within India itself.

One of the broad conclusions to emerge is the need for much more radical changes in the Indian economy and society, in order to achieve the basic goals that were unambiguously outlined at the time of India's independence, but which still remain largely unaccomplished. The problem with the economic reforms currently under way is not that they are not needed, nor that they are overexacting, but that they are basically inadequate and unbalanced.[2] The departures are too moderate — and too tolerant of parts of the established tradition of economic planning in India. More — rather than less — radicalism is needed at this time. In this first essay, an attempt is made to put that general case forward.[3] This is followed, in subsequent chapters, by the regional studies that look respectively at the experiences of Uttar Pradesh, Kerala, and West Bengal.

[1] This diagnosis has been developed in greater detail in the companion volume (Drèze and Sen, 1995).

[2] For a more comprehensive development of this line of analysis and its extensive implications, see Drèze and Sen (1995).

[3] The sections that follow have much in common with the first Lakdawala Lecture ('Beyond Liberalization: Social Opportunity and Human Capability'), which I gave in New Delhi, at the Institute of Social Sciences, on 29 June 1994.

3. INTRINSIC VALUE AND INSTRUMENTAL ROLE OF HUMAN CAPABILITIES

In his famous speech on India's 'tryst with destiny', on the eve of independence in August 1947, Jawaharlal Nehru reminded the country that the task ahead included 'the ending of poverty and ignorance and disease and inequality of opportunity'. Some achievements have indeed been made in these general areas, including the elimination of substantial famines, fairly successful functioning of our multiparty democratic system, and the emergence of a very large and quite successful scientific community — achievements that compare favourably with what has happened in many other parts of the world. However, it is not hard to see that much of the task that Nehru had identified remains largely unaccomplished, and that we have fallen quite far behind the best performers. We have to ask what obstacles we face, how they can be eliminated, and whether we are already on course in remedying the underlying deficiencies.

Nehru's list of the tasks that India faces is well worth remembering in taking stock of where we are, and more particularly where we are *not*. As Nehru pointed out, the elimination of ignorance, of illiteracy, of remediable poverty, of preventable disease, and of needless inequalities in opportunities must be seen as objectives that are valued for their own sake. They expand our freedom to lead the lives we have reason to value, and these elementary capabilities are of importance on their own.[4] While they can and do contribute to economic growth and to other usual measures of economic performance, their value does not lie only in these instrumental contributions. Economic growth is, of course, important, but it is valuable precisely because it helps to eradicate deprivation and to improve the capabilities and the quality of life of ordinary people.

We must not make the mistake — common in some circles — of taking the growth rate of GNP to be the ultimate test of success, and of treating the removal of illiteracy, ill-health, and social deprivation

[4] The capability perspective in assessing individual advantage and social progress has been presented and analysed in Sen (1980, 1985a, 1985b), Drèze and Sen (1989), and Nussbaum and Sen (1993). For extensions, applications, and critiques, see also Rawls (1982, 1993), Roemer (1982, 1994), Atkinson (1983, 1989), Nussbaum (1988), Arneson (1989, 1990), Pogge (1989), Crocker (1991), Cohen (1989, 1990, 1994), Hossain (1990), Schokkaert and van Ootegem (1990), van Parijs (1990), Sugden (1993), Herrero (1994), among other contributions.

as — at best — possible means to that hallowed end. The first and the most important aspect of Nehru's listing of what we have to do is to make clear that the elimination of illiteracy, ill-health, and other avoidable deprivations are valuable for their own sake — they are 'the tasks' that we face. The more conventional criteria of economic success (such as a high growth rate, a sound balance of payments, and so forth) are to be valued only as means to deeper ends. It would, therefore, be a mistake to see the development of education, health care, and other basic achievements *only* or *primarily* as expansions of 'human resources' — the accumulation of 'human capital' — as if people were just the *means* of production and not its ultimate *end*. The bettering of human life does not have to be justified by showing that a person with a better life is also a better producer.

This issue of intrinsic importance is an appropriate starting point, because we must assert first things first, but our analysis cannot, of course, stop at basic issues only. Something that is of intrinsic importance can, *in addition*, also be instrumentally momentous, without compromising its intrinsic value. Basic education, good health, and other human attainments are not only directly valuable as constituent elements of our basic capabilities, these capabilities can *also* help in generating economic success of a more standard kind, which in turn can contribute to enhancing the quality of human life even more. Many of the ingredients of a good quality of life — including education, health, and elementary freedoms — clearly do have instrumental roles in making us more productive and helping us to generate more outputs and incomes. As I shall presently discuss, the lessons of economic and social progress across the world over the last few decades have forcefully drawn attention to the instrumental importance of education, health, and other features of the quality of human life in generating fast and shared economic growth (on top of the direct intrinsic importance they have). It will, of course, be a mistake to see the enhancement of human capabilities as being invariably effective in raising economic performance, since the political economy of *actual use* can be very different from the *potential* possibilities generated. But without generating those possibilities the question of their use would not even arise, and this is a lesson that many other countries have learned with very good effect.

In looking back at what Jawaharlal Nehru saw as our 'tryst with destiny', we must both assert (1) the inalienable eminence of basic capabilities and the quality of life in judging the success of economic and social policies, and (2) the contingent but significant practical importance of many of these capabilities (especially those related to education, health, and elementary freedoms) in promoting economic growth, and through it further advancing the quality of life that people can enjoy. While the improvement of human life is its own reward, it also offers — as it happens — other rewards which in turn can create the possibilities of further augmentation of the quality of life and our effective freedom to lead the lives we have reason to seek.

The subject of development economics, since its inception in its modern form in the nineteen-forties, has been full of sombre theses of a multitude of 'vicious circles', and there is a general air of pessimism that has characterized this discipline. In that context, the importance of this 'virtuous circle' in achieving economic and social progress can scarcely be overemphasized.

4. ON LEARNING FROM OTHERS AND FROM INDIA

India can learn a lot from the experiences of other countries which have done, in different ways, better than we have. More on that presently, but we must also note the fact that India has much to learn from India itself. We live in a most diverse country, and in many spheres our records are extremely disparate. The average levels of literacy, life expectancy, infant mortality, etc., in India are enormously adverse compared with China, and yet in all these respects Kerala does significantly better than China. For example, in adult female literacy rate, India's 39 per cent is well behind China's 68 per cent, but Kerala's 86 per cent rate is much higher than China's. Indeed, as will be presently shown, in terms of rural female literacy, Kerala has a higher achievement than *every* individual province in China. Similarly, compared with China, Kerala has higher life expectancies at birth (69 for males and 74 for females, compared with China's 68 and 71 years, respectively), a lower fertility rate (1.8 *vis-à-vis* China's 2.0), and a much lower rate of infant mortality (17 and 16 per thousand live births, respectively, for boys and girls in 1991, compared with China's 28 and 33 years, respectively).[5]

[5] The sources of these data include Coale (1993), Office of the Registrar General of India (1993), World Bank (1994), UNDP (1994), and Drèze and Saran (1995); see also the Statistical Appendix in the companion volume (Drèze and Sen, 1995). The life expectancy estimates for India for 1991 are 'provisional' and draw on

There are a great many things that we can learn from within the country, by using the diversity of our experiences, particularly in the use of public action.[6] In some respects, Kerala — despite its low income level — has achieved more than even some of the most admired high-growth economies, such as South Korea. All this has to be recognized and its lessons used in policy-making elsewhere in India. But at the same time, we must also note that Kerala has much to learn from the experiences of other countries on how to stimulate economic growth. Kerala's performance in that sphere has been quite dismal, even compared with many other Indian states. The political economy of incentives is of crucial importance in translating the potential for economic expansion, implicit in human development, into the reality of actual achievement in the economic sphere. Kerala has to learn as well as teach.

While the encouragement of economic incentives and opportunities has varied between different parts of the country, there has been a generally counterproductive regulational environment in India that has restrained economic growth all over the country over many decades. We can profit a good deal from trying to understand what other countries have been able to do in generating economic growth and in utilizing that growth for improving qualities of human life. In the recent reforms, this issue of learning from the experiences of more successful economic performers has loomed large. I shall presently have more to say on the lessons to draw from the experiences of other countries, and in that context, I shall have to argue that some crucial features of the experiences of the more successful countries may have been seriously missed. But before that, the importance of removing counterproductive controls and regulations must be discussed.

5. COUNTERPRODUCTIVE REGULATIONS AND NECESSARY REFORMS

Comparison of India with the experiences of other countries is often made to motivate changes in economic policy, for example, to

---

unpublished works at the Registrar General's Office, for which we are most grateful.

[6] See the chapters that follow, on the experiences of three particular states: Uttar Pradesh (Jean Drèze and Haris Gazdar), West Bengal (Sunil Sengupta and Haris Gazdar), and Kerala (V.K. Ramachandran) and ending with a paper on inter-district comparisons of mortality, fertility, and gender differences (Murthi, Guio, and Drèze).

defend a programme of economic reforms — involving liberalization of trade, deregulation of governmental restrictions, encouragement of private initiative, and so on. In this context, attention is paid to the remarkable achievements of South Korea, Hong Kong, Singapore, Thailand, and other countries — including China in recent years — which have made splendid use of market-based economic opportunities. Such comparisons are indeed illuminating, and there is much to learn from these countries.

The counterproductive nature of some of the governmental restrictions, controls, and regulations has been clear for a long time. They have not only interfered with the efficiency of economic operations (especially for modern industries), but also have often failed lamentably to promote any kind of real equity in distributional matters. The privileges were often exploited for the sectional benefit of those with economic, political, or bureaucratic power, or those with the opportunity to influence people with such power. A radical change was certainly needed for these basic reasons, in addition to the short-run crises that actually prompted the change that did occur.

The scope of and rewards from greater integration with the world market have been and are large, and India too can reap much more fully the benefits of economies of scale and efficient division of labour that many other countries have already successfully used.[7] While greater reliance on trade is sometimes seen as something that compromises a country's economic independence, that view is hard to sustain. Given the diversity of trading partners and the interest of the different partners to have access to the large economic market in India, the fear that India would be an economic prisoner in the international world of open exchange is quite unfounded. This does not deny the importance of getting the terms and conditions right, including having fair regulations from GATT (or its successor) and other international institutions. But in general there is little reason for fearfully abstaining from the benefits offered by the greater use of the facilities of international trade and exchange.

---

[7] The actual scope of international division of labour depends to a great extent on the importance of economies of scale, which the recent literature on growth and trade has illuminatingly explored; see particularly Krugman (1986, 1987), Romer (1986, 1987a, 1987b), Helpman and Krugman (1990), and Grossman and Helpman (1991).

I am not commenting here on the appropriateness or sufficiency of the exact pattern of current economic reforms that is being introduced in India. Rather, I am pointing to the necessity and general desirability of economic reforms that remove counterproductive regulations and restrictions and allow greater use of the opportunities of international exchange. There is a strong case for such a change, and that case is not overwhelmed, in general, by any real reasons for fearing exploitative trading relations. The wisdom of going in this direction does not, however, deny the importance of many other policy changes that are also needed, on a priority basis, to pursue economic prosperity through greater integration with the world market.

6. India and China: Comparisons and Contrasts

In judging how India has been doing, it is useful to contrast its experiences with those of China. Whenever India is compared with much smaller countries, such as Hong Kong or Singapore, which have very successfully integrated with world markets, there is understandable scepticism about the relevance of these comparisons; these are effectively city states and can do many things that a country of the size of India cannot. In contrast, China, which is of a similar size — in fact larger — than India, provides an interesting and instructive comparative picture. This is not just because of size (though that is relevant too), but also because China too started off from being in a state of much poverty and deprivation. Also, the Chinese civilization, like the Indian, has a long tradition of trade and commerce (along with traditional, non-market, social conventions), and furthermore, both India and China have the additional similarity of having large expatriate communities which could play important instrumental roles in achieving more integration with the world of international commerce and trade. The comparison with China is, thus, quite significant in understanding where India is and in scrutinizing what it can and should do.

Table 1 presents comparative figures on adult literacy rates in India and China. India is well behind China in this field — particularly so in the realm of female literacy. In addition to the figures for the Indian average, Table 1 also gives data for two states within India that respectively do much better (Kerala) and

TABLE 1. *Adult Literacy Rates, 1991*

	Males	Females
India	64	39
China	87	68
Kerala	94	86
UP	56	25

Source. Census data (see Drèze and Sen,
1995, Statistical Appendix).

much worse (Uttar Pradesh) than the Indian average. Uttar Pradesh's male and female literacy rates of 56 and 25 per cent, respectively, lie very much behind China's 87 and 68 per cent, but on the other side, Kerala's 94 and 86 per cent lie well ahead of China's achievements.

China too is, of course, a heterogeneous country of many provinces. Fig. 1 presents the data for rural literacy rates for males and females for the Indian states and the Chinese provinces put together. Several features of this comparison are obvious from the figure. First, the Chinese provinces generally do very much better than the Indian states. Second, nevertheless the best performer among all the Indian states and Chinese provinces put together is Kerala, and the worst performer is Tibet, so that the extremes go in the opposite direction to the relative pictures of means and modes. Third, while Kerala is comfortably on top, following Kerala come a whole bunch of Chinese provinces before the next Indian state comes into the league. Similarly, while Tibet is indubitably at the bottom, above it come a big group of Indian states before we get to the next low performing Chinese province. Finally, there is some evidence in Fig. 1 that with the exception of Tibet, the Chinese provinces are more closely bunched together than are the Indian states. It is that bunched modal achievement of China that is so far above the run of Indian states.

Table 2 turns to matters of life and death, and presents the comparative picture of life expectancies at birth, infant mortality rates, total fertility rates, and female–male ratios in the population. Again, China is well ahead of India on the average, and tremendously ahead of Uttar Pradesh, but still significantly behind Kerala in each of these respects.

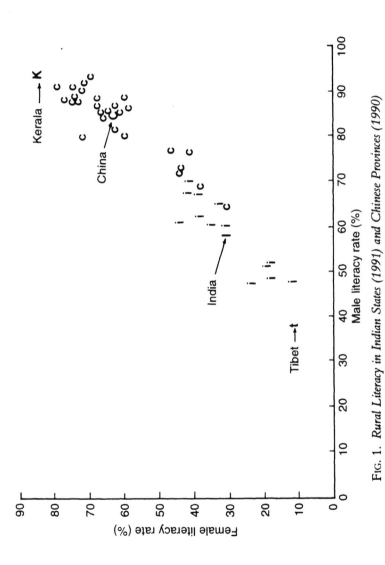

FIG. 1. *Rural Literacy in Indian States (1991) and Chinese Provinces (1990)*

TABLE 2. *Life and Death, 1991*

	Life Expectancy		Infant Mor- tality Rate	Female– male Ratio	Total Fer- tility Rate
	Males	Females			
India	59	59	80	0.93	3.6
China	68	71	31	0.94	2.0
Kerala	69	74	17	1.04	1.8
UP	57	55	98	0.88	5.1

Source. Drèze and Sen (1995), Statistical Appendix.

The distinction of Kerala is particularly striking in the field of gender equality. The female–male ratio in the population tends to be well above unity, because of the survival advantages that females have over males in terms of age-specific mortality rates whenever they receive comparable attention and care. In Europe and north America, the female–male ratio tends to be around 1.05 on the average, though it would have been somewhat lower had there not been extra male mortality in past wars the demographic effects of which still linger. In contrast, in many countries in Asia and north Africa, the female–male ratio is well below unity, and this is the case in India too.[8] But China's female–male ratio of 0.94, while higher than India's 0.93, is not really very high, whereas Kerala's ratio is close to 1.04, and is much higher than unity even after note is taken of greater emigration of men out of the state. This is a comparable ratio to that obtaining in Europe and north America and shows how much more equal Kerala is in terms of some elementary matters of gender parity, compared with China as well as the rest of India.

But leaving out the particular issue of gender equality, China's overall performance is enormously better than India's. While Kerala does better than China in terms of life expectancy, fertility rates, and infant mortality, the gap between the two, in each of these fields, is typically a good deal less than that between the average pictures of India and China.

---

[8] On this subject, see my paper, 'Missing Women', in the *British Medical Journal* (Sen, 1992), and the literature cited there. For a general review of the literature (including critiques of the estimates of Drèze and Sen, 1989, and of Ansley Coale, 1991) and some new estimates of his own, see Klasen (1994).

7. INDIA'S EDUCATIONAL BACKWARDNESS AND LESSONS OF KERALA

In view of the remarkable expansion of higher education in India (we send about six times as many people to the universities and other higher educational establishments as China does, relative to its population), it is extraordinary how little we have progressed in basic education. When I gave my Lal Bahadur Shastri Memorial Lectures in 1970 (entitled 'The Crisis in Indian Education'), the contrast between our attention to higher education and neglect of elementary teaching had seemed intolerably large.[9] But that gap has, if anything, *grown* rather than shrunk over the last 25 years. I had tried to argue that there were deep-seated class biases in the pressures that have determined Indian educational priorities, and that the inequalities in education are, in fact, a reflection of inequalities of economic and social powers of different groups in India.[10] The educational inequalities both *reflect* and help to *sustain* social disparities, and for a real break, much more determined political action would be needed than has been provided so far by either those in office, or by the parties that have led the opposition. The weakness, in this field, of even parties of the 'left' is particularly striking, given the fact that elementary education has been one of the few really solid achievements of the countries led by communist parties — in places as diverse as Soviet Union, China, Cuba, and Vietnam.

The traditionally elitist tendencies of the ruling cultural and religious traditions in India may have added to the political problem here. Both Hinduism and Islam have, in different ways, had considerable inclination towards religious elitism, with reliance respectively on Brahmin priests and on powerful Mullahs, and while there have been many protest movements against each (the medieval poet Kabir fought against both simultaneously), the elitist hold is quite

[9] 'The Crisis in Indian Education', Lal Bahadur Shastri Memorial Lecture, given in New Delhi on 10–11 March 1970, for The Institute of Public Enterprise, Hyderabad. Reprinted in Malik (1971) and partially in Chaudhuri (1972).

[10] The argument, presented in my Lal Bahadur Shastri Lecture (Sen, 1970), that 'the rot in Indian education is ultimately related to the structure of Indian society' (reprinted in Malik, 1971, p. 273) unfortunately continues to hold, and there has been in the last quarter of a century quite inadequate public effort to overcome the legacy of those social inequalities.

strong in both these religions. This contrasts with the more egalitarian and populist traditions of, say, Buddhism. Indeed, Buddhist countries have typically had much higher levels of basic literacy than societies dominated by Hinduism or Islam. Thailand, Sri Lanka, and Myanmar (Burma) are good examples.

There is even some evidence that when Western imperialists conquered countries in Asia and Africa, they tended to expand — rather than counteract — the biases that had already existed in the local cultures. For example, the British in India took little interest in elementary education, but were quite keen on creating institutions of higher learning in the good, old Brahminical mode, whereas the same British in Buddhist Burma gave much encouragement to the expansion of elementary teaching, even though they tended to do rather little for higher education.[11]

The point of this passing thought is not to argue that India must remain imprisoned by its past, but only to indicate the necessity of explicitly addressing the questions of both *ancient* and *modern* biases that shape Indian educational policies — reflecting prejudices of class divisions as well as of traditional cultures. The difficulty in getting even 'left-wing' parties interested in combating inequalities in education relates to the general social atmosphere in India (including the nature of the leadership of the different parties) which takes some major disparities as simply 'given' and not particularly worth battling against (in view of other — perceived to be more 'pressing' — challenges).

There is, however, some encouraging information in the remarkable heterogeneity that characterizes India in the field of elementary education. Advances of basic education have often come from forces that have railed against traditional politics (including protests against the historical hold of caste practices), or against traditional cultures (sometimes in the form of missionary activities). While the latter

---

[11] The relevance of these issues was briefly discussed in my paper 'How Is India Doing?', *The New York Review of Books*, 1982; see also Drèze and Sen (1995), chapter 6. On a personal note, as a young child in Mandalay, I remember being struck by the throng of Indian professors in Burma (my father was one of them for a while) coming from a country with extremely little literacy to one where most people appeared, even then, to be able to read and write. The divergence between India's extensive development of higher education and its extraordinary neglect of basic education comes out most sharply in contrast with the opposite tendency in countries like Burma.

may explain the higher achievements in elementary education in, say, Goa or Mizoram, Kerala has had the benefit of both types of breaks (education-oriented lower-class movements as well as missionary activities), in addition to the good fortune of having royal families in Travancore and Cochin that happened to be atypically in favour of elementary education.

In drawing policy lessons from Kerala's experience of public action, note must be taken of two particularly instructive features. First, a real difference has been made by political activism in the direction of educational expansion for the lower-caste — and lower-class — groups. In the general picture of political apathy towards elementary eduction that is characteristic of much of India, Kerala is a big exception, and the results vindicate the attention that has been paid to this.[12] There is, thus, much evidence here of the importance of political leadership and initiative and of popular involvement in making a real difference in the realization of basic capabilities of the people at large.[13] The lessons to draw are of relevance not only for policy-makers and political leaders in office, but also for opposition parties and the politically-conscious public at large.

Second, the historical heterogeneity *within* Kerala itself is also quite instructive. When the state of Kerala was created in independent India, it was made up, on linguistic grounds, of the erstwhile native states of Travancore and Cochin, and the region of Malabar from the old province of Madras in British India (what is now mostly Tamil Nadu). The Malabar region, transferred from the Raj, was very much behind Travancore and Cochin in social development (including literacy and life expectancy — and mortality rates generally). But by the eighties, Malabar had so much 'caught up' with the

---

[12] See particularly V.K. Ramachandran's chapter on Kerala in this volume. Ramachandran goes through the long history of Kerala's educational expansion, and the emergence and development of other forms of public intervention, and outlines the role of public participation and local leadership in bringing about the changes the results of which make Kerala stand out so sharply in India.

[13] West Bengal, the state other than Kerala in which left-wing parties have been in office for substantial lengths of time, have tended in the past to share the conservative scepticism (common in India) of elementary education, and its record in school education, while better than that of many states, has been relatively indifferent. However, there has been in very recent years a shift of governmental policy in the direction of emphasizing elementary education, and there are some early signs of rapid progress beginning to be made in this field. See the chapter on West Bengal, by Sunil Sengupta and Haris Gazdar, in this volume.

rest of Kerala that it could no longer be seen in divergent terms.[14] The initiatives that the state governments of Kerala took, under different 'managements' (led by the Communist Party as well as by the Congress), succeeded in transforming Malabar into being basically at par with the rest of Kerala. Since Kerala has had a rather special history, it is important to note that a region need not be imprisoned in the fixity of history, and much depends on what is done here and now. In this too Kerala itself offers a lesson for the rest of India on what can be done by determined public action, even without having the favourable historical circumstances of Travancore and Cochin.

TABLE 3.   *Literacy and Schooling: India (1987–88)*

	India	Kerala	UP
I. Rural literacy rate (Children 10–14)			
Males	73	98	68
Females	52	98	39
II. Percentages of rural children attending school			
Age 5–9: Males	52	87	45
Females	40	83	28
Age 10–14: Males	66	93	64
Females	42	91	31
III. Percentage of children 12–14 ever enrolled			
Rural: Males	74	100	73
Females	49	98	32
Urban: Males	89	100	81
Females	81	99	61

Source.   Drèze and Sen (1995), Table 6.1, based on Census and National Sample Survey data.

The heterogeneity within India is illustrated and explored in Table 3 which gives information on the literacy rates of rural children in India as a whole and in the two states of Kerala and

[14] On this, see T.N. Krishnan (1994).

Uttar Pradesh. It turns out that while nearly all the children in the age group of 10 to 14 years are literate in Kerala, one-third of the UP male children and more than three-fifths of the UP female children of that age group are clearly illiterate. The picture is similarly dismal for school attendance for India as a whole and even more so for Uttar Pradesh.

Finally, it is totally remarkable that in rural India in the age group 12 to 14 years, more than a *quarter* of the boys have *never* been enrolled in any school and more than *half* the girls have *never* been enrolled either. As expected, in Kerala nearly all the boys and girls of this age group have had some schooling, and on the other side, in Uttar Pradesh the percentage of rural children of this age group who have been totally out of school are even higher than in India as a whole. In fact more than two-thirds of the UP girls between 12 and 14 have never had the benefit of any schooling at all. This is an appalling picture of neglect of basic education, and shows how very backward the bulk of India is — in terms of an important element of 'the task' that Nehru identified in 1947 — and furthermore, how abysmal the failure is in India's largest state. With more than 140 million people, had Uttar Pradesh been a country on its own, it would have been one of the largest countries in the world and would have been — or close to being — the lowest in terms of school education in the entire world.

TABLE 4. *Adult Literacy Rates, 1990: Developing Countries*

	Total	Female
India[a]	52	39
China	78	68
Average of low-income countries excluding China and India	55	44
Zimbabwe	67	60
Botswana	74	65
Kenya	69	58
Nigeria	51	39
Ghana	60	51

Note. [a] Age 7+, 1991.
Source. Drèze and Sen (1995), Statistical Appendix, Table A.1, for India and China; *World Development Report 1994*, Table 1, for other countries.

Indeed, in the field of elementary education, India is not only behind China or Sri Lanka or South Korea, but also worse off than the average of 'low income countries other than India and China' (as defined by the World Bank), the comparative data for which are given in Table 4. Even in comparison with sub-Saharan Africa — perhaps the most problematic region in the world now with its record of recurrent famines — India does not shine. While it just about matches the literacy rates of Nigeria, it falls well behind the achievements of many of the African states, including Botswana, Zimbabwe, Kenya, and Ghana (Table 4). If India's relative performance is 'middling' in many fields of economic and social development, its record is far below that — close to the very bottom — in the fields of literacy and elementary education.

8. THE ECONOMIC HANDICAP OF EDUCATIONAL BACKWARDNESS

While education and the development of human ability and skill must not be valued *only* as instruments to other ends, their instrumental importance must *also* be acknowledged (as was discussed earlier). In the analysis of 'growth-mediated' social progress, public education can be both *favourable* to economic growth (through expanding the opportunities of economic expansion) and *favoured* by economic growth (through generating more resources for such support).[15]

The economic roles of school education, learning by doing, technical progress, and even economies of large scale can all be seen as contributing — in different ways — to the centrality of direct human agency in generating economic expansion. Recent work on economic growth has brought out sharply the role of labour, education, and experience, and the so-called 'human capital'. This has helped to fill the large gap identified as a 'residual' in the basic neo-classical model of economic growth, and recent growth theory has done much to bring out the function of direct human agency in economic growth, over and above the contribution made through the accumulation of physical capital. Our attempt to learn from the experiences of 'the East Asian miracle' and other cases of growth-

---

[15] On this, see Drèze and Sen (1989), chapter 10.

mediated progress cannot ignore the wealth of insights that the recent theoretical and empirical analyses have provided.[16]

The crucial role of education and skill makes it all the more essential to pay attention to public policy to expand basic education and to promote skill formation. The role of widespread basic education has been quite crucial in countries that have successfully grown fast making excellent use of world markets: for example, the so-called four 'tigers' in East Asia (namely South Korea, Hong Kong, Singapore, and Taiwan), and more recently, China and also Thailand. The modern industries in which these countries have particularly excelled demand many basic skills for which elementary education is essential and secondary education most helpful. While some studies have emphasized the productive contribution of learning by doing and on-the-job training, rather than the direct impact of formal education, the ability to achieve such training and learning is certainly helped greatly by basic education in schools prior to taking up jobs.[17]

In the context of learning from the experiences of the fast-growing economies of East Asia, it is important to recognize that all these countries — South Korea, Hong Kong, Singapore, Taiwan, Thailand, and post-reform China — had enormously higher levels of elementary education at the time they went for fast economic growth and greater integration with the world economy. The point is not that these countries have a much higher base of elementary education *now* than India currently has, but that they *already had* radically higher levels of elementary education in the nineteen-seventies, when they went rapidly ahead, compared with what India has *now*.

---

[16] On different aspects of the relations involved, see Krugman (1986), Romer (1986), Barro (1991), Stokey (1991), Young (1991), Mankiw, Romer, and Weil (1992), Lucas (1993), among other contributions.

[17] Despite having quite a different focus of emphasis in the past, the World Bank has also acknowledged these connections in its recent study of 'the East Asian miracle', which draws on a vast range of empirical works: 'We have shown that the broad base of human capital was critically important to rapid growth in the HPAEs [high-performing Asian economies]. Because the HPAEs attained universal primary education early, literacy was high and cognitive skill levels were substantially above those in other developing economies. Firms therefore had an easier time upgrading the skills of their workers and mastering new technology' (World Bank, 1993, p. 349).

Table 5 presents some comparative figures on this. India's current level of adult literacy at 52 per cent is not only enormously lower than the current figures for China, Thailand, South Korea, or Hong Kong, but compares very unfavourably with the adult literacy rates of around 70 per cent at the time these countries respectively launched their rapid economic expansion (from 1980 in China and around 1960 or thereafter in Hong Kong, South Korea, and Thailand).

TABLE 5. *Adult Literacy Rates, 1960–90*

	1960	*1980*	*1992*
India	28	36	52[a]
South Korea	71	93	97
Hong Kong	70	90	≈ 100
China	n.a.	69	80
Thailand	68	86	94

Note. [a] Age 7+, 1991.
Source. Drèze and Sen (1995), p. 38.

There has been an astonishing failure of adequate public action in expanding elementary and secondary education in India. While 'too much' government has been identified, with some plausibility, as a problem of past policies in India, in fact in the field of basic education (and also those of elementary health care, land reforms, and social security), 'too little' government action — rather than 'too much' — has been the basic problem.[18] This is not to deny that India can quite possibly achieve high rates of growth of GNP or GDP even with present levels of massive illiteracy. It is more a question of the strength and the nature of the economic expansion that can occur in India today, and the extent to which the growth in question can be participatory.[19]

The social opportunities offered by market-based economic growth, particularly of integration with modern world markets, are severely limited when a very large part of the community cannot read or write or count, cannot follow printed or hand-written

[18] These issues are discussed extensively in the companion volume (Drèze and Sen, 1995).

[19] On the characteristics of participatory growth and their relevance in enhancing living conditions, see Drèze and Sen (1989), chapter 10.

instructions, cannot cope easily with contemporary technology, and so on. The objective of integration with the world market — important as it is — is deeply hampered by India's unusually low level of basic educational development. The inequality in Indian educational policies and achievement thus translates into inequalities in making use of new economic opportunities. The *distributive* failure supplements the effect of educational backwardness in restricting the *overall* scale of expansion of employment-generating modern production.

The persistence of endemic illiteracy and educational backwardness in India has many adverse effects. It limits, in general, the freedom and well-being of the Indian masses, and has a direct role in the relative deprivation of women in particular. It sustains high levels of mortality and fertility rates.[20] It contributes to the comparative lack of pressure for social change, and to the moderateness of political demand and pressure for effective public attention in such fields as health care.[21] But in addition the lack of elementary education also makes the goals of economic expansion very much harder to realize. We have to face here two quite distinct but interrelated problems that limit the attainment and use of economic growth. First, elementary education is extremely important for successful integration with the world market. The nature and range of the commodities sold by, say, South Korea since the seventies or China from the eighties bring out clearly how crucial basic education is for catering to the world market, with production to specification and reliable quality control. Second, the wider the coverage of the population that takes part in the integration with the world market, the more 'participatory' the process of growth would tend to be, raising the income-earning power of large parts of the nation. Even if India were to grow very fast with its highly technical industries (making use of special skills that India has cultivated and drawing on the trained middle-class labour force), such as modern computer software or engineering products, the bulk of the Indians may still receive little reward from it.

[20] The paper in this volume by Murthi, Guio, and Drèze presents an extensive inter-district comparison of the relations between women's and men's education and employment opportunities, on the one hand, and the levels of mortality and fertility rates, on the other.

[21] On the relation between education and other aspects of social choice, see Tapas Majumdar (1983, 1993).

To make a relevant comparison, in the sixties and the seventies the Brazilian economy grew very fast but achieved rather little reduction of poverty — in economic as well as social terms. The lack of participatory nature of that growth was extremely important in that outcome. Comparing Brazil's problems with patterns of more inclusive growth processes in east Asia tends to bring out the big difference made by participatory growth, and the specific role of widespread basic education in east Asia.[22] India stands in some danger of going Brazil's way, rather than South Korea's, and there is something quite important to choose there.

9. THE ROLE OF PRE-REFORM CHINA IN ITS POST-REFORM SUCCESS

In learning from China, we have to pay particular attention to what has been achieved in China in the post-reform period. But if the analysis presented here is correct, we must resist the common tendency now to 'rubbish' what China had already done before the reforms. The spread of basic education across the country is particularly relevant in explaining the nature of Chinese economic expansion in the post-reform period. The role of mass education in facilitating rapid and participatory growth has been quite crucial in the integration of the Chinese economy with the world market. The big step in the direction of mass education was decisively taken in China in the pre-reform period. The literacy rates in China by 1982 were already as high as 96 per cent for males in the 15–19 age group, and 85 per cent even for females in that age group. This social asset made participatory economic expansion possible in a way it would not have been in India *then* — and is extremely difficult in India even *now*.

A similar thing can be said about widespread health care and systems of nutritional attention, which China developed in the pre-reform period, but from which post-reform China has benefited a great deal. The importance of basic health and nutrition in economic development has received much attention in the

[22] See particularly Birdsall and Sabot (1993a, 1993b) and McGuire (1994). On aspects of the Brazilian experience in particular, see also the article by Ignacy Sachs in Drèze and Sen (1990). On aspects of South Korean economic development, see also Amsden (1989) and Wade (1990).

recent literature.[23] In assessing the economic success of post-reform China, the groundwork done in the pre-reform period would have to be adequately acknowledged.

Another area in which the Chinese post-reform expansions have benefited from pre-reform achievements is that of land reforms, which has also been identified as having been of great importance in the east Asian economic development in general.[24] In China, things went, of course, much further than land reforms, and the extremism of communal agriculture certainly was a considerable handicap for agricultural expansion in the pre-reform period. But that process of collectivization of land had also, *inter alia*, abolished landlordism in China. When the Chinese government opted for the 'responsibility system', it had a land tenure pattern that could be readily transformed into individual farming without intermediaries, not weighed down by the counteracting weight of tenurial handicaps (as in many parts of India).[25]

It is interesting that the institutional developments that have favoured participatory economic growth throughout east Asia (in particular, the spread of basic education and health care, and the abolition of landlordism) had come to different countries in the region in quite different ways. In some cases, even foreign occupation had helped, for example, in the land reforms in Taiwan and South Korea. In the case of China, the pre-reform governments had carried out, for programmes of their own, radical changes that proved to be immensely useful in the economic expansion based on marketization in the post-reform period.

These connections are extremely important to note in having an adequately informed interpretation of the Chinese successes of recent years, and in drawing lessons for it for other countries. If India has to emulate China in market success, it is not adequate just to liberalize economic controls in the way the Chinese have recently done, without also creating the social opportunities that post-reform China enjoyed through education, health care, and land reform — to a great extent inherited from pre-reform achievements of that

[23] See, for example, Dasgupta and Ray (1986, 1987).

[24] See, for example, Amsden (1989), Wade (1990), and World Bank (1993).

[25] Within India, West Bengal has done much more than any other state in carrying out land reforms. On this see the chapter on rural poverty in West Bengal (by Sunil Sengupta and Haris Gazdar). But the traditional inequities in land holdings are very strong in many parts of India.

experimental country. The force of China's market economy rests on the solid foundations of social changes that had occurred earlier, and India cannot simply jump on to that bandwagon without paying attention to the enabling social changes — in education, health care, and land reforms — that made the market function in the way it has in China.

10. ECONOMIC DEVELOPMENT THROUGH SOCIAL OPPORTUNITY

The central issue in economic development is to expand the social opportunities open to the people. In so far as these opportunities are compromised — directly or indirectly — by counterproductive regulations and controls, by restrictions on economic initiatives, by the stifling of competition and its efficiency-generating advantages, and so on, the removal of these hindrances must be seen to be extremely important. The expansion of markets has a crucial role to play in this transformation.

But the creation and use of social opportunities on a wide basis requires much more than the 'freeing' of markets. They call emphatically for an active public policy that could enable people to use the opportunities that the possibility of more trade — domestic and international — offers. Perhaps above all, it calls for a rapid expansion of basic education — overcoming the massive illiteracy and educational backwardness that characterize much of India.[26] This requires the provision of literacy and elementary education as fundamental opportunities for all (rather than leaving the majority of women and a large proportion of men illiterate), and the spread of secondary education on a very much wider basis (rather than that opportunity being confined fairly narrowly to particular classes). India's record in both these respects is quite dismal, despite the fact that literacy and school education have been part of the rhetoric of Indian planning since independence.

That rhetoric continues and there is perhaps even some intensification of it, but change in this field is still extremely slow, and there is little practical evidence of serious priority being attached

---

[26] There is also considerable evidence that the rate of return to basic education tends to be higher in countries that are more 'open', with less restriction on trade. On this and related issues, see Birdsall and Sabot (1993a, 1993b).

to it in the way that liberalization and market reforms are receiving. Table 6 presents growth rates of expenditure and teaching inputs in elementary schools over the decades, and while the percentage growth rates of recurring expenditures have moved up, that increase has not been adequate to compensate for the increase in relative costs (including teachers' salaries). Indeed, judged in 'real' terms, the percentage expansion of the number of teachers has actually fallen steadily from the fifties, to the sixties, to the seventies, and through the eighties. That trend has not been reversed recently — to some extent quite the opposite has happened. The number of primary school teachers per unit of population has *fallen* between 1980–1 and 1990–1. Since the economic reforms, there seems to have been a further fall, and there has in fact been a decline in the absolute number of primary school teachers between 1991–2 and 1992–3.[27]

TABLE 6.   *Growth Rates of Expenditure and Teaching Inputs in Elementary Schools (percentage per year)*

	Recurring expenditure at 1970–71 prices	Number of teachers	Teacher–population ratio
1950–51 to 1960–61	8.5	5.6	3.6
1960–61 to 1970–71	5.8	4.5	2.3
1970–71 to 1980–81	2.8	2.7	0.5
1980–81 to 1984–85	11.1	2.1	0.0
1984–85 to 1989–90	10.8	1.6	– 0.5

Source.   Drèze and Sen (1995), p. 122.

There is little evidence that the seriousness of India's educational backwardness has been officially recognized in any practical way by New Delhi. This is particularly odd, since — as was discussed earlier — basic education is not only important for the well-being and freedom of the people and for social change, but also for the success of India's economic reforms. The prospects of participatory growth

[27] On this, see Tyagi (1993), p. 82. On the decline of real per-capita government expenditure on education after 1991, see Prabhu (1995).

in India and India's ability to make good use of the opportunities of integration with the world market are significantly compromised by the extraordinary backwardness of basic education in this country.

There are also other expansions of social opportunity that call for urgent attention. These include the need for more widespread and better health care, greater access to provisions of social security, more effective and sweeping land reforms, and in general, enabling the more constrained sections of the population to lead a less restrictive life, including being more free to make use of the facilities that the spread of markets could provide.

11. The Need for a Bigger Departure

Policy debates in India have to be taken away from the overwhelming concentration on issues of liberalization and marketization. The nostalgia of the old debates 'Are you *pro* or *anti* market?', or 'Are you *in favour* or *against* state activities?' seem to have an odd 'hold' on all sides, so that we concentrate only on some issues and ignore many — often more important — ones. While the case for economic reforms may take good note of the diagnosis that India has too much government in some fields, it ignores the fact that India also has too little government activities in many other fields, including basic education and health care, which makes people's lives miserable and which also limits the possibility of economic expansion. We may need 'more markets', but we also have to go 'more *beyond* the markets'. What needs curing is not just 'too little market' or 'too much market', but 'too little market' in some areas and 'too little *beyond* the market' in others.[28]

To emulate the use of markets in China or South Korea, without taking note of their vast and highly productive experience in public education and health care, and without understanding the role of these governmental activities in encouraging economic expansion cannot be adequate. It is, at best, 'piece-meal copying' of others — not really 'learning' from others. We have to go well beyond liberalization to get somewhere.

What applies to learning from abroad holds also for the lessons

---

[28] The argument in this direction has been more extensively presented in the companion volume (Drèze and Sen, 1995).

that we can get from the divergent experiences within India. In the chapters that follow, the experiences of Uttar Pradesh, Kerala, and West Bengal are studied in some detail. While their successes in raising living standards and the quality of life have varied greatly, all the states do need to pay more attention to creating the economic conditions for fast, participatory growth of their respective economies. But that message cannot be seen to be one of just reducing the role of government control and regulations. There are positive initiatives to be taken for raising the human capabilities that make life worthwhile and which can also — given the appropriate economic climate — serve as the basis of fast and participatory economic growth.

The radicalism that is needed cannot be met by just removing restraints through deregulation and reform, and it must also embrace the positive duties of a responsible government to create social opportunities that are valuable in themselves and which can also help the process of economic development. While learning from the successes abroad, we have to take note of the totality of the experiences in making them so successful, and in applying these lessons from elsewhere, we have to bear in mind the need for a fuller view of the government's role. The contrasts between the experiences of different states in India and their enormous variations in achieving social progress are of interest not only for their direct role in raising well-being and in reducing human deprivation, but also for the indirect part they can play in enhancing the nature and quality of economic growth.

The fundamental changes that are needed in India cannot be met just by moderate reforms that only focus on reducing the negative activities of the government, neglecting the positive functions that it can perform in bringing social opportunities within the reach of all. The studies of the contrasting experiences of the Indian states that follow are aimed at providing insights into — and understanding of — a crucial aspect of the needed radicalism. It supplements the focus on learning from abroad which has been such an important motivating factor in the recent economic debates in India. The lessons from within India have to be fitted firmly into the understanding we can gain from experiences abroad.

REFERENCES

Amsden, Alice (1989), *Asia's Next Giant: Late Industrialization in South Korea* (Oxford: Oxford University Press).

Anand, Sudhir and Martin Ravallion (1993), 'Human Development in Poor Countries: On the Role of Private Incomes and Public Services', *Journal of Economic Perspectives*, 7 (Winter).

Arneson, R. (1989), 'Equality and Equality of Opportunity for Welfare', *Philosophical Studies*, 56.

—— (1990), 'Primary Goods Reconsidered', *Nous*, 24.

Atkinson, A.B. (1983), *Social Justice and Public Policy* ((Brighton: Wheatsheaf, and Cambridge, MA: MIT Press).

—— (1989), *Poverty and Social Security* (New York: Harvester Wheatsheaf).

Barro, Robert (1991), 'Economic Growth in a Cross Section of Countries', *Quarterly Journal of Economics*, 106.

Birdsall, Nancy and Richard H. Sabot (1993a), 'Virtuous Circles: Human Capital Growth and Equity in East Asia' (mimeo, Washington, DC: World Bank).

Birdsall, Nancy and Richard H. Sabot, eds. (1993b), *Opportunity Foregone: Education, Growth and Inequality in Brazil* (Washington, DC: World Bank).

Chaudhuri, Pramit, ed. (1972), *Aspects of Indian Economic Development* (London: Allen & Unwin).

Coale, Ansley J. (1991), 'Excess Female Mortality and the Balance of the Sexes: An Estimate of the Number of "Missing Females" ', *Population and Development Review*, 17.

—— (1993), 'Mortality Schedules in China Derived from Data in the 1982 and 1990 Censuses', Office of Population Research, Princeton University, Working Paper 93-7.

Cohen, G.A. (1989), 'On the Currency of Egalitarian Justice', *Ethics*, 99.

—— (1990), 'Equality of What? On Welfare, Goods and Capabilities', *Recherches Economiques de Louvain*, 56.

—— (1994), 'Amartya Sen's Unequal World', *New Left Review*.

Crocker, David (1991), 'Toward Development Ethics', *World Development*, 19.

Dasgupta, Partha (1993), *An Inquiry into Well-being and Destitution* (Oxford: Oxford University Press).

Dasgupta, Partha and Debraj Ray (1986), 'Inequality as a Determinant of Malnutrition and Unemployment: Theory', *Economic Journal*, 96.

Dasgupta, Partha and Debraj Ray (1987), 'Inequality as a Determinant of Malnutrition and Unemployment: Policy', *Economic Journal*, 97.

Drèze, Jean and Mrinalini Saran (1995), 'Primary Education and Economic Development in China and India: Overview and Two Case Studies', in Kaushik Basu, Prasanta Pattanaik and Kotaro Suzumura, eds., *Choice, Welfare and Development* (Oxford: Oxford University Press).

Drèze, Jean and Amartya Sen (1989), *Hunger and Public Action* (Oxford: Clarendon Press).

—— (1995), *India: Economic Development and Social Opportunity* (Oxford and Delhi: Oxford University Press).

Drèze, Jean and Amartya Sen, eds. (1990), *The Political Economy of Hunger*, 3 volumes (Oxford: Clarendon Press).

Grossman, Gene M. and Elahanan Helpman (1991), *Innovation and Growth in the Global Economy* (Cambridge, MA: MIT Press).

Helpman, Elahanan and Paul R. Krugman (1990), *Market Structure and Foreign Trade* (Cambridge, MA: MIT Press).

Herrero, Carmen (1994), 'Capabilities and Utilities', mimeo, Universidad de Alicante, Spain.

Hossain, I. (1990), *Poverty as Capability Failure* (Helsinki: Swedish School of Economics).

Klasen, Stephan (1994), ' "Missing Women" Revisited', mimeo, Harvard University, forthcoming in *World Development*.

Krishnan, T.N. (1994), 'Social Intermediation and Human Development: Kerala State, India', mimeo, Centre for Development Studies, Thiruvananthapuram.

Krugman, Paul R. (1986), *Strategic Trade Policy and the New International Economics* (Cambridge, MA: MIT Press).

—— (1987), 'The Narrow Moving Band, the Dutch Disease, and the Consequences of Mrs Thatcher: Notes on Trade in the Presence of Scale Economies', *Journal of Development Economics*, 27.

Lucas, Robert (1993), 'Making a Miracle', *Econometrica*, 63.

Majumdar, Tapas (1983), *Investment in Education and Social Choice* (Cambridge: Cambridge University Press.

—— (1993), 'The Relation between Educational Attainment and Ability to Obtain Social Security in the States of India', research paper, World Institute for Development Economics Research, Helsinki.

Malik, S.C., ed. (1971), *Management and Organization of Indian Universities* (Simla: Indian Institute of Advanced Study).

Mankiw, Gregory, David Romer, and David Weil (1992), 'A Contribution to the Empirics of Economic Growth', *Quarterly Journal of Economics*, 107.

McGuire, James W. (1994), 'Development Policy and its Determinants in East Asia and Latin America', forthcoming in *Journal of Public Policy*.

Nussbaum, Martha (1988), 'Nature, Function and Capability: Aristotle on Political Distribution', *Oxford Studies in Ancient Philosophy*.

Nussbaum, Martha and Amartya Sen, eds. (1993), *The Quality of Life* (Oxford: Clarendon Press).

Office of the Registrar General of India (1993), *Sample Registration System: Fertility and Mortality Indicators 1991* (New Delhi: Ministry of Home Affairs).

Pogge, T.W. (1989), *Realizing Rawls* (Ithaca, NY: Cornell University Press).

Prabhu, K. Seeta (1995), 'Structural Adjustment and Financing of Elementary Education: The Indian Experience', *Journal of Educational Planning and Administration*, 9.

Rawls, John (1982), 'Social Unity and Primary Goods', in Amartya Sen and Bernard Williams, eds., *Utility and Beyond* (Cambridge: Cambridge University Press).

—— (1993), *Political Liberalism* (New York: Columbia University Press).

Roemer, John (1982), *A General Theory of Exploitation and Class* (Cambridge, MA: Harvard University Press).

—— (1994), 'Primary Goods, Fundamental Preferences and Functionings', mimeo, University of California, Davis.

Romer, Paul M. (1986), 'Increasing Returns and Long-Run Growth', *Journal of Political Economy*, 94.

—— (1987a), 'Growth Based on Increasing Returns due to Specialization', *American Economic Review*, 77.

—— (1987b), 'Two Strategies for Economic Development: Using Ideas and Producing Ideas', in World Bank, *Proceedings of the World Bank Annual Conference on Development Economics 1992* (Washington, DC: World Bank).

Schokkaert, E. and L. van Ootegem (1990), 'Sen's Concept of the Living Standard Applied to the Belgian Unemployed', *Recherches Economiques de Louvain*, 56.

Sen, Amartya (1970), 'The Crisis in Indian Education', Lal Bahadur Shastri Memorial Lecture, The Institute of Public Enterprise, Hyderabad; reprinted in Malik (1971) and partially in Chaudhuri (1972).

Sen, Amartya (1980), 'Equality of What?', in S. McMurrin, ed., *Tanner Lectures on Human Values*, vol. I (Cambridge: Cambridge University Press); reprinted in Sen, *Choice, Welfare and Measurement* (Oxford: Blackwell; Cambridge, MA: MIT Press, 1982).

—— (1982), 'How Is India Doing?', *The New York Review of Books*.

—— (1985a), *Commodities and Capabilities* (Amsterdam: North-Holland).

—— (1985b), 'Well-being, Agency and Freedom: The Dewey Lectures 1984', *Journal of Philosophy*, 82.

—— (1992), 'Missing Women', in *British Medical Journal*, 304 (March).

Stokey, Nancy (1991), 'Human Capital, Product Quality and Growth', *Quarterly Journal of Economics*, 106.

Sugden, R. (1993), 'Welfare, Resources, and Capabilities: A review of *Inequality Reexamined* by Amartya Sen', *Journal of Economic Literature*, 31.

Tyagi, P.N. (1993), *Education for All* (New Delhi: National Institute of Educational Planning and Administration, revised edition).

UNDP (1994), *Human Development Report 1994* (New York: UNDP).

van Parijs, Phillip (1990), 'Equal Endowments as Undominated Diversity', *Recherches Economiques de Louvain*, 56.

Wade, Robert (1990), *Governing the Market: Economic Theory and the Role of the Government in East Asian Industrialization* (Princeton: Princeton University Press).

World Bank (1993), *The East Asian Miracle* (Oxford: Oxford University Press).

—— (1994), *World Development Report 1994* (Oxford: Oxford University Press).

Young, Alwyn (1991), 'Learning by Doing and the Dynamic Effects of International Trade', *Quarterly Journal of Economics*, 106.

2

UTTAR PRADESH:
THE BURDEN OF INERTIA[*]

Jean Drèze
Haris Gazdar

1. INTRODUCTION

Why Uttar Pradesh?

One of the lessons emerging from a wide range of recent development experiences is that public action can play a powerful role in
promoting essential aspects of the quality of life, even at an early
stage of development. The literature on this subject includes a
number of instructive case studies, such as that of Kerala appearing
in this book. In this paper, we investigate an example of the other
side of the same coin, i.e. the penalties of inaction.

Uttar Pradesh can also be seen as a case study of development
in a region of India that currently lags behind much of the rest of
the country in terms of a number of important aspects of well-being
and social progress. The region is characterized *inter alia* by exceptionally high levels of mortality, fertility, morbidity, undernutrition,
illiteracy, and social inequality, and a slow pace of poverty decline.[1]

* We are grateful to Sudhir Anand, Roli Asthana, Rukmini Banerji, Sajitha
Bashir, Bela Bhatia, Gaurav Datt, Keshav Desiraju, Stuart Gillespie, B.K. Joshi, Shiva
Kumar, Nidhi Mehrotra, Aditi Mehta, Aya Okada, Vimala Ramachandran, V.K.
Ramachandran, Jesse Ribot, Amartya Sen, Sunil Sengupta, Amarjeet Sinha, Rohini
Somanathan, and R.V. Vaidyanatha Ayyar for helpful discussions, and to Geeta
Gandhi Kingdon for detailed comments on a draft of this paper. We are also indebted
to Shanti Rabindran and Usman Saadat for excellent research assistance. Finally,
we would like to thank C.P. Sharma (Agricultural Economics Research Centre,
University of Delhi), Chote Lal, and members of the Samaj Seva Sanstha in Manik-
pur, for their invaluable help with the field work.

1 For some relevant indicators, see the Statistical Appendix in the companion
volume Drèze and Sen (1995); on the issue of poverty decline, see Datt and Ravallion

This region consists of four large, adjacent states of north India: Bihar, Madhya Pradesh, Rajasthan, and Uttar Pradesh. There are important differences between these four states, and it would be a mistake to consider them as a single entity. But the causes of backwardness in these different states, nevertheless, appear to have much in common, and comparative investigations have pointed to many broad similarities in the social, cultural, and even political make-up of these states.[2] A case study may help to understand the causes of retarded development in this region.

Aside from supplying a useful case study, Uttar Pradesh deserves a good deal of attention in its own right. In fact, a large part of India's total population — one could even say of the world population — is involved: at the time of the 1991 census, Uttar Pradesh had a population of 139 million, larger than that of any country in the world other than China, India, Indonesia, Brazil, Russia, and the United States.[3] Understanding what goes on in Uttar Pradesh, and what can be done about it, is in some ways just as important as to study Bangladesh or Ethiopia.

The plan of the chapter is as follows. After some methodological clarifications in the remainder of this section, we turn in section 2 to the available evidence on living conditions in Uttar Pradesh. We also discuss the respective contributions of slow economic growth and ineffective public action to the persistence of endemic deprivation in this region. The issue of ineffective public action is illustrated in section 3 with a case study of basic education in rural areas. Section 4 presents further comments on the causes of educational backwardness in Uttar Pradesh. Section 5 explores the general phenomenon of public inertia in this region, and some of its social and political roots. Concluding remarks are presented in section 6.

Ravallion (1995); on nutritional indicators, see the recent anthropometric evidence derived from the National Family Health Survey (e.g. Gillespie, 1995).

[2] See, for instance, Sopher (1980a), and other contributions on the cultural and social geography of India in Sopher (1980b); see also Karve (1965), Rudolph and Rudolph (1972), Dyson and Moore (1983), Caldwell and Caldwell (1987), Satia and Jejeebhoy (1991), among others.

[3] The four states mentioned earlier, taken together, had a population of 335 million in 1991 (about 40 per cent of India's total population).

Methodological Clarifications

Before we begin, three methodological clarifications are in order. First, some of the analysis presented in this paper (particularly in sections 2 and 3) is essentially comparative in nature — it deals with how Uttar Pradesh has done in different fields in comparison with other states or regions of India. The presentation of comparative data will gain in clarity if we choose one 'reference region' with which Uttar Pradesh is consistently compared. We have decided against taking India itself as the reference region, simply because the four north Indian states mentioned earlier have a large weight in the all-India average (e.g. they account for 40 per cent of the total population). Since the motivation of this paper is partly to study Uttar Pradesh as a case of this collection of states, a comparison with a region of which these four states are a large component would not be particularly helpful. Specifically, such a comparison would tend to hide the sharp contrasts that exist between these states and the *rest* of India. As an alternative, we have adopted 'South India' (defined as the union of Andhra Pradesh, Karnataka, Kerala, and Tamil Nadu) as the reference region.

This reference region may be considered as a relatively 'advanced' part of India, in terms of many of the indicators used in this paper. The advanced character of this region, however, should not be exaggerated. The largest of the four south Indian states, Andhra Pradesh, is in some important respects (e.g. literacy levels) much closer to the large north Indian states than to Kerala or Tamil Nadu. The state of Kerala, of course, has exceptional achievements in some fields, but it only accounts for 15 per cent of the total population of south India. Basic calculations of indicators such as life expectancy, literacy, domestic product, etc., suggest that south India is often not very different from the rest of India *outside* Bihar, Madhya Pradesh, Rajasthan, and Uttar Pradesh. In any case, none of what follows depends on south India being 'representative' of India outside the large northern states — we simply propose it as a helpful benchmark. From time to time, we will also refer to the specific contrast between Uttar Pradesh and Kerala, which is particularly relevant to the concerns of this book.

The 'South India' figures presented in this paper have been calculated as weighted averages of the state figures. The weights used are different for different indicators. In most cases, we have been able to use the weights relevant to the respective exercises (e.g. population aged 7 and above for the 7+ literacy rate, male population for the female–male ratio, number of births for the infant mortality rate, etc.). In a few cases, some approximation has been necessary, because the exact weights were not available. But the margin of error involved in the approximations is, in every case, small enough to be ignored for our purposes.

The second clarification concerns the reference period used in the presentation of different indicators. Comparisons between different states, and related statistical exercises used in this paper, are sometimes sensitive to the choice of reference period. In order to have an impartial rule in this respect, the most recent year for which the relevant information could be obtained has been chosen as the reference year in each case (except when there was a specific reason for focusing on a different year). In a few cases, we have had to use 1981 census data, because the corresponding information from the 1991 census had not been released at the time of writing.

Finally, this paper makes considerable use of field-based observations, derived *inter alia* from village studies as well as`from our own field work, to take the analysis beyond what emerges from more aggregative secondary data alone.[4] This type of information will be useful, for instance, in understanding patterns of gender relations, the functioning of public institutions, and the nature of rural politics. These field observations are not, of course, representative of the state in a statistical sense. This qualification will have to be borne in mind as we go along, but it does not prevent field-based investigations from providing valuable insights into different aspects of the economy and society of Uttar Pradesh.

---

[4] We have made particularly intensive use of the numerous village studies that have been carried out in different parts of Uttar Pradesh. The early work in this regard includes Olper and Singh (1952), Marriott (1952), Dube (1958), Khare (1962, 1964), Berreman (1963), Park and Tinker (1963), Rastogi (1964, 1965, 1966), Elder (1970), Yogendra Singh (1970), and Wiser and Wiser (1970). A more comprehensive list of references for the period up to the early seventies can be found in Lambert (1976). More recent field-based studies that we have drawn upon include, among others, Miller (1976), Hale (1978), Miriam Sharma (1978), S.S. Sharma (1981), Simmons et al. (1982), Macdorman (1986), Danda (1987), Khan (1988), Wadley and Derr (1989), Zamora (1990), Cohn (1990), Misra (1991). Bhoosnurmath (1991), Saith and Tankha (1992), Jagpal Singh (1992), Minturn (1993), Moller (1993), Vlassoff (1993), Gupta (1994), Kingdon (1994), Ravi Srivastava (1995), and Mehrotra (forthcoming).

2. LIVING CONDITIONS IN UTTAR PRADESH

2.1 Background

Uttar Pradesh is primarily an agricultural state, with a high proportion (just above 80 per cent) of its population living in rural areas,
and primarily engaged in the agrarian economy. Although urbanization and non-agricultural employment have been increasing over
time, conditions of production in agriculture and the distribution
of agrarian assets (particularly cultivable land) remain the most
important determinants of the material condition of the population.

Two recent developments in the region's agrarian history can
be regarded as significant turning points. The first came with the
reforms of land revenue and property rights that followed India's
independence, generally known as '*zamindari* abolition'. These reforms abolished the role of private intermediaries in the land
revenue system, and led to a clearer definition of private property
rights in land. The structure of land ownership has remained, more
or less, the same since then. These early reforms coincided with
the post-independence adoption of social and economic development as official goals of public policy. The second development
was the spread, in the nineteen sixties and seventies, of modern
agricultural practices in western Uttar Pradesh, and their subsequent diffusion to other regions of the state.

Although neither of these two episodes has been particularly
dramatic (compared, for instance, with land reforms and productivity growth in other developing regions, including parts of India),
they do define the broad parameters of change in the economic
circumstances of the bulk of the population. The land reforms
limited the powers of large feudal landlords, and gave ownership
rights to a vast majority of tenant farmers who previously did not
own land.[5] The reforms did not, however, eradicate landlessness,
nor did they prevent the persistence of massive inequalities of land
ownership in the state. The land ownership structure has changed

---

[5] Prior to zamindari abolition, legal ownership of land in Uttar Pradesh was
vested with between 3 to 8 per cent of rural households (see Hasan, 1989, and
Stokes, 1975, for various estimates). After zamindari abolition the proportion of
rural households owning some land ranged from 70 to 90 per cent depending on
the precise ownership criterion (see H.R. Sharma, 1994, for results of the 1953–4
round of the National Sample Survey).

little in Uttar Pradesh in the forty years since the abolition of zamindari.[6]

TABLE 1. *India, Uttar Pradesh and South India: Selected Indicators*

	India	Uttar Pradesh	South India
Population, 1991[a] (million)	846	139	196
	(74)	(80)	(70)
Life expectancy at birth, 1990–2 (years)			
Female	59.4	54.6	64.0
Male	59.0	56.8	60.9
Death rate, age 0–4, 1991 (per 1,000)			
Female	27.5	38.4	17.8
Male	25.6	33.2	18.9
Literacy rate, age 7+, 1991 (%)			
Female	39	25	49
Male	64	56	68
Average per-capita consumer expenditure, 1987–8 (Rs/month at 1970–1 prices)			
Rural	41.2	37.7	43.2
Urban	61.2	55.1	57.1
Head-count ratio, 1987–8 (percentage of the population below the poverty line)			
Rural	45	48	41
Urban	37	42	42

Note. [a] In brackets, the proportion of the population living in rural areas (percentage).

Source. Drèze and Sen (1995), Statistical Appendix, based on data presented in Nanda (1992), Government of India (1993a), Tendulkar et al. (1993), and derived from the 1991 census, the National Sample Survey, and the Sample Registration System. The life expectancy figures are unpublished estimates supplied by the Office of the Registrar-General. The figures for 'South India' have been calculated as weighted averages of the relevant state-specific figures.

[6] Ranked by their ownership of land, the bottom 40 per cent of all rural households in Uttar Pradesh owned 2.5 per cent of the total area in 1953–4, while the top 10 per cent owned 46 per cent of the area. More or less the same size distribution was observed in 1982 (H.R. Sharma, 1994).

Technological change led, over time, to a significant expansion of private agricultural incomes, and also laid the basis for some diversification of economic activity.[7] In the absence of major redistributive programmes, however, the gradual expansion of private incomes only led to a slow decline in conventional indicators of poverty. This, combined with the fact that other bases of improvement in human well-being (such as efficient public services and widespread literacy) were severely neglected over the same period, resulted in comparatively limited achievements in terms of the elimination of endemic deprivation. Some relevant evidence is presented in Table 1, and discussed in further detail below.

2.2   Basic Demographic Indicators

The demographic evidence on survival chances in Uttar Pradesh provides a helpful starting point for our enquiry. As discussed in the companion volume (Drèze and Sen, 1995), the central goal of development can be seen as the expansion of human 'capabilities'.[8] Further, there is an obvious case for considering survival as one of the basic capabilities of primary interest. Some mortality and longevity indicators for Uttar Pradesh are given in Table 2, along with the corresponding figures for South India.

As this table indicates, life in Uttar Pradesh is short and precarious. Female life expectancy, for instance, is still below 55 years, and the under-five mortality rate is as high as 141 per thousand. To put things in perspective, these figures are not very different from, say, the corresponding estimates for sub-Saharan Africa (53 years and 160 per thousand, respectively).[9] Among all major Indian states, Uttar Pradesh has the highest under-five mortality rate, the second-highest crude death rate, and the third-lowest life expectancy figure.[10] The

[7] See Sharma and Poleman (1993), Ranjan (1994), and the literature cited there. The impact of agricultural change in Uttar Pradesh has also been analysed in a number of village studies, including Bliss and Stern (1982), Saith and Tankha (1992), Srivastava (1995), Drèze, Lanjouw, and Sharma (forthcoming).

[8] On this, see also Amartya Sen's contribution in this volume.

[9] *Human Development Report 1994*, pp. 208–9.

[10] Until the mid-eighties, Uttar Pradesh had the highest levels of infant and child mortality among major Indian states, by a long margin, and also the lowest level of life expectancy. There has been some progress in this respect in recent years,

number of maternal deaths per 100,000 live births in Uttar Pradesh was estimated to be as high as 931 in the mid-eighties. Only five countries in the world, among those for which official figures are available, had higher estimated maternal mortality rates at that time: Somalia, Bhutan, Ghana, Gambia, and Congo.[11]

Survival indicators in Uttar Pradesh are quite dismal not only in comparative international terms, but also in relation to what has been achieved in the more advanced Indian states. For instance, a new-born girl can expect to live *20 years longer* if she is born in Kerala rather than in Uttar Pradesh. And the probability that she will die before the age of one is more than six times as high in Uttar Pradesh as in Kerala (Government of India, 1993a, p. 31). Even the demographic gap between Uttar Pradesh and South India as a whole is quite striking (Table 2).

The demographic evidence on child survival is consistent with independent evidence on child nutrition. According to the recent National Family Health Survey, Uttar Pradesh comes second to Bihar (among India's major states) in terms of the incidence of undernutrition among children below the age of five.[12]

Aside from low survival chances, the demographic characteristics of Uttar Pradesh include high fertility rates. In fact, according to the latest available figures (Table 2), Uttar Pradesh has the highest birth rate among all Indian states, as well as the highest fertility rate. Uttar Pradesh has made comparatively little progress so far in terms of the 'demographic transition' from high to low levels of mortality and fertility.

2.3   Educational Levels

Empirical analyses of the determinants of demographic outcomes in India have consistently brought out the crucial role of literacy in

---

leading Uttar Pradesh to 'overtake' Madhya Pradesh and Orissa, where the decline of mortality has been relatively slow during the eighties.

[11] *Human Development Report 1991*, p. 143. Maternal mortality rates in industrialized countries such as Norway or Belgium are below 5 per 100,000 live births; this is an aspect of human well-being for which inequalities between the poorest and richest countries of the world are extraordinarily large.

[12] Gillespie (1995), based on weight-for-age data for 1992–3.

TABLE 2. *Demographic and Health Indicators*

	Uttar Pradesh [a]	South India	States doing 'worse' than Uttar Pradesh
Life expectancy at birth, 1990–2 (years)			
Female	54.6 (14)	64.0	Madhya Pradesh, 53.5
Male	56.8 (13)	60.9	Madhya Pradesh, 54.1
			Orissa, 55.9
Other mortality-related indicators			
Crude death rate, 1992 (per 1,000)	12.8 (14)	8.4	Madhya Pradesh, 12.9
Under-five mortality rate, 1992–3 [b]	141 (15)	82	none
Estimated maternal mortality rate, 1982–6 (per 100,000 live births)	931 (14)	365	Rajasthan, 938
Fertility indicators			
Total fertility rate, 1991	5.1 (15)	2.6	none
Crude birth rate, 1990–2	35.8 (15)	23.5	none
Female–male ratio, 1991			
Females per 1,000 males	879 (14)	979	Haryana, 865

Notes. [a] In brackets, Uttar Pradesh's rank among 15 'major states' for which the relevant data are available: Andhra Pradesh, Bihar, Gujarat, Haryana, Himachal Pradesh, Karnataka, Kerala, Madhya Pradesh, Maharashtra, Orissa, Punjab, Rajasthan, Tamil Nadu, Uttar Pradesh, West Bengal. The ranking is based on arranging the states in increasing order of the relevant indicator, except in the case of life expectancy and female–male ratio (decreasing order).

[b] Probability of dying before age 5.

Sources. Life expectancy: unpublished estimates (based on SRS data) supplied by the Office of the Registrar-General. Crude death rate: *Sample Registration System 1992*, Statement 26, p. 30. Under-five mortality rate: International Institute for Population Sciences (1994a), Table 34, p. 85. Maternal mortality rate: Mari Bhat et al. (1992), Table 4. Total fertility rate: SRS data presented in Government of India (1993a), pp. 20 and 40. Crude birth rate: *Sample Registration Bulletin*, January 1994, pp. 22–9 and 46–53. Female–male ratio: Nanda (1992), p. 13, based on 1991 census data. The figures for South India have been calculated as weighted averages of the relevant state-specific figures.

reducing mortality and fertility rates.[13] In particular, the four states that are commonly identified as lagging behind the rest of the country in terms of the demographic transition (Bihar, Madhya Pradesh, Rajasthan, and Uttar Pradesh) also turn out to be the four states with the lowest literacy levels.[14] The 1991 census indicates that, for persons aged 7 and above, the literacy rate in these four states ranges from 38 per cent in Bihar to 44 per cent in Madhya Pradesh as against 59 per cent in South India (with an even larger north–south gap in the younger age-groups).

The poor educational record of these four states is particularly striking in the case of female literacy. In Uttar Pradesh, only one woman out of four in the 7+ age group was able to read and write in 1991 (see Table 3). Further, aggregate literacy figures tend to hide sharp variations between different regions and population groups, implying extremely low achievements for the most disadvantaged groups at a more disaggregated level. While the 7+ female literacy rate in Uttar Pradesh as a whole was 25 per cent in 1991, the figure goes down to 19 per cent for rural areas, 11 per cent for the scheduled castes, 8 per cent for scheduled castes in rural areas, and 8 per cent for the whole rural population in the most educationally backward districts. Currently-available data from the 1991 census do not permit further disaggregation, but the 1981 census figures suggest that, in Uttar Pradesh, female literacy remains close to zero for large sections of the society. For instance, the crude female literacy rate among scheduled castes in rural areas in 1981 was below 1.5 per cent in 18 out of Uttar Pradesh's 56 districts, and below 2.5 per cent in a *majority* of districts.[15]

It might be added that, despite its far-reaching individual and social significance, literacy alone is not a momentous achievement in terms of the amount of learning involved. If we consider more demanding criteria of educational attainment, such as the completion of primary or secondary education, the achievement rates are

[13] On this, see the contribution by Murthi, Guio, and Drèze in this volume, and the literature cited there.

[14] We ignore the state of Arunachal Pradesh in north-east India, which has a tiny population of less than one million persons, mainly from the 'scheduled tribes'. Arunachal Pradesh has a lower level of male literacy than the four states in question, but a higher level of female literacy (Bose, 1991, p. 62).

[15] Nuna (1990), pp. 113–14.

correspondingly lower. For instance, in 1992–3, only half of all literate males in Uttar Pradesh, and 40 per cent of literate females, had completed the cycle of eight years of schooling involved in the primary and middle stages.[16] Many children in Uttar Pradesh, if they are literate at all, acquire this skill on the basis of a fleeting passage through the educational system.[17]

TABLE 3.　*Uttar Pradesh: Educational Achievements and Participation* [a]

	Male	Female
Literacy rate, age 7+, 1991 (%)		
Rural	52 (63)	19 (41)
Urban	70 (83)	50 (68)
Rural and urban combined	56 (68)	25 (49)
Literacy rate, age 7+, 1991: scheduled castes in rural areas (%)	39 (49)	8 (28)
Literacy rate, age 10–14, 1987–8 (%)		
Rural	68 (84)	39 (72)
Urban	76 (90)	69 (85)
Proportion of children aged 12–14 who have never been enrolled in a school, 1986–7 (%)		
Rural	27 (14)	68 (28)
Urban	19 (7)	39 (22)
Proportion of rural children attending school, 1987–8 (%)		
Age 5–9	45 (75)	28 (68)
Age 10–14	64 (74)	31 (58)

Note. [a] In brackets, the corresponding South India figures (calculated as weighted averages of the relevant state-specific figures).

Sources. Compiled from Nanda (1992, 1993), Tyagi (1993), Sengupta (1991), Visaria et al. (1993), based on census and National Sample Survey data.

[16] Calculated from International Institute for Population Sciences (1994b), Table 3.6.

[17] Not infrequently, the sojourn in the educational system is so short that the child in question does not even become literate. In the village of Palanpur (Moradabad district), a survey carried out in 1983–4 showed that, in a village with 960 residents, as many as 56 adults were illiterate despite having been to school (Drèze and Saran, 1995).

As far as the specific issue of literacy is concerned, the most sobering feature of the educational situation in Uttar Pradesh is the persistence of high levels of illiteracy in the *younger* age groups. It is not just that a lot of adults are illiterate, pulling down the average literacy rate, with most people in the younger age groups being literate.[18] Even in the younger age groups, illiteracy is endemic, especially in rural areas. In the late eighties, the incidence of illiteracy in the 10–14 age group was as high as 32 per cent for rural males and 61 per cent for rural females, and more than *two-thirds* of all rural girls in the 12–14 age group had *never* been to school (see Table 3). Uttar Pradesh is nowhere near the realization of the constitutional goal of free and compulsory education for all children up to the age of 14, which was supposed to have been reached by 1960.

2.4   Gender Inequality and Female Deprivation

The persistence of endemic illiteracy is not Uttar Pradesh's most distinctive social failure. In fact, the other large north Indian states (Bihar, Madhya Pradesh, and Rajasthan) fare no better than Uttar Pradesh in that respect. There is another field, however, in which Uttar Pradesh seems to fare worse than most, if not all, other Indian states — that of gender equality.

One basic indicator of the disadvantaged position of women in Uttar Pradesh is the female–male ratio in the population (see Table 4). In 1991, the number of females per 1,000 males in Uttar Pradesh was as low as 879. One Indian state has an even lower female–male ratio: Haryana, bordering on western Uttar Pradesh, where there were only 865 females per 1,000 males in 1991. However, disaggregated figures show that the 'epicentre' of the problem of low female–male ratios is not in Haryana but in western Uttar Pradesh. That region, which has more than one-third

---

[18] That pattern applies in Kerala, where, in 1987–8, the incidence of illiteracy was about 23 per cent in the population as a whole, but under 3 per cent in the 10–14 age group (Sengupta, 1991, based on National Sample Survey data). It also applies to many Chinese provinces (Drèze and Saran, 1995). In the educationally advanced states of India outside Kerala, such as Himachal Pradesh, Tamil Nadu, and Maharashtra, illiteracy is now quite low among male adolescents (e.g. below 15 per cent in 1987–8, for the 10–14 age group), but remains high for adolescent females; see Sengupta (1991).

of the population of the entire state and nearly three times the population of Haryana, has a female–male ratio of only 0.84.

TABLE 4. *Female Disadvantage*

	Uttar Pradesh	South India
Females per 1,000 males (1991)		
All ages	879	979
Age 0–6	928	962
Gender bias in survival		
Ratio of female to male death rates (1991)		
Age 0–4	1.16	0.94
Age 5–14	1.17	0.97
Age 15–34	1.26	0.84
Maternal mortality rate, per 100,000 live births (1982–6)	931	365
Gender gap in life expectancy (1990–2)		
Female–male difference in years	–2.2	+3.1

Sources. Calculated from Mari Bhat et al. (1992), Nanda (1992), Government of India (1993a), Visaria et al. (1993), and Drèze and Sen (1995), Statistical Appendix — all based on census, National Sample Survey, and Sample Registration System data.

Some brief international comparisons may help to put this extraordinary number in perspective. The only countries with a female–male ratio lower than 0.84, among all those listed in *Human Development Report 1994* (pp. 146–7), are the following: Kuwait (0.76), Bahrain (0.73), Qatar (0.60), and United Arab Emirates (0.48). These exceptionally low female–male ratios are overwhelmingly attributable to male in-migration. If we exclude cases of exceptional male in-migration, the country with the lowest female–male ratio in the world is Pakistan, with 92 females per 100 males. This is considerably above Uttar Pradesh (which, incidentally, has a much *larger* total population than Pakistan), not to speak of western Uttar Pradesh. Uttar Pradesh is not just a setter of world records when it comes to the female deficit in the population, it is virtually in a league of its own.

The main cause of Uttar Pradesh's low female–male ratio is the considerable female disadvantage in survival from birth until the mid-thirties (Table 4). For the 0–4 age group, female death rates in

Uttar Pradesh are 16 per cent higher than male death rates, in contrast with the typical pattern of strong female *advantage* in that age group, which applies even in South India.[19] The female disadvantage in childhood is especially influential, since mortality rates tend to be particularly high in the younger age groups. Further, the link between excess female mortality in childhood and parental neglect of female children in this region of India is well documented.[20] Uttar Pradesh's low female–male ratio is a tangible reflection of anti-female discrimination.

The effects of female disadvantage in child survival are enhanced by even greater gender disparity in death rates between the ages of 15 and 35. This is in contrast to South India, where in the same age group the gender gap changes in *favour* of females (Table 4). Much of the excess female mortality in this age group in Uttar Pradesh reflects the combined effects of high maternal mortality and high fertility. The average number of births per woman is about twice as high in Uttar Pradesh as in South India, and the risk of maternal death from a particular birth is almost three times as high (see Tables 2 and 4). Anti-female discrimination in infancy and childhood, combined with high levels of fertility and maternal mortality, imply that female life expectancy at birth in Uttar Pradesh is 2.2 years below the corresponding figure for males — in contrast with a three-year *advantage* of females over males in South India.

Before concluding on this issue, it is worth mentioning that the female–male ratio in Uttar Pradesh is not only low, it has also been steadily *declining* since the beginning of this century — from 0.94 in 1901 to 0.88 in 1991. It is difficult to explain this steady decline of the female–male ratio in Uttar Pradesh without invoking the persistence, and possible accentuation, of unequal gender relations.[21]

[19] For further discussion of gender bias in mortality as a cause of low female–male ratios in India, see chapter 7 in the companion volume (Drèze and Sen, 1995), and the literature cited there.

[20] There is a large literature on this subject. See Miller (1981), Das Gupta (1987b, 1994), Basu (1992), Khan (1988), Khan et al. (1986, 1989), Jeffery et al. (1989), Harriss (1990), Minturn (1993), among others. For clear evidence of strong 'boy preference' in Uttar Pradesh (in contrast with much more gender-neutral patterns in South India), see the National Family Health Survey data on desired family composition; e.g. International Institute for Population Sciences (1994a, 1994b).

[21] On this issue, see Drèze and Sen (1995), chapter 7, and also the chapter by Murthi, Guio, and Drèze in this volume.

The general process of modernization and development seems to have done very little, so far, to reduce gender inequality in Uttar Pradesh.

2.5   A Question of Poverty?

Poverty and Well-being

It might be tempting to think that the main cause of Uttar Pradesh's low achievements in terms of survival chances, child nutrition, fertility decline, basic education, gender equality, and related aspects of well-being, lies in high levels of poverty.[22] There is, however, little evidence to support this hypothesis. Of course, there is plenty of poverty in Uttar Pradesh; in 1987–8, almost half of the population was estimated to live below the 'poverty line'.[23] But the incidence of poverty is also high in India as a whole. In fact, poverty indicators for Uttar Pradesh and India have been quite close to each other in most years for which the relevant data are available, as Fig. 1 illustrates.[24] Differences in poverty levels between Uttar Pradesh and India as a whole cannot explain why Uttar Pradesh does so much worse than average in terms of a wide range of indicators of well-being.

To prevent a possible misunderstanding, we should emphasize that we have no intention of diminishing the significance of high poverty levels in Uttar Pradesh, either as an *indicator* of material deprivation in that state, or as a *cause* of other kinds of deprivations. Obviously, the low level of incomes in Uttar Pradesh is a major

[22] In this section, we use the term 'poverty' in the sense that has become conventional in the literature on poverty in India, i.e. low per-capita expenditure. This conventional interpretation has to be distinguished from the notion of poverty as a failure of basic capabilities (on which see Sen, 1985, 1992).

[23] Tendulkar et al. (1993), Table A.5, based on the 43rd round of the National Sample Survey. The poverty line is meant to indicate the level of per-capita expenditure at which minimal calorie requirements are met, given the observed consumption patterns. Too much stress should not be placed on this interpretation, however, given the problematic nature of the notion of 'calorie requirements' (see Dasgupta and Ray, 1990, and Osmani, 1990), and related methodological problems (see EPW Research Foundation, 1993, for an overview).

[24] On this, see also the review of poverty estimates in EPW Research Foundation (1993).

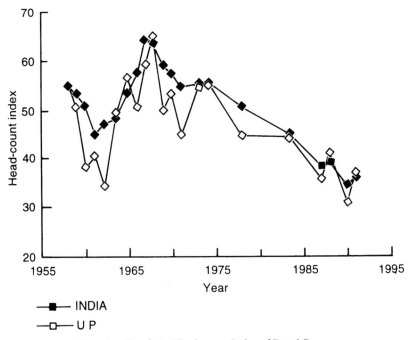

FIG. 1. *Trends in Head-count Index of Rural Poverty
in Uttar Pradesh and India, 1958–91*

Source. Unpublished figures calculated by Dr Gaurav Datt, World Bank, based
on National Sample Survey data.

constraint on individual and social opportunities. The point is that,
in this particular respect, Uttar Pradesh is not very different from
India as a whole, so that the causes of Uttar Pradesh's extraordinary
backwardness in terms of basic social achievements (such as child
survival and elementary education) have to be sought elsewhere.

The same point applies, with even greater force, when we compare
Uttar Pradesh and Kerala. Both states, according to the available
estimates, had similar levels of poverty (as measured by the head-
count ratio) in 1987–8, the latest year for which state-specific estimates of the head-count ratio are available.[25] They are, however,

[25] See, for instance, Tendulkar et al. (1993). The incidence of poverty in Kerala
seems to have declined quite rapidly in recent years (see Datt and Ravallion, 1995).
However, for most of the period from independence until the eighties, the incidence
of poverty in Kerala appears to have been, if anything, higher than in Uttar Pradesh
(see EPW Research Foundation, 1993).

poles apart in the scales of literacy and mortality indicators. The proportion of illiterates among females aged 7 and above, for instance, is more than five times as high in Uttar Pradesh as in Kerala (75 per cent and 14 per cent, respectively), and a similar observation applies to, say, the infant mortality rate (98 per thousand in Uttar Pradesh, compared with 17 per thousand in Kerala).[26] Even in a comparison between Uttar Pradesh and South India, much the same pattern applies, with South India doing much better than Uttar Pradesh in terms of literacy and child survival, despite similar levels of poverty. As will be argued further on, these astonishing contrasts have much to do with the nature of public action in the respective states.

East and West

The hypothesis that material poverty is not the main cause of Uttar Pradesh's social failures receives some support from a consideration of regional contrasts within the state. The main clue in this respect comes from a comparison of eastern and western Uttar Pradesh. These two regions, with roughly equal population sizes, account for about three-quarters of the total population of the state. The western region, which has enjoyed significant economic growth during the last three decades, is now considerably more prosperous than the eastern one. The head-count ratio of rural poverty in western Uttar Pradesh, for instance, was only 26 per cent in 1987–8, compared with 43 per cent in eastern Uttar Pradesh (see Table 5). Similarly, real wages in western Uttar Pradesh appear to be about twice as high as in the eastern region.

In spite of this economic advantage, western Uttar Pradesh fares no better than eastern Uttar Pradesh in terms of the available in- dicators of well-being and social advancement. This applies, for instance, to mortality and fertility levels. In 1981 (the latest year for which region-specific mortality data are available), western Uttar Pradesh had a *higher* child mortality rate than eastern Uttar Pradesh, with a particularly large east–west gap for female children (see Table 5). Western Uttar Pradesh also has considerably higher fer- tility levels.[27] Similarly, western Uttar Pradesh has failed to take advantage of its comparative prosperity to achieve any kind of lead

[26] See Drèze and Sen (1995), Statistical Appendix; the figures apply to 1991.
[27] On this, see also Table 8 below.

TABLE 5. Uttar Pradesh: Regional Contrasts

Region	Share of total UP population, 1991 (%)	Child mortality rate, 1981[a]		Female–male ratio, 1991	Estimated rural birth rate, 1988–90 (per 1,000)	Literacy rate, age 7+, 1991 (%)		Incidence of rural poverty, 1987–8[b]	Index of real wages for male agricultural labourers, 1989–92[c]
		Female	Male			Female	Male		
Himalayan	4.3	106	110	955	32.4	43	76	8	–
Western	35.6	170	145	841	39.7	27	55	26	7.3
Central	17.4	164	158	855	37.8	28	55	36	–
Eastern	37.9	154	144	923	37.4	21	55	43	3.5
Southern	4.8	166	147	846	37.1	24	58	50	–
All Regions	100.0	160	146	879	38.0	25	56	35	4.2
South India	–	91	104	979	25.3	49	68	30	4.5

Notes. [a] Probability of a new-born child dying before age 2 (multiplied by 1,000). This is considered to be the most reliable among the district-level estimates of infant and child mortality that have been calculated from 1981 census data (see Government of India, 1988, p. 2; and Government of India, 1989, p. 2). As recommended in these publications, we have used the 'graduated estimates', whenever available.

[b] Head-count ratio (percentage of the population below the poverty line). Note that these estimates are not directly comparable with those presented in Table 1, since they are based on a lower 'poverty line'.

[c] In Rs/day at 1970–1 prices.

Sources. Birth rates: Swamy and Sinha (1994), pp. 84–5, and *Sample Registration Bulletin*, July 1994, pp. 15–20; real wages: calculated by Bipul Chatto-padhyay (Institute of Economic Growth, Delhi) based on data published in *Agricultural Wages of India*, various issues; child mortality rates: calculated from 1981 census data presented in Government of India (1988), pp. 196–210, and Nuna (1990), p. 119, using estimates of birth rates in Mari Bhat (1995) for constructing appropriate weights; incidence of poverty, 1987–8: Drèze and Srinivasan (1995), based on a special tabulation of the National Sample Survey (43rd round); female–male ratios and literacy rates: calculated from Nanda (1992), pp. 13, 210–14, and 294–306. For each indicator, this table presents the latest available figures at the time of writing.

in the field of literacy and education. And as we saw earlier, gender inequality seems to be more extreme in western Uttar Pradesh than in any other part of the state.

All this does not mean that living conditions in general are no better in western than in eastern Uttar Pradesh. The fact that the incidence of poverty, based on conventional measures, is much lower in the former region, is an achievement of major importance. But the absence of any outstanding achievement in western Uttar Pradesh in many crucial fields, despite a significant lead in terms of income-based indicators, points once again to the importance of other neglected bases of social progress, such as public involvement in the fields of basic education and health care as well as women's effective participation in society and politics.

2.6 The Role of Public Services

The preceding observations suggest that the primary failure of economic development in Uttar Pradesh does not relate so much to the low level of private incomes (a problem which the state shares with much of the rest of India) as to the transformation of private incomes into well-being achievements. One of the relevant determinants of these achievements is the reach and functioning of public services. In this respect, the record of Uttar Pradesh is extraordinarily poor.

Some preliminary indications of this failure are given in Tables 6 and 7, which also include corresponding figures for South India.[28]

[28] It should be mentioned that some of the indicators presented in Table 6 reflect not only the provision and utilization of public services, but also some contribution

TABLE 6. Selected Indicators Relating to Public Services

	Uttar Pradesh	South India	Kerala
Health			
Percentage of recent births (1992–3) preceded by			
Tetanus vaccine	44	85	94
Antenatal checkup	30	73	97
Proportion of births taking place in medical institutions, 1991 (%)	4	50	92
Proportion of children aged 12–23 months who have received some vaccination, 1992–3 (%)	57	87	89
Proportion of villages with medical facilities, 1981 (%)	10	20	96
Number of hospital beds per million persons, 1991	340	964	2,418
Education			
Proportion of rural settlements of 300 persons or more having primary school, 1986 (%)	47.7	87.6	75.2
Proportion of primary schools held in 'open space', 1986[a] (%)	17.2	3.4	0.0
Proportion of primary schools with only one or two teachers, 1986 (%)	41	66	1.3
Proportion of rural children aged 12–14 who have ever been enrolled in a school, 1986–7 (%)			
Females	32	72	98.2
Males	73	86	99.6

of *private* services in the relevant fields. The operational basis of private provisioning, however, tends to be quite similar in different states, so that the observed *contrasts* are primarily a reflection of differences in the scope and functioning of public services. In some cases, as with schooling, another important factor is the nature of government support for private institutions geared to the provision of essential services (for instance, 'private aided' schools have played a major role in Kerala's outstanding experience of educational expansion).

Table 6 *(cont'd)*

	Uttar Pradesh	South India	Kerala
Other services			
Proportion of the rural population receiving subsidized cereals from the public distribution system, 1986–7	2	63	88
Per-capita supply of foodgrains through the public distribution system, 1986–7 (kg/year)	3	28	60
Proportion of rural households with electricity connection, 1991	11	41	42

Note. [a] *Not* including schools held in 'tents', 'thatched huts', or '*kachcha* buildings'.

Source. Compiled from Government of India (1992a, 1993a, 1993b), Tyagi (1993), Visaria et al. (1993), International Institute for Population Sciences (1994a, 1994b), Parikh (1994), and the *District Census Handbooks* of the 1981 census. The original sources are: Census of India 1981, Census of India 1991, National Sample Survey, National Family Health Survey, Fifth All-India Educational Survey, Sample Registration System. For further details on sources, and for state-specific figures, see Drèze and Sen (1995), Statistical Appendix.

The figures speak for themselves. Whether we look at health care provisions, or at educational facilities, or at the public distribution system, or indeed at almost any essential public services for which relevant data are available, Uttar Pradesh stands out as a case of resilient governmental inertia as far as public provisioning is concerned. Here again, the contrast with Kerala is particularly striking, but even the contrast with South India is quite startling.

Interestingly, these contrasts cannot be plausibly explained in terms of differences in levels of government expenditure alone. The proportions of government expenditure allocated to health and education, for instance, are similar in Uttar Pradesh and South India. In absolute terms, per-capita government expenditure on education in Uttar Pradesh is only 23 per cent below the corresponding figure for South India, with a similar proportionate gap in the case of health.[29]

[29] Calculated from *Reserve Bank of India Bulletin*, March 1993, Appendix II; the figures relate to 1990–1.

TABLE 7.   *Percentage of Villages with Selected Public Amenities, 1992–3*

	Uttar Pradesh	South India	Kerala
Health facilities			
Any health facility	23	43	98
Primary health centre or sub-centre	20	38	96
Trained birth attendant	33	61	46
Mobile health unit	0.4	15	27
Other institutions			
Anganwadi	19	55	99.5
Fair price shop	38	65	97
Cooperative society	14	32	87
Mahila mandal	5	28	89
Youth club	14	33	96

Source.   International Institute for Population Sciences (1994a, 1994b), Tables 11.3 and 11.4, based on the National Family Health Survey 1992–3.

The restricted scope and quality of public services in Uttar Pradesh, in comparison with South India, seems to have less to do with the level of government expenditure than with distorted *patterns* of social spending as well as with the defective *functioning* of the services in question. We will return to this issue, with special reference to the low effectiveness of the schooling system in Uttar Pradesh. The state of health services is no less alarming, especially in rural areas, as numerous studies have documented.[30]

One particular aspect of the dismal functioning of health services in Uttar Pradesh is worth specific mention, since it relates closely to other themes of this paper, including the central role of gender inequality and women's oppression in Uttar Pradesh's social failures. This concerns the large-scale displacement of health care services in rural Uttar Pradesh by family planning campaigns, focusing mainly on female sterilization, and often involving heavy-handed methods.

[30] See, for instance, the studies of health care in Uttar Pradesh and other north Indian states carried out by the Operations Research Group (Khan et al., 1980, 1986, 1988, 1989) and the Public Systems Group (Indian Institute of Management, 1985, Shah, 1989, Murthy 1992); also Budakoti (1988), Jeffery et al. (1989), Maurya (1989), among others.

A few testimonies, taken from recent studies of health care services in the state, may be worth citing on this point:

'the rampages of the family planning programme are particularly devastating . . . [the] preoccupation with attaining of the given family planning targets has had devastating effects on the other health activities' (Budakoti, 1988, pp. 153–4);

'the sterilization target achievement has the highest priority or rather the single priority' (Maurya, 1989, p. 167);

'under [health and nutrition education programmes] the ANMs/FHWs [Auxiliary Nurse Midwives and Family Health Workers] were motivating the people only for adoption of family planning practices to achieve their targets' (Ashok Kumar, 1990, p. 70);

'as from the highest level to the lowest everybody is asking regarding sterilization targets . . . health workers under the pretext of work of motivating sterilization cases neglect other work' (Shah, 1989, p. 120);

'in [rural and tribal] blocks it was observed that the visits of the medical and para-medical staff were irregular as most of the time they were busy with family planning and other campaigns' (Krishnamurthy and Nadkarni, 1983, p. 51);

'during the main months for family planning campaigns (usually December to March) virtually all energies of maternal and child health staff may be directed towards those ends [i.e. family planning targets]' (Jeffery et al., 1989, p. 216);

'in every scheme relating to the welfare of the rural poor, the beneficiaries are asked to practice family planning by undergoing vasectomy, or to sponsor vasectomy cases in order to avail of the benefits provided by schemes' (H.N. Singh, 1993, p. 35).[31]

It is important to note that the neglect of public services in Uttar Pradesh is not confined to specific programmes, such as those for

[31] Note that there is no evidence of the situation having improved since the studies cited here have been completed. Family-planning targets have apparently been renamed 'expected levels of achievement' (Visaria and Visaria, 1994), but the pressure to meet these targets has not relented in the least, judging from wide-ranging discussions with health and family-planning experts (see also Ramasundaram, 1995, for a startling testimony). One of them, a senior bureaucrat, after admitting that the testimonies cited here are still entirely relevant today, and that the government's family planning programme in north India still has a tendency to antagonize a large part of the population, cheerfully added: 'Opposition is the beauty of democracy.'

which data are presented in Tables 6 and 7. Rather, it is a case of comprehensive failure of social provisions in a wide range of fields, including basic education, land reform, child immunization, public distribution, maternal health, social security, public works, environmental protection, anti-poverty programmes, among others. There are few exceptions to this pattern. Nor is it easy to cite any example of a successful or innovative public programme relating to the promotion of human well-being on a widespread basis. We will return to this issue, and to the social and political roots of these failures, in section 5.

2.7 Women's Agency

The issue of gender inequality in Uttar Pradesh was introduced in section 2.3, mainly from the point of view of its consequences for women's well-being. Another crucial aspect of unequal gender relations in Uttar Pradesh is the suppression of women's *agency* in society, with extensive implications not only for the well-being of women but also for economic development and social progress in the society as a whole. The social importance of women's agency is discussed in the last chapter in this volume with specific reference to demographic outcomes, but it is relevant in other fields as well, including those of political and social change.[32]

In Uttar Pradesh, extreme social restrictions on women's freedom of movement and activities suppress women's agency by physically confining them to the domain of the household, and even diminish their ability to act effectively within that domain.[33] Low female participation in education is one aspect of this general pattern of women's limited interaction with the outside world. Similarly, less than half of all married women in Uttar Pradesh have regular exposure to *any* mass medium (compared to nearly 80 per cent in both Tamil Nadu and in Kerala).[34] Women's limited opportunities to acquire education

[32] Even economic growth and poverty decline in India seem to be positively related to female labour-force participation; on this, see Drèze and Srinivasan (1995).

[33] There is extensive ethnographic evidence on the particularly restrictive nature of gender relations in Uttar Pradesh. See, for instance, Karve (1965), Mandelbaum (1970), Sopher (1980b), Macdorman (1986), Jeffery et al. (1989), Minturn (1993), and Agarwal (1994).

[34] International Institute for Population Sciences (1994a, 1994b), Tables 3.12 and 9.14.

and information (whether through schooling, social interaction, mass media, or other means) is bound to affect their ability to play an informed role in the family and society.

Another indication of the restricted agency roles of women in Uttar Pradesh is the low level of female labour-force participation. Female labour-force participation is an important indicator of gender relations in at least two respects. First, there is much evidence that gender inequality within the family (e.g. the survival disadvantage of girls *vis-à-vis* boys) tends to be lower when adult women have wider opportunities for gainful employment.[35] Second, participation in gainful employment is one indication of the general participation of women in society, outside the narrow confines of domestic work.

The 1991 census counts only 8 per cent of women in Uttar Pradesh as 'main workers' (persons involved in economically productive employment for at least half of the year).[36] The corresponding figures for India and South India are 16 and 24 per cent, respectively. Among all Indian states, only Punjab and Haryana have lower female labour-force participation rates than Uttar Pradesh (4 and 6 per cent, respectively). As with female–male ratios, female labour-force participation rates are even lower in western Uttar Pradesh (2.5 per cent) than in Punjab or Haryana.[37] The fact that the talents and initiative of most women in Uttar Pradesh are overwhelmingly focused on domestic work represents a colossal suppression of their potential contributions in other fields.

Some of the connections between women's agency and social progress are discussed in the companion volume (Drèze and Sen, 1995) on the basis of broad comparisons between Indian states. It is worth noting that even *within* Uttar Pradesh, some important regional patterns seem to have much to do with gender relations and women's agency. The contrast between the hills and the plains is particularly relevant here. One important feature of the Himalayan region of Uttar Pradesh (consisting of eight districts in the northern part of the state) is a high level of female labour-force participation

[35] On this, see Rosenzweig and Schultz (1982), Kishor (1993), and the chapter by Murthi, Guio, and Drèze in this volume.

[36] The instructions to census investigators state that 'household duties' are not to be counted as economically productive.

[37] The figures in this paragraph are calculated from Nanda (1991), Table 6, based on the 1991 Census 'provisional population totals'.

— higher, in fact, than the average for India and even South India. Interestingly, this is also the only region of Uttar Pradesh where the female–male ratio is above unity, and where female children have a survival advantage over male children (see Table 8). The Himalayan region is also a relatively 'progressive' region of Uttar Pradesh in many other respects (e.g. it has considerably lower rates of mortality, fertility, and illiteracy), and it is quite plausible that these achievements partly reflect a more active and equal participation of women in the society as a whole.[38]

We end on this subject by noting that, like female–male ratios, female labour-force participation rates in Uttar Pradesh appear to have decreased rather than increased since the beginning of the century (there may, in fact, be a causal connection between these two distinct trends). According to census data, the ratio of female to male participation in the labour force was 0.43 in 1901, but only 0.13 in 1991. Changes of definitions and survey techniques may have contributed to this apparent decline, but are unlikely to account for the whole of it (especially since the tendency, in recent decades at least, has been to promote a more *inclusive* definition of female labour-force participation). Here again, there is little evidence of economic development having done very much for gender equality in Uttar Pradesh.

2.8 Discussion

Uttar Pradesh is one of India's most backward states, as far as the living conditions of the population are concerned. The proximate causes of that backwardness include a high level of poverty, as measured by conventional indices such as the head-count ratio. In that particular respect, however, Uttar Pradesh does not really stand out among Indian states. In order to explain, say, the exceptionally high levels of mortality and fertility in Uttar Pradesh, we have to take note of other social failures that have intensified the deprivations associated with low income levels. The contrasts between

---

[38] Similarly, the failure of the western region of Uttar Pradesh to achieve any kind of lead in health and educational matters compared with the eastern region, in spite of considerably higher incomes, may well relate to the particularly restricted social roles of women in the western region.

TABLE 8. Gender-Related Indicators for UP Regions, 1981

Region	Female–male ratio		Ratio of female q(2) to male q(2) [a]	Female labour force participation rate [b] (%)	Crude female literacy rate (%)	Percentage of girls aged 5–14 who are attending school	Total fertility rate
	All ages	Age 0–9					
Himalayan	959	960	0.96	24.2	24.1	40.7	5.2
Western	835	879	1.17	1.4	15.4	22.3	6.4
Central	868	937	1.03	3.7	15.9	22.6	5.8
Eastern	944	931	1.07	7.1	10.7	17.1	5.7
Southern	858	895	1.13	7.4	14.0	21.1	5.5
All Regions	885	913	1.10	5.3	14.0	21.1	5.5
South India	981	984	0.88	21.6	33.5	52.4	3.8

Notes. [a] q(2) is the probability of a new-born child dying before age 2 (as in Table 5).
[b] Proportion of 'main workers' in the total female population.

Sources. Calculated from district-level data published in Nuna (1990), Nanda (1992, pp. 294–306), Government of India (1989), Census of India 1981, Primary Census Abstract, Part II-B, Census of India 1981, Part IV-A, Social and Cultural Tables, Tables C-1, C-2, and C-4, and Census of India 1981, General Economic Tables, Part II. Each regional figure is a weighted average of the relevant district figures, with the size of the relevant population group in each district being taken as the relevant weight. In the case of male (female) q(2), the relevant weight for each district is the number of male (female) births; in the absence of district-level data on the number of births by gender, we have used the total number of births in the district as weight.

Uttar Pradesh and South India point to three social failures of deep significance: low levels of education, the restricted role of women in society, and the poor functioning of public services.[39]

These three particular failures (which are, of course, interrelated) do not exhaust the range of relevant influences, but they certainly play a central role in the persistence of endemic deprivation in Uttar Pradesh. Consider, for instance, the problem of high infant mortality. In Uttar Pradesh, a large proportion of infant deaths are due to tetanus and diarrhoea.[40] In both cases, cheap and effective means are available for preventing or curing the disease (vaccination, in the case of tetanus, and oral rehydration, in the case of diarrhoea). If so many children continue to die of tetanus and diarrhoea in Uttar Pradesh, it is not primarily because their parents are too poor to do something about it.[41] More influential reasons are: (1) inadequate public provisions for primary health care (including child immunization), especially in rural areas; (2) low educational levels, leading *inter alia* to a poor understanding of the causes and possible prevention of these elementary diseases, and to ineffective utilization of the services that are available;[42] and (3) the suppression of women's

[39] As was discussed earlier, the first two also have to be interpreted as *aspects* of human deprivation in Uttar Pradesh. As discussed by Amartya Sen in his contribution to this book (see also Drèze and Sen, 1995), human capabilities — such as literacy or participation in society — should be seen as having both intrinsic importance, as constituents of well-being, and instrumental importance, as means of enhancing *other* aspects of well-being. The failure of public services, on the other hand, is mainly of instrumental importance in this context.

[40] In a study based on data from rural Uttar Pradesh, Simmons et al. (1982) find tetanus to be one of the most common causes of neonatal death. They also find that diarrhoea and low birth-weights (and not the amount of food intake) are the main causes of malnourishment among children. A sample survey carried out in 1981–2 finds that neonatal mortality due to tetanus in rural Uttar Pradesh is higher than in any other state, and five times as high as the all-India average (Biswas, 1990, p. 48).

[41] On the relatively weak link between per-capita income and child survival in India, see the chapter by Murthi, Guio, and Drèze in this volume.

[42] In many parts of rural Uttar Pradesh, it is still common for umbilical cords to be cut with unsterilized sickles, for children to be left entirely unimmunized, for cooked food to be left uncovered for long hours before consumption, and for extraordinary beliefs to be entertained about the causes of simple diseases such as tetanus or diarrhoea (personal observations). On the highly uninformed nature of many beliefs and practices relating to health care in north India and Pakistan, see also Prasad et al. (1969), Mull (1991), Minturn (1993), Khan (1988), Khan et al. (1986, 1989), among others.

informed agency in the family and society, including in matters relating to child survival.[43]

Underlying the specific failures relating to public services, elementary education, and women's agency, is a deeper failure to achieve the kind of basic social change that facilitates progress in these fields. One aspect of the 'inertia' that accounts for slow social progress in Uttar Pradesh is the apathy of the state, but an equally important factor is the failure of civil society to challenge oppressive patterns of caste, class, and gender relations. The society of Uttar Pradesh remains steeped in traditional inequalities, which makes it that much harder to achieve widespread literacy, to run efficient public services, or to promote the agency of women in social and political matters. For instance, the conservative nature of gender relations makes it very difficult for women to work as teachers or doctors in rural areas, even if they have the required qualifications.[44] Similarly, as will be discussed further on, the resilience of caste and gender inequalities is a strong obstacle to the spread of basic education. And the highly divided nature of the rural society in Uttar Pradesh has seriously constrained the scope for collaborative public action (e.g. the provision of local public services) at the village level. In that sense, social change — or lack or it — occupies centre-stage in the story of Uttar Pradesh's past failures and possible future achievements.

We will return to this in section 5. Before that, the next two sections present a more detailed empirical investigation of some of the issues we have been concerned with so far, with special reference to primary education.

[43] In the case of girls, there is the additional issue of a low value being placed on female survival. The disadvantaged position of women in Uttar Pradesh implies *both* (1) a low level of female well-being (evident inter alia in massive excess female mortality), and (2) a reduced ability of women to do something for themselves *and* for other members of the society (leading, for instance, to high mortality rates for male as well as female children).

[44] As several studies have documented, the involvement of women as doctors and teachers often has a positive influence on the functioning of health and education services, e.g. because women prefer to be treated by female doctors (Indian Institute of Management, 1985), or because parents are reluctant to send their daughters to school unless they are taught by female teachers (Gupta et al., 1993, p. 55). In Uttar Pradesh, an overwhelming majority of doctors and teachers in rural areas are male (Indian Institute of Management, 1985; Government of India, 1994a); in Kerala, by contrast, about two-thirds of all primary-school teachers are female (Government of India, 1994a).

3. Schooling in Uttar Pradesh: A Field Investigation

3.1 The Setting

In this section, we report the findings of an informal field investigation of the functioning of primary schools in rural Uttar Pradesh. The enquiries we have carried out (in February–March 1994) essentially consist of unannounced visits to primary schools, supplemented by detailed discussions with local residents, teachers, officials, and activists. Altogether, we have visited 16 villages in four different districts: Moradabad, Rae Bareli, Pratapgarh, and Banda. In each district, we had made prior contact with a local person, who accompanied us to different villages around the place where he or she lived.

This method obviously falls short of guaranteeing a representative sample of villages and schools, and the findings reported below should be read in that light. If we think that they are worth reporting, it is because this informal investigation brings out striking regularities in the functioning of primary schools in different areas, which cannot reasonably be attributed to chance.[45]

Our survey involved unannounced visits to all government schools in the sample villages. The majority of these schools were primary schools, although some sample villages also had a 'middle' or secondary school.[46] In this section, the term 'sample schools' specifically refers to the government primary schools of the sample villages. All the sample villages, except two, had at least one government primary school. Some of them also had a private school. Although we collected a good deal of indirect information on these private schools, we only visited a few.

The sample villages are spread over four of the five 'regions' of Uttar Pradesh, namely Western (Moradabad), Central (Rae Bareli), Eastern (Pratapgarh), and Southern (Banda).[47] Rae Bareli

---

[45] In some respects, our findings also bear remarkable similarity to those of similar field-based studies in Uttar Pradesh as well as in other educationally backward regions of India. See particularly Prasad (1987), Kingdon (1994), A. Sinha (1995), and Sinha and Sinha (1995).

[46] In Uttar Pradesh, primary, 'middle', and secondary schools are those with classes up to and including the fifth, eighth, and tenth grade, respectively.

[47] This regional division follows the National Sample Survey (see Jain et al., 1988, for a list of the constituent districts). The fifth region, 'Himalayan', is not included in our sample.

and Pratapgarh districts, however, are adjacent to one another. In terms of agro-climatic zones and social conditions, then, our surveys effectively covered three distinct regions of the state: Moradabad in western Uttar Pradesh, a 'Green Revolution' district with a relatively dynamic economy; Rae Bareli and Pratapgarh on the central–eastern border, formerly a stronghold of Thakur zamindars (whose presence is still felt), where agricultural growth is of more recent origin and non-agricultural activities are quite limited; and the eastern part of Banda in southern Uttar Pradesh, where an overwhelmingly scheduled-caste and *adivasi* population still lives in the oppressive shadow of powerful 'Dadu' Brahmin landlords.

In Moradabad district, our investigation focused on Palanpur, a village familiar to one of us, and the surrounding villages. On Palanpur itself, a good deal of useful information is available from earlier household surveys, covering the 1957–94 period.[48] Some use of that supplementary information will be made in this section and the next one.

3.2   Accessibility of Primary Schools

As was mentioned earlier, all but two of the sample villages had at least one government primary school. The two villages without a government primary school (one in Pratapgarh, the other in Banda) were relatively small.[49] In both cases, local residents cited tangible political factors as being responsible for the absence of a school. In the Pratapgarh village, we were told that local Thakur landlords, who wielded a great deal of power, had obstructed the provision of a primary school. In Banda, we visited a scheduled-caste village where a school officially sanctioned under a scheduled-caste development scheme had failed to materialize. Instead, the school was built in a neighbouring high-caste settlement within the same administrative area. These two exceptions, while affecting a relatively small number of persons, are of some political significance, in so far as they illustrate the absence of a well-accepted social consensus on the need to universalize primary education in Uttar

[48] See Bliss and Stern (1982) and Drèze, Lanjouw, and Sharma (forthcoming); the schooling situation in Palanpur is also discussed in Drèze and Saran (1995).

[49] In fact, both 'villages' are officially considered as hamlets within larger residential units recognized as villages for administrative purposes.

Pradesh, and the lack of effective political organization among disadvantaged groups (on which more further on).

Even these two villages, however, were within walking distance of government primary schools in neighbouring villages or settlements. In this respect, the sample villages were not atypical of rural Uttar Pradesh as a whole, where the proportion of the population living more than two kilometres away from a primary school is only around 2 per cent (Tyagi, 1993, p. 54). In other words, the existence and accessibility of schools does not seem to be the main cause of persistent educational backwardness in this region (even though much scope remains for improving the schooling infrastructure, as will be discussed shortly). As we move from schools to *schooling*, however, the educational situation in rural Uttar Pradesh appears in an extremely poor light.

3.3   Physical Condition of Schools

The first thing that struck us on approaching most of the sample schools was the dilapidated condition of the buildings, and, linked to that, the poor utilization of whatever facilities were available. Not a single one of the schools we visited had full use of the building. Buildings were not usable due to prolonged decay, pending repairs, incomplete construction, and lack of maintenance. In one village, the school building was being used by the local landlord as a cattle shed. In another, the headmaster (who was from outside the village) had made part of the school buildings his residence.

In several villages, we found evidence of school buildings falling into disrepair due to lack of maintenance, and then being abandoned in favour of new school buildings rather than repaired. In some of these cases, even the new building was not usable.[50] The most commonly-used part of the school building was the veranda, where children of all grades were often huddled together. This space provides some shelter from the elements, but is open on three sides

---

[50] It was a common complaint that buildings were left incomplete. Relatively minor construction jobs such as floor levelling, plastering of walls, fitting of doors and windows, and so on, were often left undone. Poor construction standards, exposure to the elements, and lack of use and maintenance, led to many buildings being abandoned altogether.

and hardly conducive to concentrated study. In many cases we found teachers and children sitting under trees near the school building.

The facilities available in most of the sample schools were minimal. Typically, the school building was completely bare, except for the occasional table and chair used by the headmaster. In several cases, we heard that whatever furniture had existed earlier had been appropriated by the village headman, the school teacher, or other influential local residents. Widely-used teaching material was limited to notebooks, slates, and some basic textbooks.

The pathetic physical condition of the sample schools is in sharp contrast with the claims recently made by the Government of India in connection with the expansion of schooling infrastructure under Operation Blackboard. This scheme was initiated in 1987–8 with the stated objective of providing all primary schools with some essential facilities, including '(i) a building comprising at least two reasonably large all-weather rooms with a verandah and separate toilets for boys and girls, (ii) at least two teachers in every primary school, as far as possible one of them a woman, and (iii) essential teaching learning equipment including blackboards, maps, charts, toys, and equipment for work experience' (Government of India, 1994a, p. 31). Recent reports of the Department of Education state that Operation Blackboard had been 'implemented' in 91 per cent of the country's primary schools by the end of 1992–3, rising to 99.9 per cent by the end of 1993–4.[51] In contrast with these cheerful statements, there is no evidence of Operation Blackboard having had much practical impact in the sample schools.[52]

3.4   Teacher Attendance and Teaching Practices

Teacher absenteeism was endemic in the sample schools. By all accounts, this is the most basic problem of the schooling system in the sample villages.

[51] Government of India (1994a), p. 31, and Government of India (1995), p. 109.

[52] In a recent survey of primary schools in three districts of Uttar Pradesh (Bashir et al., 1993a), a majority of schools reported being in possession of the teaching aids supplied by Operation Blackboard. However, 'most of these aids and toys are lying in brand new condition in trunks, cupboards or at the head teacher's residence' (p. 89), and only 10 per cent of teachers report using any teaching aids other than the prescribed textbooks (p. 64).

One indication of the magnitude of this problem is the simple fact that *two-thirds* of the teachers in the sample schools were absent, for one reason or another, at the time of our unannounced visit. In other words, the attendance rate of teachers in these schools is only around one-third.[53] Only two of the fifteen schools we visited had full attendance of teachers at the time of our visit. In some cases, particularly when the school had only one teacher, the absence of the teacher(s) implied that the school remained closed for the day. On several occasions, we found that a school had been closed without prior notice for the day, or a large part of it, because the teacher(s) had decided to engage in some other activity.

Another aspect of the problem of teacher absenteeism is that most teachers come late and leave early. We rarely found a school to be open on time in the morning, or after 12.30 in the afternoon, when the lunch break is supposed to begin. Schools rarely reconvene after this break. In effect, therefore, the school day lasts for under three hours on average (when the school opens at all).[54]

The consequences of low teacher attendance are all the more serious given that the official number of days of teaching in a year is quite low in the first place — about 220 according to government figures.[55] Combined with a teacher attendance rate of about one-third, this implies that the actual number of full teaching days per teacher per year in the sample schools may be as low as 75 or so.

Further, we found that teachers actually performed very little teaching *even when they were present.* In fact, no active teaching was taking place in any of the fifteen sample schools at the time of our visit.[56] At best, the teacher(s) had given exercises to the pupils.

[53] The last statement is based on the fact that the times of our visits were more or less randomly distributed over the period of the day when schools are officially open. Our findings on teacher absenteeism are consistent with the District Primary Education Programme (DPEP) baseline survey for Uttar Pradesh. In the latter case, half of the teachers were absent at the time of the investigators' visits, despite the fact that the teachers had been informed beforehand of the likely dates of these visits (Dr Sajitha Bashir, personal communication).

[54] The situation appears to be somewhat better in urban areas, but even there teacher absenteeism and shirking are serious problems. In her survey in Lucknow city, Kingdon (1994) found that government schools supplied on average 3.2 hours per day of teaching to grade 8 children.

[55] Mehrotra (1995), Table 2, based on data published by the Ministry of Human Resource Development.

[56] We did observe some teaching in the primary 'section' of several schools that

When they were present at all, teachers in the sample schools were found to be engaged in one or more of the following activities: supervising children; playing cards; talking with each other; talking with visitors (other than ourselves!), reading comics; preparing rolls for the forthcoming election of the management committee of a local credit cooperative.

In effect, the primary schools we visited were little more than child-minding centres (that too, working only occasionally). In most cases (even when more than one teacher was present), we found that all the children had been assembled together in one place, irrespective of age or grade, and were only expected to maintain a semblance of order. Some of them were working on exercises given by the teacher, and others were teaching themselves or each other. But many more were just playing or passing time. Supervision took one of the following forms: watching the children from a desk or chair; asking one senior child to maintain order; letting the children look after themselves. In many schools, the ambience was nothing short of chaotic.

These direct observations were amply confirmed by informal conversations with parents and local residents. Shirking and absenteeism on the part of school teachers was widely perceived as the fundamental problem of government schools in *all* the sample villages. The quality of whatever teaching does take place is also a matter of widespread popular concern.

3.5   Female Teachers

None of the sample schools had a female teacher. Even in the few schools that had separate primary sections for girls, we did not

---

also had an upper primary or secondary section. These schools, which tend to be located in larger villages, usually have a relatively large number of teachers, supervised by a headmaster. The scope for shirking is somewhat lower in these schools than in small primary schools where, more often than not, a single teacher is actually present, and acts as his or her own supervisor. In 1986, 29 per cent of all primary schools in India had a single teacher (if any!), and another 32 per cent had only two teachers (Tyagi, 1993, p. 88). In Uttar Pradesh, two-teacher schools are effectively reduced to single-teacher schools for a large part of the year, given the widely-observed fact that, in these schools, teachers 'frequently take turns in attending' (Middleton et al., 1993, p. 11).

encounter any female teacher. We were told that female teachers typically work in larger agglomerations, or in villages close to main roads.

This explanation is, indeed, the most plausible way of reconciling our field observation with official statistics, which indicate that 18 per cent of all primary-school teachers in Uttar Pradesh are female (Government of India, 1994a, p. 289). The distribution of female teachers, it appears, is highly uneven, with the teaching staff of primary schools being almost exclusively male in large parts of the state, especially the less accessible ones.[57]

The uneven distribution of female teachers in Uttar Pradesh is only one aspect of the issue of gender imbalance in teaching. Even the average of 18 per cent for the state as a whole is low; the corresponding figures for South India and Kerala are 39 per cent and 66 per cent, respectively.[58] In fact, among *all* Indian states, Uttar Pradesh has the lowest proportion of female teachers. Further, the proportion of female teachers in Uttar Pradesh has been declining in recent years, in spite of the supposed emphasis of official policy on a rapid expansion of female involvement in primary-school teaching.[59]

The low number and declining proportion of female teachers in Uttar Pradesh, and their particularly low presence in rural areas, relate to the restrictive and unequal nature of gender relations in that state. As was discussed earlier, women's labour-force participation in Uttar Pradesh is extremely low, and female access to the public domain is also very limited. The low involvement of women in teaching is one reflection of this general suppression of women's agency in society. Further, the patriarchal environment makes it very difficult for female teachers to reside in (or commute to) rural areas on their own, and nor can a married female teacher expect her husband to follow her if she is posted at some distance from his own place of work.

[57] According to the Fifth All-India Educational Survey, 40 per cent of female teachers in Uttar Pradesh are posted in urban areas, as opposed to 13 per cent of male teachers (National Council of Educational Research and Training, 1992, vol. II, Table 122).

[58] Calculated from Government of India (1994a), p. 289.

[59] The proportion of female teachers in Uttar Pradesh dropped from 21 per cent to 18 per cent between 1986 and 1992–3 (National Council of Educational Research and Training, 1992, and Government of India, 1994a).

The absence of female teachers in a large majority of rural schools in Uttar Pradesh may well be a serious constraint on the expansion of primary education, and particularly of female education. There is, indeed, some evidence that parents often have greater confidence in sending their daughters to school if the school has some female teachers.[60] The presence of female teachers in most schools is also important in so far as schooling is as much a socialization experience as a process of formal learning. The virtual exclusion of women from teaching positions in Uttar Pradesh diminishes the quality and diversity of that socialization experience, for girls *and* boys.[61]

3.6   Enrolment and Attendance

In all the sample schools, the number of pupils actually present at the time of our visit was well below — often as much as 50 per cent below — the number of children officially enrolled. Teachers also report that attendance levels vary a great deal over the year.[62] While there are many cases of children not turning up for long periods (and often eventually dropping out), the most common pattern is one of erratic attendance, with children dropping in and out of school according to circumstances.

One particular aspect of this pattern is a high level of child absenteeism during periods of high activity in the agricultural cycle. Pupil absenteeism, for instance, was said to be widespread at harvest time. It might be added that public examinations are usually held in late April, which is the time of the wheat harvest in Uttar Pradesh. This basic conflict between the schooling and agricultural calendars

[60] According to Gupta et al. (1993), for instance, in north India 'reluctance to have daughters taught by male teachers may begin as early as 7 to 8 years of age' (p. 55). A recent survey carried out in Nepal also finds that employing female teachers leads to 'lower repetition rates and higher attendance rates, especially among female children' (CIET International, 1995, p. 1).

[61] On aspects of the social importance of female teaching in India, see Narayana (1995). On issues relating to the socialization of girl children, the content of education, and the reproduction of gender inequalities, see Chanana (1988, 1990) and Devi (1992).

[62] This is consistent with our own direct observations for the village of Palanpur in Moradabad district, which we had the opportunity to visit on several occasions in 1993 and 1994.

is a telling indication of the lack of sensitivity of official policy to the needs of the rural poor.[63]

Teachers, in general, did not think that actively encouraging school attendance was part of their responsibility. This attitude contrasts with the accepted practice in schools run by voluntary organizations, which often employ people to bring children. It also contrasts with accounts of how schools functioned in the past in the sample villages. According to local residents, the teachers used to consider the monitoring and promotion of school attendance as an ordinary part of their duty.

The proportion of female children among attending children was, on average, about one-third (with a similar proportion for enrolled children). This is quite close to the ratio of female enrolment to total primary-level enrolment in Uttar Pradesh as a whole (39 per cent).[64] In some of the middle schools, the proportion of girls was higher. One reason for this is that boys are disproportionately en-rolled in private schools, which are more important at the middle than at the primary level.

School fees in government schools were nominal: around 10 paise per month in class 1, rising to around 1.50 rupees per month in class 5. Very often school fees were in arrears. In a number of schools, it was standard practice for teachers to continue the registra-tion of a pupil even if his or her fees were overdue, if necessary by paying the fees out of their own pockets. The motives for doing so were not altogether altruistic. In the sample schools, monitoring of teachers by district educational authorities is primarily based on periodic inspection of the school register.[65] In order to avoid being transferred, a teacher has to ensure that enrolment does not fall below the official norm. By paying school fees in the names of

[63] This problem has been known for many years (see e.g. Sen, 1970, for an early discussion and Kingdon, 1996 for a recent analysis), but no action has been taken so far. According to some researchers, resistance of teachers' unions to the required changes in the schooling calendar is one major reason for this inertia (Vimala Ramachandran, former advisor to the Department of Education, personal com-munication).

[64] Government of India (1994a), p. 280. The last figure pertains to all recognized schools, government and private.

[65] This inspection often takes place at the office of the inspector rather than at the school. In his study of schooling in rural Andhra Pradesh, Prasad (1987) also found that school inspectors showed great reluctance to visit rural schools per-sonally.

children who have actually dropped out (or have never been enrolled in the first place), teachers are able to maintain inflated registers and to reduce the chances of being transferred.[66]

3.7   Private Schools and Implicit Privatization

Little information exists on private schooling facilities in rural Uttar Pradesh. According to official statistics, less than 3 per cent of all primary schools in rural Uttar Pradesh are managed by private institutions.[67] These statistics, however, only cover *recognized* private schools ('aided' and 'unaided'), and field investigations — including our own — suggest that unrecognized private schools account for a much larger share of all private schools.

In most of the areas we visited, the network of government primary schools (classified as 'local body' schools in official statistics) was supplemented with formal and informal schools operated by private individuals or institutions. Most of these schools were unrecognized, and therefore unaided. Roughly speaking, private schools were of two types:[68] (1) profit-oriented schools managed on commercial principles, and (2) non-profit educational institutions run by voluntary organizations such as religious missions, development agencies, community institutions, and charitable trusts.

In the sample villages, the first type was more common than the second, except in Banda district where there was an active network

[66] This practice was widespread among the sample schools. Its implications for the reliability of official enrolment data are obvious enough. The long-standing problem of inflated enrolment figures in India is another example of a well-known but unaddressed flaw of the schooling system. The official figure for the gross enrolment ratio at the primary level in India is well above 100 per cent (Government of India, 1994a, p. 281), but this cheerful figure does not stand up to scrutiny; see Drèze and Sen (1995) for further discussion.

[67] National Council of Educational Research and Training (1992), vol. I, Table 53. For a thorough discussion of different types of school management in Uttar Pradesh, and of their respective performance in Lucknow, see Kingdon (1994).

[68] This is a somewhat simplified classification, which does not do full justice to the diversity of private schooling establishments. Some private schools, for instance, are based on a mixture of pecuniary and philanthropic motives (as when better-educated but unemployed youth decide to set up an informal school, both to earn some income as well as to contribute to the advancement of their village or community).

of schools run by voluntary organizations. The discussion in this section therefore concentrates on profit-oriented private schools. As far as non-profit schooling institutions are concerned, we will only note in passing that these institutions, while few in number, are often well-run and well-attended. The high attendance and low drop-out rates in these schools, where teachers and managers often have a genuine commitment to the promotion of basic education (especially among disadvantaged groups), demonstrates that low attendance in government schools has more to do with the abysmally low standards of teaching and management in these schools than with any lack of interest in education on the part of children and their parents. There are indeed cases where, in the same village, a well-run philanthropic school is packed with enthusiastic children (girls as well as boys) while the local government school exudes a familiar atmosphere of desertion, apathy, and decay.[69]

Turning to profit-oriented private schools, one obvious characteristic of these schools is that they charge substantial fees. The actual level of fees varies a good deal between different schools and regions. In the sample villages, the average fee in private primary schools was of the order of 15 rupees per child per month. This is roughly equivalent to three kilograms of wheat, or to the daily wage of an agricultural labourer in central or eastern Uttar Pradesh (in Moradabad district, wages are a little higher, but so are school fees).

Private-school teachers are poorly qualified and poorly trained. It is generally agreed that government teachers are more competent. But private-school teachers, unlike government teachers, turn up for work and do their job. They have a strong incentive to do so, since they might lose their job if attendance declines due to poor teaching standards. In short, teachers in private schools are accountable to parents in a way that simply does not apply in the case of government teachers. This is so in spite of private-school teachers earning much lower salaries than government teachers. In private schools, teachers are often employed on a part-time basis for less than 500 rupees per month, compared with a starting salary of 2,200

---

[69] For similar observations in a low-income area in Delhi, see Banerji (1995). The high general level of parental motivation for education in our sample villages came up again and again in discussions with parents (with some important qualifications, notably relating to gender and caste, on which see section 4.3), and the performance of the schooling system has to be evaluated in that light.

rupees per month for a government teacher (also effectively part-time!).

School attendance in private schools is significantly male-dominated, for two reasons. First, many parents are more reluctant to pay school fees for female than for male children. Second, attending a private school often involves commuting to a different village, something which female children are not easily allowed to do.[70] The pro-male bias of private schooling is one reason why female children are the first victims of the poor functioning of government schools, as will be discussed further on.

A crucial problem faced by private schools in rural areas is that it is hard for many of them to obtain official recognition (*maanyata*) from the government. Without maanyata, private schools cannot issue recognized primary-school certificates. The standard way of dealing with this problem of non-recognition is the following: children are taught in private schools until grade 5, when they are transferred to government schools for the sole purpose of obtaining a certificate. Most private schools establish informal links with local government schools in order to implement this procedure. This system is advantageous not only to private schools, whose existence depends on it, but also to government teachers, who are able to maintain inflated rolls as a result (since the children in question are officially enrolled in government schools). Inflated rolls ensure, as was mentioned earlier, that government teachers are not transferred to other schools due to low enrolment.

The system of 'fifth-grade transfer' described in the preceding paragraph is only one way in which public schooling in Uttar Pradesh has been, in effect, partly privatized. Another form of implicit privatization observed in some of the sample villages is the practice of government teachers hiring private teachers to mind the children while they do something else (this is viable for the government teachers, given the large salary differentials between government and private teachers). Some government teachers also give private tuitions in return for fees (during or outside their normal working hours), sometimes to the same children whom they are supposed to teach at school.

[70] Kingdon (1994) finds that private-school enrolment in the city of Lucknow is also male-dominated. In the absence of official statistics on unrecognized private schools, there is little state-level information on the gender gap in private-school enrolment.

3.8   Failure of Public Schooling

The picture emerging from this field investigation is quite bleak, to put it mildly. Teaching and management standards in government schools are extremely poor, and play a major part in the persistence of low attendance levels. Even those children who do attend government schools receive very little education, due to high rates of teacher absenteeism and shirking as well as to crude teaching methods.

Our own observations about the dearth of teaching in the sample schools were amply corroborated by local residents, who tend to be highly critical of the functioning of the schooling system. Most local residents also take the view that teaching standards in government schools have significantly *deteriorated* during the last two or three decades. Specifically, it is widely agreed that the extent of teacher absenteeism and shirking has dramatically increased over this period. What is discouraging is not just that so little teaching goes on in government schools, but also that there is no sign of any improvement in that respect. On the contrary, the system has, by all accounts, decayed over time. Further, pupil–teacher ratios in Uttar Pradesh have risen at an alarming rate in recent years, e.g. by almost *fifty per cent* between 1981–2 and 1992–3 (Tyagi, 1993, p. 84). In that sense, the current evolution of government schooling in rural Uttar Pradesh seems to be characterized by a remarkable decline in effective quantity as well as in quality.

This finding may seem hard to square with the fact that literacy rates, after all, keep increasing even in Uttar Pradesh (as elsewhere in India). An important part of the answer may lie in the recent expansion of private schooling facilities, described as 'mushroom growth' by some experts.[71] This development, itself partly a response to the decay of the public schooling system, may have made an important contribution to the continued expansion of educational achievements in Uttar Pradesh. It is also likely that the demand for primary education has rapidly increased in Uttar Pradesh in recent years (due to rising incomes, higher levels of parental literacy, and

[71] Geeta Gandhi Kingdon, personal communication based on research in progress (see also Kingdon, 1996). The author's own household survey reveals that 86 per cent of primary-school children in urban Lucknow attend private schools. According to a recent survey carried out by the National Council of Applied Economic Research, the proportion of school-going children attending private schools in rural Uttar Pradesh is 27 per cent — by far the highest figure among all Indian states (Shariff, 1996).

related factors), inducing a larger proportion of parents to send their children to school despite the declining quality of teaching in government schools. The fact remains that, had the system of public schooling in rural areas expanded in quantity and quality, instead of stagnating, educational achievements in Uttar Pradesh would now be much higher than they actually are. The slow but steady improvements that have taken place in overall indicators of literacy and education in recent years have occurred *in spite* of the persistent inadequacy of public schooling at the village level, rather than *as a result* of positive government policies.

4. PUBLIC POLICY AND SCHOOLING DECISIONS

As the field investigation discussed in the preceding section brings out, the failures of schooling in rural Uttar Pradesh are fairly extensive, and their roots are deep. Transforming the educational situation is not just a question of increasing public spending on education, or of accelerating the quantitative expansion of educational facilities, or of introducing ad hoc 'schemes' to supplement the basic schooling system, or of undertaking a short-term 'campaign' for total literacy. Such initiatives would certainly be useful (and have been lacking in Uttar Pradesh, in comparison with many other Indian states), but the primary issue is to ensure that every village in the state has a well-equipped, well-staffed, well-functioning, and well-attended primary school. This section discusses a few basic issues relating to that essential goal.

At a general level, it may be useful to distinguish between the broad issues of *provision* and *utilization* of schooling facilities. While different authors have tended to put different emphases on each, a successful expansion of educational achievements obviously depends both on the adequate provision (and functioning) of schooling facilities and on the widespread utilization of these facilities. Both aspects are considered in this section.

4.1 Provision and Accountability

Our field investigation suggests that the physical supply of schooling infrastructure is no longer the main constraint on educational expansion at the primary level, in the sense that the vast majority of the rural population lives within short distance of a primary school. This diagnosis is corroborated by secondary data. According to the Fifth All-India Educational Survey, in 1986, 89 per cent of the rural population in Uttar Pradesh lived within 1 km of a primary school, and 98 per cent lived within 2 km.[72]

Considerable scope remains, however, for expanding and improving the schooling infrastructure in rural Uttar Pradesh. For instance, effective access of young girls to primary schools may depend on these schools being located within the village or hamlet where they live, given that it may be socially unacceptable for them to wander outside the village.[73] In 1986, less than half of all rural settlements of 300 persons or more in Uttar Pradesh had a primary school, compared with 77 per cent in India as a whole and 88 per cent in South India. In that respect, Uttar Pradesh was the worst-performer among all Indian states.[74] Similarly, effective access of all female children to primary education may depend on a strong presence of female teachers in the local schools. And in that respect, too, as we saw earlier, Uttar Pradesh is at the rock-bottom of the scale among all Indian states.

The reach of the schooling system, thus, is not quite universal, despite a major expansion of physical infrastructure in the post-independence period. We have also noted how the facilities available in the sample schools are, in most cases, extremely poor. Having said this, the most striking weakness of the schooling system in rural Uttar Pradesh is not so much the deficiency of physical infrastructure as the poor functioning of the existing facilities. The

[72] Tyagi (1993), p. 54. The corresponding all-India figures are 94 per cent and 99 per cent, respectively.

[73] A household survey conducted in Palanpur (Moradabad district) in 1983–4, at a time when the village school was non-functional, found that only three girls in the whole village were attending school in neighbouring villages (compared with twenty-nine boys). See Drèze and Saran (1995) for further discussion. Limited mobility of girls outside the village is also a serious constraint on female education beyond the primary level, given that middle and secondary schools tend to be more distant than primary schools (see Macdorman, 1986).

[74] *Fifth All-India Educational Survey* (National Council of Educational Research and Training, 1992, vol. I, Table 17). The situation for predominantly scheduled-caste rural settlements (of 300 persons or more) was even worse. Less than a third of these in Uttar Pradesh had a primary school, compared to 83 per cent in South India.

specific problem of endemic teacher absenteeism and shirking, which emerged again and again in the course of our investigation, plays a central part in that failure. This is by far the most important issue of education policy in Uttar Pradesh today.[73]

The main constraint in the sample villages is not that there are too few teachers (though this is certainly the case, too), but that the appointed teachers spend an alarmingly small part of their time teaching. Many of them regard teaching as part-time secondary employment, which they combine with other — often more valued — economic pursuits. Even when they are present at the school, with no opportunity to pursue other productive activities, they have little motivation to engage in active teaching.

There is a sharp contrast, in this respect, between government and private schools. In private schools, there is virtually no problem of teacher absenteeism or shirking. Unlike government teachers (whose earnings are not linked to performance), private-school teachers have strong incentives to work hard, since failure to do so easily leads to dismissal. Indeed, in a private school the manager or headmaster is accountable to the parents, who pay fees and expect tangible teaching services in return.[76] A shirking teacher, therefore, cannot expect much protection or indulgence from his or her superiors. There is a chain of accountability that stretches from the providers of the service to its ultimate recipients.

In government schools, this chain of accountability is extremely weak. Notionally it exists in the form of the school inspection system, whose agents (the government-employed school inspectors) may be thought of as acting on behalf of the users. The links, however, are fragile and tenuous. Users of the service (i.e. parents and the community at large) have little direct control over the activities of the school teachers or inspectors. The only control they have is through their political representatives who can approach the

---

[75] The Ramamurti Committee, set up by the government in 1991 to review the National Education Policy of 1986, also identified teacher absenteeism as one of the major constraints on educational development (see Bandyopadhyay, 1991). The revised National Education Policy of 1992, however, has nothing concrete to say on this issue. Nor does the problem receive any serious attention in the companion 'plan of action' (Government of India, 1992b).

[76] For a broader discussion of the relative efficiency of public and private schooling in Uttar Pradesh, see Kingdon (1994); see also Bashir (1994) on Tamil Nadu, and Jimenez et al. (1991) for an overview.

district educational authorities. In practice this amounts to very little, since basic education is low on the political agenda, and also because the holders of political power are more interested in using the schooling establishment as a means of extracting and dispensing public resources for their own advantage than in promoting the cause of widespread literacy.

In the absence of any effective control by the actual users, teachers are only subject to routine formal supervision from the government machinery. This official supervision mechanism, too, is quite ineffective, and it is worth considering exactly where it breaks down. One part of the story, which has already been mentioned, is that school teachers have permanent jobs. Given that it is virtually impossible to fire a shirking teacher, the official disciplining device consists of transfers. In practice, teachers are transferred only if the number of children in the school falls below stipulated norms. Correspondingly, the 'inspection' system is almost exclusively based on sporadic review of the school registers by school inspectors.

There is evidence that government school teachers do take the threat of transfer seriously enough to ensure that the required enrolment levels are maintained, at least on paper. Their response to this threat, however, is not less shirking, but manipulation of records to avoid sanction. This, as we have seen, takes the form of fictitiously enrolling children who have effectively dropped out (or who have never attended school in the first place), if necessary by paying fees on their behalf. Another method is to register private-school pupils in government schools. The phenomenon of widespread absenteeism and shirking of government teachers in the sample villages is ample testimony of the inadequacy of the official monitoring system.

We conclude on this subject with a few supplementary remarks. First, informal observations suggest that teacher absenteeism and shirking are more common in village schools, particularly those with few teachers, than in schools situated in towns or large villages. Schools with a comparatively large number of teachers tend to be organized on hierarchical lines, with greater scope for supervision and peer pressure, and less opportunity for collusive shirking. Larger schools are also more visible, and therefore more exposed to public scrutiny. Another possible factor is that, among schools situated in larger agglomerations, there is a modicum of competition for child enrolment, making it harder for a school to get away with non-provision of teaching services. It is in the small and relatively isolated village schools, where one or two teachers are expected to act as their own supervisors, that the problem of inadequate work incentives seems to be most acute. A corollary of this observation is that the strengthening of teaching staff in small village schools may have an important role to play in improving teaching practices.

Second, teacher absenteeism is facilitated by the existence of a significant nexus between the local elites and the public schooling system. Many teachers have close relations with the local elite, not only because of their relatively high earnings by local standards, but also because political connections were often instrumental in getting them appointed in the first place. There is a problem of 'adverse selection' here, as high salaries attract candidates with privileged political or social connections.[77] The crucial role played by school teachers at the time of elections, census enumerations, and related events is another common basis of expedient alliances with the local elite. Based on these alliances, many teachers have ample political protection, further helping them to evade scrutiny and avoid sanctions.

Third, to be fair to the teachers, it should be mentioned that their professional environment is in many ways extremely demotivating.[78] While their salaries are quite high by local standards, and while many of them have privileged connections, teachers seem to enjoy little general social esteem, and their status in the government hierarchy is low. More importantly, the working conditions in village schools (including the frequent need to cope with multi-grade teaching) make the task of conscientious teaching highly challenging. In these circumstances, it is not surprising that even teachers who are otherwise strongly motivated find it hard to maintain high teaching standards.

Finally, it is difficult to see how the problem of lack of accountability of the schooling establishment can be effectively addressed without the active involvement of concerned parents and local communities. The current emphasis of public policy on the

---

[77] There are other interesting examples of rent extraction based on the nexus between the schooling establishment and the local elite. In several sample villages, for instance, the headman was involved as a contractor in the construction and repair of local school buildings. There are handsome profits to be made from such activities, particularly by leaving the work unfinished or by using inferior materials.

[78] On this, see also Government of India (1986).

'decentralization of school management', based on *panchayati raj* institutions, can be seen as giving some recognition to that need. But there has been far more promise than action, as far as decentralization is concerned. As things stand, village-level and even block-level representative institutions have virtually no control over any significant decisions relating to school management. Further, given the current political links between the schooling establishment and the rural elite, formal decentralization cannot be expected to achieve very much unless it goes hand in hand with more active political mobilization of disadvantaged groups.[79] A genuine transformation can only be achieved if schooling is taken up as a major political issue by popular organizations and social movements.

4.2 Poverty and the Demand for Schooling

Poverty is often assumed to be the main reason why many Indian parents do not send their children to school. One version of this story, which is particularly popular in official circles, is that poor parents cannot afford to send their children to school because their labour makes a crucial contribution to the household economy.

In the absence of firm empirical evidence on this issue, it is difficult to assess the actual importance of poverty as an obstacle to widespread schooling.[80] Literacy rates and school attendance certainly do go down as one considers progressively poorer sections of the population.[81] What is far from clear, however, is to what

[79] For further discussion of this point, see chapter 5 in the companion volume (Drèze and Sen, 1995).

[80] It is worth noting that the paucity of empirical evidence is itself a reflection of the low attention which basic education has received in the literature on Indian development. Most household surveys (including the National Sample Survey) include information on literacy and school attendance, which could have been used with good effect to examine issues such as the determinants of school attendance, the circumstances that lead to children dropping out, and intra-household inequalities in schooling decisions. Few studies, however, have investigated these issues in any depth. For some recent contributions in this field, see Minhas (1992), Kingdon (1994), Subramanian (1994), Banerji (1995), Labenne (1995), Mehrotra (forthcoming).

[81] See e.g. National Sample Survey data (42nd round, 1986–7) presented in *Sarvekshana*, January–March 1991.

extent this correlation reflects an income effect as such, rather than the influence of some other variables that are themselves correlated with income. Examples of possibly relevant variables include the literacy of parents, the quality of available schooling facilities, and the social support which different sections of the population receive in pursuit of their educational aspirations.[82] What looks like a problem of poverty may often turn out, on closer examination, to have more to do with other factors.

To illustrate this point, consider literacy rates in different per-capita expenditure groups in rural and urban areas. According to National Sample Survey data, in 1986–7 the literacy rate in the second-highest quintile of the per-capita expenditure (PCE) scale in rural areas was 48 per cent. The literacy rate in the *lowest* quintile of the PCE scale in urban areas was a little *higher* (50 per cent), even though the average PCE in that group was only half as high as the average PCE in the former group. To put it another way, *everyone* in the first group is above the official 'poverty line', while *no-one* in the second group is, and yet the literacy rates in the two groups are very similar. One plausible reason for this contrast is the better access of the urban population to schooling facilities.

Recent empirical investigations tend to confirm that the importance of poverty as a cause of persistent illiteracy has often been exaggerated, and other influences underplayed. In a recent analysis of inter-district variations in child labour, for instance, Labenne (1995) finds that poverty has relatively little explanatory power after controlling for adult literacy, schooling facilities, caste, and gender. Maharatna (1995), based on a study of child activities in rural West Bengal, argues that the opportunity cost of child labour is quite low even among very poor rural households. S. Sinha (1995), drawing on many years of experience with child labourers in rural Andhra Pradesh, also argues that 'parents do want their children to be educated and poverty as a limiting factor is highly overrated' (p. 40).[83]

---

[82] Recent studies of the demand for schooling place growing emphasis on these 'non-income' factors (see, for instance, Colclough, 1993).

[83] The last author also presents an illuminating analysis of the political economy of the 'poverty' argument: 'It should be clearly understood that acceptance of the premise that poverty compels parents to send their children to work is extremely convenient to those charged with the responsibility of reducing if not eliminating child labour because in such a case, improving the economic status of the parents becomes the focal point of attention. This is neither the responsibility of the labour or the education department and the buck can be passed elsewhere' (pp. 32–3).

Our own field investigation lends some support to this diagnosis. In government schools, fees are extremely low (almost symbolic, at the primary level), and we found no evidence of non-fee payments being demanded from parents by school authorities. There are some cash costs in the form of items such as clean clothes, slates, and books, but even these are not high given the highly informal mode of operation of small village schools (uniforms, for instance, are not required). The opportunity cost of children's time is certainly an important consideration for some parents, but school hours are short, and schooling can be combined with a substantial contribution to the household economy at other times.

The point is that the willingness of parents to bear these costs, such as they are, and to coax their children into going to school, may depend crucially on the *quality* of the schooling services they obtain in return.[84] The importance of material deprivation as a factor of non-attendance, therefore, has to be evaluated in the light of the poor functioning of the schooling system in many areas. In this connection, it is worth recalling the strong popular appeal of well-functioning primary schools managed by voluntary organizations, even among economically deprived groups (see section 3.7). These positive experiences indicate the possibility of achieving widespread literacy in the younger age groups even when a large part of the population is still quite poor.[85] This is not to deny that poverty makes it harder to send one's children to school, or that this disincentive requires specific attention in public policy, in addition to the issue of school management and teaching practices.

4.3   Educational Achievements and Social Inequality

As we saw earlier, one feature of the educational situation in Uttar Pradesh is the existence of large disparities in literacy achievements

[84] On this point, see also Mehrotra (forthcoming). The quality of schooling affects not only the motivation of parents, but also that of children. And as Bashir et al. (1993b) note in their survey of primary schools in three districts of Uttar Pradesh: 'Many parents . . . mentioned that the continuing of their child's education would depend on the child's interest' (p. 6).

[85] For similar assessments, see Weiner (1991), Banerji (1995), Maharatna (1995), Mehrotra (1995), S. Sinha (1995). Kerala's experience, discussed in Ramachandran's contribution to this volume, is another crucial illustration of the possibility of rapid educational expansion at an early stage of development.

between different regions and social groups. The problem of low average literacy rates is compounded by large inequalities, reflected in abysmally low literacy rates for the most disadvantaged sections of the population. Scheduled-caste women, for instance, remain almost entirely illiterate in a majority of districts (see section 2.3).

Similar disparities can be observed at the village level. To illustrate, Table 9 presents some information on literacy rates and school attendance in the village of Palanpur (Moradabad district) in 1993.[86] As this table indicates, gender and caste-based inequalities in educational achievements can be extremely large even *within* a single village. It is remarkable, for instance, that the female literacy rate in Palanpur varies from zero among the Jatabs (Palanpur's main scheduled caste, also known as Chamars) to 100 per cent among the Kayasths (who have a long tradition of involvement in clerical occupations and consider schooling as an essential part of every child's upbringing).[87]

These contrasts suggest that there is more to the problem of educational backwardness in Uttar Pradesh than the failure of the state to provide adequate schooling facilities. Different sections of the population in Palanpur have access to similar facilities, and yet their educational achievements show enormous variations. These contrasts may relate, to some extent, to differences of income between different groups, but this is only a small part of the story. Gender differences in literacy rates, for instance, are sharp in all income groups (and even if they were confined to low-income groups, one would still have to explain why girls are discriminated against within those groups). Similarly, caste-based differences in educational achievements are statistically significant even after controlling for differences in income levels.[88]

[86] It is worth mentioning that literacy rates in Palanpur are very close to the corresponding figures for Moradabad district as a whole. For instance, in 1991 the rural male and female literacy rates in the district (age 7+) were 37 and 10 per cent, respectively, compared with 37 and 9 per cent in Palanpur in 1993. This village cannot, therefore, be dismissed as a 'basket case', despite its astonishingly poor record of educational expansion (on the latter, see Drèze and Saran, 1995, and Drèze, Lanjouw, and Sharma, forthcoming).

[87] Even though the Kayasth population in Palanpur was quite small in 1993, this contrast is unlikely to be fortuitous. Indeed, the same pattern applies for each of the five surveys that have been conducted in Palanpur since 1957–8. Similar caste-based contrasts in educational achievements have also been observed elsewhere in India. See, for instance, the chapter on West Bengal in this volume.

[88] For instance, probit analysis of the determinants of school attendance in

TABLE 9. *Literacy and School Attendance in Palanpur, 1993*

Caste/ community	Number of persons	Percentage of literates among persons aged 7 and above		Percentage attending school among children aged 6–10 [a]	
		Male	Female	Male	Female
Thakur	283	56	19	50	46
Kayasth[b]	8	100	100	–	–
Murao	294	39	2	63	25
Muslim	140	20	2	31	29
Jatab	133	12	0	33	0
Others	275	38	8	61	31
Total	1,133	37	9	51	29

Notes. [a] *All* schools (including private schools and government schools in nearby villages) are taken into account in these attendance figures.

[b] There were no Kayasth children between the ages of 6 and 10 in 1993.

Source. Household survey carried out by the authors. Except for the 'others' group, different castes/communities have been listed in rough descending order of status in the local social hierarchy. The Jatabs are Palanpur's main 'scheduled caste'.

The female disadvantage in basic education links with some deep-rooted features of gender relations in Uttar Pradesh.[89] The gender division of labour, which relegates most adult women (including those with relatively good education) to domestic work, diminishes the perceived 'returns' of investment in female education. The prevailing norms of village exogamy and patrilocal post-marital residence imply that these returns (and other benefits of female education) flow primarily to a daughter's future in-laws rather than to her parents. And marriage transaction patterns may act as a tangible disincentive against female education, given that an educated daughter is expected to marry a *more educated* man, often

---

Palanpur indicates that children from Muslim and Jatab families are less likely to attend school than children from other families, even after controlling for per-capita income and the education of parents.

[89] On this, see also Drèze and Saran (1995), and Drèze and Sen (1995), chapter 6.

implying higher dowry payments.[90] The remarkably backward state of female education in Uttar Pradesh fits in a tight web of mutually-reinforcing gender inequalities and patriarchal practices.

The reasons why caste continues to be an important determinant of educational achievements and school attendance, independently of income and parental education, are less obvious. It is hard to ascertain, for instance, to what extent the schooling system discriminates against children of disadvantaged castes. Judging from our field investigation, blatant forms of caste-based discrimination (e.g. denying access to schooling facilities to certain castes, or requiring children of different castes to sit separately at school) have by and large disappeared, and nor is there much evidence in other studies of the survival of such practices.[91] More subtle forms of discrimination, however, seem to remain quite widespread. Some examples include (1) discrimination against scheduled-caste settlements in the location of schools, (2) teachers refusing to touch scheduled-caste children, (3) children from particular castes being special targets of verbal abuse and physical punishment by the teachers, (4) low-caste children being frequently beaten by higher-caste classmates.[92]

[90] Hard-boiled neo-classical analysis *à la* Becker might suggest that the 'externalities' of investment in female education are internalized through *lower* dowry payments. But the real world seems to work quite differently, judging from the fact that the fear of having difficulties marrying a well-educated daughter is very real for many parents in rural India (see Drèze and Sen, 1995, p. 135, and the studies cited there, and also Macdorman, 1986, and Bashir et al., 1993b, p. 17). It is quite possible, however, that as levels of *male* literacy in a particular community rise beyond a certain threshold, female education becomes an asset rather than a liability from the point of view of marriage prospects, because most young men aspire to marry a literate bride (see e.g. U. Sharma, 1980, Jejeebhoy and Kulkarni, 1989, and Minturn, 1993, for some relevant evidence).

[91] Blatant discrimination has not disappeared altogether. In Banda district, for instance, there have been cases of active interference of Dadu Brahmin landlords with the schooling of scheduled-caste people. For similar observations elsewhere, see Wadley and Derr (1989) and Banerjee (1994).

[92] To illustrate: 'SC children refuse to go to school, being afraid and hurt of the scorns thrown at them' (Shami, 1992, p. 26, about a village school in Madhya Pradesh); 'the majority of the [school-going] children are Rajputs and the SC children are so often rebuked and hit by the teachers that they have virtually stopped going to school' (Varma, 1992, about a Bihar village); 'these [scheduled-caste] children often sat at the back. The teacher hardly paid any attention to them' (Bashir et al., 1993b, pp. 20–1, on a village school in UP). See also Mehrotra (forthcoming)

There are other ways in which caste is likely to remain an important determinant of educational achievements, even in the absence of discriminatory practices in the schooling system. The ability of parents to assess the personal and social value of education depends, among other things, on the information they have at their disposal. If their entire reference group is largely untouched by the experience of being educated, that information may be quite limited. Even if some aspects of the general value of education (e.g. the economic returns to male education) are relatively obvious, they may be perceived as alien to certain groups, and relevant only to 'others'.[93] In Palanpur, for instance, it is taken for granted that Kayasth children go to school, and the benefits which Kayasth households have been able to derive from their high education levels are widely understood, but that experience is not necessarily considered by (say) Jatab parents as relevant for themselves. Jatabs and Kayasths are seen to have different roles in society, and the perceived value of education is contingent on these assumed roles.

It is tempting to conclude from this discussion that educational expansion in Uttar Pradesh depends crucially on a transformation of social attitudes and practices that have little to do with the provision of schooling facilities, or even with public policy in general. This assessment has to be qualified in at least two ways.

First, educational backwardness in Uttar Pradesh primarily reflects the *combined effects* of (1) the state's failure to provide adequate schooling facilities, and (2) social norms and practices that have been detrimental to the widespread utilization of available facilities. Consider, for instance, the problem of endemic female illiteracy in Palanpur. Negative attitudes to female education (themselves related, as was discussed earlier, to the patriarchal nature of gender relations in Uttar Pradesh) certainly have had much influence here. That influence, however, has been magnified by the non-functioning of the

---

on peer beating, and Lata (1995), p. 32 for further examples. On the disadvantaged access of scheduled-caste settlements to schooling facilities in Uttar Pradesh (in contrast with South India, where no such bias can be observed), see National Council of Educational Research and Training (1992), vol. I, Table 17.

[93] On the role of caste (and tribe) based peer reference in forming social attitudes, particularly with regard to education, see Sharma (1981) and Bara et al. (1991). A related issue is the elitist nature of the school curriculum and teaching methods, which may further discourage the participation of children from disadvantaged social backgrounds; on this, see Kamat (1985) and particularly Kumar (1994).

village school over long periods of time. Many parents have dealt with the failure of the local school by sending their boys to school in neighbouring villages, but very few have done the same for girls. In fact, in 1983–4 only three girls were studying outside the village. All three of them were Kayasth; other parents simply considered it socially unacceptable to allow their daughters to wander outside the village. The failure of the state to provide adequate schooling facilities in Palanpur, therefore, is also a crucial part of the story. Similar remarks apply to the promotion of education among disadvantaged castes.

Second, it would be a mistake to consider that public policy is concerned with the provision side alone. The official goal of public policy, ever since independence, has been a rapid move towards universal education until the age of 14. If that goal cannot be achieved simply by expanding schooling facilities, the state has a responsibility to address other relevant constraints (including, for instance, the conservatism of social attitudes towards female education). Schooling decisions are, ultimately, private decisions taken at the household level. But these decisions are responsive to social norms and external incentives that can often be decisively influenced through government policy and public action.[94]

4.4 Education and Politics

The challenge of educational reform in Uttar Pradesh is extremely exacting. In the absence of any kind of accountability to the public, the system of government schools has been comprehensively corrupted. The failure of the schooling system, in combination with persistent inequalities of class, caste, and gender, has kept even the most elementary educational achievements out of reach of large sections of the population.

The most remarkable feature of the educational situation in Uttar

---

[94] Some illustrations may help. In the course of a similar investigation in Kerala in February 1995, we found that most primary schools there closely monitored school attendance, and contacted parents in the event where a child fails to turn up at school for a number of days. Similarly, most schools provided midday-meals, had an active parent–teacher association, and were supported by crèche facilities for pre-school children. None of these practices were observed in any of the schools we visited in Uttar Pradesh.

Pradesh is that this state of affairs seems to be passively accepted by the general public. At the village level, we found that most parents were extremely critical of the schooling system, but had little sense of (or faith in) the possibility of making organized demands for change. In some cases, this inertia was quite extreme. In Palanpur, for instance, the village school was virtually non-functional for as long as ten years, between 1983 and 1993, due to systematic absenteeism on the part of the local teacher (who also happened to be the son of the headman, a prosperous high-caste landowner). This blatant abuse did not trigger any organized protest, or any serious discussion in the village panchayat.[95]

A similar pattern of inertia applies at the state level. For one thing, there are no signs of the government of Uttar Pradesh taking any bold initiatives in the field of basic education, in spite of the alarming nature of the current situation. On the contrary, it is easy to cite many examples of continued indifference. One of the most telling symptoms in this respect is the sustained *decline* of real per-capita public expenditure on education in recent years — by almost 20 per cent between 1991–2 and 1993–4.[96] The number of primary-school teachers per capita has also steadily gone down in recent years (see Fig. 2), further aggravating the spiralling decline of teacher–pupil ratios in the eighties.[97] Similarly, the state government has taken little interest in the Total Literacy Campaign, even after the considerable potential of that campaign had been well demonstrated in several other states.[98] The under-utilization of large grants earmarked for the promotion of elementary education (received from international agencies as well as the central government) is yet another symptomatic indication of the low priority given to basic education by the state government. Here again, official neglect has

[95] Note the parallel with a similar observation reported many years ago by Iqbal Narain (1972) in an enlightening account of educational politics in Rajasthan: 'all the villagers may be dissatisfied with a school teacher, yet if he is in the good books of the *sarpanch* and *pradhan* he is not transferred' (p. 152).

[96] On this, see Prabhu (1995), p. 37. Over the same period, there has also been some decline in many other states, but at a much slower rate than in Uttar Pradesh.

[97] On the latter, see Tyagi (1993), p. 84. The number of primary-school teachers per 1,000 pupils declined from 26 to 17 between 1981–2 and 1992–3.

[98] On this, see Ghosh et al. (1994). The authors, after noting that the Total Literacy Campaign had made little impact in the most educationally backward states, including Uttar Pradesh, argue that this poor response is primarily due to a 'low political commitment to the eradication of illiteracy' in those states (p. 39).

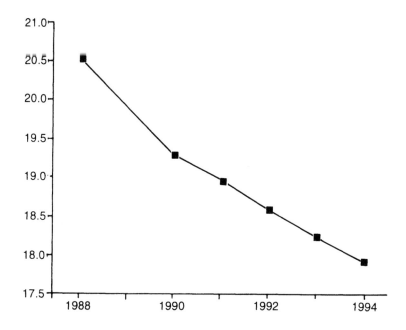

FIG. 2. *Number of Teachers per 10,000 Persons in Uttar Pradesh.*
Source. Calculated from annual reports of the Department of Education, Ministry of Human Resource Development, New Delhi.

provoked little challenge from opposition parties, interest groups, the media, or the general public.

The privileged background of most political leaders, the undemocratic nature of village politics, and the role of the schooling system as a means of patronage, all play a part in this continued neglect of the obvious need for educational reform in Uttar Pradesh. This neglect also fits in a general pattern of lack of responsiveness of Uttar Pradesh politics to the basic needs of the citizens; we will come back to that in the next section. In the specific context of basic education, it is worth adding that the absence of any strong political demand for educational reform in Uttar Pradesh illustrates the elementary — yet widely overlooked — fact that literacy is a crucial tool of effective participation in democratic politics. Widespread illiteracy makes it that much harder for disadvantaged groups to ensure that their needs receive due attention in public debates and political contests, and the apathy of the leadership towards these needs, in turn, is responsible for the persistence of widespread illiteracy.[99]

This self-sustaining circle is a central feature of Uttar Pradesh politics, and also has much relevance in interpreting Indian politics in general. On the positive side, these observations suggest that the expansion of basic education, and the political campaigns and social movements that might lead to that expansion, have a central role to play in the transformation of Indian politics. In particular, the value of basic education as a tool of political empowerment deserves much more attention from political and social leaders than it has received so far.

5. The Burden of Inertia

5.1 Aspects of Public Inertia

The crisis of rural schooling is not an isolated example of the dismal functioning of public services in Uttar Pradesh. As we saw in section 2, much of the backwardness of the state in terms of demographic transition, health indicators, educational achievements, and gender inequality can be plausibly linked to similar failures of state intervention and public action in a wide range of domains.

Although the main focus of our fieldwork was on the schooling system, we were also able to form a judgement on the functioning of other public programmes, such as primary health care, nutritional interventions, poverty alleviations schemes, and public works in the sample villages. Direct observation as well as extensive discussions with local residents strongly suggest that the standards of operation of most of these programmes in the sample villages are no higher than those of the schooling system. To illustrate, most of the sample villages had no semblance of functioning public health services (even

---

[99] It is perhaps no coincidence that the Total Literacy Campaign has its antecedents in campaigns initiated by political and social organizations in Kerala and Tamil Nadu, one of whose primary concerns was political mobilization of illiterate people (see Rao, 1993). The link between universal basic education and political participation is also strong in the history of developed economies (see e.g. Simon, 1965, on the correlation between educational and electoral reform in Britain).

in cases where a health centre had been officially set up or sanctioned). Similarly, none of the sample villages showed any sign of serious activity under the *'anganwadi'* programme (officially known as the Integrated Child Development Scheme), which is supposed to have wide rural coverage; many residents, in fact, had not even heard of the programme, even in cases where an anganwadi officially existed in their village.[100]

The failure of public intervention in Uttar Pradesh extends well beyond the provision of public goods and services. Most of the major developmental and redistributive programmes have gone in and out of fashion without making much of an impact. Whether these were state government programmes (such as agrarian reforms and panchayati raj) or central government schemes for which the state government acts primarily as an implementation agency (e.g. the Integrated Rural Development Programme or the Jawahar Rozgar Yojana), the pattern has consistently been one of inadequate commitment, ineffective implementation, and insignificant results.

Beyond the abolition of the zamindari system which took place all over India soon after independence, no serious effort at agrarian reforms ever made any headway in Uttar Pradesh. Even the enactment of basic land ceiling laws took the best part of a decade after the abolition of zamindari. Land ceilings, when they were finally enacted, were higher than in any other state, and numerous loopholes — both in the law and in its application — enabled the landlords to retain much of their initial holdings.[101] Voluntary programmes of land distribution such as Bhoodan and Gramdan also had very limited results.[102] Even land which was assigned to the village community (known as *gram sabha* land) as opposed to individual landlords was appropriated in many places by vested political interests.[103]

Even for programmes such as the public distribution system (PDS), the Integrated Rural Development Programme (IRDP), and

[100] For similar findings on a wide range of public services and government programmes in 8 villages of Uttar Pradesh, see A. Sinha (1995). For a detailed case study, based on Palanpur (Moradabad district), see Drèze, Lanjouw, and Sharma (forthcoming).

[101] See e.g. Singh and Misra (1964) and Haque and Sirohi (1986). On the political aspects of this failure to institute major land reforms, see also Kohli (1987) and Hasan (1989).

[102] For a contemporaneous account of the failure of Gramdan at the village level, see Planning and Research Action Institute (1966). See also Church (1974).

[103] For some examples, see Shankar (1991a) and Saith and Tankha (1992).

the Integrated Child Development Scheme (ICDS), where the role of the state government is essentially to implement transfers of various kinds to target groups (as opposed to directly redistributing assets between different classes), the gap between promise and delivery has been wide indeed. Uttar Pradesh has the lowest per-capita supply of foodgrains through the PDS among all major states (S. Jha, 1994). Field-based studies of IRDP, the main national anti-poverty programme, have produced much evidence of systematic abuse and corruption.[104] *'Antyodaya'* village programmes have suffered more or less the same fate (Vais, 1982). The ICDS programme in Uttar Pradesh is described by one of its own former Directors as 'a complete write-off' and a *'bakwas* (nonsensical) scheme'.[105]

This comprehensive failure of public services, and of development-oriented interventions in general, can be seen to have two mutually-reinforcing roots: (1) the state's low commitment to broad-based development and social equity, and (2) the failure of civil society to challenge that apathy, and more generally to promote social needs and the interests of disadvantaged groups. The crisis of rural schooling, discussed in the preceding section, provides a good illustration of these issues. The poor condition of schooling facilities, and the absence of an adequate number of teachers (especially female teachers), reflect the low commitment of state authorities to the goal of universalization of basic education. The chaotic functioning of schools (reflected, for instance, in a wide gap between stipulated and actual teaching hours) is also the responsibility of the state, but the failure of village communities to discipline school teachers plays a part in that outcome as well. Further, entrenched social inequalities (including oppressive caste

---

[104] See Singh and Singh (1989), Drèze (1990a), Shankar (1991b), Saith and Tankha (1992), and A. Sinha (1995), among others. Fraudulent practices include large-scale selection of ineligible beneficiaries, disregard for the prescribed norms of consultation with villagers, and endemic extortion of bribes by bank managers, *gram sevaks*, and other government officials. Interestingly, the implementation flaws of recent anti-poverty schemes have much in common with those of earlier agricultural extension programmes. See, for instance, H.K. Singh (1958) on the appropriation of benefits of the National Extension Service by large landlords.

[105] Keshav Desiraju (IAS), former ICDS Director for Uttar Pradesh, personal communication. A recent field investigation in rural areas of Allahabad district found most anganwadis to be non-functional (Nidhi Mehrotra and Sangeeta Goyal, personal communication). As was mentioned earlier, this is also our own experience in the sample villages.

and gender relations) hinder collective action for improved schooling facilities, and also restrict the utilization of whatever schooling
is actually supplied.

5.2 State Apathy and Public Accountability

It may be argued that state apathy in the field of social policy is
an all-India phenomenon, and that there is nothing special about
Uttar Pradesh in this respect. This is not quite accurate. Many
other states, in fact, have a much better record not only of implementing social programmes sponsored by the central government, but also of taking important *initiatives* in this field. Health
care in Kerala, social security in Tamil Nadu, employment guarantee in Maharashtra, panchayati raj in Karnataka, drought relief in
Gujarat, primary education in Himachal Pradesh, land reform in
West Bengal, are some examples.[106] These initiatives have not been
uniformly successful, but the point of interest here is that they
indicate some responsiveness of state policy to developmental
concerns and social needs. In Uttar Pradesh, however, there are
no important examples of such initiatives, and the most consistent
feature of state policy in these fields is one of resilient inertia.

The problem of low commitment to social needs in terms of
government policy is amplified by ineffective implementation at the
local level. Schools do exist but teachers are frequently absent; health
care facilities are provided, but are used to promote female sterilization; poverty alleviation programmes are launched, but end up being
used as instruments of patronage by the rural elite. The sanctioning
of programmes and resources at the state level is meaningless if
implementation bears no resemblance to stated policy objectives.

As was discussed in the previous section with reference to school
education, the absence of accountability in the public sector plays a
major part in this implementation failure. The breakdown of formal
monitoring procedures (e.g. the school inspection system) is one
aspect of the problem. In the absence of any credible threat of
sanction (even in the relatively weak form of transfer rather than

---

[106] For some relevant studies on these different initiatives, see Guhan (1981,
1990), Drèze (1990b), Mahendra Dev (1993a, 1993b), Crook and Manor (1994),
Visaria and Visaria (1995), Goyal (1995), among others; also the chapters on Kerala
and West Bengal in this volume.

dismissal), teachers and other government employees have little incentive to do their duty. While public-spirited individual initiatives can make a positive difference, the main issue is that of institutional corruption.[107]

The formal monitoring procedures, however, are quite similar all over India, and it is not clear why they should be particularly ineffective in Uttar Pradesh (and its neighbours) in comparison with other states. One relevant consideration here is that, aside from formal monitoring procedures, the informed vigilance and articulated demands of the public also have a role to play in ensuring the proper functioning of local public services. The fact that a village teacher shirks, for instance, is much easier to observe for the residents of that village than for a government inspector. If the concerned residents are able to organize and have means of putting pressure on the village teacher (either directly or through government institutions), their vigilance can be an effective disciplining device. Similarly, if the users of local public services are aware of their entitlements and resolved to defend them, it is that much harder for the local government doctor to appropriate the furniture of the village health centre, for the ration-shop manager to sell her supplies on the black market, for the headman to sell the village trees for his own benefit, and for anyone to steal the electricity wires.[108] This brings us to the issue of local democracy and village politics.

5.3 Village Institutions and Local Governance

In pre-independence Uttar Pradesh, the institutional basis of local governance largely derived from the network of social and economic relations associated with zamindari and *jajmani*. The powerful zamindars dealt with higher levels of political authority, and sometimes also played a role in matters of collective interest at the

[107] Corruption has become the working norm of most government departments in Uttar Pradesh; see, for instance, Gupta (1994). In our field work, we did encounter occasional examples of public-spirited individual initiatives. A sub-divisional magistrate in Pratapgarh, for instance, was credited for having resolutely tackled local teacher absenteeism, with some temporary success. The situation reverted back to 'normal', however, soon after she was transferred.

[108] Each of these examples of 'abuse' has been observed in one or more of our sample villages.

village level. The jajmani system defined patron–client relations pertaining not only to private transactions but also to some public goods and services. While the services of non-agricultural castes such as carpenters, smiths, barbers, etc., were privately consumed, some castes were responsible for services of a more public nature such as sweeping, sanitation, drainage, and street maintenance.[109] Even schooling was largely organized on the basis of traditional caste obligations (in this case involving Brahmin teachers) in many villages.[110] This system of customary obligations was, of course, highly unequal and extremely unjust.[111]

The abolition of zamindars after independence undermined the basis of their political authority and economic power. These reforms, and the development of market relations, also hastened the decline of patron–client relations. While many traditional activities became more and more market-based, a similar transition could not be expected in the case of activities with a large element of public consumption. This led to some erosion of public provisions that had been previously organized on the basis of customary obligations and patron–client relationships.

A well-documented example of this phenomenon concerns the decay of collective irrigation facilities after the abolition of zamindari. Many studies have noted how the latter development led to the collapse of traditional arrangements for the creation and maintenance of village tanks and related irrigation facilities in different parts of India.[112] Similarly, there is some evidence of a deterioration

[109] For detailed accounts of the jajmani relation and their decline over time in various parts of Uttar Pradesh, see Elder (1970), Wadley and Derr (1989), Wiser and Wiser (1970), among others; on the provision of public services within the framework of jajmani or other patron–client relationships in pre-independence India, see also Matthai (1915).

[110] On traditional schooling arrangements in rural India, see Matthai (1915), and especially Dharampal (1983).

[111] Scholarly assessments of village society under jajmani have undergone significant change from the initial stress on reciprocity and harmony to the subsequent recognition of exploitation and oppression. See, for instance, the changing perceptions of jajmani in Karimpur, a village of western Uttar Pradesh which has been studied over a period of seventy years (Wiser, 1936, Derr and Wadley, 1987, Wadley and Derr, 1989).

[112] See e.g. P. Jha (1994), Mahapatra (1994), and Janakarajan (1995) for evidence of this problem in Bihar, Tamil Nadu, and Orissa, respectively. In the case of irrigation, of course, this decline of collective facilities was more than compensated, in due course, by private investment in irrigation devices.

in collective arrangements for the supply of cleaning, drainage, and sanitary services based on customary obligations in the early post-independence period.[113]

The collapse of the pre-independence social order after zamindari abolition, and the replacement of the hierarchical system of customary obligations by more impersonal labour relations, were important steps in the emancipation of the labouring classes. These positive developments were not accompanied, however, by a corresponding adaptation of collective arrangements for the provision of collective goods and services.[114] Nor was state intervention successful, in Uttar Pradesh, in providing a sound basis for such arrangements. The challenge of creating an effective system of participatory local governance remains largely unmet.

5.4 Accountability, Democracy and Factionalism

In Uttar Pradesh as elsewhere in India, local government bodies (Panchayati Raj Institutions) are now constituted on the basis of elections. To the extent that government employees are ultimately answerable to political representatives, it may be argued that the public has an opportunity to exercise some control on the quality of local public services and related matters. There are, in fact, interesting cases where an improved practice of local democracy (based on administrative decentralization and/or political organization) is considered to have led to some progress in the quality of development programmes. It has been reported, for instance, that democratic decentralization in Karnataka in the late eighties led to a major improvement in the performance of village teachers and health workers.[115] Similarly, the comparatively successful implementation

[113] See, for instance, Khare (1964) and A. Singh (1977). In contrast, Elder (1970) gives an interesting account of how, in a village where jajmani was still alive and well, the landlords persuaded a Bhangi (sweeper) family to settle in the village in return for a small plot of land.

[114] Some of the early optimism in the ability of village communities to smoothly take over the task of 'community development' was based, perhaps, on idealized notions of harmonious village communities. See, for instance, Danda (1987) for an account of the breakdown of collective efforts in a village considered promising in the early years of community development.

[115] Ford Foundation (1992), based on the recent Krishnaswamy Report; see also Vyasulu (1993) and Crook and Manor (1994).

of land reform and poverty alleviation programmes in West Bengal has built on systematic political activism at the local level.[116] The experience of Village Development Boards in Nagaland is another example of positive achievements of local democratic institutions.[117]

In Uttar Pradesh, however, the decentralized Panchayati Raj Institutions have failed to provide anything like an effective basis of local democracy and accountability. Elections have not been held on a regular basis, and when they are held, they are dominated by factional rivalries at the expense of social concerns. Privileged groups (usually high-caste landlords) have exercised a tight control on local government institutions,[118] and used them to their private advantage at the expense of public needs. This has been a consistent pattern from the early years of zamindari abolition when decentralization was first implemented.

Decentralization was perceived as a problematic issue from the very start. Those familiar with rural inequalities warned that de-volution of political power might well result in the enhanced tyranny of dominant elite groups.[119] As a matter of fact, it soon became clear that political power at the village level remained with the propertied classes. Contrary to common expectations based on an idealized view of harmonious village coexistence, the introduc-tion of new elected bodies led to exacerbated tensions in the early years.[120] Some of these tensions were due to the assertion by the newly-enfranchized poor of their rights *vis-à-vis* the dominant elites made up of erstwhile zamindars and their allies.[121] A number of

[116] See the chapter on West Bengal in this volume, and the references cited there.

[117] See e.g. Gokhale (1988) and Maithani and Rizwana (1992).

[118] For instance, a recent study of panchayat institutions in Dobhi block of eastern Uttar Pradesh (H.N. Singh, 1993) found that as many as two-thirds of the headmen in 82 surveyed villages belonged to the Thakur caste — the traditional landowning upper caste in that region, notorious for oppressive subjugation of the lower castes. Among the available village studies for Uttar Pradesh (see footnote 4), a large majority of those that provide information on the village headman describe him as a high-caste landlord (usually Thakur or Brahmin).

[119] See e.g. Berreman (1963) for an early study on the prospects for community development in Uttar Pradesh under conditions of extreme social and economic inequality, and Srinivas (1962) on the danger of political devolution in India leading to 'the tyranny of the dominant caste' (p. 32).

[120] See e.g. Chandra (1958), Dube (1958), Khare (1962), Marriott (1958), and Zamora (1990).

[121] See, for instance, village studies by H.A. Singh (1969) and K.K. Singh (1967).

studies, however, show that following an initial period of ferment starting around zamindari abolition, the situation settled, often to the advantage of the landlords.[122] Although economic and political changes led to some relative decline of the old elite groups of high-caste landlords, these groups continued to dominate village politics, and captured the new Panchayati Raj Institutions by means foul or fair. These institutions rapidly became instruments of elite power rather than popular control.[123]

While political changes at the time of zamindari abolition undoubtedly gave new freedoms to the poorest sections in Uttar Pradesh, there was also much continuity in the forms and bases of political mobilization. The jajmani system of patronage and dependence was a system of factional alignment *par excellence*, and factions remained the basis for political mobilization even after the abolition of zamindari and the disappearance of jajmani.[124] Factional strife has been an influential part of political life in much of India, but this has been particularly so in Uttar Pradesh. Not only have political parties been organized around factional lines at all levels, even within parties factional struggle has been one of the primary preoccupations.[125]

At the village level, factions are typically multi-caste and multi-class coalitions, often organized around alignments based on social

[122] It is interesting to note that in two separate village studies undertaken in different districts of eastern Uttar Pradesh (Zamora, 1990, for Jaunpur, and Y. Singh, 1970, for Basti), similar political developments were observed in the period immediately following the abolition of zamindari and the institution of elected panchayats. In both villages, low-caste tenants initially asserted their political independence from the former (Thakur) zamindars but the latter returned to power within ten years, having demoralized their poorer opponents by threats of economic sanction and by exploiting factional divisions among the former tenants.

[123] See e.g. Khare (1962), Park and Tinker (1963), Retzlaff (1962), and Kantowsky (1968), for village studies in various parts of the state.

[124] See for instance Y. Singh (1970) on change and continuity in the relations between *jajmans* (patrons) and *prajas* (clients), and in their roles as political leaders and followers. A similar picture emerges from the fictionalized history of one particular village in eastern Uttar Pradesh in the popular Hindi novel *Adha Gaon* by Rahi Masoom Raza.

[125] On the predominance of factional considerations at the state level, see also Kohli (1987) and Brass (1965, 1990). P.K. Srivastava (1991) shows that factional battles have figured prominently in the election of Chief Ministers in Uttar Pradesh throughout its electoral history.

and economic rivalry within the village and led by the main landowning families.[126] Caste, or more precisely sub-caste kinship groups, have acted as natural units of local factional mobilization. Inter-faction rivalries are often little more than economic and social competition between families of similar stature, which can be considerably enhanced by securing access to state resources.[127] Thus, the appropriation of public resources and the dispensation of patronage play an important role in sustaining and nurturing factional politics. Developmental or welfare programmes, in particular, are often regarded by faction leaders as useful channels for the recruitment and reward of supporters.[128] A headman, for instance, is more likely to use his influence to protect a delinquent headmaster, and thereby gain a useful ally, than to take the side of the parents, who include enemies as well as supporters.[129]

It is difficult to think of political systems where factions do not exist, or play no important role.[130] What is remarkable about Uttar Pradesh politics, however, is that for nearly two decades after independence, factions remained the *only* significant basis of mobilization, and even nominal reference to ideology or policy were nearly absent from the mainstream. Human deprivation and social inequality did not figure as important political concerns at all.[131] In this regard, political developments in Uttar Pradesh differed markedly

[126] Hardiman (1994) argues against the use of the term 'faction' in studies of Indian politics, on the grounds that it adds nothing to the more precise and widely applicable term 'class collaboration'. Without disagreeing with his contention that a 'faction' is essentially an elite-led coalition which coopts sections of the economically exploited, we retain the use of the term since it aptly captures the specific form which class collaboration has taken in the context of village India.

[127] On this phenomenon, see e.g. Government of Uttar Pradesh (1964a, 1966), Dubey (1965), Rastogi (1965, 1966), Sahay (1969), Y. Singh (1970), M. Sharma (1978), Fukunaga (1993), among other relevant village studies.

[128] See, for instance, Khare (1962) and Hale (1978). The situation in Uttar Pradesh can be seen as an extreme form of the general relationship between public resources and private patronage in Indian political life. See Bardhan (1988) for an analysis of this phenomenon.

[129] On the use of the schooling system, both public and private, as a channel of patronage, see contributions by Narain (1972) on Rajasthan and Gould (1972) on Uttar Pradesh in Rudolph and Rudolph (1972).

[130] In fact, early studies that identified factionalism as an important feature of rural politics in Uttar Pradesh often considered it as a necessary stage in the process of political development (see e.g. Brass, 1965).

[131] On this, see particularly Hasan (1989).

from, say, West Bengal, where class organizations have been important early on, and also from Maharashtra and the south Indian states,
where 'low-caste' organizations have played an important role in
shaping political life.[132] In the late sixties, when a challenge to
caste-based social inequality did finally emerge on the political agenda in Uttar Pradesh, it was led by the relatively well-off 'middle'
castes, and factional politics continued to exercise a predominant
influence.

One of the most harmful aspects of factional politics has been
that rewards for political allegiance are made in the form of access
to public resources such as public-sector employment (including
teaching positions in village schools), government subsidies (e.g.
through IRDP loans), and building contracts (including those for
school buildings). Moreover, this system of patronage-based governance is not simply a localized phenomenon, it has corrupted political institutions at all levels. Leading political parties have played a
critical role in the development of this perverted system of governance.[133] In these circumstances, it would be naive to expect state
action to promote social opportunities on a wide basis, or the electoral process to act as a sound instrument of accountability.

Factionalism in Uttar Pradesh can be regarded both as a sign of
social conservatism and as an obstacle to social change. The political
economy of factionalism and patronage can be seen as a manifestation of the success of the rural elites in marginalizing the concerns
of the poor and the disadvantaged from the political agenda. Under
these conditions, the immense potential of democratic politics as a
basis for social change has been largely wasted so far.[134] The factional
basis of local politics has also suppressed the emergence of other
types of mobilization, including class-based coalitions, anti-caste
movements, and women's organizations. The failure of civil society
in Uttar Pradesh to rise beyond faction-based politics has played an
important role in slowing down social change and preserving the
traditional balance of political power.

[132] See e.g. Bose (1993), and the chapter on West Bengal in this volume. On
anti-Brahmin movements in a number of Indian states, see Srinivas (1966), O' Hanlon (1985), and various contributions in Frankel and Rao (1989).

[133] See, for instance, Kohli (1987), Hasan (1989), and Brass (1990).

[134] For a startling case study of 'deficient democracy' in Uttar Pradesh, see Lieten
(1994); the problem of lack of real local democracy analysed in that study has also
been noted in many of the village studies cited earlier in this chapter.

5.5 Political Participation and Social Inequality

Social and political life in Uttar Pradesh seems to be marked by two related features: pervasive inequality and resilient conservatism. Traditional patterns of caste and gender relations continue to exert a strong influence (with, for instance, women's social role remaining overwhelmingly confined to domestic work). Political mobilization still follows old patterns dominated by factionalism and patronage. And extreme inequalities of political power continue to exclude large sections of the population from effective participation in the democratic process.

To some extent, these problems apply elsewhere in India as well. In many other states, however, popular movements have had some success in fostering social change and in altering the balance of political power. In West Bengal and Kerala (discussed elsewhere in this book), political mobilization along class lines has led to far-reaching reforms concerned with land tenure and participatory democracy. Kerala further stands out for other social pursuits based on popular movements, such as resistance to caste discrimination and the universalization of basic education. Besides Kerala, Tamil Nadu, Karnataka, and Maharashtra have seen important socio-cultural movements against caste oppression, which have also taken up the issues of educational deprivation and political marginalization.[135] Social and political movements of this type have been comparatively weak — though not altogether absent — in Uttar Pradesh, or for that matter in large parts of the northern region.

It is beyond the scope of this paper to ascertain the ultimate roots of social and political inertia in Uttar Pradesh. Our primary aim has been to highlight the role of public inertia (involving the state as well as civil society) as a cause of persistent human deprivation in the state. Identifying the roots of this inertia would require detailed historical enquiry. In this section, a more modest attempt is made to understand how certain features of class, caste, and gender relations in Uttar Pradesh have made it that much harder to achieve rapid social change in the post-independence period.

---

[135] See, for instance, Srinivas (1966), Kakrambe (1983), O'Hanlon (1985), and Omvedt (1994) for accounts of such traditions, particularly in 'peninsular' India (south India and Maharashtra).

Agrarian Structure and Agrarian Politics

In the post-independence period, agrarian politics in Uttar Pradesh have revolved around producer interests (such as input subsidies and procurement prices), and the leadership of agrarian movements has remained firmly in the hands of relatively prosperous land-owners. After zamindari abolition, there was little political impetus for further land reform, whether in the form of land redistribution or tenancy reform. Zamindari abolition weakened the position of 'feudal' landlords, but strengthened the class of smaller landlords and peasants. Rapid technological change in agriculture, starting in the late sixties, further enhanced the economic position of landown-ing farmers.

Another relevant feature of the agrarian structure in Uttar Pra-desh is that it does not include a large class of landless labourers. Although land ownership in Uttar Pradesh is highly unequal, a relatively small proportion of the population is entirely landless. Relatedly, Uttar Pradesh has the second-lowest proportion of agri-cultural labourers in the rural male labour force among all major states, and the second-highest proportion of rural male workers reporting cultivation as their primary occupation (Nanda, 1992). This factor, too, has contributed to the predominance of producer interests and prosperous farmers in agrarian politics. In contrast with Kerala and West Bengal, where a significant proportion of the rural population had no direct stake in the existing structure of property rights, the potential constituency for class-based mobilization geared to radical agrarian reform and related goals has been a relatively small one in Uttar Pradesh. There is strong evidence, in fact, to suggest that land reforms under zamindari abolition were consciously de-signed to prevent the possibility of class-based political mobiliza-tion.[136] Landowners, even poor ones with marginal holdings, found themselves supporting rich farmer-led mobilization on producer interests, rather than challenging, alongside the landless, the highly unequal distribution of land.

It is also worth noting that even among the 'farmers movements', those based in Uttar Pradesh (mainly in the western part of the state), have been known for their hostility to demands relating to

[136] See, for instance, the analysis of the role of Charan Singh, widely regarded as one of the main architects of zamindari abolition in Uttar Pradesh, in Hasan (1989) and Byres (1988).

wage labour, women's emancipation, and economic equality. In contrast, the main farmers' organization in Maharashtra (which, like its counterpart in western Uttar Pradesh, is also primarily concerned with producer issues such as input and output prices) has given serious consideration to these concerns.[137] In Uttar Pradesh, the economic interests of groups other than prosperous farmers have neither been incorporated in the farmers' movements, nor had enough political weight to achieve much independent expression.

Caste and Class

Another distinguishing feature of the agrarian structure of Uttar Pradesh is the dominant position of certain 'high' castes with combined privileges of land ownership and ritual status.[138] Specifically, dominant landowners in Uttar Pradesh frequently belong to high-ranked castes with a martial tradition, commonly identified as Kshatriya, Thakur, or Rajput.[139] This is in contrast with much of south India and Maharashtra, where dominant landowners often belong to castes that rank much lower in the ritual hierarchy (on this, see Srinivas, 1962). The conjunction of temporal power and ritual authority in Uttar Pradesh has made it that much harder to challenge the prevailing inequalities of caste and class.

The emergence of strong anti-caste movements, in particular, would have been quite difficult in such circumstances. While anti-caste and 'anti-high-caste' movements have a long and significant history in many parts of India, such movements are of relatively recent origin in Uttar Pradesh.[140] In Maharashtra and much of

---

[137] On this contrast, see Omvedt (1995).

[138] We use the term 'dominant caste' in the sense discussed by Srinivas (1960, 1987), i.e. that of a caste which through a combination of numerical strength and economic advantage (usually land ownership) holds political power at a local level.

[139] Why these martial castes are there in the first place is a different matter. Their influence in this region has a long history, going back at least to the Mahabharata epic, which is built around the story of warring Kshatriya families. The hold of martial castes on the land is understandable, given that land ownership has often had to be won or defended through violent means in the past, especially perhaps in this fertile region frequently exposed to raids and invasions.

[140] There have been sporadic attempts, earlier on, at caste-based mobilization based on a critique of the ideology of caste hierarchy; see e.g. Gooptu (1990) for an account of Chamar-led agitation in urban centres of Uttar Pradesh in the 1920s. These initiatives failed, however, to give rise to sustainable political organizations.

south India, where the dominant landowning groups themselves often belonged to low-ranked castes in terms of ritual status, sections of the rural elite were initiators and active participants in these movements.[141] By contrast, the landowning martial castes of Uttar Pradesh (particularly in the central and eastern regions), far from initiating any challenge to the caste hierarchy, have actively repressed such initiatives.

The situation has been somewhat different in parts of western Uttar Pradesh, where the agrarian economy is dominated by Jats, who are not highly ranked in the ritual caste hierarchy. Anti-Brahmin rhetoric was liberally employed by Charan Singh in the sixties to build an alliance of 'backward' castes under the leadership of Jat landowners. It is important to note, however, that a wide gulf (in terms of both economic and ritual status) separates landowning castes such as the Jats from dispossessed 'untouchable' castes such as the Chamars. This gulf came to be reflected in the hostility of the peasant movements to the interests of scheduled-caste agricultural labourers.[142]

Recent years have seen a growing mobilization of scheduled castes in Uttar Pradesh politics, notably under the leadership of the Bahujan Samaj Party (BSP).[143] Thus far, this movement has not gone much beyond electoral coalition-building and other relatively narrow objectives such as caste-based reservation of public-sector employment. It remains to be seen whether these new coalitions are sustainable, and whether they are capable of putting the needs of disadvantaged groups on the political agenda.

---

[141] On the regional patterns of class–caste relations in India, and on the history of various 'low-caste' movements in Maharashtra and south India, see Srinivas (1966), O'Hanlon (1985), Frankel and Rao (1989).

[142] Byres (1988) notes that the tone of Charan Singh's movement was 'anti-Brahmin' on the one hand, but contemptuous of the scheduled castes on the other. See also Omvedt (1995) on the anti-labour stance of the new farmers' movements of western Uttar Pradesh.

[143] Interestingly, the current Chief Minister of the state is a scheduled-caste woman (Mayawati, a BSP leader). While this is certainly a path-breaking development, its origin is also reminiscent, in some ways, of the phenomenon of unprincipled factionalism discussed earlier. Indeed, the main political force within the coalition which brought Mayawati to power is the Bharatiya Janata Party (BJP), a party staunchly opposed to 'low-caste politics'.

Resilient Patriarchy

Many scholars have noted that the patriarchal culture of north India is particularly strong among dominant landowning communities, such as the Rajputs and Jats. Some notable features of this culture, many of which can be plausibly related to the material circumstances of agrarian or landowning communities, include the practices of patriliny and patrilocality, a strong emphasis on the ideology of the joint family, and a pronounced gender-based division of labour.[144] Among the martial castes, these patriarchal practices are compounded by an obsession with 'honour', the preservation of which depends partly on women adhering to conservative norms of behaviour ranging from seclusion to *sati*.[145] The traditions and values of these martial castes have had a strong influence on other dominant landowning castes, reinforcing their patriarchal culture.

Gender relations among the labouring classes have tended to be less unequal, partly due to the influence of much higher rates of female labour-force participation.[146] As we saw earlier, however, in Uttar Pradesh these classes are relatively unimportant in numerical terms, compared with other states. This is one reason why gender relations in Uttar Pradesh have been overwhelmingly influenced by the fiercely patriarchal practices of the propertied classes.

These links between caste, class, and gender relations in Uttar Pradesh have been a factor not only of extreme gender inequalities but also of great *resilience* in these unequal patterns. In the absence of any organized opposition to the prevailing caste hierarchy, for instance, disadvantaged castes in Uttar Pradesh have often attempted to elevate their status by emulating rather than challenging the culture

[144] An extreme manifestation of this patriarchal culture is the practice of female infanticide, which used to be common among Rajputs, Jats, and other dominant landowning communities of north India, and contributed to remarkably low female–male ratios in these communities. On these issues, see Panigrahi (1972), Miller (1981, 1993a), Kishwar (1995), and also related analyses in Caldwell and Caldwell (1987), Harris (1993), Agarwal (1994), Karve (1994), among others.

[145] On this aspect of the culture of the martial castes in Uttar Pradesh, see Minturn (1993); also Hitchcock (1975). On the general links between militarism and patriarchy in different societies, see Harris (1993).

[146] On this influence, see the chapter by Murthi, Guio, and Drèze in this volume, and the literature cited there. On the contrasting status of women among Jat landowners and scheduled-caste labourers in north India, see Horowitz and Kishwar (1982) and Majid (1986).

of the higher castes, including (and perhaps especially) their patriarchal practices.[147] The introduction of restrictions against widow remarriage among low-ranked but upwardly-mobile castes, and the spread of dowry among communities which used to practice brideprice, are two well-documented trends that can be interpreted along these lines.[148] While the phenomenon of Sanskritization is not confined to Uttar Pradesh or north India, it may have been particularly detrimental to gender equality in that region, where the castes considered as 'role models' (mainly the landowning martial castes, rather than the Brahmins as in much of south India) have an extremely patriarchal tradition.

Recent patterns of change in female–male ratios in Uttar Pradesh make interesting reading in this light. As discussed in the companion volume (Drèze and Sen, 1995, chapter 7), the female–male ratio in Uttar Pradesh has steadily declined since the beginning of this century, from 0.94 in 1901 to 0.88 in 1991. The last figure is quite typical of the female–male ratios that were *already* found among the martial and dominant landowning castes of Uttar Pradesh in 1901 (e.g. 0.89 among Rajputs, 0.85 among Jats, 0.80 among Gujjars), and the overall decline of the female–male ratio in Uttar Pradesh has largely taken the form of female–male ratios among *other* groups declining to values around or even below 0.9 from much higher levels. These trends are quite consistent with the notion that the patriarchal culture of the dominant castes has been spreading to other groups in recent decades.

A related issue of some importance is that of women's freedom of action and participation in gainful employment and non-domestic activities. As we noted in section 2, female labour-force participation rates in Uttar Pradesh (outside the Himalayan region) are exceptionally low even by Indian standards, and so is the participation of women in non-domestic activities in general. This is one aspect of the dominant patriarchal culture, which has not diminished in the least — and may have spread — in recent decades. Restrictions on

[147] On this phenomenon of 'Sanskritization', see Srinivas (1962, 1966, 1989). On the history of caste-based social mobility in rural Uttar Pradesh, see also Cohn (1990) and Wiser and Wiser (1970).

[148] On the transition from bride-price to dowry among some scheduled castes of Uttar Pradesh, see e.g. Macdorman (1986) and Wadley and Derr (1989); on widow remarriage, see Kolenda (1983) and other studies cited in Drèze (1990c) and Chen and Drèze (1995).

women's freedom of movement and activities have been an especially important factor of inertia in gender relations, in so far as they
have made it extremely difficult for women to act collectively.[149] As
women's movements elsewhere in India have amply demonstrated,
organized action is essential to challenge patriarchal norms, since
individual rebellion is all too easily repressed.

Inequality and Repression

The preceding discussion may help to understand the resilient nature of social inequalities in Uttar Pradesh, and of the resulting
disparities of political power. It is important to emphasize that the
main issue is not just economic inequality in the conventional sense
of the term (e.g. inequality of income or land ownership). In fact,
there is little evidence of economic inequality being particularly high
in Uttar Pradesh compared with other Indian states.[150] What is more
relevant is the particular form which social and economic inequalities have taken, and the mutually-reinforcing nature of different types of inequality (relating in particular to class, caste, and
gender).

The high concentration of power and privileges deriving from
the combined effects of inequalities based on class, caste, and
gender has made for an environment that is extremely hostile to
social change and broad-based political participation. One particular
symptom of this problem is the brutal repression of social and
political movements geared to the emancipation of disadvantaged

[149] This problem has been further reinforced by the practices of patrilocal
residence and village exogamy, which further isolate women from each other and
from their natal families. In all these respects, the situation of women has been
considerably more favourable in south India, where (in addition to higher female
labour-force participation rates) the kinship system gives greater scope to female
autonomy and solidarity. On the north–south contrast and other regional differences
in kinship systems, see Karve (1965), Sopher (1980b), Dyson and Moore (1983),
Caldwell and Caldwell (1987), Kishor (1993), Agarwal (1994), and Agnihotri (1994),
among others.

[150] In 1987–8, the Gini coefficients of per-capita consumer expenditure in major
Indian states were fairly evenly distributed between 0.26 and 0.33, with Uttar
Pradesh (0.293) very close to the middle of this interval (see Drèze and Sen, 1995,
Statistical Appendix, Table A.3). Nor are inequalities of land ownership in Uttar
Pradesh likely to be particularly large compared with other states, given the relatively
small proportion of landless households.

groups. Attempts by women to claim their property rights, or by agricultural labourers to claim higher wages, or by members of the scheduled castes to resist high-caste oppression have often been met with violence, rape, and murder.[151] The much-discussed 'criminalization of politics' in Uttar Pradesh fits in this general pattern of violence-based social control.[152] One plausible reading of the recent social history of Uttar Pradesh is that the prevailing patterns of class, caste, and gender inequality have made it particularly difficult for disadvantaged groups to cope with repressive violence.

6. Concluding Remarks

In drawing lessons from Uttar Pradesh's development experience, we must avoid the trap of regarding this state either as typical of India as a whole, or as a special case of little significance for other states. Much of India is very different from Uttar Pradesh, as we have discussed with particular reference to the contrast with South India. At the same time, large parts of India *are* like Uttar Pradesh in some important respects. In particular, the social failures that have hindered Uttar Pradesh's development (e.g. widespread illiteracy, pervasive inequality, endemic corruption, and the suppression of women's agency in society) are not confined to that state alone. These failures are, in many cases, particularly prominent in Uttar Pradesh, where their human consequences also come into sharper focus, but this feature enhances rather than diminishes the relevance of this regional perspective on Indian development. It is on this understanding that we conclude with some general observations on the interpretation and wider significance of the case study presented in this paper.

[151] For some examples (from Uttar Pradesh and elsewhere in north India), see e.g. Saith and Tankha (1992), M. Sen (1993), Kumar (1993), Srivastava (1995, forthcoming), and Bhatia (forthcoming). For further discussion of the phenomenon of endemic violence in Uttar Pradesh, see Oldenburg (1992).

[152] According to the Chief Election Commissioner, 180 of Uttar Pradesh's 425 Members of Legislative Assembly (MLAs) have criminal cases pending against them, at least 52 of which involve 'heinous crimes' such as rape and murder. See Singh and Ahmed (1995), who consider that Uttar Pradesh surpasses all other states (even Bihar) in this respect, and that the crime–politics nexus 'seems to have overwhelmed politics in Uttar Pradesh' (p. 119).

To put first things first, we should restate the basic fact that Uttar Pradesh is one of the regions in India that lags behind as far as many basic indicators of development are concerned. If this point is worth reiterating, it is because Uttar Pradesh has not usually been seen in that way, at least not until recently. As we saw in section 2, Uttar Pradesh does not differ very much from India as a whole in terms of conventional poverty indicators, and given the overwhelming influence of these indicators in policy debates, the state has not been the object of any special concern in development planning. Further, Uttar Pradesh is often seen as one of the 'progressive' Green Revolution regions that have — it is often argued — received too much rather than too little official attention and government support (e.g. in the form of agricultural credit and infrastructure investment). This assessment, too, is based on neglecting important indicators of human deprivation in the state, such as mortality and illiteracy. Interestingly, it is the widespread concern with high *fertility* in the northern region, including Uttar Pradesh, which eventually led to greater attention being paid to 'social development' in the so-called BIMARU states (Bihar, Madhya Pradesh, Rajasthan, and Uttar Pradesh).

Second, as far as the *causes* of endemic deprivation in Uttar Pradesh are concerned, low per-capita incomes and slow economic growth are only part of the story. Indeed, poor economic performance in terms of these and other standard indicators is a problem which Uttar Pradesh shares with many other Indian states. The issue of economic performance is, of course, very serious, but there are many other failures to address in transforming living conditions in Uttar Pradesh. Among the relevant failures are aborted land reforms, the displacement of health care services by family-planning programmes, the decay of the public schooling system, the widespread corruption of poverty alleviation programmes, the suppression of women's informed agency in society, and the fragile basis of local democracy. Underlying these diverse problems is a basic failure of public action — whether of a collaborative or adversarial type — to focus on the promotion of social needs, particularly those of disadvantaged sections of the population.

Third, this case study of Uttar Pradesh makes particularly interesting reading in the light of Kerala's development achievements, discussed in Ramachandran's contribution to this volume. Just as Kerala's experience illustrates what can be achieved through determined public action at an early stage of development, Uttar Pradesh illustrates the penalties of inertia. Even the specific fields of action which have been so central to Kerala's achievements (e.g. land reform, gender relations, basic education, local democracy) turn out to be remarkably similar to those where public inertia in Uttar Pradesh has exacted such a heavy price. This particular contrast is of major significance in understanding the divergent development performances of different Indian states and their practical implications.

Fourth, the persistence of widespread illiteracy in Uttar Pradesh (even in the younger age groups, and particularly among females) is an issue of great importance on its own, both as an *aspect* of human deprivation in that state and as a *cause* of other kinds of deprivation. A wide range of recent empirical investigations have brought out the diverse individual and social roles of basic education, including those connected with economic growth, demographic change, social equity, political participation, and personal development. In the light of these recent findings, the promotion of basic education in Uttar Pradesh and other educationally backward states is undoubtedly one of India's foremost development priorities. Unfortunately, as the field investigation reported in sections 3 and 4 brings out, the functioning of government schools in rural Uttar Pradesh is extraordinarily poor as things stand, and probably deteriorating. The central issue seems to be the absence of any kind of accountability of the schooling establishment. Reforming the schooling establishment is no easy task, and the prospects of real change seem to depend crucially on basic education in Uttar Pradesh becoming a major political issue.

Fifth, this case study highlights the crippling effects of social inequality on development achievements. In Uttar Pradesh, extreme inequalities of political power have severely distorted the priorities of state intervention and the implementation of most development programmes. The low participation of disadvantaged groups in the political process, in turn, reflects the continuing influence of sharp inequalities relating not only to class but also to caste and gender. Even the failure to achieve widespread literacy fits in this general pattern, reflected *inter alia* in the elitist biases of educational policy and the lack of accountability of the schooling establishment. These observations are of some general importance, given the frequent tendency to see inequality through the narrow prism of income distribution, and to consider inequality as a secondary issue compared with the overriding objective of reducing poverty. This perspective fails to recognize (1) that social inequality is not just a matter of income distribution, (2) that social change, including the elimination of oppressive inequalities, is an integral part of development, and (3) that social inequality can be a major obstacle to the successful pursuit of a wide range of other development objectives.

Sixth, Uttar Pradesh's development experience has some bearing on current debates about economic reform in India. The current focus of economic reforms, as well as of the *critiques* of these reforms, is overwhelmingly on the specific question of liberalization.[153] Without denying the importance of the issues that have been debated in that context, this focus is seriously inadequate. As this case study of Uttar Pradesh illustrates, the social failures that account for the persistence of endemic deprivation in India are wide-ranging and deep-rooted, and the requirements of real reform go much beyond economic liberalization.[154]

Finally, the transformation of development priorities and achievements in Uttar Pradesh is a challenge not only for the state but also for the public. The agency of the state is obviously central to this transformation, but the decisions of the state and the effectiveness of government initiatives are themselves contingent on the nature and content of democratic politics. In the present political climate, it would be naive to expect the government to initiate a major reorientation of development priorities on its own, or on the basis of bland expert advice. Ultimately, this is a political battle, which calls for more effective enfranchisement of disadvantaged groups as well as better articulation of social needs. The other case studies presented in this book illustrate the feasibility of substantial changes in the balance of political power in Indian states. Even the recent political history of Uttar Pradesh itself includes some hopeful signs of change. The social failures of Uttar Pradesh are quite daunting, but the potential rewards of action are correspondingly high, and the costs of continued inertia even higher.

[153] As one commentator insightfully put it at a recent seminar on economic reform, the government's reform programme has three components: deregulation, fiscal adjustment, and liberalization of international trade (Dr Amresh Bagchi, National Institute of Public Finance and Policy).

[154] This general issue is explored in greater depth in the companion volume (Drèze and Sen, 1995).

REFERENCES

Agarwal, Bina (1994), *A Field of One's Own: Gender and Land Rights in South Asia* (Cambridge: Cambridge University Press).

Agnihotri, Satish (1994), 'Missing Females: A Disaggregated Analysis', mimeo, University of East Anglia, forthcoming in *Economic and Political Weekly*.

Ahmad, A. and S.C. Nuna (1990), *School Education in India* (New Delhi: NIEPA).

Anon (1991), 'Note on Participation in Education — All India', *Sarvekshana*, 14 (3), January–March.

—— (1992), 'Morbidity and Utilization of Medical Services: NSS 42nd Round', *Sarvekshana*, 15 (4), April–June.

Bandyopadhyay, R. (1991), 'Education for an Enlightened Society: A Review', *Economic and Political Weekly*, 16 February.

Banerjee, Sumanta (1994), 'Obstacles to Change', *Economic and Political Weekly*, 26 March.

Banerji, Rukmini (1995), 'Urban Poverty and the Context of Primary Schooling in India', mimeo, Spencer Foundation, Chicago.

Bara, D., R. Bhengra, and B. Minz (1991), 'Tribal Female Literacy: Factors in Differentiation among Munda Religious Communities', *Social Action*, 41 (4).

Bardhan, Pranab (1988), 'Dominant Proprietary Classes and India's Democracy', in Kohli (1988).

Bashir, Sajitha (1994), 'Public Versus Private in Primary Education: Comparisons of School Effectiveness and Costs in Tamil Nadu', Ph.D. thesis, London School of Economics.

Bashir, Sajitha, et al. (1993a), *Education for All: Baseline Survey of Three Districts of Uttar Pradesh, India* (New Delhi: New Concept Consultancy Services), vol. 1.

—— (1993b), *Education for All: Baseline Survey of Three Districts of Uttar Pradesh, India* (New Delhi: New Concept Consultancy Services), vol. 2.

Basu, Alaka Malwade (1989), 'Is Discrimination in Food Really Necessary for Explaining Sex Differentials in Childhood Mortality?', *Population Studies*, 43 (2).

—— (1992), *Culture, the Status of Women and Demographic Behaviour* (Oxford: Clarendon Press).

Berreman, G.D. (1963), 'Caste and Community Development', *Human Organisation*, 22 (1).

Bhoosnurmath, Kashinath (1991), 'People's Perception of Importance of Education: A Field Experience in Dehradun District', *The Administrator*, 36.

Biswas, C. (1990), 'Health and Nutritional Level of Children in Uttar Pradesh, with Special Reference to Allahabad', Occasional Paper No. 56, Govind Ballabh Pant Social Science Institute, Allahabad.

Bliss, Christopher and Nicholas Stern (1982), *Palanpur: The Economy of an Indian Village* (Oxford: Oxford University Press).

Bose, A. (1991), *Demographic Diversity of India* (Delhi: B.R. Publishing).

Bose, Sugata (1993), *Peasant Labour and Colonial Capital: Rural Bengal Since 1770* (Cambridge: Cambridge University Press).

Brass, Paul R. (1965), *Factional Politics in an Indian State* (Berkeley and Los Angeles: University of California Press).

—— (1985), *Caste, Faction and Party in Indian Politics: Volume Two — Election Studies* (Delhi: Chanakya Publications).

—— (1990), *The Politics of India since Independence* (Cambridge: Cambridge University Press).

Byres, T.J. (1988), 'Charan Singh, 1902–87: An Assessment', *Journal of Peasant Studies*, 15 (2).

Budakoti, D.K. (1988), 'Study of the Community and Community Health Work in Two Primary Health Centres in Chamoli District of Uttar Pradesh', M.Phil. Dissertation, Centre for Social Medicine and Community Health, Jawaharlal Nehru University, New Delhi.

Caldwell, Pat and John Caldwell (1987), 'Where There is a Narrower Gap between Female and Male Situations: Lessons from South India and Sri Lanka', paper presented at a Workshop on Differentials in Mortality and Health Care, BAMANEH/SSRC, Dhaka.

Chanana, Karuna (1990), 'Structures and Ideologies: Socialisation and Education of the Girl Child in South Asia', *Indian Journal of Social Science*, 3 (1).

Chanana, Karuna (ed.) (1988), *Socialisation, Education and Women: Explorations in Gender Identity* (New Delhi: Orient Longman).

Chandra, P. (1958), 'Hindu Social Organisation in Village Majra', *Eastern Anthropologist*, 11 (3–4).

Chen, Marty and Jean Drèze (1995), 'Recent Research on Widows in India', *Economic and Political Weekly*, 30 September.

Church, R. (1974), 'The Impact of Bhoodan and Gramdan on Village', *Pacific Affairs*, 48 (1).

CIET International (1995), 'Nepal Multiple Indicator Surveillance:

Summary of Preliminary Results (Formal Education)', mimeo, CIET International, New York.

Cohn, B.S. (1990), *An Anthropologist among the Historians and Other Essays* (Delhi: Oxford University Press).

Colclough, Christopher (1993), *Educating All The Children: Strategies for Primary Schooling in the South* (Oxford: Clarendon).

Crook, R.C. and J. Manor (1994), 'Enhancing Participation and Institutional Performance: Democratic Decentralisation in South Asia and West Africa', report to the Overseas Development Administration, January.

Danda, A.K. (1987), *A Rural Community in Transition* (New Delhi: Inter-India Publications).

Das Gupta, Monica (1987a), 'Informal Security Mechanisms and Population Retention in Rural India', *Economic Development and Cultural Change*, 36 (1).

—— (1987b), 'Selective Discrimination against Female Children in Rural Punjab', *Population and Development Review*, 13.

—— (1994), 'Life Course Perspectives on Women's Autonomy and Health Outcomes', paper presented at a meeting of the Population Association of America, Miami, May.

Dasgupta, Partha and Debraj Ray (1990), 'Adapting to Undernourishment: The Biological Evidence and Its Implications', in Drèze and Sen (1990), vol. I.

Datt, Gaurav and Martin Ravallion (1995), 'Why Have Some Indian States Done Better than Others at Raising Rural Living Standards?', mimeo, World Bank.

Derr, Bruce W. and Susan S. Wadley (1987), 'Changing Patterns of Employment in Karimpur: 1925–1984', paper presented at the Wisconsin Conference on South Asia, Madison, November.

Devi, M.D. Usha (1992), 'Research Perspective for Understanding Women's Education', *Economic and Political Weekly*, 13–20 June.

Dharampal (1983), *The Beautiful Tree: Indigenous Indian Education in the Eighteenth Century* (New Delhi: Biblia Impex Pvt. Ltd.).

Drèze, Jean (1990a), 'Poverty in India and the IRDP Delusion', *Economic and Political Weekly*, 29 September.

—— (1990b), 'Famine Prevention in India', in Drèze and Sen (1990), vol. II.

—— (1990c), 'Widows in Rural India', Discussion Paper No. 26, Development Economics Research Programme, STICERD, London School of Economics.

Drèze, Jean, Peter Lanjouw, and Naresh Sharma (forthcoming),

'Economic Development in Palanpur, 1957–94', to be published in P. Lanjouw and N. Stern (eds.), *A Sort of Growth: Palanpur 1957–94* (Oxford: Oxford University Press).

Drèze, Jean and Mrinalini Saran (1995), 'Primary Education and Economic Development in China and India: Overview and Two Case Studies', in K. Basu, P. Pattanaik, and K. Suzumura (eds.), *Choice, Welfare and Development* (Oxford: Clarendon).

Drèze, Jean and Amartya Sen (1989), *Hunger and Public Action* (Oxford: Clarendon Press).

—— (1995), *India: Economic Development and Social Opportunity* (Delhi and Oxford: Oxford University Press).

Drèze, Jean and Amartya Sen (eds.) (1990), *The Political Economy of Hunger*, 3 volumes (Oxford: Clarendon Press).

Drèze, Jean and P.V. Srinivasan (1995), 'Poverty in India: Regional Estimates, 1987–8', Working Paper No. 36, Centre for Development Economics at the Delhi School of Economics.

Dube, S.C. (1958), *India's Changing Villages: Human Factor in Community Development* (London: Routledge and Kegan Paul).

Dubey, S.M. (1965), 'Role of Kinship and Ideology in Rural Factionalism: A Study of Factions in a Village of Eastern U.P. with Special Reference to the Role of Patti', *Eastern Anthropologist*, 18 (1).

Dumont, L. and D. Pocock (eds.) (1957), *Contributions to Indian Sociology* (Paris: Mouton).

Dyson, Tim and Mick Moore (1983), 'On Kinship Structure, Female Autonomy, and Demographic Behavior in India', *Population and Development Review*, 9 (1).

Elder, J.W. (1970), 'Rajpur: Change in the Jajmani System of an Uttar Pradesh Village', in Iswaran (1970).

EPW Research Foundation (1993), 'Poverty Levels in India: Norms, Estimates and Trends', *Economic and Political Weekly*, 21 August.

Frankel, Francine R. and M.S.A. Rao (eds.) (1989), *Dominance and State Power in Modern India: Decline of a Social Order*, 2 volumes (Delhi: Oxford University Press).

Fukunaga, Masaaki (1993), *Society, Caste and Factional Politics* (New Delhi: Manohar).

Fuller, C.J. (1989), 'Misconceiving the Grain Heap: A Critique of the Concept of the Indian Jajmani System', in J. Parry and M. Bloch (eds.), *Money and the Morality of Exchange* (Cambridge: Cambridge University Press).

Ghosh, A., U.R. Ananthamurthy, A. Béteille, S.M. Kansal, V. Mazumdar, and A. Vanaik (1994), 'Evaluation of Literacy Campaigns in

India', report of an independent Expert Group appointed by the Ministry of Human Resource Development (New Delhi: Ministry of Human Resource Development).

Gillespie, Stuart (1995), 'Nutrition Trends in India: Latest Data', mimeo, UNICEF, New Delhi.

Gokhale, A.M. (1988), 'Panchayati Raj in Nagaland', mimeo, Department of Rural Development, Ministry of Agriculture, New Delhi.

Gooptu, Nandini (1990), 'Caste, Deprivation and Politics: The Untouchables in U.P. Towns in the Early Twentieth Century', paper presented at a Workshop on Labour and Dalit Movements held at the School of Oriental and African Studies, London.

Gould, Harold (1972), 'Educational Structures and Political Processes in Faizabad District, Uttar Pradesh', in Rudolph and Rudolph (1972).

Government of India (1986), *The Teacher and Society: Report of the National Commission on Teachers* (New Delhi: Government of India Press).

—— (1989), 'Child Mortality, Age at Marriage and Fertility in India', Occasional Paper No. 2 of 1989, Demography Division, Office of the Registrar General, New Delhi.

—— (1991a), *Family Welfare Programme in India: Yearbook 1989–90* (New Delhi: Ministry of Health and Family Welfare).

—— (1991b), 'Provisional Population Totals: Rural–Urban Distribution', Census of India 1991, Series 1, Paper 2 of 1991, Office of the Registrar General, New Delhi.

—— (1991c), 'Provisional Population Totals: Workers and their Distribution', Census of India 1991, Series 1, Paper 3 of 1991, Office of the Registrar General, New Delhi.

—— (1992a), *Health Information of India: 1991* (New Delhi: Central Bureau of Health Intelligence, Ministry of Health and Family Welfare).

—— (1992b), *National Policy on Education 1986: Programme of Action 1992* (New Delhi: Ministry of Human Resource Development).

—— (1993a), *Sample Registration System: Fertility and Mortality Indicators 1991* (New Delhi: Office of the Registrar General).

—— (1993b), 'Housing and Amenities: A Brief Analysis of the Housing Tables of 1991 Census', Census of India 1991, Paper 2 of 1993, Office of the Registrar General, New Delhi.

—— (1994a), *Annual Report 1993–94 (Part 1) of the Department of Education* (New Delhi: Ministry of Human Resource Development).

—— (1994b), *Report of the Group to Examine the Feasibility of Implementing the Recommendations of the National Advisory Committee set up to Suggest*

Ways to Reduce Academic Burden on School Students (New Delhi: Department of Education).

Government of India (1995), *Expenditure Budget 1995–96*, vol. 2 (New Delhi. Ministry of Finance).

Government of Uttar Pradesh (1964a), 'Factionalism and Leadership Change in Bhurbharal: A Case Study of Panchayat Elections', Report of the Planning and Research Action Institute, Lucknow.

—— (1964b), 'Female Leadership in Deintikar Gram Sabha', Report of the Planning and Research Action Institute, Lucknow.

—— (1966), 'Decision-makers in a Gramdan Village', Report of the Planning and Research Action Institute, Lucknow.

Guhan, S. (1981), 'Social Security: Lessons and Possibilities from the Tamil Nadu Experience', Bulletin, Madras Development Seminar Series, 11 (1).

—— (1990), 'Social Security Initiatives in Tamil Nadu 1989', Working Paper No. 96, Madras Institute of Development Studies.

Gupta, Akhil (1994), 'Blurred Boundaries: The Discourse of Corruption, the Culture of Politics and the Imagined State', mimeo, Department of Anthropology, Stanford University.

Gupta, D.B., A. Basu, and R. Asthana (1993), 'Population Change, Women's Role and Status, and Development in India: A Review', mimeo, Institute of Economic Growth, Delhi University.

Hale, S. (1978), 'The Politics of Entrepreneurship in Indian Villages', *Development and Change*, 9 (2).

Haque, T. and A.S. Sirohi (1986), *Agrarian Reforms and Institutional Changes in India* (New Delhi: Concept).

Hardiman, David (1994), 'The Indian "Faction": A Political Theory Examined', in R. Guha (ed.), *Subaltern Studies I: Writing on South Asian History and Society* (Delhi: Oxford University Press).

Harlan, Lindsey and Paul B. Courtright (eds.) (1994), *From the Margins of Hindu Marriage: Essays on Gender, Religion and Culture* (New York: Oxford University Press).

Harris, Marvin (1993), 'The Evolution of Human Gender Hierarchies: A Trial Formulation', in Miller (1993b).

Harriss, Barbara (1990), 'The Intrafamily Distribution of Hunger in South Asia', in Drèze and Sen (1990), vol. I.

Hasan, Zoya (1989), 'Power and Mobilization: Patterns of Resilience and Change in Uttar Pradesh Politics', in Frankel and Rao (1989).

—— (1995), 'Shifting Ground: Hindutva Politics and the Farmers' Movement in Uttar Pradesh', in Tom Brass (ed.), *New Farmers' Movements in India* (Ilford: Frank Cass).

Hitchcock, John T. (1975), 'The Idea of the Martial Rajput', in M. Singer (ed.), *Traditional India: Structure and Change* (Jaipur: Rawat Publications).

Horowitz, B. and Madhu Kishwar (1982), 'Family Life — The Unequal Deal', *Manushi*, 11.

Indian Institute of Management (1985), *Study of Facility Utilization and Programme Management in Family Welfare* (Ahmedabad: Public Systems Group, Indian Institute of Management).

International Institute for Population Sciences (1994a), *National Family Health Survey: India 1992–93* (Bombay: IIPS).

—— (1994b), *National Family Health Survey 1992–93*, State volumes (Bombay: IIPS).

Iswaran, K. (ed.) (1970), *Change and Continuity in India's Villages* (New York: Columbia University Press).

Jain, A.K. and Moni Nag (1985), 'Female Primary Education and Fertility Reduction in India', Working Paper No. 114, Center for Population Studies, The Population Council, New York.

Jain, L.R., K. Sundaram, and S.D. Tendulkar (1988), 'Dimensions of Rural Poverty: An Inter-Regional Profile', *Economic and Political Weekly*, Nov. (special issue); reprinted in Krishnaswamy (1990).

Janakarajan, S. (1995), 'Village Resurvey: Some Issues and Results', paper presented at a workshop on The Village in Asia Revisited held at the Centre for Development Studies, Thiruvananthapuram, January.

Jeffery, P., R. Jeffery, and P. Lyon (1989), *Labour Pains and Labour Power: Women and Child-bearing in India* (London: Zed).

Jejeebhoy, S. and S. Kulkarni (1989), 'Demand for Children and Reproductive Motivation: Empirical Observations from Rural Maharashtra', in S.N. Singh et. al. (eds.), *Population Transition in India*, Delhi: B.R. Publishing.

Jena, B. and R.N. Pati (eds.) (1989), *Health and Family Welfare Services in India* (New Delhi: Ashish).

Jha, Praveen Kumar (1994), 'Changing Condition of Agricultural Labourers in Post-independent India: A Case Study from Bihar', Ph.D. thesis, Centre for Economic Studies and Planning, Jawaharlal Nehru University, New Delhi.

Jha, Shikha (1994), 'Foodgrains Price and Distribution Policies in India: Performance, Problems and Prospects', Preprint No. 134, Indira Gandhi Institute of Development Research, Bombay; forthcoming in *Asia-Pacific Development Journal*.

Jimenez, E., M.E. Lockheed, and V. Pacqueo (1991), 'The Relative

Efficiency of Private and Public Schools in Developing Countries', *World Bank Research Observer*, 6 (2).

Kakrambe, S.A. (1983), *Karamveer Bhaurao Patil and Mass Education Movement: Impact on Maharashtra* (Bombay: Somaiya Publications).

Kamat, A.R. (1985), *Education and Social Change in India* (Bombay: Somaiya Publications).

Kantowsky, D. (1968), 'Local Politics in Rameshvar, a Multi-caste Village in Eastern U.P., India', Seminar Paper No. 7, in collected seminar papers on Autonomy and Dependence in 'Parochial' Politics, Institute of Commonwealth Studies, University of London.

Karve, Irawati (1965), *Kinship Organisation in India* (Bombay: Asia Publishing House).

—— (1974), *Yuganta: The End of an Epoch* (Hyderabad: Orient Longman).

—— (1994), 'The Kinship Map of India', in Uberoi (1994).

Khan, M.E. (1988), 'Infant Mortality in Uttar Pradesh: A Micro-level Study', in A.K. Jain and P. Visaria (eds.), *Infant Mortality in India: Differentials and Determinants* (New Delhi: Sage).

Khan, M.E., R. Anker, S.K. Ghosh, Dastidar, and S. Bairathi (1989), 'Inequalities between Men and Women in Nutrition and Family Welfare Services: An Indepth Enquiry in an Indian Village', in J.C. Caldwell and G. Santow (eds.), *Selected Readings in the Cultural, Social and Behavioral Determinants of Health*, Health Transition Series, No. 1 (Canberra: Health Transition Centre, Australian National University).

Khan, M.E., S.K. Ghosh, Dastidar, and R. Singh (1986), 'Nutrition and Health Practices among the Rural Women: A Case Study of Uttar Pradesh', *Journal of Family Welfare*, 33 (2).

Khan, M.E., R.B. Gupta, C.V.S. Prasad, and S.K. Ghosh, Dastidar (1988), *Performance of Health and Family Welfare Programme in India* (Bombay: Himalaya Publishing House).

Khan, M.E., C.V.S. Prasad, and A. Majumdar (1980), *People's Perceptions about Family Planning in India* (New Delhi: Concept).

Khare, R.S. (1962), 'Group Dynamics in a North Indian Village', *Human Organisation*, 21 (3).

—— (1964), 'A Study of Social Resistance to Sanitation Programmes in Rural India', *Eastern Anthropologist*, 17 (2).

Kingdon, Geeta Gandhi (1994), 'An Economic Evaluation of School Management-Types in Urban India: A Case Study of Uttar Pradesh', Ph.D. Thesis, St. Antony's College, Oxford.

Kishor, Sunita (1993), ' "May God Give Sons to All": Gender and Child Mortality in India', *American Sociological Review*, 58.

Kishwar, Madhu (1995), 'When Daughters are Unwanted', *Manushi*, 86 (Jan.–Feb.).

Kohli, Atul (1987), *The State and Poverty in India: The Politics of Reform* (Cambridge: Cambridge University Press).

Kohli, Atul (ed.) (1988), *India's Democracy: An Analysis of Changing State–Society Relations* (Princeton, NJ: Princeton University Press).

Kolenda, Pauline (1983), 'Widowhood among "Untouchable" Chuhras', in A. Ostor, L. Fruzzetti, and S. Barnett (eds.), *Concepts of Person: Kinship, Caste and Marriage in India* (Delhi: Oxford University Press).

Krishnamurthy, M.G. and M.V. Nadkarni (1983), 'Integrated Child Development Services: An Assessment', report prepared for UNICEF, New Delhi.

Kumar, Ashok (1990), 'The ICDS Projects in North Indian States: A Study of Selected Blocks', National Institute of Public Cooperation and Child Development, Lucknow.

Kumar, Krishna (ed.) (1994), *Democracy and Education in India* (London: Sangam Books).

Kumar, Radha (1993), *The History of Doing: An Illustrated Account of Movements for Women's Rights and Feminism in India, 1800–1990* (London: Vision).

Labenne, Sophie (1995), 'Analyse Econométrique du Travail des Enfants en Inde', M.Sc. thesis (unpublished), Department of Economics, Université de Namur, Belgium.

Lambert, Claire M. (ed.) (1976), *Village Studies: Data Analysis and Bibliography — Volume 1: India 1950–1975* (Essex: Bowker Publishing Company, for the Institute of Development Studies at the University of Sussex, Brighton).

Lata, Divya (1995), 'An Assessment of Early Child Care and Education Programmes Supported by SCF in India', mimeo, Save the Children Fund (UK), New Delhi.

Lieten, G.K. (1994), 'The North Indian Kulak Farmer and His Deficient Democracy', Occasional Paper 1994, 4, Indo-Dutch Programme on Alternatives in Development, Indian Council of Social Science Research, New Delhi.

Macdorman, M. (1986), 'Contemporary Marriage Practices in North India: Evidence from Three Uttar Pradesh Villages', Ph.D. thesis, Australian National University, Canberra.

Mahapatra, R.K. (1994), 'Food Crises in Kalahandi: 1960/61–1992/93',

M.Phil. Dissertation, Centre for Economic Studies and Planning, Jawaharlal Nehru University, New Delhi.

Maharatna, Arup (1995), 'Children's Work, Activities, Surplus Labour and Fertility: A Case Study of Peasant Households in Birbhum, West Bengal', paper presented at the second workshop on Applied Development Economics, 6–10 January 1996, Centre for Development Economics at the Delhi School of Economics.

Mahendra Dev, S. (1993a), 'India's (Maharashtra) Employment Guarantee Scheme: Lessons from Long Experience', paper presented at a workshop on Employment for Poverty Alleviation and Food Security, convened by the International Food Policy Research Institute, Washington, DC, October 1993.

—— (1993b), 'Social Security in the Unorganized Sector: Lessons from the Experience of Kerala and Tamil Nadu', mimeo, Indira Gandhi Institute of Development Research, Bombay.

Majid, A. (1986), 'Women's Contribution to Household Income Among Agricultural Labourers of Punjab', Research Study No. 86/2, Agricultural Economics Research Centre, University of Delhi, Delhi.

Mandelbaum, D.G. (1970), Society in India (Berkeley: University of California Press).

Mari Bhat, P.N., K. Navaneetham, and S.I. Rajan (1992), 'Maternal Mortality in India', paper presented at a workshop on Health and Development in India held at the India International Centre, 2–4 January 1992; also published in M. Das Gupta, T.N. Krishnan, and L. Chen (eds.) (1995), *Women's Health in India: Risk and Vulnerability* (Bombay: Oxford University Press).

Marriott, McKim (1952), 'Social Change in an Indian Village', *Economic Development and Cultural Change*, 1.

Matthai, John (1915), *Village Government in British India* (London: T. Fisher Unwin).

Maurya, K.N. (1989), 'An Analysis of Causative Factors Responsible for Low Utilisation of Health and Family Welfare Services', in Jena and Pati (1989).

Mehrotra, Nidhi (1995), 'Primary Education in Rural India: A Field Report', mimeo, Department of Education, University of Chicago.

—— (forthcoming), 'Primary Schooling in Rural India: Determinants of Demand', Ph.D. thesis, University of Chicago.

Middleton, John, et al. (1993), 'Uttar Pradesh Basic Education Project: Staff Appraisal Report', Report No. 11746–IN, Population and Human Resources Operations Division, World Bank, Washington, DC.

Miller, Barbara (1981), *The Endangered Sex* (Ithaca: Cornell University Press).

Miller, Barbara (1993a), 'On Poverty, Child Survival and Gender: Models and Misperceptions', *Third World Planning Review*, 15.

Miller, Barbara (ed.) (1993b), *Sex and Gender Hierarchies* (Cambridge: Cambridge University Press).

Miller, D.B. (1976), *From Hierarchy to Stratification: Changing Patterns of Social Inequality in a North Indian Village* (London: Oxford University Press).

Minhas, B. (1992), 'Educational Deprivation and its Role as a Spoiler of Access to Better Life in India', in A. Dutta and M.M. Agrawal (eds.), *The Quality of Life* (Delhi: B.R. Publishing).

Minhas, B.S., L.R. Jain, and S.D. Tendulkar (1991), 'Declining Incidence of Poverty in India in the 1980s', *Economic and Political Weekly*, 6–13 July.

Minturn, Leigh (1993), *Sita's Daughters: Coming Out of Purdah, The Rajput Women of Khalapur Revisited* (New York: Oxford University Press).

Moller, Joanne (1993), 'Inside and Outside: Conceptual Continuities from Household to Region in Kumaon, North India', unpublished Ph.D. thesis, London School of Economics.

Mull, Dorothy (1991), 'Traditional Perceptions of Marasmus in Pakistan', *Social Science and Medicine*, 32.

Murthy, Nirmala (1992), 'Issues in Health Policies and Management in India', paper presented at a Workshop on Health and Development in India, 24 January 1992; also published in M. Das Gupta, T.N. Krishnan, and L. Chen (eds.) (1995), *Women's Health in India: Risk and Vulnerability* (Bombay: Oxford University Press).

Nanda, Amulya Ratna (1991), 'Provisional Population Totals: Workers and Their Distribution', Census of India 1991, Series 1, Paper 3 of 1991, Office of the Registrar General, New Delhi.

—— (1992), 'Final Population Totals: Brief Analysis of Primary Census Abstract', Census of India 1991, Series 1, Paper 2 of 1992, Office of the Registrar General, New Delhi.

—— (1993), 'Union Primary Census Abstract for Scheduled Castes and Scheduled Tribes', Census of India 1991, Series 1, Paper 1 of 1993, Office of the Registrar General, New Delhi.

Narain, Iqbal (1972), 'Rural Local Politics and Primary School Management', in Rudolph and Rudolph (1972).

Narayana, D. (1995), 'Education by Women as a Leading Factor in Fertility Reduction in India', paper presented at a Workshop on Fertility Change in India and Brazil, Center for Population and Development Studies, Harvard University, April.

National Council of Educational Research and Training (1992), *Fifth All-India Educational Survey*, 2 volumes (New Delhi: NCERT).

National Institute of Public Cooperation and Child Development (1992), *Statistics on Children in India. Pocket Book 1992* (New Delhi: NIPCCD).

Nuna, Sheel C. (1990), *Women and Development* (New Delhi: National Institute of Educational Planning and Administration).

O'Hanlon, Rosalind (1985), *Caste, Conflict and Ideology: Mahatma Jotirao Phule and Low Caste Protest in Nineteenth-Century Western India* (Cambridge: Cambridge University Press).

Oldenburg, Philip (1992), 'Sex Ratio, Son Preference and Violence in India: A Research Note', *Economic and Political Weekly*, 5–12 December.

Olper, M.E. and R.D. Singh (1952), 'Economic, Political and Social Change in a Village of North Central India', *Human Organisation*, 11 (2).

Omvedt, Gail (1993), *Reinventing Revolution: New Social Movements and the Socialist Tradition in India* (London: M.E. Sharpe).

Osmani, Siddiq R. (1990), 'Nutrition and the Economics of Food: Implications of Some Recent Controversies', in Drèze and Sen (1990), vol. I.

Panigrahi, Lalita (1972), *British Social Policy and Female Infanticide in India* (New Delhi: Munshiram Manoharlal).

Parikh, Kirit (1994), 'Who Gets How Much from PDS: How Effectively Does It Reach the Poor?', mimeo, Indira Gandhi Institute of Development Research, Bombay.

Park, R.L. and I. Tinker (eds.) (1963), *Leadership and Political Institutions in India* (Princeton: Princeton University Press).

Prabhu, K. Seeta (1995), 'Structural Adjustment and Financing of Elementary Education: The Indian Experience', *Journal of Educational Planning and Administration*, 9.

Prasad, B.G., et al. (1969), 'A Study of Beliefs and Customs in a Lucknow Village in Relation to Certain Diseases, Menstruation, Childbirth and Family Planning', *Indian Journal of Social Work*, 30 (1).

Prasad, K.V. Eswara (1987), *Wastage, Stagnation and Inequality of Opportunity in Rural Primary Education: A Case Study of Andhra Pradesh* (New Delhi: Ministry of Human Resource Development).

Raju, S. (1988), 'Female Literacy in India: The Urban Dimension', *Economic and Political Weekly*, 29 October.

Ramasundaram, S. (1995), 'Implementation of Family Welfare Programme: An Overview', CSD Papers, Series 1, Centre for Sustainable Development, Lal Bahadur Shastri National Academy of Administration, Mussoorie.

Ranjan, Sharad (1994), 'Rural Non-farm Employment in Uttar Pradesh, 1971–1991: A Regional Analysis', M.Phil. thesis, Centre for Development Studies, Thiruvananthapuram.

Rao, Nitya (1993), 'Total Literacy Campaigns: A Field Report', *Economic and Political Weekly*, 8 May.

Rastogi, P.N. (1964), 'Factionalism, Politics and Crime in a U.P. Village', *Eastern Anthropologist*, 17 (3).

—— (1965), 'Factions in Kurmipur', *Man in India*, 45 (4).

—— (1966), 'Polarisation at Thakurpur: The Process and the Pattern', *Sociological Bulletin*, 15 (1).

Retzlaff, R.H. (1962), *Village Government in India: A Case Study* (New York: Asia).

Rosenzweig, Mark R. and T. Paul Schultz (1982), 'Market Opportunities, Genetic Endowments, and Intrafamily Resource Distribution: Child Survival in Rural India', *American Economic Review*, 72.

Rudolph, S.H. and L.I. Rudolph (eds.) (1972), *Education and Politics in India: Studies in Organization, Society, and Policy* (Cambridge, MA: Harvard University Press).

Sahay, B.N. (1969), 'Leadership, Conflict and Development Programme in a North India Village', in L.P. Vidyarthi (ed.), *Conflict, Tension and Cultural Trend in India* (Calcutta: Punthi Pustak).

Saith, Ashwani and Ajay Tankha (1992), 'Longitudinal Analysis of Structural Change in a North Indian Village: 1970–1987', Working Paper No. 128, Institute of Social Studies, The Hague.

Saldhana, Denzil (1994), 'The "Socialisation" of Critical Thought: Responses to Illiteracy Among the Adivasis in Thane District', in Kumar (1994).

Satia, J.K. and S.J. Jejeebhoy (eds.) (1991), *The Demographic Challenge: A Study of Four Large Indian States* (Delhi: Oxford University Press).

Sen, Amartya (1970), 'Aspects of Indian Education', Lal Bahadur Shastri Memorial Lecture at the Institute of Public Enterprise, Hyderabad; reprinted in S.C. Malik (ed.), *Management and Organization of Indian Universities* (Simla: Institute of Advanced Study), and partly reprinted in P. Chaudhuri (ed.) (1971), *Aspects of Indian Economic Development* (London: Allen and Unwin).

—— (1985), *Commodities and Capabilities* (Amsterdam: North-Holland).

Sen, Amartya (1992), *Inequality Reexamined* (Oxford: Clarendon Press and Cambridge MA: Harvard University Press).

Sen, Mala (1993), *India's Bandit Queen* (New Delhi: Indus).

Sengupta, S. (1991), 'Progress of Literacy in India during 1983 to 1988', *Sarvekshana*, April–June.

Shah, M.H. (1989), 'Factors Responsible for Low Performance of Family Welfare Programme', in Jena and Pati (1989).

Shami, N. (1992), 'Socio-Economic Survey of Village Patna Khurd', training assignment, Lal Bahadur Shastri National Academy of Administration, Mussoorie.

Shankar, K. (1991a), 'Politics of Land Distribution in Uttar Pradesh', *Economic and Political Weekly*, 27 April.

—— (1991b), 'Integrated Rural Development Programme in Eastern UP', *Economic and Political Weekly*, 12 October.

Shariff, Abusaleh (1996), 'Elementary Education in India: Differentials and Determinants', paper presented at the second workshop on Applied Development Economics, Centre for Development Economics at the Delhi School of Economics, 6–10 January.

Sharma, H.R. (1994), 'Distribution of Landholdings in Rural India, 1953–54 to 1981–82: Implications for Land Reform', *Economic and Political Weekly*, 24 September.

Sharma, Miriam (1978), *The Politics of Inequality: Competition and Control in an Indian Village* (New Delhi: Hindustan Publishing Corporation).

Sharma, Rita and Thomas T. Poleman (1993), *The New Economics of India's Green Revolution* (Ithaca: Cornell University Press).

Sharma, S.S. (1981), 'Harijan Influentials in a North Indian Village', *Journal of Social and Economic Studies*, 9 (2).

Sharma, Ursula (1980), *Women, Work and Property in North-West India* (London: Tavistock).

Simmons, G.B., C. Smucker, S. Bernstein, and E. Jensen (1982), 'Post-Neonatal Mortality in Rural India: Implications of an Economic Model, *Demography*, 19 (3).

Simon, Brian (1965), *Education and the Labour Movement: 1870–1920* (London: Lawrence and Wishart).

Singh, Avtar (1977), 'Community Structure and Technological Development', *Contributions to Asian Studies*, 10 (43).

Singh, Baljit and Shridhar Misra (1964), *A Study of Land Reforms in Uttar Pradesh* (Honolulu: East–West Center).

Singh, H.A. (1969), 'Strains in Leadership Structure: From Status

Groups to Pluralism in an East U.P. Village', *Economic and Political Weekly*, 3 May.

Singh, H.K. (1958), 'Class of People Benefited by Agricultural Programmes of N.E.S.', *Journal of Social Sciences*, 1 (2).

Singh, H.N. (1993), 'Social Background and Role Performance of Village Pradhans', Occasional Paper No. 10, Institute of Social Sciences, New Delhi.

Singh, Jagpal (1992), *Capitalism and Dependence: Agrarian Politics in Western Uttar Pradesh, 1951–1991* (New Delhi: Sage).

Singh, J.P. and R.P. Singh (1989), 'A Study of Employment and Income in Agriculture under the Jurisdiction of IRDP in Sultanpur District', *Narendra Deva Journal of Agricultural Research*, 4 (2).

Singh, K.K. (1967), *Patterns of Caste Tension* (Delhi: Asia).

Singh, N.K. and F. Ahmed (1995), 'Crime and Politics: The Nexus', *India Today*, 31 August.

Singh, Yogendra (1970), 'Chanukera: Cultural Change in Eastern Uttar Pradesh', in Iswaran (1970).

Sinha, Amarjeet (ed.) (1995), *Village Visit Reports*, compendium of selected field reports of the 60th Foundational Course, Lal Bahadur Shastri National Academy of Administration, Mussoorie.

Sinha, Shantha (1995), 'Child Labour and Education Policy in India', CSD Papers, Series 1, Centre for Sustainable Development, Lal Bahadur Shastri National Academy of Administration, Mussoorie.

Sopher, David (1980a), 'The Geographical Patterning of Culture in India', in Sopher (1980b).

Sopher, David (ed.) (1980b), *An Exploration of India: Geographical Perspectives on Society and Culture* (Ithaca, NY: Cornell University Press).

Srinivas, M.N. (1960), *India's Villages*, second edition (Bombay: Asia Publishing House).

—— (1962), *Caste in Modern India and Other Essays* (Bombay: Asia Publishing House).

—— (1966), *Social Change in Modern India* (Berkeley and Los Angeles: University of California Press).

—— (1987), *The Dominant Caste and Other Essays* (Delhi: Oxford University Press).

—— (1989), *The Cohesive Role of Sanskritization and Other Essays* (Delhi: Oxford University Press).

Srivastava, P.K. (1991), *State Government and Politics in India* (New Delhi: Mittal Publications).

Srivastava, Ravi S. (1995), 'Beneath the Churning: Change and Resilience in Producer Strategies in Uttar Pradesh Agriculture', paper presented at a workshop on The Village in Asia Revisited held at the Centre for Development Studies, Thiruvananthapuram, January.

Srivastava, Ravi S. (forthcoming), 'Agrarian Change and the Labour Process', in P. Robb and U. Patnaik (eds.), *Meanings of Agriculture* (Delhi: Oxford University Press).

Srivastava, Saraswati (1976), 'Uttar Pradesh: Politics of Neglected Development', in I. Narain (ed.), *State Politics in India* (Meerut: Meenakshi Prakashan).

Stokes, E. (1975), 'The Structure of Landholding in Uttar Pradesh 1860–1948', *Indian Economic and Social History Review*, 12.

Subramanian, Shankar (1994), Gender Discrimination in Intra-Household Allocation in India', paper presented at the Second Applied Development Economics Workshop, 6–10 January 1996, Centre for Development Economics at the Delhi School of Economics, Delhi.

Tendulkar, S.D., K. Sundaram, and L.R. Jain (1993), 'Poverty in India, 1970–71 to 1988–89', Working Paper, ILO-ARTEP, New Delhi.

Tyagi, P.N. (1993), *Education for All: A Graphic Presentation*, second edition (New Delhi: National Institute of Educational Planning and Administration).

Uberoi, Patricia (ed.) (1994), *Family, Kinship and Marriage in India* (Delhi: Oxford University Press).

Vais, R.R. (1982), 'An Evaluation of Antyodaya Programme in Uttar Pradesh', Research Study No. 81/6, Institute of Development Studies, University of Delhi.

Varma, Jyotsna (1992), 'Lanka Kachuara: A Village Divide', training assignment, Lal Bahadur Shastri National Academy of Administration, Mussoorie.

Visaria, Leela and Pravin Visaria (1995), 'Acceleration of Fertility Decline in Tamil Nadu since 1981: Some Hypotheses', Working Paper, Gujarat Institute of Development Research, Ahmedabad.

Visaria, P., A. Gumber, and L. Visaria (1993), 'Literacy and Primary Education in India, 1980–81 to 1991', *Journal of Educational Planning and Administration*, 7 (1).

Visaria, Pravin and Leela Visaria (1994), 'Demographic Transition: Accelerating Fertility Decline in 1980s', *Economic and Political Weekly*, 17–24 December.

Vlassoff, C. (1980), 'Unmarried Adolescent Females in Rural India: A Study of the Social Impact of Education', *Journal of Marriage and the Family*, 42 (2).

Vlassoff, C. (1993), 'Against the Odds: The Changing Impact of Education on Female Autonomy and Fertility in an Indian Village', paper presented at a Workshop on Female Education, Autonomy and Fertility Change in South Asia, New Delhi, 8–10 April.

Vyasulu, Vinod (1993), Management of Poverty Alleviation Programmes in Karanataka: An Overview', paper presented at a workshop on Poverty Alleviation in India held at the Institute of Development Studies, Jaipur, February.

Wadley, S.S. and B.W. Derr (1989), 'Karimpur 1925–1984: Understanding Rural India Through Restudies', in P. Bardhan (ed.), *Conversations Between Anthropologists and Economists* (Delhi: Oxford University Press).

Weiner, Myron (1991), *The Child and the State in India: Child Labor and Education Policy in Comparative Perspective* (Princeton: Princeton University Press).

Wiser, W.H. (1936), *The Hindu Jajmani System* (Lucknow: Lucknow Publishing House).

Wiser, W. and C. Wiser (1970), *Behind Mud Walls, 1930–60* (Berkeley: University of California Press).

Zamora, M.D. (1990), *The Panchayat Tradition: A North Indian Village Council in Transition 1947–1962* (New Delhi: Reliance Publishing House).

3

AGRARIAN POLITICS AND RURAL DEVELOPMENT IN WEST BENGAL*

Sunil Sengupta
Haris Gazdar

1. WHY LOOK AT RURAL WEST BENGAL?

West Bengal, and its neighbouring states of Bihar and Orissa, have had some of the highest proportions of rural population below the poverty line ever since these indicators have been published for Indian states. In 1987–8, the latest year for which state-wise poverty indicators were available at the time of writing, nearly three–fifths of the rural population in West Bengal lived below the poverty line.[1] West Bengal is India's most densely-populated state, with a population density of 766 persons per square kilometre in 1991 compared with around 270 persons per square kilometre in India as a whole.[2] Although the proportion of the population living in urban areas is a little higher in West Bengal than in India as a whole (27.4 per cent and 25.7 per cent in 1991, respectively), the pace of urbanization

* We gratefully acknowledge discussion with Nripen Bandyopadhya, Boudhayan Chattopadhyay, Jean Drèze, Madan Gopal Ghosh, Barbara Harriss-White, Jackie Loh, Debanshu Majumder, Mamta Murthi, V.K. Ramachandran, Ben Rogaly, and Amartya Sen. We owe a special debt to the staff of the research project 'Rural Poverty, Social Change and Public Policy' based at Visva-Bharati, Santiniketan, and the residents of villages they surveyed. Sri Benoy Krishna Chowdhury was a constant source of encouragement and help throughout the period of the project and after. This chapter was finalized while one of us (Gazdar) was visiting the Centre for Development Economics. We are grateful for the Centre's support.

[1] The main source of such data in India is the National Sample Survey Organization (NSSO). Reported results are from Minhas, Jain, and Tendulkar (1991). For studies on earlier trends in rural head-count ratios and the consumption of cereals etc., see Jose (1984) and Maitra (1988).

[2] See Bose (1991), pp. 49 and 58.

has been slower in West Bengal than in the rest of the country during the entire post-independence period. Over the same period, the state's relative position in terms of industrial output has undergone prolonged stagnation and relative decline. In 1960–1, nearly 23 per cent of India's industrial output was produced in West Bengal. This fell to about 10 per cent in 1980–1, and to under 7 per cent by the end of the eighties.[3] Starting out as a region of early industrial development, West Bengal lost its predominant position and failed to reverse the trend of relative industrial decline that set in from around the mid-sixties.

In the absence of industrial (and other non-agricultural) development, the agrarian economy remained the mainstay for the overwhelming majority of the rural population. Despite reasonable agricultural potential, however, output in this sector also remained stagnant from the fifties to the early eighties.[4] In short, high population density, undeveloped agricultural potential, and stagnation in industry have been characteristic features of the limitations to economic opportunity faced by the people of the state. It was under these rather bleak economic conditions that West Bengal experienced a radical change in the course of its state-level politics in the late seventies.

1.1 Change on the Horizon

West Bengal has had the unparalleled distinction among Indian states, of being ruled, since 1977, by a coalition of left-wing parties, that have advocated class-based politics and are publicly committed to improving the position of the poor in rural areas as a matter of priority. There has been wide interest in the experience of the state since the Left Front coalition, led by the Communist Party of India (Marxist) or CPM, came to office over a decade and a half ago. The Left Front government came to power following a period of intense political strife in rural as well as urban areas, on the promise of vigorous agrarian and political reform. The electoral support of the Left Front in rural areas has been overwhelming. Since its initial

[3] Government of West Bengal (1993).

[4] Furthermore, there was little diversification of employment away from agriculture in the rural areas. See, for instance, Chandrasekhar (1993) and Gazdar (1992).

victory in the 1977 state elections, it has won three consecutive state elections by convincing margins, and its candidates have received a steady share of around 70 per cent of the popular vote in rural local government *(panchayat)* elections for four successive terms.

The antecedents of the Left Front's victory in 1977 lie in the political history of West Bengal. Not only had class-based left-wing politics found a receptive home in Calcutta, once a major centre of anti-colonial struggle, there had also been a history of active involvement in peasant movements and organizations on the part of the communists since the nineteen thirties. By the late sixties the communist parties had considerable following in rural areas, and when state politics underwent a crisis with a split in the ruling Congress party, the CPM, in alliance with other left-wing parties, formed coalition governments with the breakaway Bangla Congress in 1967 and 1969. The total period for which this coalition (known as the 'United Front') ruled was around thirteen months.

The late sixties were a period of unprecedented ferment in the rural areas for the redistribution of land ownership and the more effective implementation of existing agrarian-reform legislation in the state. In particular, peasant organizations encouraged their supporters to take the initiative in the identification and appropriation of landholdings above the legally permitted limits, that had been 'concealed' by landlords in apprehension of land-redistribution laws using various administrative and legal loopholes. This movement of the landless and the small and marginal farmers escalated after the formation of United Front governments whose constituents included parties that had led peasant organizations.[5]

The United Front governments were short-lived, and fell under the combined pressures of a Congress-ruled centre on the one hand, and escalating violence in the peasant revolt on the other. The Congress party returned to power in West Bengal after this period until it was defeated at the state elections in 1977 by the CPM-led

[5] The political formations which emerged in that period included the largely Maoist C.P.I. (M–L), or Communist Party of India (Marxist–Leninist), also known as 'Naxalites', who remained outside the United Front, and were, indeed, opposed to participation in government. The Naxalites initiated land seizures from big landlords in north Bengal soon after the formation of the first United Front government. This was followed within four months by a major call to their supporters by the left-wing constituents of the United Front itself for the unearthing of concealed land. The latter came to be known as the 'land grab' movement.

'Left Front' consisting mainly of the left-wing constituents of the erstwhile United Front.

The emergence and consolidation of a political front with ideological commitment to economic equity, and with a wide base of support in rural areas, has significant implications that stretch well beyond West Bengal itself.[6] If the development experience over much of India has been plagued by the political domination of propertied elites, with little or no interest in pro-poor interventions, here is the case of a state where the situation appears to be quite different. This difference deserves attention not only for what it might reveal about the potential for change within West Bengal, but also for the lessons which might be elicited from the experience of one state for the rest of India, and indeed for other developing countries.

To state that change was desperately needed, particularly in the economic conditions of the rural poor, would be no exaggeration. About the only favourable feature of the Left Front's inheritance in 1977 was its reasonably assured political base. The economic situation was characterized by extremely high rates of rural poverty, stagnation in agriculture, relative decline in the non-agricultural sectors, high and rising demographic pressure, and the near absence of economic diversification. Furthermore, by choice or by political necessity, the Left Front had to play by the rules of India's capitalist democracy. Any economic and political reforms had to be consistent with the established politico-legal framework, and had to be implemented under conditions, where, for most of this period, the constituents of the Front were on opposition benches at the centre.

Agrarian reforms and the reorganization of the system of local governance were initiated early on and they have attracted much attention in scholarly as well as political circles. The period since the late seventies has, indeed, seen many changes in West Bengal. In contrast to the situation in 1977, by 1994, West Bengal had experienced a sustained period of agricultural growth stretching over a decade. Its rural poverty indices had registered marked declines, and there was new optimism about the potential for industrial rejuvenation. But there have been positive changes in other parts of

[6] This opportunity has been noted by a number of observers. Kohli (1987), for instance, notes that 'West Bengal, ruled by a party that is communist in name and organization but "social-democratic" in ideology and practice, highlights the redistributive possibilities within India's contemporary democracy and capitalism' (p. 9).

India also. Whether, and which reforms of the Left Front played a positive (or indeed negative) role, is a matter for analysis and debate.[7] We hope to contribute to this discussion by focusing on some essential aspects of the well-being of the population: poverty alleviation, health, and education.

We are interested, therefore, not only in the programme of the Left Front, and whether, or to what extent, the government was successful in implementing it, but also in how this programme relates to the conditions and needs of the poor in rural West Bengal. Section 2 discusses the political antecedents of the Left Front in West Bengal, and the context in which the agrarian reforms agenda came to occupy the centre-stage in state politics. Evidence on the implementation of agrarian-reforms is examined, and the scope that the various reform measures offer in terms of poverty alleviation and the reduction of inequality is explored. In section 3 we evaluate the performance of agriculture in the state, and analyse trends in rural consumption, poverty, and inequality over the last two decades or so. An attempt is made to interpret these trends in output, consumption, and distribution within the context of the eastern region (i.e. the neighbouring states of Bihar and Orissa) and to assess the relative impact of land reforms on the livelihoods of the poor. Non-income aspects of well-being, such as health and education, are discussed in section 4. West Bengal's record in the expansion of literacy and the lowering of mortality rates is compared with that of other Indian states. Section 5 offers concluding remarks and sums up the achievements as well as the failures of public policy in West Bengal in the expansion of the well-being of the rural population. We return to the political factors associated with the emergence of the Left Front, and discuss how they might have helped as well as hindered the process of social and economic development.

[7] Some of the early developments under the Left Front were reviewed, for instance, by Ghosh (1981), Rudra (1981), and Sengupta (1981) among others in a special section of the *Economic and Political Weekly* in 1981 (see vol. 16, nos. 5–6). Since then, there has been wide scholarly interest in public policy in the state. Besides dealing with specific aspects of economic and political development quite a number of these studies — Acharya (1993), Bhattacharyya (1993, 1994), Kohli (1987, 1990), Lieten (1992), Mallick (1992, 1993), Webster (1992), Westergaard (1986), and Williams (1995), for instance — have also attempted to formulate overall assessments of the Left Front government.

1.2   A Note about Data

A variety of data-sources are used in this paper to build a picture of West Bengal's experience over the last two decades or so. Of the primary sources of data, special mention needs to be made of the work of a research project of the World Institute for Development Economics Research (WIDER) based at the Visva-Bharati University at Santiniketan between 1987 and 1990. This project, entitled 'Rural Poverty, Social Change and Public Policy' collected and analysed data on a wide range of issues relating to rural poverty, incomes, owner-ship of land and other assets, impact of land reforms, food consump-tion, nutrition of children, literacy, and occupational mobility. One of us (Sengupta) was closely associated with the planning, implemen-tation, and direction of the project from its inception.

The core of the project consisted of collecting and processing socio-economic data from six villages in the various agro-climatic zones of West Bengal, on the basis of detailed household and in-dividual questionnaires. Much of the social and economic data, such as caste background, land ownership and operation (including the impact of agrarian-reform legislation), and household income, was based on a complete enumeration of all households. Likewise, all relevant individuals were covered to obtain information related to individuals such as educational attainment, wage earnings, and nu-tritional status. In all, the surveys covered 749 households, and 3,972 individuals. These surveys were carried out between 1987 and 1989, with teams of field researchers spending around six months in each of the villages. Four of the six villages surveyed are in south Bengal, two (Kuchli and Sahajapur) in Birbhum district, and one each in the districts of Medinipur (Bhagabanbasan) and Purulia (Simtuni). The other two villages are in the north Bengal districts of Jalpaiguri (Magurmari) and Koch Behar (Kalmandasguri). We draw upon results of these surveys to complement insights from a variety of published secondary data. The terms 'WIDER villages', 'WIDER data', and 'WIDER surveys', etc., refer to these surveys.[8]

The six survey villages vary greatly in their size as well as eco-nomic conditions (see Table 1). While each village may not actually

---

[8] More detailed information on these and other activities of the project can be found in Majumder and Sengupta (1990), Misra and Sengupta (1990), Sengupta (1991), Gangopadhyay (1990), Mukherjee (1990), and Gazdar (1992).

be representative of the area in which it is located, the six villages taken together capture a good deal of the diversity found in rural West Bengal. All villages save one (Magurmari in Jalpaiguri, which is close to some centres of traditional industry such as *biri*-making) are predominantly agricultural. Two of these (Kuchli in Birbhum and Bhagabanbasan in Medinipur) had access to shallow ground-water irrigation, and were relatively prosperous on this account. Simtuni, in Purulia, is a small, predominantly-tribal village with almost no landlessness, but with extremely poor soil and water conditions. Kalmandasguri in Koch Behar is also poorly endowed in terms of agricultural potential. Sahajapur, in Birbhum district, is the largest village and had over 200 households at the time of the survey, the majority of whom had been landless prior to the agrarian reforms. In terms of agricultural potential, this village stood some-where between the relatively high-productivity Kuchli and Bhaga-banbasan, and the poorly-endowed Simtuni and Kalmandasguri, as it had access to some canal irrigation and deep groundwater, but not to shallow groundwater.

TABLE 1. *Income and Poverty in WIDER Villages*

	Kuchli (Birbhum)	*Sahajapur (Birbhum)*	*Bhagabanbasan (Medinipur)*	*Simtuni (Purulia)*	*Magurmari (Jalpaiguri)*	*Kalmandasguri (Koch Behar)*
Number of households	142	227	134	75	99	89
Households below official poverty line (per cent)	40.4	52.3	16.5	62.5	56.6	72.7
Per cent of workers in agriculture	86	63	69	87	13	67
Mean per-capita household annual income (rupees)	1647	1544	2213	1160	1441	1212

Note.   The name of the district is given in parenthesis.
Source. WIDER village surveys, 1987–9.

Secondary data sources used in this paper include socio-economic data from the decennial census, expenditure data collected by the

National Sample Survey Organisation (NSSO), agricultural output data published by the Centre for the Monitoring of the Indian Economy (CMIE), and demographic information from the Sample Registration System. Most of the arguments presented below for West Bengal draw on these widely accepted secondary data sources for empirical support. We attempt to use the primary and secondary data sources in a complementary way, with references to village-level information coming within the context of the state-level picture, by way of elaboration and substantiation.

2. POLITICAL ECONOMY OF THE REFORM PROGRAMME

It is not surprising that the rural programme of the Left Front has attracted interest in India and abroad. The statistics of the state's performance in the fields of agrarian and political reforms are impressive enough. By the end of 1991, for instance, West Bengal, whose share of India's cropped area was only around 3 per cent, accounted for nearly a fifth of all cultivable land redistributed under agrarian-reform legislation in India. Over 40 per cent of all land-redistribution beneficiaries in India were to be found in the state.[9] While legislation for the protection of tenants from arbitrary evictions exists in many parts of the country, in West Bengal steps were taken to make this legislation effective, by official recording of tenancy leases. Over 1.4 million tenants were thus registered. In addition to these agrarian reforms, the Left Front government initiated the revitalization of the local government Panchayati Raj Institutions (PRIs) on a scale unprecedented in the country. Unlike almost anywhere else in India, regular elections to all three tiers of the PRI structure have been held on four separate occasions since 1978 in West Bengal.

Agrarian reform and democratic decentralization have been persistent themes in Indian debates on rural development since independence and even before. West Bengal has gone further than nearly all states in the implementation of the former, and arguably further than any state in the implementation of the latter. Whether it has gone far enough to substantially affect the conditions of the rural poor is an important question.

[9] Government of India (1992).

2.1   Agrarian Setting and Agrarian Reforms

Agrarian reforms in India have been concerned with one or several of the following issues: abolition of intermediaries in the revenue-collection system; security of tenure for sharecroppers and tenants; imposition of land-ownership 'ceilings' and the redistribution of private-property rights to 'ceiling-surplus' land from landlords to the landless and the land-poor; consolidation of fragmented land-holdings. These measures either pre-suppose, or at the very least avoid conflict with, the acceptance of private-property rights in land.[10] The first, that is, the abolition of intermediaries, was aimed at establishing these property rights in areas where the *zamindari* system of revenue intermediation had prevailed.[11] This was accomplished soon after India's independence. Of the other measures, land consolidation does not have major redistributive implications.[12] Among agrarian-reform measures that have been enacted in India, the reform of tenancy and implementation of 'ceiling laws' offer the greatest possibilities for the redistribution of economic claims from the well-off to the poor in rural areas, and it is in precisely these areas that West Bengal has a good record.[13]

The basis of the zamindars' economic position lay not in their outright ownership of landed property, but in their function as revenue agents of the government. While the zamindars did, indeed, hold transferable legal titles to land, these, in fact, implied unrestricted rights to land-revenue collection, but not effective control over the land itself. This remained vested with the *ryots* as the system

[10] It is worth noting that agrarian reforms in India are not institutional reforms at all, in the sense that they have been in China, where each successive reform has brought in its wake *new* forms of individual and collective rights over land.

[11] Under this system, which was in operation in parts of British-ruled India (having been initiated in Bengal in 1793), intermediary rights in the collection of revenue over agricultural land were made permanent and transferable. The class of intermediaries thus created was known as *zamindars*, who had fixed revenue obligations to the state coffers for specified areas of land. They were entitled, of course, to raise much greater amounts if they wished.

[12] Land consolidation also happens to be one area of agrarian reform where West Bengal's record compares unfavourably with other states. This is arguably a serious omission given the high degree of fragmentation of landholdings in West Bengal and the possibility of large efficiency gains as a result of consolidation.

[13] See Bergmann (1984), for instance, for a comparative study of agrarian reforms in Indian states.

predated the revenue categories created by the colonial administration.[14] With the abolition of revenue intermediation after India's independence (in West Bengal under the Estates Acquisition Act of 1953), private property rights over land became the main determinants of economic position. In the case of West Bengal, these rights reverted to the ryots.[15]

The fact that a very large section of the rural population in West Bengal had few rights in land was significant, both for the way in which agrarian politics developed, and also for the redistributive possibilities offered by the programme of land reforms. There are few precise estimates of the total number of landless households, but a large proportion of agricultural labourers and tenant farmers are clearly in this category. At the time of the 1981 census, men relying mainly on agricultural labour for their livelihood numbered nearly 4 million workers, comprising over a third of the rural male workforce.[16] Assuming that most men reporting agricultural labour as their main occupation belonged to landless or virtually landless households, the incidence of landlessness in West Bengal must have been at least one-third, and possibly more.[17] This is very high in comparison with most other Indian states. Micro-level data corroborate these observations about the high incidence of landlessness. In the WIDER villages, for instance, nearly half of all households were landless prior to the land reforms. Estimates of the number of tenant farmers *(bargadars)* vary between 1.5 to 2 million households, equivalent to nearly a quarter of all rural households in 1981.[18]

There is likely, of course, to be some overlap between the categories of agricultural labourer and tenant farmer. Some agricultural-labourer households would, undoubtedly, have leased-in land, while members of bargadar households might well have hired themselves

---

[14] See Bose (1993) for a detailed analysis of the status of various claims over land during this period.

[15] It is worth noting that over time, the system of intermediary interests had evolved into a multi-layered hierarchy, with the zamindars at the top, but with many levels of 'sub-infeudation' in between (see Islam, 1988). The system was, for all intents and purposes, moribund, and post-independence legislation declared its demise.

[16] Census of India, 1981.

[17] Strictly speaking, this reasoning assumes that labour-force participation rate is similar among landless and landed households.

[18] On the probable number of bargadar tenants, see Lieten (1992), p. 160.

out as wage labourers. Despite this overlap, for an understanding of how agrarian politics developed in West Bengal, it is useful to keep an eye on the fairly distinctive class histories of these two groups in the agrarian economy. Bose (1993) traces the historical origins of the large class of landless labourers in the zamindari era to the 'demesne-labour complex' — i.e. the substantial practice of self-cultivation by large landowners of their privately-owned *(khas)* holdings by means of tied labour. This, according to Bose, was more prevalent in the western parts of undivided Bengal that were to eventually constitute West Bengal. The bargadars, on the other hand, owed their origins as a class to the system of sharecropping in which the relatively more autonomous tenants were the main source of labour for the relatively heterogeneous class of landlords known as *jotdars*. It is this latter group of the landless and the land-poor (i.e. the bargadars), and not the tied labourers, that were the main base of the early peasants' movement in Bengal.

The post-zamindari agrarian structure of West Bengal has been alternately understood as having been dominated by big landlords and small-to-middle farmers. Bose (1986) has shown convincingly that the jotdars of Bengal were not a homogeneous group in terms of land, resources, and power.[19] The absolute domination of big jotdars was confined largely to parts of north Bengal, where they enjoyed virtual monopoly over property rights in land.[20] In much of West Bengal, although large landlords existed, and indeed were strengthened when their ranks were joined by former zamindars who acquired *khas* land in anticipation or as the result of zamindari abolition, their numbers were few, they were regionally dispersed, and they lacked state-wide collective and coherent leadership.[21]

Agricultural census data on landholdings are consistent with this characterization of land-ownership patterns in West Bengal. By 1971, only 2 per cent of the holdings were larger than 4 hectares,

[19] Although jotdar literally means owner of land, the term is commonly used to refer to the class of landlords who lease out land.

[20] A similar situation prevailed in parts of the 24-Parganas district in south Bengal. Large landlords in this area were known as *lotdars*, and their holdings consisted mainly of allotments of recently reclaimed land.

[21] Kohli (1990) notes the relative absence of state-level caste-based mobilization of propertied classes in West Bengal in contrast with a number of other Indian regions. This might have been another factor in the relative political weakness of the large landlords.

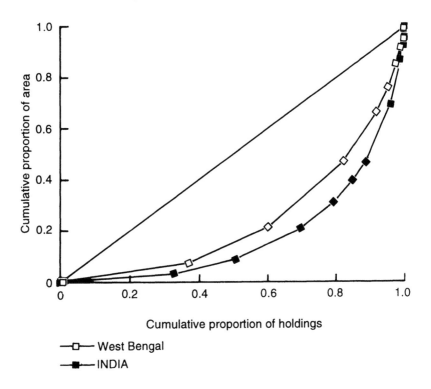

FIG. 1. *Distribution of Landholdings in West Bengal and India, 1971*
Source. Agricultural Census 1971.

compared to 11 per cent in India as a whole. These holdings accounted for only 15 per cent of total cropped area, compared to 53 per cent in India.[22] These proportions are misleading to some extent, since the average size of holdings is lower in West Bengal than in the rest of India. Fig. 1, however, shows the Lorenz curves for the *distribution* of landholdings in West Bengal and India as-a-whole in 1971. It is clear from the figure that landholdings were more equally distributed in West Bengal than the country as-a-

[22] We cite figures for 1971 from Agricultural Census of India 1971, as these predate most of the land redistribution, and present the pre-reforms picture. Agricultural census data, however, are only of limited use, since they report operational holdings rather than ownership holdings. Even so, it is worth noting that West Bengal had a less unequal distribution of operational holdings than India as a whole.

whole. The agrarian structure was thus characterized by a relatively high incidence of landlessness on the one hand, and the relatively equal distribution of landholdings (among those with land) on the other.

While bargadars had played an active part in the development of the peasant movement in Bengal,[23] by the late sixties it was the demand for the redistribution of ownership rights that came to the fore of the agrarian agenda. In an economy where private-property rights in land had come to form the basis of agrarian production, the labourers and the bargadar tenants, comprising nearly half of all rural households, shared the common feature of having little or no access to such rights. The propertied classes, on the other hand, were dominated numerically as well as in terms of area of land owned by smaller farmers. It was in this context of extremely high incidence of land deprivation, and of relative political and economic isolation of the large landlords, that peasant organizations such as the Krishak Sabha built up considerable support among tenants, marginal farmers, and the landless, and were able to thrust the demand for agrarian reforms on to the agenda of state politics.[24]

The political power of the big landlords was effectively challenged in the late sixties when wide sections of the small and medium-sized landowners threw their lot in with the struggle of the landless and the land-poor.[25] The 'middle' and 'rich' peasants played a pivotal role in turning the balance of power away from the large landlords, and very often, their involvement in left politics and their support of peasant organizations put them in positions of leadership at local levels.[26] It was this broad alliance of the landless

[23] The famous Tebhaga ('two-thirds share') movement in the nineteen-forties, for instance, was largely concerned with crop shares and tenant security.

[24] For a more detailed statement of this thesis, see Sengupta (1981).

[25] See, for instance, Sengupta (1981), Bose (1993), and Acharya (1993) among the many accounts of West Bengal's agrarian history that place the turning point of rural politics at the late sixties. An event which marked this change was the split in the state Congress party and the formation of the Bangla Congress, reflecting the political division within the propertied classes.

[26] There is considerable ambiguity in the use of terms such as 'middle' peasant or 'rich' peasant, and large landlord. They have tended, however, to dominate the political discourse, and retain some social relevance. Operationally, these categories are often thought of as representing different rates of application of family and non-family labour on owned land, with peasants, including 'rich' ones using family labour alongside some hired help.

and the land-poor, led by peasant organizations under the slogan of 'peasant unity', with sections of the propertied classes occupying strategic positions, which was to form the electoral base of the Left Front.

These developments which were based on mobilization for agrarian reform, and were particularly aimed at the empowerment of some of the poorest sections of the rural population (namely the landless and the land-poor), were quite revolutionary in the Indian context. However, the legal–institutional framework within which these agrarian politics were to play themselves out was the fairly conservative one that had emerged in India at the time of independence. Agrarian reforms in a West Bengal led by left-wing parties allied to peasant organizations were, as elsewhere in India, limited to the marginal redistribution of private-property rights in land, increasing the crop share for tenants, and giving them security of tenure.

2.2 Redistribution of Land Ownership

If the intended beneficiaries of the land-redistribution programme are the landless and land-poor households, our estimate of their numbers, based upon the 1981 Census, range around 2.5 million households, or just over a third of all households in rural West Bengal. The actual number of beneficiaries of land redistribution in the state by the end of 1993 was around 2.15 million. If all the beneficiaries were indeed landless to begin with, nearly 90 per cent of the landless would have received some land. This last figure may well be an overestimate (given the possibility that some non-landless have benefited from land distribution, and that the incidence of landlessness may have been higher than one-third to start with), but it does suggest that the scale of land redistribution in West Bengal has been comparable with the magnitude of the problem of landlessness.

Although land-ceiling laws had been in operation since the abolition of zamindari in 1953, much of this achievement is of relatively recent origin. Loopholes in these laws were utilized to the fullest by owners of ceiling-surplus land to take evasive action. *Benami* transfers, that is, the transfer of property into names of friends, relatives, and even unwitting tenants, were frequent.[27] Furthermore, implementation was the responsibility of petty land officials, most of whom were recruited from the land-revenue officials of the erstwhile zamindars, and were sympathetic to the landlords.[28]

The demand for the proper implementation of ceiling laws played an important role in the galvanization of support for left parties among the landless and land-poor. The parties of the United Front fought and won the state elections in the late sixties on the slogan of locating and distributing the benami lands, and the proper implementation of the existing ceiling laws. The United Front governments also drafted amendments to the land-reform legislation, and these have remained the basis of land redistribution since. Previously, the basic ceiling had been 25 acres *per person*. The amended ceiling laws changed the basis of ceilings from individuals to households. They also lowered these ceilings considerably. Households consisting of 2 to 5 persons are now allowed to own up to 12.35 acres of irrigated land or 17.39 acres of unirrigated land, respectively. There are higher allowances for larger households, but the absolute limit has been set at 17.29 acres of irrigated or 24.12 acres of unirrigated land.

Nearly twice as much land was vested with the state between 1967 and 1970 under the two United Front ministries, as had been vested up to then for the entire period since the abolition of zamindari in 1953.[29] In terms of area of land vested and redistributed, therefore, the real breakthrough in West Bengal had occurred well before the Left Front came to office in 1977. Some 625,000 acres of land had been redistributed by then (Table 2), and West Bengal already had a commanding position in the implementation of ceiling laws in comparison with other Indian states.

After 1977, during the Left Front period, a further 287,000 acres, representing under a third of the total area redistributed, were assigned (Table 2). The number of beneficiaries, however, increased by almost a million, and more than doubled. The contrast between the pre- and post-1977 land redistribution reflects a number of important differences in the approach to land reforms between the

---

[27] See Basu and Bhattacharya (1963) for a comprehensive account of the early implementation of agrarian-reforms legislation.

[28] On this point, see Bandyopadhyay (1986).

[29] On the redistribution of land under the United Front, see Ghosh (1981).

Left Front and its predecessors in the United Front. Before commenting on these, it is important to set the record right on some confusion that has crept into the use of official land-redistribution statistics.

TABLE 2. *Implementation of Land Ceiling Laws in West Bengal*

	Up to 1977	Between 1977 and 1983	Between 1983 and 1991	Up to 1991
No. of beneficiaries (households)	984,032	472,443	537,141	1,993,616
Cropped area redistributed (acres)	626,284	140,417	146,688	913,389
Land distributed per beneficiary (acres)	0.64	0.30	0.27	0.46

Sources. West Bengal, *Economic Review 1977–78*, Statistical Abstract; Ministry of Rural Development, *Annual Report 1991–92*, Government of India.

A recent study of the Left Front reforms[30] concludes, for instance, that there is little to distinguish between the record of the Left Front and the preceding Congress regimes in the implementation of ceiling laws. This observation is based upon the presumption that the Congress regimes were responsible for most of the land redistributed prior to 1977. This presumption is entirely unjustifiable, as it ignores the critical role of the United Front, most of whose constituents went on to form the Left Front, in the transformation in West Bengal.[31] During the United Front period, benami lands

[30] Mallick (1992).

[31] Another serious misinterpretation of data contained in Mallick's (1992) study concerns the author's comparison of West Bengal's land-redistribution record with that of other states in India. In West Bengal, as in other states where the zamindari system had prevailed, most of the land that was declared surplus was under the land-ceiling clauses of the zamindari abolition legislation. Specific land-ceiling laws were enacted by states where the zamindari system (and therefore zamindari abolition laws) did not exist. Mallick (1993), however, arbitrarily compares the areas of

were identified and distributed by means of direct action on the part of the landless and land-poor under the guidance of peasant and political organizations.[32] The legal granting of leases often lagged behind, and much of the area that appeared to have been redistributed in the early seventies had already been acquired by the beneficiaries during the 'land-grab' movement. It was simply a question of extending *de jure* recognition of *de facto* ownership.

In contrast to the direct approach to land redistribution of the late sixties, the Left Front redistribution programme has been less dramatic and more institutionalized. Although political and peasant organizations were actively involved, the main mechanisms of redistribution were local government bodies. Another important difference was that the average area of land distributed per beneficiary was considerably smaller. In this period, beneficiaries received under a third of an acre on average, less than half the average size of allotment prior to 1977 (see Table 2). As for the background of the beneficiaries, and whether or not they came from the target groups, published secondary data are of limited use. One indication that target groups were reached comes from the fact that over half of all beneficiaries (before, as well as after 1977) were from the Scheduled Castes and Scheduled Tribes.

Our observations from village-level data provide more detailed (though less-representative) evidence on this score. They confirm that most of the beneficiaries were people who had not owned any land at all (Table 3). The few who did, owned marginal holdings. In Kuchli, Bhagabanbasan, and Kalmandasguri, beneficiary households constituted about a third of the village population, while in Sahajapur, the proportion was around a quarter. In Magurmari there was only one beneficiary household, which was in fact landed, and which received a relatively large plot of land. In all the other villages besides Magurmari, land-reform implementation appears to be consistent with the aims of policy and the official claims of achievement. Village-level data also confirm that the total area of land available

---

land redistributed under various *post*-zamindari abolition ceilings laws in Indian states, in order to substantiate his dubious claim that West Bengal's record in redistribution was no better than that of most other states. All the data on land areas redistributed that we have presented above and in Table 2 refers to the aggregate area redistributed under *all* land-ceiling legislation, as reported in Government of India (1992), and other official publications.

[32] See Ghosh (1981).

for redistribution was a relatively small proportion of total operated area in all villages with the exception of Kalmandasguri in north Bengal. This pattern is not unrepresentative given the domination of small farmers in West Bengal's agrarian structure.

TABLE 3. *Land Redistribution in WIDER Survey Villages*

	Kuchli (Birbhum)	*Sahajapur (Birbhum)*	*Bhagabanbasan (Medinipur)*	*Simtuni (Purulia)*	*Magurmari (Jalpaiguri)*	*Kalmandasguri (Koch Behar)*
Area redistributed (acres)	28.2	12.0	8.8	6.5	0.8	19.5
Per cent of total cropped area	11	4	4	4	1	18
Number of landless households	65	131	39	2	71	42
Beneficiaries of redistribution	64	56	49	13	1	30
Landless beneficiaries	43	52	34	1	0	23
Landless non-beneficiaries	22	79	5	1	71	19
Average area per beneficiary (acres)	0.44	0.21	0.18	0.50	0.75	0.65

Average household income of landless assignees from wage labour and assigned land (in rupees)

Wages	3945	4013	3643	–	–	3900
Land	1573	418	893	–	–	1527

Proportion of total household income of landless assignees from assigned land (per cent)

	29	9	20	–	–	28

Note. The names of the districts are given in parenthesis.
Source. WIDER village surveys 1987–9.

Two of the main administrative objectives of the land-redistribution programme appear to have been fulfilled in the villages surveyed in the WIDER project: there were no households with above-ceiling holdings, and beneficiaries were, by and large, from the target group. Village data, however, highlight some important limitations of land redistribution based on ceiling laws as a comprehensive redistributive system.

Of the six villages surveyed, there were four (Kuchli, Sahajapur, Bhagabanbasan, and Kalmandasguri) where the landless poor benefited from land redistribution. The two villages where the impact was minimal were Simtuni, which had no landlessness to begin with, and Magurmari, where due to proximity to a town, there was a high rate of participation in the non-agricultural economy. Sahajapur in Birbhum was the most populous village in our sample and also had a high proportion of landless households. A majority of the landless households (over 60 per cent of them) in that village received no land at all. This was in spite of the fact that the average area distributed per beneficiary was quite modest. In fact, if all landless households had received some land, the average area per beneficiary would have amounted to under a tenth of an acre. If the Sahajapur pattern of beneficiary selection was typical of the state in general, a large proportion of the 2.5 million or so estimated poor landless households would not have received any land.

The availability of ceiling-surplus land for redistribution depends, of course, on the initial distribution of land ownership, and the level at which the ceiling is fixed. For any given level of land ceiling, the more equal the initial distribution, the smaller the area of land that would be available for redistribution. Conversely, for a given distribution of land ownership, the lower the land ceiling, the larger the ceiling-surplus area (as well as potential losers from land redistribution). If the area per beneficiary is fixed, the extent to which the target group can be covered would depend on the initial distribution and the land ceiling. The relatively less unequal land-ownership structure in West Bengal (among those who own land) implies that only modest areas of land are available for redistribution unless ceilings are drastically reduced.

In actual fact none of these policy targets (land ceilings, area per beneficiary, number of potential losers, or indeed the number of intended beneficiaries) is exogenously fixed and all are subject to negotiation and political judgement including electoral calculus.

The class alignment between small-holders and the landless which emerged in the late sixties, and which formed the basis of the Left Front's electoral support could be sustained by maximizing the *number* of the landless beneficiaries while ensuring that most of the small-holders and indeed other landowning groups who constituted Left Front supporters were not adversely affected. The small size of the average area of land assigned appears to have been an outcome of such a calculus.

The impact of assigned land on the livelihoods of landless beneficiaries in the WIDER villages brings into focus three important features of the land-redistribution programme in West Bengal. Firstly, in spite of its administrative success, land redistribution under existing ceiling laws has been marginal in the sense that it ameliorated but did not resolve class contradictions, or significantly alter class relations, between the land-rich and the land-poor. For landless beneficiaries in all villages, wage labour remained, by far, the most important source of earning (Table 3).

Secondly, although they remained *primarily* dependent on wage labour for their livelihoods, income from assigned land made a substantial contribution to the incomes of the landless beneficiaries. It accounted for nearly three-tenths (29 and 28 per cent, respectively) of total earnings in Kuchli and Kalmandasguri, a fifth (20 per cent) in Bhagabanbasan, and under a tenth (9 per cent) in Sahajapur.

Thirdly, although implementation appeared to have been fair in all villages (with the exception of Magurmari) its impact on the livelihoods of the poor varied greatly between villages. In absolute terms, the beneficiaries in Sahajapur received marginally more land, on average, than their counterparts in Bhagabanbasan, and yet their earnings from land were under half of the latter (Table 3). The higher cropping intensity in Bhagabanbasan accounted for the difference. In Kuchli and Kalmandasguri, average areas per beneficiary were higher. The final impact of land redistribution on the livelihoods of the poor depended on the initial distribution of landholding within the village (i.e. the availability of surplus land), as well as the local agro-economic conditions (i.e. the productivity of land). As an instrument for reducing income inequality, then, the land-redistribution programme with its focus on localized redistribution was successful in reducing intra-village inequalities, but was largely ineffectual in dealing with inter-village inequalities or, indeed, inter-regional inequalities where these were determined by agro-climatic variations.

2.3 Tenancy and 'Operation *Barga*'

Tenant farmers (or bargadars) had long been regarded as a vulnerable and exploited section of the rural population. The development of the peasant movement in Bengal was closely associated with activism for the rights of tenants.[33] For decades, demands of higher crop shares, security of tenure (including the right to inherit tenancy), and legal endorsement of tenancy agreements have been raised and fought for by peasant organizations.

Operation Barga, preparations for which began soon after the Left Front assumed office, has been described as a culmination of these movements.[34] The Left Front government's amended tenancy legislation incorporated all the key demands over which peasant movements and organizations had fought. Tenancy was made inheritable, crop shares were fixed at between two-thirds and three-quarters depending on the sharing of inputs, and clauses in earlier legislation that provided loopholes for eviction of tenants were plugged.[35] Eviction of tenants was the main obstacle to the enforcement of other demands such as higher crop shares. The threat of eviction and the availability of other tenants who might accept lower terms, made it impossible for a tenant to sustain a bargaining position *vis-à-vis* the landlord.[36] Recording of tenancies and enhancement of their legal status were rightly identified as the necessary conditions for other aspects of the legislation to work. Operation Barga was launched in 1978 with the primary purpose of recording tenancy leases.

Government claims of having recorded 1.44 million sharecroppers have been accepted widely. Disagreements exist about whether

[33] Communists led the peasants movement in Bengal in the mid-thirties for abolition of fixed-produce rent. This demand was met in 1938 during Provincial Autonomy rule in Bengal when the fixed-rent system was outlawed. Later in the forties the Tebhaga movement demanded a two-thirds share for the tenant, and also that threshing of the crop and its division should be carried out in public with the tenant's right to supervise.

[34] See, for example, Lieten (1992).

[35] One such loophole was the so-called 'Resumption Clause'. This allowed landlords to evict tenants by claiming they were going to farm the land themselves.

[36] During the decisive moments of the Tebhaga struggle in the mid-forties, for instance, the threat of eviction was instrumental in weakening the resolve of the bargadars of western Bengal (Bose, 1993). There were also large-scale evictions of tenants in many areas of West Bengal in the late fifties in response to the stepping up of the sharecroppers' movements in the post-zamindari abolition period.

there are significant numbers who are not recorded.[37] Since estimates of the number of tenant households range between 1.5 and 2 million, at least in terms of reaching a substantial part of the target group, Operation Barga has been a success. There is support for this assessment from other sources also. A survey of 414 *kisani* bargadars[38] in the Nanoor area of Birbhum found that 370 or nearly 90 per cent had been registered.[39] Out of these 370, however, 16 had since been evicted, most of them in exchange for outright ownership of small plots of land.[40] Lieten (1992) who surveyed a kisani village in Birbhum also found that most of the tenants had registered.

Bargadars accounted for less than ten per cent of all households in the WIDER villages and the area under tenancy ranged from 3 to 17 per cent of total cropped area (Table 4). In two of the south Bengal villages (Kuchli and Bhagabanbasan) the land area under annual lease was 5 per cent or less of the total cropped area of the village. Nearly two-thirds of all leases were found to have been recorded. The only village with a relatively high share of land under tenancy (Magurmari in north Bengal) also had two-thirds of the bargadars, accounting for over 90 per cent of leased area, registered. Although a majority of the leases, and most of the area under these leases had been registered, there was still a significant proportion of the transactions that were not.

The real test of the success of the campaign is its effect on the share of the produce that actually goes to the tenant. The evidence on crop shares, mainly to be found in village-level surveys, is mixed. The Nanoor study found that only a third of the recorded bargadars interviewed received the stipulated 75 per cent share. An earlier study of villages in Birbhum and other areas found that the legally

[37] See Lieten (1992) for a detailed discussion of contending statistics.

[38] Kisani is a form of sharecropping traditionally practised in Birbhum district and in parts of Bardhaman and Murshidabad districts adjoining Birbhum. Tenants received a one-third share of the output, in contrast with the more prevalent half-share, with the landlord providing all non-labour inputs.

[39] Sengupta (1991) and Gangopadhyay (1990).

[40] This practice of bargadars surrendering their tenancy rights in exchange for the ownership of a smaller area of land cannot be equated with the outright evictions of earlier years. The landowners in this particular area felt obliged to part with a small portion of their holding in order to guarantee unrestricted property rights over larger parts of it. This reflects the relatively better bargaining position enjoyed by bargadars.

stipulated share was rarely given.[41] A survey that included both recorded and unrecorded tenants in two regions of Medinipur district found that recorded bargadars consistently received a greater share of the crop than unrecorded ones.[42]

TABLE 4. *Land Tenancy and Registration of Leases in WIDER Survey Villages*

	Kuchli (Birbhum)	*Sahajapur (Birbhum)*	*Bhagabanbasan (Medinipur)*	*Magurnari (Jalpaiguri)*	*Kalmandasguri (Koch Behar)*
Area under annual leases (acres)	13.8	22.3	6.6	11.6	10.1
As per cent of total cropped area	5.0	7.8	3.0	17	9.2
Per cent of annually leased area registered	68	52	68	91	72
No. of annual leases	12	17	12	9	10
No. registered	4	10	9	6	8
Area seasonally leased (acres)	25.0	2.9	9.7	0.0	1.1
No. of seasonal leases	49	10	13	0	2

Note. The names of the districts are given in parenthesis.
Source. WIDER village surveys 1987–9.

Operation Barga has been able to extend security of tenure to tenants who previously faced the constant threat of eviction, and this has translated into higher crop shares for tenants, even though these are frequently lower than the legally stipulated shares. Time and again the propertied classes in rural India (including West Bengal) have acted in anticipation of redistributive policies by deploying legal loopholes and taking preemptive action. The expeditious recording

[41] Westergaard (1986) reports, for instance, that the prevalent share in kisani areas was 40 per cent — much lower than the legally stipulated 75 per cent, but higher, than the traditional 33 per cent.
[42] See Bhaumik (1993).

of land leases under Operation Barga, thus made tenancy security laws enforceable for the first time. The campaign approach that was adopted for this task showed that redistributive public policy need not stand helpless in the face of evasive and collusive strategies of propertied classes. To this extent, then, Operation Barga was successful in meeting its objectives.

There are a number of questions, however, about the economic wisdom of tenancy regulation in general, and the continued relevance of such regulation as a redistributive measure in the context of present-day West Bengal in particular. In theoretical models, sharecropping is usually understood as a way of combining different inputs under conditions of uneven endowments of land, labour, creditworthiness, and other inputs, on the one hand, and the absence of markets due to informational asymmetries, on the other. Tenancy in general, and sharecropping in particular, are not therefore, in themselves, causes of economic inequality and exploitation, but simply the means of organizing agricultural production under conditions of inequality in the ownership of assets.

Tenancy regulation and the legal enforcement of crop shares have potentially redistributive functions if tenants are universally poorer than landlords (since such reforms are primarily concerned with strengthening the tenant's position), and if crop shares are at least partly determined by the respective bargaining positions of the two parties. Even under these conditions, however, tenancy regulation is likely to be a less effective means of bringing about greater equality in incomes than the outright redistribution of property rights in land (if inequality in land ownership is, indeed, the main source of income inequality). Moreover, although the traditional pattern of rich landlords leasing land out to poor tenants may have been a valid generalization in the zamindari period, tenancy relations may no longer correspond neatly with class relations.[43]

The long-term effects of tenancy regulation on productivity and economic efficiency are not easy to discern by theoretical reasoning alone. On the positive side, security of tenure does provide greater incentives for longer-term investments by tenants in improving land quality. If, on the other hand, sharecropping contracts are second-best institutional responses to imperfections or failures in various

---

[43] The rise of 'reverse' tenancy, that is, the leasing in of land by large landowners from smaller ones, usually to take advantage of scale economies in irrigation or other inputs, has been widely noted in West Bengal. See, for instance, Bhaumik (1993).

input markets, then conferring legal status on these contracts might hinder their eventual replacement by more efficient forms of input sharing. The secular decline, over the three decades *preceding* Operation Barga, in the proportion of agricultural holdings in the form of pure tenancy leases may well have been a response to changing economic and demographic conditions that allowed for such improvements in efficiency.[44]

Another argument against tenancy regulation is that statutory intervention might impose uniformity and rigidity on an otherwise complex and changing set of economic relations. Rudra (1981) has argued, for instance, that the diversity of crop shares that existed in West Bengal reflected diverse cost-sharing arrangements, and legal fixing of shares without improving the registered bargadars' access to institutional credit would leave them credit-constrained.[45]

Indeed, in a political climate generally favourable to recording, the failure of some tenants to register cannot be put down simply to coercive pressure by landlords. There may be advantages in preserving amicable relations with a landlord who also acts as a source of credit.[46] Lieten (1992) found in his village study that most of the bargadars who had failed to register had done so because they wished to maintain cooperative relations with their landlords. Bhaumik (1993) found evidence of greater economic interaction between the landlords and unrecorded tenants than recorded tenants. He also found that the caste backgrounds of the vast majority of the unrecorded tenants was similar to that of the lessors. Both groups were predominantly from the general caste, as opposed to the domination of Scheduled Caste and Scheduled Tribe tenants among the recorded lessees. This caste-wise pattern of recording tenancies possibly reflects the different levels of cooperation and conflict between landlords and tenants with and without mutual kinship and other social ties.

---

[44] For evidence of this decline, see the results of various NSS rounds reported in Bhaumik (1993).

[45] The law does allow for some flexibility. Tenant crop shares of 60 per cent (as opposed to 75 per cent) are set for leases where costs are shared. This still does not fully take into account the range of possible arrangements.

[46] It should be noted that Operation Barga, and agrarian reforms in general, strengthened the *collective* bargaining position of the landless and the land-poor. In this sense there is a 'positive externality' of tenancy recording that benefits unrecorded tenants also.

Although on the surface a tenancy contract appears to be mainly about the leasing of land, in actual fact it may embody a great diversity of economic relationships. Even the best of regulatory laws is bound to overlook some of these complexities, and may, therefore, hinder the development of mutually gainful economic transactions. There is some evidence that tenancy regulation in West Bengal might have had such an effect. This is in spite of the fact that many landlords and tenants have ignored the regulations and have chosen to continue with traditional crop and cost-sharing arrangements. In his survey of tenancy contracts, for instance, Bhaumik (1993) finds that the relatively more recent tenancy contracts are less likely to be recorded than long-standing ones. Since there is no legal restriction for a tenant filing a claim to be registered, a potential lessor is constrained in his choice of tenants to those with whom he shares a relationship of trust. Since the landless and the land-poor continue to participate voluntarily in unrecorded contracts, an unwanted side-effect of tenancy regulation from the distributional point of view might have been the restriction in the supply of new leases.

Recent years have seen the emergence of seasonal leasing contracts mainly in the summer months in regions where groundwater irrigation has been developed. This form of leasing is regarded as casual and does not come within the ambit of tenancy laws. It has become a profitable venture, as it allows households with access to groundwater to take in neighbouring fields and thus to enjoy benefits of scale economies. In Kuchli and Bhagabanbasan (the two villages in our study which have extensive irrigation throughout the year), the total area leased seasonally, and the number of seasonal leases, exceeded the area and number of long-term annual contracts (Table 4). Although larger farmers with access to groundwater irrigation lease in plots of land from smaller landowners in the neighbourhood of their water source, seasonal leasing is not limited to the larger farmers, by any means. In Kuchli, over 43 out of the 49 seasonal leases were taken by households with less than 2 acres, and in Bhagabanbasan, the corresponding number was 9 out of 13. In spite of the long-term decline in the incidence of sharecropping, its resilience as the basis of new rental contracts provides some support for the view that as a *form* of contract it fulfils important economic functions.

In sum, while tenancy regulation has, clearly, enhanced the bargaining position of tenants, the efficiency effects of such a system are not likely to have been unambiguously positive.[47] On the one hand, regulation may perpetuate contracts that might no longer be economically efficient. On the other hand, it acts as a constraint on the emergence of new contracts that are potentially profitable. Moreover, the parties to this form of economic transaction no longer correspond closely to different classes, as they might have done at the time of the Tebhaga struggle and other similar mobilizations. As a means of redistributing economic claims from the rich to the poor, therefore, tenancy regulation is less effective than it might have been in the past, and is, in any case, second-best to the outright transfer of property rights in land.

It is critical to grasp that the regulation of a particular form of economic transaction was incidental to the change in the balance of power between the dominant propertied classes and the poor. The real engine of that change was the successful mobilization of claims on economic resources on the part of large sections of the poor. The fact that this mobilization took place around the issue of tenancy security is partly a result of the history of agitation on this issue by left-wing political parties and peasant organizations. Although Operation Barga was one of the flagship reforms of the Left Front government, its effectiveness as a redistributive programme (compared to land redistribution) and its value as a productivity-raising measure need to be interpreted with some caution.

The political impact, however, of an energetic campaign for the creation of tenancy rights for nearly one-and-a-half million households immediately after the election of the new government was extremely significant indeed. It sent a strong signal to the supporters as well as the opponents of the Left Front that the change of regime was real and that the new administration was serious about implementing agrarian reforms.

2.4   Local Democracy and Political Consolidation

Besides agrarian reforms, the main plank of the Left Front rural programme was the revitalization of the local government Panchayati Raj Institutions (PRIs). West Bengal is the only state in India

---

[47] Indeed the precise effects of tenancy regulation on efficiency need closer scrutiny of theoretical as well as empirical material than we have been able to conduct (see Banerjee and Ghatak, 1995 for one recent investigation).

where elections to panchayats have been held on a regular basis and contested along party-political lines.[48] The reform of local government was initiated soon after the Left Front government was formed in 1977. The first elections were held in 1978, and since then there have been three further polls. The success of Left Front candidates in these elections has been overwhelming and consistent. Their share of the popular vote has remained around 70 per cent. Indeed, the recent central government legislation on the reform of PRIs includes key aspects of the West Bengal experience such as a multi-tier structure (with direct electoral representation at each tier), regular elections, reservation of seats for Scheduled Caste and Scheduled Tribe candidates, and a similar quota for women.

Post-reform PRIs have come to represent an alternative structure of authority to the police, civil service officers, and other official departments such as revenue and irrigation, in the rural areas.[49] This is a significant departure from past practice in West Bengal, as well as from the present situation in much of India where the system of administration inherited from colonial times has retained much of its authority in spite of a plethora of formally representative bodies.

West Bengal PRIs have also been compared favourably in field-based investigations of the implementation of poverty-alleviation programmes. The Integrated Rural Development Programme (IRDP), which, in essence, is a subsidized credit scheme is one of the major anti-poverty programmes of the Indian government, whose implementation is entrusted to state governments. This provides a useful basis for inter-state comparison.[50] Most beneficiaries in West Bengal were found to be from the target group, and transactions costs of obtaining the loan were relatively small. This contrasted with other parts of India where beneficiaries were often the well-off relatives of

[48] Notable among other states that have taken initiatives in the decentralization of power is Karnataka. Here, many policy functions were devolved to the PRIs in the early eighties. Failure to hold regular elections, however, was one of the factors that led to the reversal of these gains (see Crook and Manor, 1994). See also Raghavalu and Narayana (1991) for a comparison of West Bengal's record with PRIs with other states besides Karnataka, including Kerala and Andhra Pradesh.

[49] Bhattacharyya (1993) reports from his field study that the traditional relationship between the administrative bureaucracy and the PRIs has changed significantly to the advantage of the latter in West Bengal.

[50] See Drèze (1990) and Swaminathan (1990) for comparative assessments of the implementation of IRDP. The former is based on field studies in parts of rural West Bengal, Uttar Pradesh, and Gujarat; the latter on West Bengal and Tamil Nadu.

panchayat officials, and intended target groups faced high transactions costs including the bribing of officials. This is not to say that IRDP or similar programmes have actually achieved what they set out to in West Bengal. The only aspect of implementation that we have focused on is the selection of beneficiaries, as in schemes such as IRDP where the target groups are administratively identified, the scope for leakage is quite high. In other matters, such as the choice of investment project, training of beneficiaries, backup services, etc., the record of West Bengal is not much better than most other parts of India.[51] In a study focused on the implementation of the Jawahar Rozgar Yojana (JRY), which is a government-run employment generation programme for the rural poor, Echeverri-Gent (1992) found that the scheme was run efficiently, served the target groups, and was relatively free of corruption.[52]

One explanation for the relatively better implementation of these programmes in West Bengal is that there was greater popular participation. It is now widely accepted that one of the key aspects of rural development is the participation of the rural people directly in the process of planning as well as the implementation of programmes. Local people have better information about their own needs and conditions. In the case of targeted poverty-alleviation programmes, 'objective' measures such as household income may be inappropriate indicators of poverty status for a wide range of reasons. Identification of the poorest using other criteria, including the perceptions of villagers, can yield quite different results from formal income criteria.[53] Local participation in implementation has the advantage of bringing local information into the picture.

Popular Participation and Electoral Democracy

In West Bengal, however, participation has not, by and large, taken the form of *gram sabha* (village assembly) meetings where allocations

---

[51] See, for instance, Raychaudhuri and Biswas (1994).

[52] Taken together, the IRDP and the JRY constituted the bulk of central government resources committed to direct poverty-alleviation programmes.

[53] In the WIDER villages, for instance, there was significant mismatch between alternative ranking of the poorest twenty households according to the investigators' perceptions based on discussion with villagers, and those based on income measures (Gazdar, 1992). A similar exercise (with similar results) was conducted in some other West Bengal villages by Mukherji (1992).

of IRDP or JRY funds have been discussed in detail. A number of studies of the working of PRIs in West Bengal indicate that decisions about expenditure priorities are rarely based on the prescribed forms of consultation (e.g. gram sabha) between panchayat leaders and the villagers they represent. This does not imply that there is no consultation or participation. In fact, there is a great deal of informal discussion of these matters. A survey of perceptions of villagers about the working of the panchayats in their villages, conducted as part of the WIDER study, also showed that in general the panchayat leaders reflected the opinions of their constituents (see Mukherjee, 1990). In particular, installation of wells and taps for potable water, and the building of roads, were considered important areas requiring attention, by villagers as well as panchayat members.

It is, in fact, mainly through the electoral process (which has been institutionalized and regularized) that popular participation has been practised in West Bengal. Village-level studies have shown that the poor, including those from socially-deprived groups such as Scheduled Castes and Scheduled Tribes, not only participate in elections as voters, but also stand as candidates.[54] It can be argued, with much justification, that real empowerment involves going well beyond participation in elections, and we return to some of these concerns later.

The fact remains, however, that electoral accountability, and the responsiveness of all major political parties to the concerns of voters, have contributed to the relatively better performance of PRIs in West Bengal compared to other states. Echeverri-Gent (1992) has argued that democratic competition between political parties has given incentives to the CPM and the Left Front leadership to 'monitor the performance of panchayat members and weed out those engaged in corruption'.[55] Westergaard (1986) found similar pressures operating in her survey villages, but did come across isolated cases where corrupt individuals were retained as candidates due to their ability to deliver votes. A number of recent studies report cases of corrupt and unscrupulous panchayat leaders, including many who were Left Front supporters. It is significant, however, that in nearly

[54] In fact, nearly all micro-level studies of panchayat elections find significant numbers of the landless, the land-poor, and people from Scheduled Castes and Scheduled Tribes among panchayat candidates and members. See, for instance, Lieten (1992, 1994b), Ruud (1995), Webster (1992), and Williams (1995).

[55] Echeverri-Gent (1992), p. 1414.

all reported cases, such leaders became electoral liabilities to their parties.[56]

Electoral competition alone cannot explain this situation. Instead of providing a forum for public accountability, such contest can, and does frequently, end up as an arena for factional rivalry within elite groups, with loyalties being divided along the lines of caste, faction, grouping, etc.[57] This certainly appears to have been the case in West Bengal before the Left Front period.[58] The CPM and the Left Front parties are themselves not immune to using caste and group loyalties to electoral advantage. This has been shown by a number of recent field-based studies of village-level politics.[59] What is important, however, is that unlike many other parts of India, caste or group-based factional rivalry is not the *only* basis on which politics are organized in rural West Bengal. A consequence of the agrarian struggles and the mass mobilization of some of the poorest people for their economic rights has been the raising of political awareness. The poor, therefore, are no longer pliable clients of local elites, but assertive and vigilant participants in local democracy.[60]

PRI Revitalization and Agrarian Reforms

The distinctive features of Panchayati Raj in West Bengal relate not so much to their formal structure as to the success that has been achieved in giving these structures some vitality. The main factors that have distinguished West Bengal's PRIs from those of other states in the formal sense are that elections have been overtly party-political, that they have been held with great regularity, and that a policy of positive discrimination in favour of women and Scheduled

[56] See, for example, Bhattacharyya (1993), Ruud (1995), and Williams (1995).

[57] See, for example, the chapter on Uttar Pradesh in the present volume and the literature cited there.

[58] See, for instance, Chattopadhyay (1992) and Dasgupta and Mukhopadhyay (1989). For similar evidence on another state, see the chapter on Uttar Pradesh in the present volume, and the literature cited there.

[59] See, for example, Bhattacharyya (1993), Ruud (1995), and Williams (1995). All these studies show that the CPM has been quite flexible in its approach to mobilization, and adept at using caste, religious, and factional loyalties for electoral advantage.

[60] This vigilance, ironically, is not always to the advantage of the Left Front parties, since their candidates with a record of corruption are also rejected by voters (see, for example, Bhattacharyya, 1995).

Caste/Scheduled Tribe candidates has been in place.[61] These factors have certainly contributed to the revitalization of the PRIs in West Bengal. But, at a more basic level, the real difference between West Bengal and other states lies in the fact that PRIs here are important arenas of political activity, that are taken seriously by the voters as well as the main political contenders at state and centre levels, and that they represent effective loci of power and governance. The political significance of the PRIs in the state owes much to the prominence given to them in the agrarian-reform programmes of the Left Front.

Panchayats have been involved from the start in the agrarian-reform programmes of the Left Front. As such, they have been part and parcel of the programme of change, including the redistribution of power from landed elites to an alliance of small farmers and the landless poor. Whereas implementation of agrarian-reform legislation has been largely a bureaucratic affair over much of India (as in West Bengal prior to the ascendancy of the left parties), and was mainly the result of direct action by beneficiaries and peasant organizations under the United Front periods, during the Left Front era the energies of the peasant and party organizations were channelized through the PRI structure. The presence of loci of political power in rural areas that were not subservient to old-standing propertied interests was critical in the implementation of the agrarian reforms.[62] In turn, the diminished economic power of the landed elites opened the door for wider participation by the poor and socially-deprived groups in political processes. The pre-eminence of the agrarian agenda in state politics, and the central role assumed by PRIs in this regard, has been responsible for their becoming active arenas of politics.

These institutions have also served the political and electoral interests of the CPM and the Left Front government by allowing

[61] These very aspects (regular party-based elections, reservation of seats for various groups) are the subject of recent central-government legislation on PRIs that the states have to follow. It is worth noting, however, that even in the case of West Bengal, these were not innovations, but that they reflected the recommendations of the Ashok Mehta Commission on PRIs in 1977, which were ignored in most other states.

[62] On the domination by large landlords of virtually all public institutions, including PRIs, prior to the Left Front reforms, see Dasgupta and Mukhopadhyay (1989) and Chattopadhyay (1992). Also see Bandyopadhyay (1986) on the resistance to change on the part of bureaucratic personnel.

them to consolidate their political support, and by giving rise to power structures that operate broadly under the control of the state government. This is neither surprising nor unusual, as within a pluralistic and competitive electoral system, any political party ought to be expected to look after its electoral interests. Where the Left Front can claim to have scored a remarkable success is in the institutionalization of agrarian reforms through the PRIs. The fact that all important political parties regularly contest the local government elections confers almost consensual validation to agrarian reforms which are now part of the new political reality.

From Activism and Agitation to Bureaucracy and Conciliation

The activities of the PRIs continue to reflect their association with the agrarian agenda of class politics pursued in the state. Not only were they involved in the early implementation of land redistribution and Operation Barga, these institutions have also acquired the role of guarantors of these newly acquired rights in property and tenancy. With the scope for further agrarian reforms seriously constrained on political as well as legal grounds, however, there have been concerns of late that the panchayats in West Bengal are 'running out of steam'. In a report to the state government, Mukarji and Bandyopadhyay (1993) warn that with the implementation of agrarian reforms being exhausted, panchayats run the risk of losing their sense of direction. On the basis of a survey of PRIs across West Bengal, they find that the activities of the panchayats are now largely confined to carrying out public works under the JRY. According to these authors, the realization of local self-government would remain incomplete without an active programme of development.

A related issue is the change in the character of PRIs over time. Webster (1992) argues that 'if the programme continues to change from being a political movement and increasingly becomes a bureaucratic strategy with its only political goal being the re-election of the Left Front to state government, it will fail in its original goals and disillusionment could easily result in the fall of the Left Front'.[63] There is a sense, however, in which the change from 'class mobilization' to a more conciliatory approach is inevitable. While the rise of the Left Front was associated with the sharpening of class conflict

[63] Webster (1992), p. 131.

in rural West Bengal and the shifting of class alliances, its consolidation has necessitated a more conciliatory approach. Consequently, an important role of PRIs has been that of mediation between conflicting claims in matters such as terms of lease and agricultural wages.

The alliance between the 'middle peasantry' and the landless and small-holder poor, which was instrumental in the successful challenge to the position of rich landlords, blurs potentially conflicting economic claims from different groups within that alliance.[64] While the landless poor and the small-holders have made political as well as economic gains, the cost has been borne, thus far, by small numbers of landlords with relatively large holdings. Other landowners (defined as middle and rich peasants) have remained relatively unscathed, and many have, in fact, acquired political power due to their association with Left Front parties.

It is easy to see that any intensification of agrarian reforms or class mobilization would pose a threat to the stability of this political alliance. Releasing more land for redistribution, for instance, would require the further lowering of land ceilings to levels that would begin to affect the smaller landowners (including 'middle peasants') adversely. Similarly, high wage claims by agricultural labourers would affect large landlords as well as those numerous smaller farmers who also hire labourers. The fact that panchayats are often involved in the mediation of such disputes puts them in a strategic position for the management of potential conflict between segments of Left Front support.

A Basis for Effective Governance

The decreasing emphasis on political activism on the part of PRIs (and indeed on the part of Left Front organizations) and the increasing emphasis on limited routine functions such as the implementation of central government ought not to be surprising. The scope for further agrarian reforms is restricted by legal as well as political considerations, and therefore programmes like the JRY and IRDP provide the mainstay of the panchayats' activities. It is possible to argue, of course, that the poor bear a disproportionately greater cost

---

[64] This alliance, incidentally, has not been an equal partnership. The 'middle peasants' have been the leaders, and the landless and the land-poor, for the most part, followers.

of maintaining the stability of the Left Front base in terms of the opportunities of further reform that are foregone. Whether or not agrarian reforms could be taken further is a complex issue, and much turns on the political judgement of the observer.

The debate about the scope for activism on the part of the Left Front organizations and the PRIs ought not to be limited, however, to agrarian reforms alone. In post-reform West Bengal, PRIs can act as instruments of public policy much more efficiently than they are able to do over most other parts of the country. Their role in the implementation of IRDP and JRY is simply an example of the potential they represent. Other interventions, such as the policy of positive discrimination in favour of the political representation of women and people belonging to Scheduled Castes and Scheduled Tribes, and the recent literacy campaign in the state, have been implemented through the PRIs. The fact remains, however, that such actions have been piecemeal, and that after the exhaustion of the agrarian-reforms agenda, the PRIs are left without a clearly defined programme. While the agrarian-reforms agenda has its own limitations, the potential created in West Bengal due to the institution of effective governance remains largely unfulfilled. We return to some of these concerns in sections 4 and 5 below.

3. Impact on Livelihoods

3.1 Agricultural Growth

After nearly two decades of stagnation, agricultural production — particularly the output of foodgrains — took off from the mid-eighties onwards. Between 1969–70 and 1979–80, total foodgrains production increased at an average rate of 2.5 per cent a year in India as a whole, and at 1.7 per cent per year in West Bengal — lagging far behind the rate of increase of population. From 1979–80 to 1989–90, however, West Bengal's foodgrains output grew at an average rate of 3.4 per cent per year, compared to India's 2.7 per cent.[65] This trend has continued into the nineties, and for the entire period from 1978 to 1991, West Bengal's trend growth rate in foodgrains output was 4.6 per cent compared with 2.8 per cent for the country as a whole.

[65] Centre for Monitoring the Indian Economy (1993).

The break in trend appears to have occurred around 1983 when, following two years of disastrous harvests, output increased by over 50 per cent from 5.9 million tonnes in 1982 to 9.2 million tonnes in 1983. Following over a decade of high rates of growth, it is possible to refer to this break in trend as a historical point of departure.[66] Saha and Swaminathan (1994) who tested for a break in trend in foodgrains output in the early eighties found it to be highly significant. They suggest a positive link between the Left Front

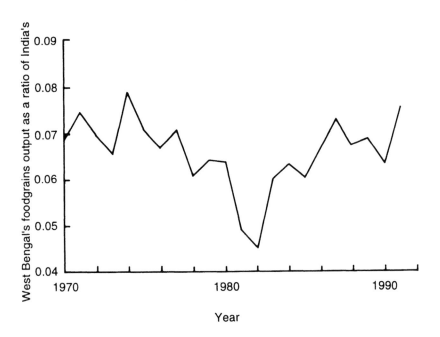

FIG. 2. *West Bengal's Share of India's Total Foodgrains Output*
Source. CMIE, *Performance of Agriculture in Major States*, July 1993.

[66] The reliability and consistency of agricultural data from West Bengal have been called into question from time to time. See, for instance, Ray (1994) for a recent intervention. Different sources of data might yield different magnitudes of growth, but the trend break appears to be robust. In line with some of the more recent work in this area, we have made use of the series for West Bengal and other Indian states compiled by the Centre for Monitoring the Indian Economy (CMIE).

reforms and agricultural performance. Harriss (1993) arrived at similar conclusions about overall trends — that there was a turn-around in West Bengal's agricultural performance — from village re-surveys, but gave greater weight in the explanation to technologi-cal developments and farmers' response to relative price changes. The dichotomy between policy-led and market-induced institution-al innovation that is implied in these two respective contributions is, in our opinion, too narrow a framework for understanding the recent developments in the agro-economy. Before addressing the explanations of growth, however, it is quite useful to place it in a temporal and geographic context.

Agricultural growth in recent years was preceded not just by stagnation, but by relative decline. The historically high growth rates have thus far simply restored the state's relative position in grain production in India as it stood in the mid-seventies. Fig. 2 plots West Bengal's share in India's total foodgrains output for the period 1970–1 to 1991–2. It shows that by the end of this period, despite rapid growth in output, West Bengal's share in India's total output of foodgrains (7.6 per cent) was only slightly higher than it had been in 1977–8 (7.0 per cent). Rapid growth in the eighties, then, has mainly taken the form of reversing and compensating for the relative declines of the seventies.

A longer view of the performance of West Bengal and the neigh-bouring states (Fig. 3) also confirms the picture of relative stagnation up to around 1982–3 and rapid growth since then.[67] Fig. 3 shows that foodgrains output declined substantially in West Bengal and somewhat less sharply in Bihar. It is clear from the plot that due to the wide fluctuations in output, the direction and significance of any trend estimates would depend to a great extent on the sample period selected. While the performance of West Bengal's agriculture has been particularly remarkable throughout the late eighties, any analysis which takes a starting point in the early eighties would tend to overestimate the upward trend.[68] Our own estimates of the trend growth rates for West Bengal vary from 4.3 per cent if the period chosen is 1983–91, to 6.6 per cent for the period 1981–91.

Furthermore, although West Bengal experienced the highest rate

[67] Fig. 3 plots the trends in the output of foodgrains, with the mean for the sample period for each region set at 100. Three-year moving-averages are used for output.

[68] See, for example, Saha and Swaminathan (1994).

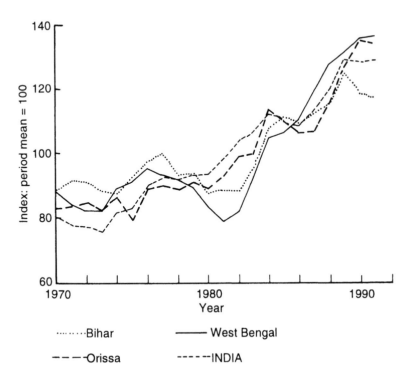

FIG. 3. *Comparative Trends in the Output of Foodgrains.*
Source. *CMIE, Performance of Agriculture in Major States,* July 1993.

of growth in the country during this period, the trend break in the early eighties also occurred in Bihar and Orissa, two states that share some of the agro-economic features of West Bengal.[69] Compared to the all-India trend growth of 2.7 per cent, and West Bengal's trend of 6.6 per cent (between 1981 and 1991), foodgrains production grew at 3.5 per cent a year in Bihar and at 4 per cent in Orissa. Explanations for the break in trend, therefore, need not be specific to West Bengal, although the higher rates of growth in the state do require specific attention.

The proximate causes of this departure from trend have been ascribed to two simultaneous processes: improved irrigation that led

[69] This was also found by Abhijit Sen and Ranja Sengupta (1995). They find a greater acceleration in West Bengal compared to the two neighbouring states.

to higher cropping intensities, particularly the area under the summer *boro* rice crop, and the adoption of higher-yielding varieties for the main *aman* rice crop. While the total production of foodgrains in 1991–2 was about 4.6 million tonnes higher than 1980–1, the respective contributions of boro and aman crops to this increase were 2.0 and 2.2 million tonnes.[70] The adoption of a higher-yielding variety of the aman crop is not, of course, unrelated to the availability of water. More control over water makes switching over to a higher-yielding but expensive seed more lucrative.[71] Another factor behind higher yields in the aman crop, however, has been the development of HYVs that are more robust and better suited to local conditions. According to farmers in Sahajapur — a village with low groundwater exploitation — the new HYV which first came to the area in 1984 had a lower yield than the HYVs that had been around earlier, but was also less vulnerable to variability in water supply, and more resilient to pests.

The effect of the development of irrigation could be inferred from the well-known study by Boyce (1987) of agricultural stagnation in Bengal (including West Bengal as well as Bangladesh). This influential work (which was published, ironically, at a time when growth was taking off), provides a useful frame of reference. Boyce (1987) showed that there was great potential for agricultural growth in Bengal, that water was the 'leading' input, and that institutional innovation for the exploitation of groundwater sources was the main binding constraint. Cooperative rather than market-based innovation was considered to be the most viable mechanism for change. Subsequent experience appears to confirm the author's optimism about the agricultural potential of West Bengal, as well as the important role of water resources, although Boyce's pessimism regarding the development of private water markets appears to have been unwarranted. Private investment in irrigation has been the main source of groundwater development, and the emergence of markets for water was the main institutional innovation.

The fact that accelerated agricultural growth in West Bengal has coincided with the Left Front agrarian reforms has provided some scope for speculation about the possible effects of reforms on

[70] Government of West Bengal (1993).

[71] There is much complementarity in the various inputs that make up the package of recent technological change. The eighties also witnessed a near trebling of fertilizer consumption in West Bengal (Government of West Bengal, 1993).

productivity. It has revived some early concerns in agricultural economics with establishing credentials for land reforms on efficiency
grounds. Some of the early political rhetoric of left parties also
carried an echo of these themes and was couched in terms such as
'unfettering the forces of production'. The fact that accelerated
growth has also taken place in eastern India as well as Bangladesh
over much the same period, however, suggests that the agrarian
reforms in West Bengal were not the main cause of the agricultural
take-off. The relative strength of growth in West Bengal compared
to its neighbouring states does, nevertheless, warrant explanation.

Specific land-reform measures, on their own, however, are unlikely candidates for this. Despite their wide coverage in terms of
beneficiaries, the redistributive reforms have only affected a relatively small proportion of total cultivable area. The amount of
cropped land distributed under ceiling laws, for instance, represents
around 6.5 per cent of total cropped area in the state, less than a
third of which was distributed after 1977. Precise estimates of the
total area registered under Operation Barga are not available, but
this is unlikely to have exceeded 15 per cent of the total cropped
area. For land redistribution and Operation Barga to be the driving
forces behind accelerated growth, these relatively small areas of land
would have had to achieve extraordinarily high rates of productivity
growth. This, clearly, has not been the case. Instead, there has been
wide adoption of HYVs for aman, and an extensive increase in
(irrigated) boro cultivation.

The dichotomization of the explanations of recent agricultural
growth in West Bengal between market versus non-market innovations, or reforms versus private incentives, is problematic
from both conceptual as well as empirical viewpoints.[72] Private
agents, after all, operate (and respond to incentives) within an
overall economic context that is conditioned to a great extent by
the distribution of assets as well as political power. It is true that
the development of the groundwater irrigation potential has been
largely down to farmers investing in tubewells for their own land
and for selling water to neighbouring farmers, while the programme
for public tubewells has been largely unsuccessful. At the same
time, however, the improved electricity supply to rural areas, which

[72] Saha and Swaminathan (1994) and Lieten (1994) suggest agrarian reforms as
the key explanation for growth, while Harriss (1993), though supportive of these
reforms in general, has focused attention primarily on private incentives.

has enabled the installation of private tubewells, is partly a reflection of the stronger bargaining position of rural producers *vis-à-vis* their urban counterparts as a result of political empowerment. Similarly, while private incentives, such as the fall in the price of fertilizers relative to rice, have led to increased consumption of fertilizers, the effective operation of local-level government has probably played a positive role in the flow of information, the timeliness of supply, and the general functioning of input delivery systems.[73]

In short, the main factors behind the agricultural take-off in West Bengal are shared with other states of the eastern region, with similar agro-economies. West Bengal's particularly strong record may reflect the state's greater agronomic potential than its neighbours. Additionally, the combined effect of agrarian and political reforms is likely to have been positive. The mechanisms through which agrarian reforms have had a positive impact, however, are likely to be those that improved the general functioning of markets and enabled agents to participate in these, rather than efficiency effects relating specifically to land redistribution or tenancy regulation.

The tendency to seek retrospective validation for agrarian reforms on efficiency grounds is surprising, since these arguments have been largely incidental to the political mobilization around agrarian issues in West Bengal, which was based squarely in redistributive terms. For practical purposes, it is sufficient to note that the recent growth record of West Bengal dispels any possible apprehensions that redistributive reforms might have had *negative* effects on efficiency.[74] The more interesting question, in our opinion, is whether and to what extent the poor have been able to participate in the growth that has occurred.

[73] This is broadly consistent with the finding that besides electricity, the consumption of other inputs did not accelerate in West Bengal in the eighties as it did in Bihar and Orissa (Sen and Sengupta, 1995). Part of the explanation for West Bengal's higher rate of growth in foodgrains output despite unchanged growth rates for most inputs must be in the more efficient use of inputs.

[74] One argument against redistributive reforms on efficiency grounds is that redistribution of land creates uncertainty about private property rights and discourages investment. In a situation of already heightened class tensions over the issue of land as in West Bengal, however, a once-and-for-all reform might well be a way of reducing uncertainty and insecurity.

3.2   Poverty, Consumption and Distribution

The most commonly used indicator of absolute poverty is the head-count ratio, or HCR, which measures the proportion of the population with incomes (or expenditures) below the poverty line. There has been wide acceptance among analysts of Indian poverty of the basic poverty line adopted by the Planning Commission over three decades ago and periodically updated since then.[75] Here, we use the series compiled by Tendulkar, Sundaram, and Jain (1993) based on the method suggested by Minhas, Sundaram, and Jain (1991).[76] For the distribution of income and expenditure, the main sources of information are the successive rounds of National Sample Surveys (NSS) which are designed to be statistically representative.

Fig. 4 traces the rural HCR for West Bengal, its neighbouring states, and India as-a-whole over the seventies and eighties. When the Left Front government came to office in 1977, West Bengal had the highest HCR of all Indian states. By 1983 it had overtaken Bihar, and in 1987 it left both Bihar and Orissa well behind. The decline in its HCR was particularly marked in the last period (1983–4 to 1987–8) when it experienced the highest proportionate decline of all the major Indian states. Besides a fall in the HCR, West Bengal registered consistent declines in distributionally-sensitive poverty indicators throughout the period from 1972–3 to 1987–8 (Tendulkar et al., 1993).

NSS samples are constructed to be representative of the population at large, but the surveys do not collect panel data. In other words, they select different villages and households for each round. There is some value in making comparisons over time with the same set of respondent households. This was done for West Bengal by Bhattacharya, Chattopadhyay, and Rudra (1987a, 1987b, 1987c, 1987d, 1987e, and 1988). These studies are based on re-surveys in 1985–6 of villages and households which were first surveyed in the 1972–3 and 1973–4 rounds of the NSS in the districts of Birbhum, Bardhaman, and Purulia. These re-surveys are valuable not only because they cover a period of great interest, but also because they provide a sound basis for inter-temporal comparisons, given their

---

[75] Details of the construction and updating of poverty lines in India are surveyed in EPW Research Foundation (1993).

[76] This series is, in our opinion, the most consistent one, as it takes into account changes in regional purchasing power parities.

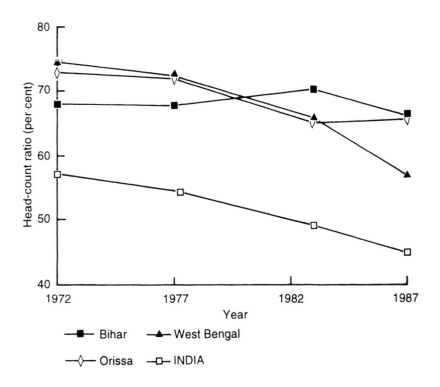

FIG. 4. *Comparative Trends in the Proportion*
of the Rural Population below the Poverty Line
Source. Tendulkar et al. (1993) based on successive rounds of NSS.

meticulous sampling and data collection method. Further, they focus on direct measures such as the consumption of various private and public goods, rather than attempting to construct income measures (which although perhaps analytically superior, are sensitive to assumptions that must be made about relative consumption weights and prices in any inter-temporal assessment).

The 'levels of living' studies found improvements in the overall level of consumption of private goods in the period between 1972–3 and 1985–6. The situation varied from one commodity group to another, but the overall picture was described by the authors as having been no more than a 'mild improvement'. The consumption of clothing, footwear, and consumer durables such as torches, wrist watches, bicycles, furniture, and utensils remained low, but nevertheless showed improvement. Housing conditions were found to have deteriorated in terms of space per capita, and while some people improved the structure of their houses (for example, from *kuchcha* to semi-*pukka*), for others it deteriorated. The per-capita consumption of most food items increased between the first survey and the re-survey. The important exception concerned cereals, the average consumption of which stagnated.

The authors of these studies rightly highlight the marginal nature of overall improvements in consumption levels. However, they prematurely dismiss the possibility that small increases in aggregate consumption might have gone hand in hand with some significant distributional improvement. They remark 'it is possible that even the mild improvements in non-food consumption affected only the upper strata of the rural population' (Bhattacharya et al., 1987a, p. 1150). This, however, is inconsistent with further results subsequently published by the same authors (Bhattacharya et al., 1988). The analysis of cereal consumption by socio-economic group presented in the latter paper shows, for instance, that per-capita consumption of cereals declined from about 0.55 kgs to just over 0.50 kgs a day for owner-cultivators, and increased from 0.43 kgs to 0.48 kgs a day for agricultural labourers.

In fact, there were substantial improvements in the distribution of expenditure between 1977 and the late eighties. The Gini coefficient which was around 0.31 in 1972–3, as well as in 1977–8, fell to around 0.29 in 1983, and to 0.25 in 1989–90. The improvement in the overall distribution of expenditure is confirmed by Fig. 5, which shows Lorenz curves for the distribution of rural household expenditure using NSS data from 1977–8 and 1989–90. The Lorenz curve for 1989–90 'dominates' (i.e. lies above) the 1977–8 curve, indicating unambiguous distributional improvement over this period.

The comparison with other states that experienced agricultural growth from around 1983 onwards is also enlightening. Between 1983 and 1989–90, the Gini coefficient for consumer expenditure in rural areas registered a decline for West Bengal and Bihar (Table 5). It is noteworthy however, that the decline (i.e. the improvement in the distribution of expenditure) was most pronounced in West Bengal. In Orissa, the Gini coefficient actually increased. In Bihar, the reduction was marginal, and, unlike West Bengal, there was no clear dominance of the 1989–90 distribution over the 1983 distribution.

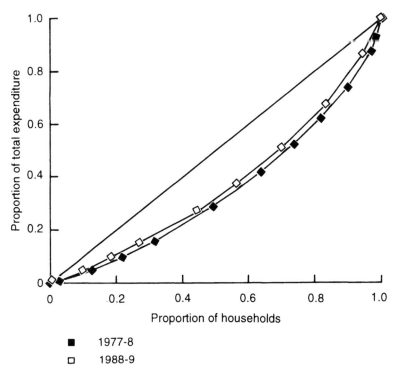

FIG. 5. *Distribution of Expenditure among
Rural Households, 1977–8 and 1988–9*
Source. National Sample Survey, 1992.

TABLE 5. *Distribution of Rural Per-capita Household
Expenditure in West Bengal, Bihar and Orissa*

	West Bengal	*Bihar*	*Orissa*
Gini coefficients			
1983–4	28.9	25.6	27.0
1987–8	27.8	26.5	28.5
1989–90	24.9	24.6	27.1
Stochastic dominance			
1989–90 over 1983–4	Yes	No	–

Source. NSSO (various).

The trend in inequality reduction observed in West Bengal between 1977 and 1983 appears to have accelerated after 1983, during the period of high growth in agricultural output.

3.3 Reform and Redistribution

Improvements in distribution imply that the consumption of the poor has risen proportionately more than that of the non-poor. This could happen if there were a transfer of income or assets to the poor (as happened with agrarian reforms), or if the economic return on their assets (i.e. wage rates) increased disproportionately, or a combination of both these processes.

Table 6 reports the modal daily wage for male labourers[77]

TABLE 6. *Daily Wage Rates for Male Agricultural Labourers (Kgs of Rice)*

	1956	1983	1987	1990
Birbhum	2.60	2.00	3.60	4.05
Kuchli	–	2.57	3.42	4.29
Sahajapur	2.64	2.61	3.30	4.00
Medinipur	3.00	2.10	3.40	5.43
Bhagabanbasan	–	3.00	3.60	–
Purulia	–	2.00	3.20	3.43
Simtuni	–	2.40	2.57	–
Koch Behar	3.00	1.90	2.30	3.54
Kalmandasguri	–	2.53	2.66	–
Jalpaiguri	4.20	2.50	3.40	3.95
Magurmari	–	2.85	2.80	–
West Bengal	2.95	2.56	3.62	5.07

Sources. Kynch (1990) for district and state average rice wages for 1956, 1983, and 1987. Agricultural Wages in India (1991) for 1990 nominal average wages for districts, converted into rice terms by applying a uniform rice price of 5.10 rupees per kg. AERC (1956) Sahajapur village survey for rice wage in Sahajapur in 1956. WIDER village surveys 1987–9 and re-surveys in 1990 for all other villages and years.

[77] The modal wage refers to the usual wage rate for casual field labour work. In fact, many different forms of labour contracts, and corresponding wage rates, can

prevailing in the WIDER villages in rice equivalent terms.[78] For the purpose of comparison we also report the average wages in the respective districts at corresponding points in time. The district average wages were calculated by Kynch (1990) using official wage series for reporting centres, and deflating them by the prevalent rice prices. It is interesting to note that the district-level wage rates are quite close to the corresponding village-level wages in most cases. Both show significant increases in recent years. State-wise secondary data on agricultural wages confirms these trends (Fig. 6) and show that the recent increases in wage rates have come after a long period of stagnation.[79]

Wage rates can rise as a result of an increase in the demand for labour with increasing cropping intensity and the adoption of technological innovations that require more intensive and timely use of labour inputs. These factors have been operating in West Bengal since the mid-eighties, in conjunction with the accelerated growth in output. In fact, trends in wage rates have closely tracked trends in output over the entire period for which consistent data are available (see Fig. 6). Another factor that might have led to higher wages is the increased bargaining power of agricultural labourers due to unionization and collective bargaining. The threat of strike action by agricultural labourers in their bargaining for higher wages, and indeed actual instances of wage strikes, are a distinguishing feature of labour relations in rural West Bengal. The fact that village panchayats play a prominent role in inter-mediating labour disputes underlines the political aspect of wage-setting in the state.[80]

---

and do exist even within a village. These other wage rates are, also, often indexed to the modal or *chuto* (casual or free) labour wage rate (see Rogaly, 1994).

[78] Since rice is the main staple, the choice of a rice index makes inter-temporal and inter-village/regional comparisons easier.

[79] The real wage series presented in Fig. 6 was calculated by Bipul Chattopadhyay (Institute of Economic Growth, Delhi), based on data published in *Agricultural Wages of India*, and using the same methodology as in Acharya (1988). Although the AWI (Agricultural Wages of India) data appear to have some methodological shortcomings, and to lead to some overestimation of wage *levels*, they seem to be reliable enough for the purpose of assessing broad *trends* in wage rates. For a good discussion of this issue, see Jha (1994).

[80] It has been noted by a number of recent micro-level studies that a strike threat has become a ritualized part of pay negotiations, in contrast with the early years of the Left Front government when strikes did raise the stakes in the bargaining process

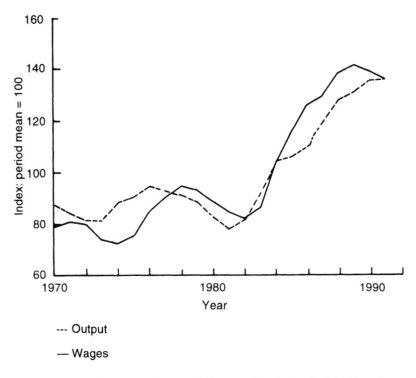

--- Output

— Wages

FIG. 6. *Trends in Wage Rates and Output of Foodgrains in West Bengal.*
Sources. Acharya (1988), Bipul Chattopadhyay (IEG, Delhi, 1994), and CMIE,
July 1993.

The rise in wage rates in West Bengal was, in fact, within the
overall context of rising wages in India as a whole, as well as in the
neighbouring states of Bihar and Orissa. Fig. 7 shows the trend in
real wages for West Bengal, Bihar, Orissa, and India as a whole.[81]
The plots show that wage rates moved in similar directions for these
states through most of the seventies and the eighties.[82] Although
wages grew fastest in West Bengal in the eighties, so did agricultural

---

(see, for instance, Rogaly, 1994, and Williams, 1995). The fact remains, however,
that wages are set collectively, with PRIs acting as arbitrators.

[81] In Figs. 6 and 7, figures on output and wages refer to three-year moving
averages, expressed in terms of percentage of the period mean in the relevant region.

[82] In terms of *level* of real wages, West Bengal was far ahead of both Bihar and
Orissa. The present discussion, however, focuses on trends rather than levels.

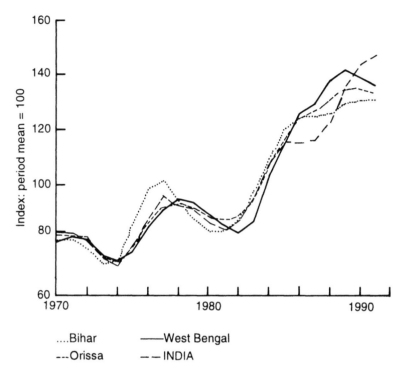

FIG. 7. *Comparative Trends in Agricultural Labourers' Wage Rates.*
Source. Acharya (1988), Bipul Chattopadhyay (IEG, Delhi, 1994)

output.[83] There is no evidence of an additional upward pressure on wages due to increased bargaining power.

In fact, the rates of growth of output and wages in West Bengal were quite similar during this period, in contrast with Bihar, Orissa, and the all-India averages, where wage rises outstripped the growth in output. Between 1980 and 1991, the trend annual growth rate of real wages in West Bengal was 5.7 per cent while output grew at 5.6 per cent per year. The corresponding rates were 4.8 and 2.7 in India as a whole, 4.8 and 2.8 in Bihar, and 5.5 and 3.3 in Orissa. Labour

---

[83] Correspondingly, when output was falling, so were real wages, as in the first few years of Left Front rule, when, arguably labour militancy would have been the highest.

organization, wage strikes, and panchayat mediation in wage-setting, therefore, do not appear to have resulted in a substantial wage premium in West Bengal. Nor are recent trends in wage rates an adequate explanation for the fact that the distribution of income improved in West Bengal, but not in the neighbouring states.

There are other aspects of the terms of employment of agricultural labourers that may have differed significantly between West Bengal and other states, and contributed to an improvement in the distribution of income.[84] One such factor is the wage differential between men and women. Our time-series data apply to male labourers and it is widely recognized that wage rates for female labourers are often lower than male wage rates. Data from the WIDER villages suggest, however, that at least in these villages no such gender gap applies (Table 7). In all villages, with the exception of Kalmandasguri in north Bengal, the average daily wages of female labourers were equal to (or even marginally higher than) those of male labourers.[85]

TABLE 7.   *Wages and Employment of Agricultural Labourers by Village and Gender*

	Average daily wage[a] (rupees)		Mean number of days employed in a year	
	Male	Female	Male	Female
Kuchli (Birbhum)	13.47	13.43	221	61
Sahajapur (Birbhum)	12.22	12.98	189	76
Bhagabanbasan (Medinipur)	14.58	14.90	158	102
Simtuni (Purulia)	14.22	14.32	104	95
Kalmandasguri (Koch Behar)	10.97	8.31	187	142

Note.   [a] Average of (total wage earnings in the year of survey/total days employed) over all agricultural labourers.
    The name of the district is given in parenthesis.
Source.   WIDER village surveys 1987–9.

[84] We have not examined changes in employment in West Bengal and other states, for want of comparable data. This, undoubtedly, may be an important issue.

[85] Table 7 omits the village Magurmari where most of the labourers were involved in non-agricultural activities.

Women perform fewer days of agricultural labour a year than men, on average, and most of their work is concentrated in periods when seasonal demand for labour is high. The absence of female disadvantage in terms of average wage, therefore, may reflect the greater concentration of women's labour time in periods when the wages are relatively high. The similar levels of average wages for men and women, in other words, are consistent with some gender discrimination in *task-specific* (or period-specific) wages. But the fact that such discrimination, if it did exist, was not strong enough to result in a difference in average wages remains significant.[86] Even if collective wage bargaining did not have a major impact on the general level of agricultural wages, it may have succeeded in narrowing — perhaps even eliminating — the gender gap in wage rates.

In the earlier discussion of land redistribution and tenancy reforms above (sections 2.2 and 2.3), we observed that these reforms involved a relatively small amount of land, and did not dramatically reduce dependence of the landless poor on wage labour.[87] The question remains as to how far they have contributed to the reduction of rural poverty in the eighties, and to the improvement of income distribution. We showed in Table 3 that in the WIDER survey villages, the contribution of income from assigned land to the total income of beneficiary households ranged from 9 to 29 per cent. The impact of land redistribution on incomes, without being dramatic, is far from insignificant, considering that small increases in income from a low base can represent considerable improvements in well-being and economic security. Further, the income effects of land redistribution may be quite substantial in comparison with those of other recent economic changes, such as wage increases. Table 8 presents some tentative calculations on this, including estimates of the respective impact of wage increases and land redistribution on the earnings of landless beneficiaries of land redistribution in the WIDER villages.

[86] Even in Simtuni, a tribal village where wage employment patterns are quite similar for men and women (e.g. there is little difference between them in terms of average number of days worked), the female average wage was as high as the male average wage (see Table 7).

[87] It is worth noting, nevertheless, that West Bengal is the only major state in India where the proportion of agricultural labourers in the male workforce declined between 1981 and 1991 (Census of India 1991). This confirms the trend noticed by Lieten (1992) and labelled by him as 'depeasantization discontinued'; the author ascribes this trend to the positive effects of land reforms.

TABLE 8. *Landless Households:*
Income from Wage Labour and Assigned Land

	Kuchli	Sahajapur	Bhagabanbasan	Kalmandasguri
Households as a proportion of all village households				
Below IRDP poverty line	0.40	0.52	0.17	0.73
Landless prior to land reform	0.46	0.61	0.30	0.43
Landless beneficiaries of land redistribution	0.30	0.24	0.26	0.23
Earnings of landless beneficiaries as proportion of IRDP poverty line [a]				
1. Total income	0.87	0.70	0.71	0.85
2. Incremental wage earnings[b]	0.15	0.13	0.09	0.03
3. Earnings from assigned land in 1987–8	0.25	0.07	0.14	0.24
4. Row (2) + Row (3)[c]	0.40	0.20	0.23	0.27
5. Row 4/Row 1[d]	46	29	32	32

Notes. [a] All earnings (except last row) are converted into fractions of the IRDP poverty line of 6400 rupees per year for households of 5 persons in 1987–8.

[b] This is the difference in real wage rates between 1987–8 and 1983, multiplied by days of employment in 1987–8.

[c] Row 4 is the total 'incremental' earnings due to wage rate increase and assigned land.

[d] Row 5 is the 'incremental' earnings as a proportion of total income.

Source.   WIDER village surveys, 1987–9.

These calculations are based on a number of simplifying assumptions. In particular, the estimated 'incremental earnings' associated with wage earnings are calculated as the difference between the wages actually earned by agricultural labourers in 1987–8 and what they would have earned from the *same* number of employment days had wages remained at the 1983 level. Similarly, the incremental income from assigned land is based on the assumption that income earned in 1987–8 from assigned land was purely additional — e.g. there was no opportunity cost in terms of foregone wage labour. These 'incremental earnings' (figures presented in Table 8) are, thus, best interpreted as estimates of the 'first-round' effects of land redistribution and wage increases.

As might be expected, these estimates vary a great deal from village to village, but they do suggest that the income effects of land redistribution are considerably larger than those of wage increases. The only exception concerns Sahajapur, where the average area distributed was particularly small, and where cropping intensity is low. In Kuchli and Bhagabanbasan, incremental income from assigned land was almost twice as high as incremental income from wage increases, even though these villages experienced relatively rapid wage increases. These survey results lend some support to the notion that the effects of land redistribution on the overall distribution of income in rural West Bengal compare favourably with the effects of economic changes such as wage increases.

In sum, the picture that emerges from the preceding analysis of available evidence on agricultural output, wages, consumer expenditure, and related variables is fairly consistent and intuitive. The decline in the head-count ratio of poverty in rural West Bengal has occurred alongside improvements in the distribution of expenditure from the late seventies onwards. Rapid agricultural growth from around 1983 onwards was a clear break from the earlier pattern of prolonged stagnation. This break from trend, however, was not unique as it occurred also in the neighbouring states of Bihar and Orissa at around the same time. Nevertheless, West Bengal's agricultural performance from 1983 onwards has been particularly impressive, and does warrant some explanation over and beyond the explanations for accelerated growth in eastern India in general. Agrarian and political reforms of the Left Front form an important part of this explanation.

Where West Bengal's experience appears to have differed rather more significantly from those of Bihar and Orissa is in the distribution of income, and the sharing of growth. Improvement in the distribution of expenditure (or consumption) predated the rise in agricultural productivity in West Bengal, and accelerated during the period of high growth. Redistribution of private property rights in land (and possibly in land use) was one of the main mechanisms in the redistribution of incomes. This is a significant point, as it highlights the redistributive potential of land reforms even where relatively small areas of land are involved. The rise in the collective bargaining power of agricultural labourers, as evidenced by their unionization, did not have a major impact on setting wage rates over and above what might have been expected due to growth in output. The crucial result of political mobilization, and the heightened collective bargaining power of the landless and land-poor, is the effective transfer of property rights. In contrast with the situation in West Bengal in the past, and with the current situation in most other states of India, the involvement of political organizations and elected local government made it possible to implement and defend these legal transfers.

Despite agricultural growth, and rising wages, there is little evidence of any reduction in inequality in the neighbouring states. Agrarian reforms in West Bengal, both through their directly redistributive functions, as well as through their contribution to the institution of effective local governance, have resulted in improvements in the material conditions of the poorest. Although class-based mobilization on the question of land did not culminate in radically altering class distinctions, the reforms did deliver tangible gains for some of the most deprived sections of society.

4. CHANGE AND STAGNATION

The discussion so far has focused on economic indicators relating primarily to private consumption, such as household income, consumer expenditure, head-count ratios, inequality indices, agricultural wages, and direct measures of consumption of food and other commodities. Private income, however, is not an adequate basis for the assessment of well-being, given that the relationship between the former and the latter can depend a great deal on personal characteristics (e.g. whether the individuals being considered are literate or illiterate), on the social environment, on the scope and quality of public services, and related factors. International comparisons, and also comparisons of different states within India, indicate that well-being achievements do vary widely even at a similar level of private income.[88]

[88] These issues are discussed in greater detail in the companion volume (Drèze and Sen, 1995); see also chapters 1 and 2 in this volume.

West Bengal itself is a significant example of a state in India that has had relatively better health and educational conditions in rural areas, in spite of having some of the lowest levels of private income. In the early eighties, for instance, seven of the thirteen major states with lower rural head-count ratios than West Bengal had higher rates of infant mortality in rural areas. West Bengal's rural IMR for 1981–3 was 95 per 1,000 live births, compared to 114 and 136, respectively, for Bihar and Orissa, which had similar head-count ratios. The rural IMR was lower in West Bengal than Assam (102), Gujarat (121), Haryana (102), Madhya Pradesh (144), Rajasthan (113), Tamil Nadu (100), and Uttar Pradesh (159), all states with lower rural head-count ratios than West Bengal.[89] The situation was much the same in the late eighties (see Fig. 8) when of the 15 major Indian states, West Bengal had a lower rural head-count ratio than two (Bihar and Orissa), but had a rural IMR that was higher than only three other states (Kerala, Punjab, and Maharashtra). Similarly, the rural literacy rate in West Bengal in 1981 (40 per cent) was higher than the corresponding figure not only in Bihar and Orissa but also in Andhra Pradesh, Haryana, Karnataka, Madhya Pradesh, Maharashtra, Rajasthan, and Uttar Pradesh — seven major states that had lower rural HCRs than West Bengal.[90]

4.1 Political Change and Public Action

Many of the factors that lie between private income and well-being are connected with the supply, demand, and utilization of public goods and services. The improvement in anthropometric indicators, for instance, depends as much on the availability of clean water, access to health services, awareness about nutritional needs, and general conditions of public hygiene, as on food intake.[91] Similarly, public health measures such as mass immunization are known to have contributed to substantial lowering of mortality rates, and progress in education is often dependent on the presence and effective functioning of a public schooling system. Public intervention,

---

[89] *Sample Registration Bulletin*, June 1992.

[90] Census of India, 1981; the figures are related to the 5+ age group.

[91] For that matter, food intake itself can also be related to public interventions in terms of the efficiency and reach of a public distribution system, or the presence of feeding programmes.

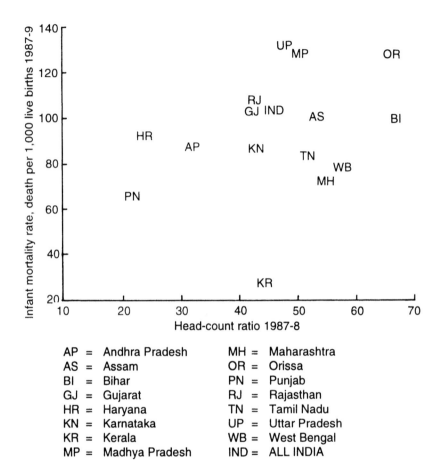

FIG. 8. *Rural Poverty (Head-Count Ratio) and Infant Mortality, 1987–8: Indian States*

Source. Sample Registration Bulletin (1992), and Tendulkar et al. (1993).

therefore, can be critical for the rapid improvement of well-being even if private consumption is expanding.

Public action may also act as a lever on other factors, such as the allocation of food, health care, or leisure time within the household, that affect the relationship between private consumption and well-being but do not necessarily involve the consumption of public goods. If gender disparities in the allocation of private (as well as public) consumption, for instance, are partly determined by the nature of female employment opportunities and property rights, then the relevant domain of public intervention might extend well beyond the supply of public goods.

On both these counts (the expansion of public services, and the promotion of social change), the political changes of the type experienced in West Bengal can be expected to have a major impact on prevailing deprivations. If the old pattern of political power being concentrated in the hands of elite groups and bureaucrats, acted as a constraint on the expansion of public services, then the changed balance of power in rural West Bengal certainly opened up new possibilities of more development-oriented governance.[92] The very fact that PRIs in West Bengal do exercise political power, and have acquired authority (in contrast to much of India where they simply provide a forum for the airing of factional rivalries), implies that greater scope exists for effective supply of public goods and related interventions.

Radical political changes have often coincided with social changes of similar depth. Changes in political regime, associated with the redistribution of economic claims in favour of disadvantaged groups, have also resulted, in a number of countries (e.g. China), in rapid improvements in the health and education conditions of the population, and of deprived groups in particular. Some of these ingredients of change have been present, though arguably not to the same extent, in the events which led the Left Front to power in West Bengal. Even if international comparisons are not entirely relevant, due to the relatively modest scope of reforms in West Bengal, examples from closer to home also suggest a link between political change and development-oriented public action. In Kerala, for instance, political formations similar to the Left Front have been credited with playing an influential historical role in the expansion of education and health care.[93] Political change, and particularly change based upon the mobilization of oppressed groups for their economic claims, can be expected to raise the consciousness amongst these groups of their social rights in other spheres. It has been suggested,

[92] Kohli (1987), for instance, characterizes the formation of the Left Front government in West Bengal as representing a change from the political economy of corruption to one of development.

[93] See, for instance, the chapter on Kerala in this volume.

for example, that political awareness in Kerala has been an important factor in raising people's awareness of health issues and their ability to demand health services.[94]

For all these reasons, political change in West Bengal represented an opportunity for social change and decisive improvements in well-being. The eradication of inequalities based on class, caste, and gender in access to health care and education represented as urgent a task as the alleviation of inequalities in access to land. Indeed, the public commitment of the Left Front parties to the eradication of gender discrimination and caste-based social inequities is on record. Highly visible policies such as the reservation of seats in Panchayati Raj bodies for women and for Scheduled Caste and Scheduled Tribe candidates have been adopted. The key question, however, is whether or not this stated political commitment resulted in actual improvements. We examine some evidence below.

4.2   Progress and Persisting Backwardness

Infant Mortality

Sample Registration System surveys show that the infant mortality rate (IMR) in rural West Bengal declined from 95 to 75 per thousand live births between 1981 and 1990 (Sample Registration System, 1992). In 1990, as in 1981, West Bengal's IMR was about 19 points below the Indian average. The decline has been sustained at a similar rate since around 1970 (this is the earliest period for which a consistent SRS series is available). Of the 15 major states for which SRS data are reported, rural West Bengal's rank rose from the sixth-lowest IMR in 1981 to the fourth-lowest one in 1990. This, however, was mainly due to the poor performance of Karnataka and Andhra Pradesh, where the IMR actually stagnated over part of this period.

West Bengal's own *rate* of decline during the eighties was not much faster than the Indian average, and was in fact surpassed or

---

[94] Nag (1989), for instance, drew attention to the contrast between Kerala and West Bengal in this regard. He observed that in Kerala health awareness grew alongside the development of political consciousness, whereas in comparison West Bengal had lagged behind on both counts. His observations, however, predate the Left Front era, when significant political changes did take place.

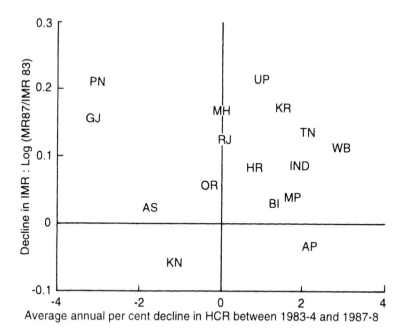

FIG. 9. *Decline in Rural Poverty (Head-Count Ratios) and Infant Mortality Rates (IMR) between 1983–4 and 1987–8*
Source. Sample Registration Bulletin (1992) and Tendulkar et al. (1993).

equalled by Bihar, Uttar Pradesh, Gujarat, Punjab, Kerala, and Tamil Nadu. Fig. 9 shows the performance of Indian states in reducing the rural IMR between 1983–4 and 1987–8 (vertical axis) and their respective changes in rural poverty (horizontal axis). West Bengal's *rate* of reduction of IMR over this short period was surpassed by seven states (Uttar Pradesh, Punjab, Maharashtra, Kerala, Gujarat,

Tamil Nadu, and Rajasthan), four of which (Punjab, Maharashtra, Gujarat, and Rajasthan) experienced either stagnation or increase in the rural head-count ratio during this period.

Child Nutrition

The WIDER village surveys included an anthropometric survey of all children below the ages of five years in the six survey villages. The measure chosen was weight-for-age, which is widely used in rural health programmes in India.[95] Besides the classification of children between the well-nourished and the under-nourished, four categories of undernourishment were used. They range from 'slight' and 'moderate' to 'severe' and 'disastrous' levels of undernourishment. If a child is found to be in the latter two categories, health centre guidelines call for clinical intervention including hospitalization if necessary.

For two of the WIDER villages (Kuchli and Sahajapur) earlier nutritional surveys — conducted in 1983 — are available (Amartya Sen and Sunil Sengupta, 1983). For these villages, there were clear signs of improvement in the nutritional status of children in the intervening five years (Table 9). Particularly, the incidence of 'disastrous' undernourishment, which affected 8 per cent of children in both villages in 1983, was almost non-existent in 1988. The incidence of 'severe' undernourishment also recorded a major decline.[96]

These observations are based on the experience of only two villages at two points in time, and, as such, need to be interpreted with caution, but the decline of undernourishment is dramatic enough to represent a significant indication of very real improvement. 'Disastrous' undernutrition of a child is more likely to result from poor health and infection than from actual shortage of food. Improvements in the supply of drinking water, better awareness of health conditions, and easier access to medical services have probably been important factors in the near eradication of extreme forms of child undernutrition from these villages.[97]

[95] The standards commonly used by *Anganwadi* health centres in West Bengal villages for the monitoring of child health are based on WHO or Harvard standards of healthy body weight at different ages.

[96] There was a corresponding rise in the proportion of less seriously undernourished children in both the villages (Table 9).

[97] There is some evidence, from other sources, of improvement in these factors.

TABLE 9. *Percentage of Children Undernourished,*
by Level of Undernourishment (Children Aged 5 or Below)

	Level of undernourishment				Index[a]
	Slight	Moderate	Severe	Clinical	
1983					
Kuchli	20	30	26	8	48
Sahajapur	21	31	33	8	54
1988–9					
Kuchli	25	37	13	0	36
Sahajapur	32	35	14	1	37
Bhagabanbasan	46	26	13	0	34
Simtuni	28	36	25	3	47
Magurmari	42	26	11	7	39
Kalmandasguri	41	37	4	4	36

Note. [a] Refer to the main text for an explanation of the index.
Sources. Sen and Sengupta (1983), and WIDER village surveys 1987–9.

The overall level of deprivation, however, has remained extremely high. In none of the villages, was the estimated proportion of undernourished children below three-quarters in 1988–9. In Simtuni, less than one in ten of the children under the age of five were adequately nourished at the time of the survey. In Magurmari and Kalmandasguri, several children were found to be 'disastrously' undernourished.

An index of undernourishment was calculated using the method of Sen and Sengupta (1983). This index gives a summary measure of the extent of undernourishment in any group. The higher the index, the worse the aggregate status of the group. If a child is disastrously undernourished, it is assigned a score of 4, for severe undernourishment it gets a score 3, for moderate and slight undernourishment scores of 2 and 1 respectively, and a well-nourished child gets a score 0. These scores are then summed up over the

---

The re-survey of NSS observations by Bhattacharya et al. (1987b) showed that access to and consumption of public health had increased somewhat in the re-survey. The most significant improvement reported was in the access to potable water.

relevant group and divided by four times the total number of children in the group (i.e. the index is 1 if all children are disastrously undernourished and 0 if all children in the group are well-nourished). Broadly, the gender and caste patterns are according to expectation — i.e. girls are more undernourished than boys, and general caste Hindu children are better nourished than children of Scheduled Caste and Scheduled Tribe families (Table 10).[98]

TABLE 10. *Index of Child Undernutrition by Caste and Gender* [a]

	Boys	Girls
General Caste Hindu	30	39
Scheduled Caste	33	39
Scheduled Tribe	37	50
Muslim	34	40

Note. [a] Refer to main text for an explanation of the index.
Source. WIDER village surveys 1987–9.

Literacy

Literacy rates increased between the 1981 and 1991 censuses in rural West Bengal from 48.6 per cent to 57.7 per cent for the 5+ population overall, and from 36.1 per cent to 47.2 for females (Table 11). These rates of increase were not spectacular by the standards of other Indian states. West Bengal's rank among the major Indian states remained unchanged for overall as well as female literacy rates between the two census years.

According to the 1991 census, West Bengal literacy rate for the 7+ male population was 68 per cent compared to the Indian average of 64 per cent, and the corresponding literacy rate for females was 47 per cent compared to the Indian average of 39 per cent. More recent changes in literacy patterns would appear in the literacy rates of younger age groups. According to NSS estimates for 1987–8, the

[98] The term 'general-caste Hindus' refers to Hindus other than those classified as Scheduled Castes or Scheduled Tribes. It is, therefore, a residual category used for the sake of convenience. This group does, nonetheless, comprise Hindu castes that claim 'higher' caste status, and in general, enjoy better economic conditions than people from the Scheduled Castes and Scheduled Tribes.

TABLE 11.   *Literacy Rates in Major Indian States, by Rank*

Overall 1981		Overall 1991	
Kerala	01.6	Kerala	90.6
Maharashtra	55.8	Tamil Nadu	63.7
Tamil Nadu	54.4	Himachal	63.5
Gujarat	52.2	Maharashtra	63.0
Himachal	51.2	Gujarat	60.9
West Bengal	48.6	West Bengal	57.7
All India	43.6		52.1
Female 1981		Female 1991	
Kerala	75.7	Kerala	86.9
Maharashtra	41.0	Himachal	52.5
Tamil Nadu	40.4	Tamil Nadu	52.3
Punjab	39.6	Maharashtra	50.5
Gujarat	38.5	Punjab	49.7
Himachal	37.7	Gujarat	48.5
West Bengal	36.1	West Bengal	47.2
All India	29.8		39.4

Sources.   Population Censuses 1981 and 1991.

literacy rate for 10–14 year old males in rural areas in West Bengal (69 per cent) was *lower* than the Indian average (73 per cent), and was lower than all states with the exception of Bihar (60 per cent), Andhra Pradesh (66 per cent), Madhya Pradesh and Uttar Pradesh (68 per cent each). West Bengal's female rural literacy rate for the same age group (61 per cent), however, was significantly higher than the Indian average (52 per cent).[99] While West Bengal's narrower gender gap in literacy rates compared to the Indian average (both according to census and NSS data) might be viewed in a positive light, it ought to be a matter of some concern that in the younger age groups this narrow gap appears to be a consequence more of an

[99] National Sample Survey Organisation (NSSO), 1987–8 round.

extraordinarily low literacy rate for males rather than an extraordinarily high one for females.

Average literacy rates conceal the true nature of the problem of education in India. Analysis of literacy rates by caste and gender (Table 12) illustrates this very powerfully. The aggregate literacy rate for the WIDER villages, for example, is not very different from that for rural West Bengal as a whole. The group-specific literacy rates, however, range from near total illiteracy for Scheduled Tribe women, to near universal literacy for general caste Hindu men. A similar picture applies with other caste groupings. In terms of public policy, then, there is not one 'literacy problem' but several. For some sections of the rural population, in fact, there is no literacy problem at all.

TABLE 12. *Literacy Rates (Percentage of Population Aged 7 and Above, Literate) by Gender and Caste*

	Female	*Male*	*Both*
Rural West Bengal[a]	38	62	50
WIDER sample	40	60	51
Caste Hindus	71	92	82
Scheduled Castes	22	43	33
Scheduled Tribes	5	24	15
Muslims	15	30	22

Note. [a] West Bengal literacy rates are from Census 1991.
Sources. Census 1991, WIDER village surveys 1987–9.

Further insights on this issue can be obtained from a consideration of changes in literacy rates over time. These can be gauged from the current literacy rates of different age cohorts. Assuming that people become literate if at all by the age of 15, and that the chances of acquiring literacy thereafter are low, literacy rates of different age cohorts can tell us something about patterns of change in literacy over time.[100] Table 13 gives literacy rates by gender and caste for people who reached the age of 15 in different periods.

[100] Strictly speaking, this 'backward projection' method also assumes that mortality rates are similar for literate and illiterate people within the relevant groups; see Drèze and Loh (1995) for further discussion.

TABLE 13. *Literacy Rates (Percentage of Population Literate)*
by Caste and Age Cohort

	Caste Hindus		Scheduled Castes		Scheduled Tribes	
Aged 15 in	*Males*	*Females*	*Males*	*Females*	*Males*	*Females*
1983–7	95	88	58	30	41	0
1978–82	95	82	38	26	30	2
1973–7	95	76	40	19	19	5
1963–72	96	77	44	11	12	0
1953–62	91	53	31	7	30	0

Source. WIDER village surveys, 1987–9.

It is striking that, at the two extremes of the literacy scale, there is no discernible trend over time: for general caste Hindu males the 1953–62 cohort was already very close to full literacy, while for Scheduled Tribe females there has been no significant departure from total illiteracy during the entire reference period. The groups in between accounted for changes in the aggregate literacy rates between the fifties and the late eighties. For general caste Hindu women, there were steady improvements throughout this period, while for Scheduled Caste and Scheduled Tribe males the changes were more recent.[101] The cohorts which displayed the most significant increases in literacy were the youngest ones, roughly corresponding to the period since the Left Front government has been in power.

4.3 Limited Initiatives

West Bengal's progress in improving health and educational conditions during the period of Left Front rule has not been extraordinary. The infant mortality rate has been declining, but its rate of change has been in line with past trends, and also in line with declining infant mortality rates in most other Indian states. Literacy rates have also improved but, here too, in relative terms the improvement has

[101] Similar patterns of change were found for primary schools enrolment in the Muhammad Bazar Block in Birbhum district over the mid-seventies onwards by Lieten (1992).

not been outstanding. If anything, among the younger age groups, West Bengal's relative position might have suffered a relative decline. Traditional patterns of deprivation along caste and gender lines persist, though the recent period does appear to mark acceleration in achievement for Scheduled Caste and Scheduled Tribe males. Whether this corresponds to a one-off or sustained improvement remains to be seen. Micro-level evidence suggests that some of the most extreme forms of undernutrition have become rare, but nutritional deprivation remains widespread and acute.

The fact that, by and large, there is no break in trends of improvement in well-being, that rates of change are not very different from country-wide averages, and that traditional patterns of deprivation persist and reproduce themselves, is in itself remarkable. More could have been expected from a state that has had a distinguished record in the implementation of agrarian reforms, led the way in the establishment of local-level democracy, broken a long spell of stagnation in agricultural production, and, most importantly, experienced significant reductions in rural poverty and inequality.

It is striking, indeed, that energetic activism on the agrarian-reforms agenda went alongside a near total absence of initiative in public policy on other factors that influence well-being. The reform of local governance failed to extend in a comprehensive manner to the public health and education systems. The successful examples of Kerala as well as other states in implementing innovative programmes such as noon meals in schools and immunization drives were conspicuous by their absence in West Bengal. The emancipation of women, which is a critical factor in the expansion of public services and overall social development, made its appearance on the public agenda only with reference to the reservation of panchayat seats.[102]

Literacy Campaign

One significant exception to the general pattern of neglect of public services was the state's implementation of the national Total Literacy Campaign, which started in 1991. The campaign was given high prominence, and the panchayats played an active role in it. The aim

[102] While some Left Front initiatives such as collective wage bargaining are likely to have led to some improvement in the relative position of women, others, such as the redistribution of property and tenancy rights almost exclusively to male heads of poor households, may have had the converse effect.

of the campaign was to mobilize large numbers of people on a non-party political basis to teach people basic literacy skills in a concentrated effort. Large numbers did indeed take part, though most of them were in fact supporters of the Left Front parties.

The precise impact of the campaign is difficult to assess at this early stage. Available results are sketchy and varied. Official claims of having completely eradicated illiteracy from some districts do seem exaggerated. The two WIDER study villages in Birbhum district (which was at one stage declared a fully literate district — the claim was later withdrawn), Kuchli and Sahajapur, were surveyed for literacy after the completion of the literacy campaign. Results indicate a significant positive impact. Nearly 60 per cent of those who were previously illiterate had achieved at least 'semi-literacy'. This has been an important achievement, even if it is much more modest than official claims of full literacy. Another survey (Sinha, Majumder, Mondal, and Chattopadhyay, 1993), carried out in some other Birbhum villages about a year and a half after the campaign, recorded a much smaller impact. Only 11 per cent of the participants surveyed had in fact learned to read and write, as against official claims of 61 per cent.

It is difficult to form a judgement about the campaign on the basis of these two surveys. A number of basic points, however, can be made. A campaign approach, while necessary for the implementation of land reforms, and probably quite useful to raise the issue of literacy all over the state, is likely to be of limited consequence if not backed up by other support measures. Neo-literates, particularly adult neo-literates, are prone to losing their newly acquired skill if it falls into disuse. A literacy campaign, therefore, cannot be the end of the process of 'skilling' the population. It can only be the beginning. Without the continued acquisition and retention of literacy skills by children and young people through regular channels of schooling, a campaign risks ending up as a flash in the pan.[103] Even if the literacy campaign has achieved its objectives, and the evidence on this is mixed, to say the least, it is no substitute for a comprehensive and effective system of public schooling that is able to actively address the needs of deprived groups on a sustained basis.

---

[103] Given that a significant proportion of CPM's local-level leadership consists of village school teachers (Bhattacharyya, 1995), it is somewhat surprising that the regular schooling system has received so little attention.

5. BEYOND THE AGRARIAN AGENDA

The Left Front government has been largely successful in implementing the programme of agrarian reform legislated by governments over the decades in response to movements of small peasants and the landless poor. These reforms involved important redistribution of economic claims from the well-off to the poor. In addition, the government has been able to consolidate these gains by transforming the Panchayati Raj Institutions into effective agents of local government.

The process of agrarian reform in West Bengal, although it covered relatively small areas of land, did affect a substantial proportion of the population. Taken together, the 1.44 million beneficiary households of Operation Barga, and the 2.15 million beneficiary households of ceiling laws, constitute around half of all rural households in West Bengal. Even if we assume that some beneficiaries of these programmes overlap, a substantial section of the population, mainly the poorest people with few assets, and those from socially deprived groups, have been direct beneficiaries. While the land struggles of the sixties marked a watershed in terms of the change in class alignments, the Left Front reforms of a decade later gave that changed balance of power concrete form by instituting redistribution of claims to land affecting millions of people. This, we believe, is not an insignificant achievement. The economic benefits to some of the most deprived sections of the rural population have been tangible. West Bengal has experienced rapid declines in rural poverty, and substantial improvements in the distribution of consumption.

Two seemingly contradictory approaches to the recent agrarian and political history of West Bengal have emerged. On the one hand, Kohli (1987) focuses attention on state action alone as the engine of social and political change. While he does acknowledge the other direction of interaction — that is, the influence of civil society on state action — his analysis gives undue pre-eminence to the ideological discipline of the CPM as an explanation of pro-poor interventions. On the other hand, attempts to restore the importance of class relations and class struggle, particularly the movement of the late sixties and early seventies in the understanding of social and political change (for instance, Bose, 1993, Acharya, 1993, and Rudra, 1981), have tended to dismiss the relatively placid and bureaucratic approach of the Left Front as having at best a marginal, and at worst a negative, impact on the situation of the poor.

There is a sense in which these two approaches describe two different aspects of the West Bengal reality. The success of the Left Front in implementing a broadly democratic system of governance has involved more than the agency of a disciplined 'social-democratic' party. Political mobilization and heightened political awareness on the part of the poor had contributed to the 'presence' of the party in the first place, and continued to play a role in imposing electoral discipline on its cadres. The reforms of the Left Front, on their part, have extended legal and institutional recognition (partly through bureaucratic channels) to the socio-political changes which were initiated in radical agrarian struggles. By so doing, the reforms have given content (be it modest) to the changed balance of power in the shape of defensible property and tenancy rights, as well as the opportunity for the exercise of civil and political rights in the shape of democratic local government.

The driving force behind the Left Front reforms has been political mobilization and the need for its consolidation. These have been the main factors in placing the agrarian question at the centre of things. The history of politicization played a major role in West Bengal, as it has done elsewhere, in setting the framework for social and political change. We have already noted some of the limitations to redistribution within this framework. The ultimate objective of the land-redistribution programme, for instance, cannot be complete equalization of land ownership, as any further lowering of the land ceiling will endanger the political constituency of the Left Front. Furthermore, the domain over which redistribution has taken place is the village, and the final impact on the livelihood of poor landless households would depend on the initial conditions (such as the distribution of land and agro-economy) in their villages.

A more serious limitation of the agrarian agenda in the West Bengal experience has been the relative continuity in some of the traditional patterns of deprivation. While patriarchy, for instance, was probably weakened as a result of collective bargaining for wages, it may have been strengthened by the creation and consolidation of private property (as well as tenancy) rights in land, mainly in favour of male household heads.

Furthermore, contrary to expectation, the political changes have not led to breaks from trend in aspects of well-being such as health and educational conditions, for which public policy and public action are known to play a critical role. West Bengal's rankings among the major Indian states in rural infant mortality and literacy rates have not undergone substantial changes. Decreases in its mortality and illiteracy rates in recent years are in line with their historical trends. Not much of the energy and activism that attended the implementation of the agrarian-reforms agenda was transferred to these areas of public policy.

The agrarian-reforms framework in general, and in West Bengal particularly, calls for a renegotiation of class-based economic claims. Within the legal context of land-reforms legislation in India, and the political context of 'peasant unity' in rural West Bengal, however, this renegotiation is limited to the marginal redistribution of private property rights in land. Even under these limitations, the agrarian-reforms agenda does provide for forms of intervention that address urgent needs of some of the most deprived groups in society. The overriding concern with the agrarian-reforms agenda, however, has also been, at least partly, responsible for the almost complete neglect of claims which might arise from other sources of social and economic inequity. The failure of public policy to act on the serious gaps between the educational and health achievements of male and female children is one such case. Indeed, the near exclusive concern of the Left Front organizations with agrarian politics, and the establishment and redistribution of property rights in land, is an important factor in their neglect of individual rights to a minimal level of education and health care.

The limits to further redistribution of land, extension of tenancy rights, and arbitration of wage demands are set both by the politico-legal framework of Indian agrarian reforms, and the electoral calculus of the ruling coalition. These limits had probably been reached as early as the mid-eighties. The continued relevance of the agrarian agenda since then owes something to the growth in agricultural output and the scope created for the wider sharing of this output. In this regard, the agrarian agenda has not outlived its usefulness. It is also clear, however, that the economic, political, and social sustainability of the Left Front reforms, as well as of the gains that these reforms imply for the poor, require ventures beyond the agrarian agenda. In matters of economic policy, the West Bengal government has shown that it is quite capable of looking beyond the agrarian agenda. Once accused of having neglected the industrial sector, the Left Front leaders are winning plaudits for their active wooing of Indian and foreign investment in the state.[104] Thus far, however, there is little evidence of innovative thinking or action on urgent matters of social policy.

The activism generated by political mobilization on agrarian issues has remained confined, by and large, to the realm of relations and forces of production in agriculture. The successful implementation of agrarian reforms and the institution of local-level democracy in the state provides some of the most favourable conditions anywhere in India for overcoming traditional patterns of deprivation along the lines of class, caste, and gender. Guarantees of local political office to members of deprived groups can help in this process, but it is in the exercise of political power for the expansion of public services, and the universalization of primary health care and education that the foundations of egalitarian and participatory economic and social development can be laid. Whether or not the Left Front parties are willing and able to take the lead in this regard remains yet to be seen.

REFERENCES

Acharya, Poromesh (1993), 'Panchayats and Left Politics in West Bengal', *Economic and Political Weekly*, 28 (22), 29 May.
Acharya, S. (1988), 'Agricultural Wages in India: A Disaggregated Analysis', *Indian Journal of Agricultural Economics*, 44 (2), April–June.
Agricultural Census of India 1971.
Agricultural Wages of India 1992–93.
Bandyopadhyay, D. (1986), 'Land Reforms in India: An Analysis', *Economic and Political Weekly*, 21 (25–6), Review of Agriculture, 21–8 June.
Banerjee, Abhijit V. and Maitreesh Ghatak (1995), 'Empowerment and Tenancy: The Economics of Tenancy Reform', mimeo, Department of Economics, Harvard University, November.
Basu, S.K. and S.K. Bhattacharya (1963), *Land Reforms in West Bengal: A Study on Implementation* (New Delhi: Oxford Book Company).

---

[104] See, for instance, the special report on the new industrial strategy of the Left Front in *Economic Times*, 12 July 1994.

Bergmann, Theodore (1984), *Agrarian Reform in India, with Special Reference to Kerala, Karnataka, Andhra Pradesh and West Bengal* (New Delhi: Agricole).

Bhattacharya, N., M. Chattopadhyay, and A. Rudra (1987a), 'Changes in Level of Living in Rural West Bengal — Private Consumption', *Economic and Political Weekly*, 11 July.

—— (1987b), 'Changes in Level of Living in Rural West Bengal — Social Consumption', *Economic and Political Weekly*, 15 August.

—— (1987c), 'Changes in Level of Living in Rural West Bengal — Housing Conditions', *Economic and Political Weekly*, 5–12 September.

—— (1987d), 'Changes in Level of Living in Rural West Bengal: Consumer Durables, Clothing and Footwear', *Economic and Political Weekly*, 31 October.

—— (1987e), 'Changes in Level of Living in Rural West Bengal: Perceptions of the People', *Economic and Political Weekly*, 28 November.

—— (1988), 'Changes in Level of Living in Rural West Bengal — Variations Across Socio-Economic Groups', *Economic and Political Weekly*, 28 May.

Bhattacharyya, Dwaipayan (1993), Agrarian Reforms and Politics of the Left in West Bengal, Ph.D. thesis (unpublished), University of Cambridge.

—— (1995), 'Manufacturing Consent: CPI(M)'s Politics of Rural Reforms in West Bengal (1977–90)', paper presented at the Workshop on Agricultural Growth and Agrarian Structure in West Bengal and Bangladesh, Calcutta, 9–12 January 1995.

Bhaumik, Sankar Kumar (1993), *Tenancy Relations and Agrarian Development: A Study of West Bengal* (New Delhi: Sage).

Bose, Sugata (1986), *Agrarian Bengal: Economy, Social Structure and Politics, 1919–1947* (Cambridge: Cambridge University Press).

—— (1993), *Peasant Labour and Colonial Capital: Rural Bengal Since 1770, The New Cambridge History of India III: 2* (Cambridge: Cambridge University Press).

Boyce, J. (1987), *Agrarian Impasse in Bengal: Institutional Constraints to Technological Change* (Oxford: Oxford University Press).

Census of India, 1981.

Census of India, 1991.

Centre for Monitoring the Indian Economy — CMIE (1993), *Performance of Agriculture in Major States (1967–68 to 1991–92)*, July 1993.

Chandrasekhar, C.P. (1993), 'Agrarian Change and Occupational Diversification: Non-agricultural Employment and Rural Development in West Bengal', *Journal of Peasant Studies*, 20 (2), January.

Chattopadhyay, Sujit Narayan (1992), 'Historical Context of Political Change in Rural West Bengal: A Study of Seven Villages in Bardhman', *Economic and Political Weekly*, 27 (13), 28 March.

Crook, R.C. and J. Manor (1994), 'Enhancing Participation and Institutional Performance: Democratic Decentralisation in South Asia and West Africa', report to the Overseas Development Administration.

Dasgupta, S. and R.S. Mukhopadhyay (1989), 'Party Politics, Panchayat and Conflict in West Bengal', *Man in India*, 69 (1).

Drèze, Jean (1990), 'Poverty in India and the IRDP Delusion', Economic and Political Weekly, 29 September.

Drèze, Jean and Jackie Loh, (1995), 'Literacy in India and China', *Economic and Political Weekly*, 30 (45), 11 November.

Drèze, Jean and Amartya Sen (1995), *India: Economic Development and Social Opportunity* (Oxford and New Delhi: Oxford University Press).

Echeverri-Gent, J. (1992), 'Public Participation and Poverty Alleviation: The Experience of Reform Communists in India's West Bengal', *World Development*, 20 (10), October.

Economic Times (1994), '"West Bengal: Back in Business", An Economic Times Survey', 12 July.

Gangopadhyay, Bodhirupa (1990), 'Operation Barga', mimeo, WIDER Project on Rural Poverty, Social Change, and Public Policy, Santiniketan.

Gazdar, Haris (1992), 'Rural Poverty, Public Policy and Social Change: Some Findings from Surveys of Six Villages', WIDER Working Paper 98, May.

Ghosh, Ratan (1981), 'Agrarian Programme of Left Front Government', *Economic and Political Weekly*, Review of Agriculture, 16 (25–6).

Government of India (1992), Ministry of Rural Development, *Annual Report 1991–92*.

Government of West Bengal (1993), *Economic Review 1992–93*.

Harriss, John (1993), 'What is Happening in Rural West Bengal?: Agrarian Reform, Growth and Distribution', *Economic and Political Weekly*, 12 June.

Islam, Sirajul (1988), *Bengal Land Tenure: The Origin and Growth of Intermediate Interests in the Nineteenth Century* (Calcutta: K.P. Bagchi).

Jha, Praveen Kumar (1994), 'Changing Conditions of Agricultural Labourers in Post-independent India: A Case Study from Bihar', Ph.D. thesis, Centre for Economic Studies and Planning, Jawaharlal Nehru University, Delhi.

Jose, A.V. (1984), 'Poverty and Income Distribution — the Case of West Bengal', in A.R. Khan and Eddy Lee (eds.), *Poverty in Rural Asia* (Bangkok: International Labour Organisation, Asian Employment Programme, ARTEP).

Kohli, Atul (1987), *The State and Poverty in India: The Politics of Reform* (Cambridge: Cambridge University Press).

—— (1990), 'From Elite Activism to Democratic Consolidation: The Rise of Reform Communism in West Bengal', in Francine Frankel and M.S.A. Rao (eds.), *Dominance and State Power in Modern India.* (Delhi: Oxford University Press).

Kynch, Jocelyn (1990), 'Agricultural Wage Rates in West Bengal and Their Trends Over Time', mimeo, Centre for Development Studies, University College, Swansea.

Lieten, G.K. (1992), *Continuity and Change in Rural West Bengal* (Delhi: Sage).

—— (1994a), 'What Has Really Happened in West Bengal: Land Reforms at the Centre Stage', mimeo, Centre for Asian Studies, Amsterdam.

—— (1994b), 'For A New Debate on West Bengal', *Economic and Political Weekly*, 29 (29), 16 July.

Maitra, T. (1988), 'Rural Poverty in West Bengal', in T.N. Srinivasan and P.K. Bardhan (eds.), *Rural Poverty in South Asia* (Oxford: Clarendon).

Majumder, Debanshu and Sunil Sengupta (1990), 'Levels of Living Among the Rural Poor in West Bengal (1987–89) — A Study of Six Villages, Part I', WIDER Project on Rural Poverty, Social Change, and Public Policy, Santiniketan, Working Paper.

Mallick, R. (1992), 'Agrarian Reform in West Bengal: The End of an Illusion', *World Development*, 20 (5).

—— (1993), *Development Policy of a Communist Government: West Bengal Since 1977* (Cambridge: Cambridge University Press).

Minhas, B.S., L.R. Jain, and S.D. Tendulkar (1991), 'Declining Incidence of Poverty in 1980s: Evidence versus Artefacts', *Economic and Political Weekly*, 6–13 July.

Misra, Anshuman and Sunil Sengupta (1990), 'Food Consumption in Selected Poor Households (1987–89) — A Study of Six Villages',

Part I, WIDER Project on Rural Poverty, Social Change, and Public Policy, Santiniketan, Working Paper.

Mukarji, Nirmal and Debabrata Bandyopadhyay (1993), 'New Horizons for West Bengal's Panchayats', A Report for the Government of West Bengal, New Delhi.

Mukherjee, Partha (1990), 'Panchayats in West Bengal', mimeo, WIDER Project on Rural Poverty, Social Change, and Public Policy, Santiniketan.

Mukherji, Neela (1992), 'Villagers' Perception of Rural Poverty through the Mapping Technique of PRA', mimeo, London School of Economics.

Nag, Moni (1989), 'Political Awareness as a Factor in Accessibility of Health Services: A Case Study of Rural Kerala and West Bengal', *Economic and Political Weekly*, 25 February.

National Sample Survey Organisation (NSSO), *Sarvekshana*, January–March 1989, 12 (3); January–March (1991), 14 (3); and other issues.

Raghavalu, C.V. and E.A. Narayana (1991), 'Reforms in Panchayati Raj: A Comparative Analysis of Andhra Pradesh, Karnataka and West Bengal', *Indian Journal of Public Administration*, 37 (1).

Ray, S. Datta (1994), 'Agricultural Growth in West Bengal', *Economic and Political Weekly*, 16 July.

Raychaudhuri, Ajivata and Rongili Biswas (1994), 'IRDP, Poverty Alleviation and Development: The Comparative Story of West Bengal, India, mimeo, Department of Economics, Jadavpur University, Calcutta.

Rogaly, B. (1994), 'Rural Labour Arrangements in West Bengal', D.Phil. thesis (unpublished), University of Oxford.

Rudra, Ashok (1981), 'One Step Forward, Two Steps Backward', *Economic and Political Weekly*, Review of Agriculture, 16 (25–6).

Ruud, Arild Engelsen (1995), 'Wealth, Power and Status Among CPM-Supporter Groups in Rural West Bengal', paper presented at the Workshop on Agricultural Growth and Agrarian Structure in West Bengal and Bangladesh, Calcutta, 9–12 January 1995.

Saha, Anamitra and Madhura Swaminathan (1994), 'Agricultural Growth in West Bengal in the 1980s', *Economic and Political Weekly*, 26 March.

Sample Registration Survey (1992), *Sample Registration Bulletin*, June.

Sen, Abhijit and Ranja Sengupta (1995), 'The Recent Growth in Agricultural Output in Eastern India, with Special Reference to the Case of West Bengal', paper presented at the Workshop on

Agricultural Growth and Agrarian Structure in West Bengal and Bangladesh, Calcutta, 9–12 January 1995.

Sen, Amartya and Sunil Sengupta (1983), 'Malnutrition of Rural Indian Children and the Sex Bias', *Economic and Political Weekly*, 18, Annual Number.

Sengupta, Sunil (1981), 'West Bengal Land Reforms and the Agrarian Scene', *Economic and Political Weekly*, Review of Agriculture, 16 (25–6).

Sengupta, Sunil, et al. (1991), 'Rural Economy and Poverty in West Bengal and the Public Policy Interventions', Report of the WIDER project at Santiniketan, September 1991.

Singh, Ashok Kumar (1988), *Peasants Revolt and Agrarian Reform* (New Delhi: Commonwealth Publishers).

Sinha, A., D. Majumder, D. Mondal, and K. Chattopadhyay (1993), 'Glimpses of Literacy Profile: An Evaluation Study of the Mass Literacy Programme in Birbhum', Report, Agro-Economic Research Centre, Visva-Bharati, Santiniketan, West Bengal.

Swaminathan, Madhura (1990), 'Village Level Implementation of IRDP: Comparison of West Bengal and Tamil Nadu', *Economic and Political Weekly*, 31 March.

Webster, Neil (1992), *Panchayati Raj and The Decentralisation of Development Planning in West Bengal: A Case Study* (Calcutta: K.P. Bagchi and Company).

Westergaard, Kirsten (1986), 'People's Participation, Local Government and Rural Development: The Case of West Bengal, India', Centre for Development Research, CDR Research Report No. 8, Copenhagen, March.

Williams, Glyn (1995), 'Panchayati Raj and the Changing Micro-Politics of West Bengal', paper presented at the Workshop on Agricultural Growth and Agrarian Structure in West Bengal and Bangladesh, Calcutta, 9–12 January 1995.

4

ON KERALA'S DEVELOPMENT ACHIEVEMENTS*

V.K. Ramachandran

1. INTRODUCTION

The most conspicuous feature of the Indian economy is that hundreds of millions of India's people live in conditions of appalling

* I began to collect material for this paper while at the Harvard Center for Population and Development Studies, and most of the work was done while at the Indira Gandhi Institute of Development Research (IGIDR), Bombay. The research was supported by WIDER and IGIDR. I am grateful to the Directors of the three institutions, Lincoln Chen, Lal Jayawardena, and Kirit Parikh for their support.

I am very grateful to friends and colleagues on the faculty and student body of the Centre for Development Studies (CDS), and to the administrative staff for their hospitality and help, and their generosity in sharing research results and the resources of the Centre with a visitor. I am grateful to the staff at the library of the CDS, the India Office Library (IOL), the Jawaharlal Nehru University Library, the Library at the office of the Central Committee of the Communist Party of India (Marxist) at A.K. Gopalan Bhavan, and the Library of the Communist Party of India at Ajay Bhavan for their help.

Amartya Sen provided the initial ideas and encouragement for this research, and Jean Drèze and he provided ideas and comments at every stage of the work. Jean Drèze did much painstaking work on the final draft of the paper; his suggestions and criticism contribute a great deal to the argument and presentation. I had helpful discussions with Nata Duvvury, Judith Heyer, Thomas Isaac, Kumari Jayawardena, Prakash Karat, T.N. Krishnan, Saraswathi Menon, Siddique Osmani, Vikas Rawal, A.K. Shiva Kumar, M.H. Suryanarayana, Madhura Swaminathan, David Washbrook and participants in a seminar at the Centre for Economic Studies and Planning, Jawaharlal Nehru University. Arundhati Mundlay helped tabulate data from the national readership surveys. P. Poovendran, Chief Cartographer, TTK Maps, Madras, drew the map. Vikas Rawal and I collected and processed the data on incomes, consumer expenditure, and prices, and wrote the Annexure together. E.M.S. Namboodiripad, P. Govinda Pillai, and M.S. Swaminathan gave me detailed interviews. Thomas Isaac, Madhura Swaminathan, and Michael Tharakan commented on drafts of this paper, and Thomas Isaac made detailed suggestions regarding the presentation of the material and the argument. I am very grateful to all of them.

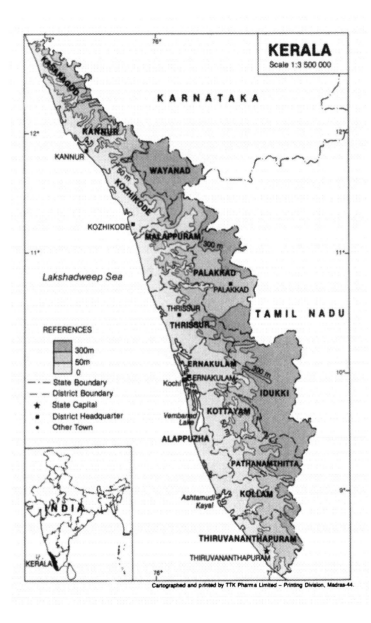

Map of Kerala

deprivation — in conditions of hunger, ill-health, homelessness, illiteracy and subject to different forms of class, caste, and gender oppression. Among the states of India there is, as is now well-known, one state — Kerala — whose performance in the spheres of social and economic development has been substantially better than the others. Kerala's accomplishment shows that the well-being of the people can be improved, and social, political, and cultural conditions transformed, even at low levels of income, when there is appropriate public action.[1] In Kerala, the action of mass organizations and mass movements against social, political, and economic oppression and the policy actions of governments have been the most important constituents of public action.

Life expectancy at birth in Kerala was 68.8 years for men and 74.4 years for women in 1990–2. The infant mortality rate in 1992 was 17 per thousand in rural Kerala and 13 per thousand in urban Kerala. There were 1040 females per thousand males in Kerala in 1991. Kerala has the lowest birth and death rates in India, and has more hospital beds relative to the population than any other state. The rate of immunization is among the highest in India, and current data indicate that girls are immunized at the same rate as boys. The rate of literacy among persons in the state who are 7 years old and above is more than 90 per cent. The most radical implementation of land reforms in India has taken place in Kerala. There have been important achievements with respect to the abolition of untouchability. Women in Kerala have made outstanding gains in the spheres of health and education. Kerala has the best public food-distribution system of India's states. The circulation of newspapers is more widespread in Kerala than elsewhere in India. The gaps between 'backward' and 'advanced' regions of the state have been narrowed substantially.

The objective of this review is to investigate the sources of Kerala's high-profile performance in respect of living standards. When studying the sources of Kerala's current levels of achievement, it quickly becomes clear that Kerala has special features in respect of a host of social circumstances. The purpose of this study, however, is not to study the specific features of Kerala's experience only in order to try and establish Kerala's exclusiveness; it is to try and draw

[1] See Centre for Development Studies (1977). On examples of the successes of direct support amidst general conditions of low-income growth, see Drèze and Sen (1989), especially ch. 12.

lessons from Kerala's experience for the rest of India and, perhaps, for other developing societies.

This paper is organized as follows. The second section discusses some basic features of Kerala's economy and society. Section 3 deals with Kerala's achievements in respect of the health status of the people. Specifically, it deals with health, nutrition, the public distribution system, and sex ratios. It also discusses some pockets of persistent health-deprivation in the state. Section 4 deals with literacy, a key facilitator of Kerala's health and demographic achievements. Section 5 discusses aspects of caste and gender relations in Kerala. Section 6 attempts to analyse changes in agrarian relations in Kerala. Section 7 reviews the part played by the major agents of social change in Kerala: it deals with the role of governments, the role of women in development, Protestant missionaries in the nineteenth-century, caste-based reform movements, and the modern left movement. Section 8 is a brief concluding section.

2. BACKGROUND

Kerala has an area of about 39,000 sq km and its population in 1991 was 29,098,518. The density of population was 749 per sq km, much higher than the Indian average of 257 per sq km, and the highest among states in India after West Bengal (767 per sq km). At the Census of 1981, the population was divided into Hindu, Muslim, and Christian groups in the proportion 58 : 21 : 21.

There are four major physiographic zones in the state, the highlands, the middle zone, the lowland plain, and the coastal plain.[2] The highland zone is part of the Western Ghats, and generally forms the eastern border of Kerala. In the midland region (alt. 300m to 600m), hill ranges extend westward from the hill zone and continue into valleys that widen as altitude declines. These are productive laterite tracts. The lowland zone (alt. 30m to 300m) varies between 20 and 100 km in width, and ends in the narrow (the average width is 10 km) coastal plain.

Kerala is a region of relatively heavy monsoon rain. There are more than 40 streams and rivers in Kerala that originate along the

---

[2] For introductory data on the state, see Gazetteer of India (1986, 1989), and Centre for Monitoring the Indian Economy (1993).

crest of the Western Ghats and flow westward into backwaters and the Arabian Sea. Kerala is a region of arresting greenness (the green, for instance, of paddy and coconut fields, of vegetable, fruit, and spice gardens, of live fences, of forests, and of cardamom, tea, and coffee plantations), of the sea, and of lakes and backwaters in the coastal plains.

Regional Divisions

The state of Kerala was established in 1956 with the reorganization of three areas, where most people spoke Malayalam, into a single state. The three areas were the Malayalam-majority regions of Travancore, Cochin, and Malabar.[3] Travancore and Cochin were princely states before Indian independence. The state of Travancore as it existed at the time of India's independence was created in the mid-eighteenth century, during and after the rule of Martanda Varma (1729–58). The state of Cochin was, similarly, a product of the late eighteenth century. The consolidation of the state followed Cochin's treaty in 1791 with the East India Company. Malabar was a district of the Madras Presidency in British India, and was absorbed into British India in stages, with the military defeat of Tipu Sultan in 1792.[4]

The distinction between the three regions is of importance in the history of Kerala's social, economic, and political development. In the nineteenth century and until the formation of Kerala, there were marked divergences in state policy in the three regions. In respect of agrarian relations, education, and health, modern administrative reforms, transport and communications, and in respect of the commercialization of agriculture and the growth of trade and commerce, the 'states' part of Kerala (Travancore and Cochin) pushed far ahead of the part that was directly under British rule. While the basic

[3] The districts of modern Kerala that correspond to regions of old Travancore (also spelled Thiruvithamkoor) are Thiruvananthapuram (formerly Trivandrum), Kollam (formerly Quilon), Pathanamthitta, Kottayam, Idukki, Alappuzha (formerly Alleppey). The districts that correspond to old Cochin are Ernakulam and Thrissur (formerly Trichur). The modern districts that correspond to the area of the old Malabar district are Malappuram, Palakkad (formerly Palghat), Kozhikode (formerly Calicut), Kannur (formerly Cannanore), Wayanad, and Kasargod.

[4] The district of Malabar also included enclaves in Cochin (the *taluk* of 'British Cochin'), two enclaves in Travancore as well as the Lakshadweep and Minicoy islands.

distinction is between the states part of Kerala and Malabar, there were also differences between Travancore and Cochin. Travancore had a more powerful and authoritarian State than Cochin, with a larger bureaucracy and a more high-profile, interventionist regime. It had a bigger and more varied resource base than Cochin,[5] and the development of capitalism in agriculture and the expansion of trade and commerce was greater in Travancore than in Cochin.

Settlement Patterns

A feature of Kerala's development performance is that there are no great disparities between achievements in the urban areas of Kerala and the rural areas. The absence of great disparities is because public policy is so targeted; public policy has been helped in this regard by the special geographical configuration of towns and villages in Kerala. The distinction between rural and urban areas is less sharp in Kerala than in other parts of the country. The literature is full of references to Kerala's 'rural–urban continuum'; a new Kerala coinage is 'rurban'.

The occupational structure of Kerala's villages also distinguishes them from villages elsewhere. There is a larger proportion of workers outside agriculture, in waged and salaried non-agricultural occupations, in Kerala's villages than in villages elsewhere. In other parts of India, the inhabited part of a village and the cultivated part — that is, where people live and where the fields are — are easy enough to distinguish. Not so in Kerala, where houses are scattered, not clustered, and are located near cultivated fields.

That Kerala's habitational pattern was distinct was noted by writers as early as Ibn Batuta. The origins of the present pattern have been ascribed to the relationship between landowning castes and the unfree tillers of the soil; they have also been traced to features of Kerala's distinct topography, hydrology, and cropping pattern.[6]

---

[5] Travancore included parts of modern Tamil Nadu — the whole of the present Kanniyakumari district and parts of Tirunelveli district.

[6] On settlement patterns in Kerala and the spatial organization of Kerala's villages, see Aiyappan (1965), pp. 33–4; Mencher (1966); Mayer (1952), p. 49; Munro (1817); Ward and Conner (1816–20), pp. 6–7. See Nagaraj (1986), T.T. Sreekumar (1990), and Casinader (1994) on aspects of the rural–urban continuum in settlement patterns, and Chattopadhyay (1994) on the influence of the biophysical environment on settlement patterns in Kerala.

The development of road transport since the nineteen-sixties, and particularly after the mid-seventies, has had the effect of accentuating the urbanization of Kerala's villages. Every village in the state is connected by motorable road. There are, as a result, increased opportunities for commuting to work for members of the non-agricultural work-force who live in villages and work in towns. The growth of retail trade, construction, and other forms of economic activity in villages after the sharp increase in the volume of remittances from workers in the Gulf countries has also contributed to the urbanization of Kerala's villages.

Kerala's villages are not the same kind of distinct socio-economic unit that villages in other parts of the country are; boundaries between villages, which have been demarcated for purposes of administration, are somewhat arbitrary. The average size of a village at the Census of 1981 was 16,967 persons (the all-India average was 911 persons).

Political Movements

After the late nineteen-thirties and until the present, the Communist Party, with its mass organizations of workers, peasants and agricultural labourers, students, youth, and women, has been the major organizer of mass political movements among the people of Kerala. The first general elections in united Kerala were won by the Communist Party; the first Communist government in India, led by E.M.S. Namboodiripad, Kerala's pre-eminent Communist, took office in Kerala in 1957. Kerala has had Communist-led, Communist-majority governments from 1957 to 1959, 1967 to 1969, 1980 to 1981, and 1987 to 1991; all other governments were Congress-majority governments. Although the Communist Party and its allies have actually been in power for relatively short periods of time, the Communist Party and the left have had a profound influence on social and political life and government policy in Kerala, and on the legislative agenda of the state since its formation.

Voter turnouts in Kerala are high. Electoral contests in Kerala are, basically, contests between the coalitions led by the Congress Party and the Communist Party of India (Marxist), or CPI(M). There are no members of the state's Legislative Assembly from the main political party of the Hindu right, the Bharatiya Janata Party (BJP); non-secular parties of the Muslim and Christian minorities are, however, active in electoral politics and in the legislature (and, indeed, can be decisive factors in the survival of coalition governments).

The Economy

Kerala's achievements are an outstanding example of the power of public action even in conditions of low-production growth; the other side of the coin, however, is that Kerala faces an acute crisis in the spheres of employment and material production (and, indeed, one does not have to be in Kerala very long to recognize the extent and intensity of unemployment in the state). People at large and political parties of the left perceive the problems of unemployment and production as the major economic problems of the immediate future; this concern also found repeated expression in the proceedings of the International Congress on Kerala Studies in August 1994. The persistence of the crisis is understood as being a threat to the polity and society, and the question has also been raised, by persons in politics, journalists, scholars, and others, whether the development achievements of Kerala's people can be sustained if the employment and production situations are not transformed.[7]

Net state domestic product (NSDP) per capita in Kerala is below the Indian average. In 1980–1, for instance, Kerala was ranked sixteenth out of 24 states and 3 Union Territories; in 1991–2, its rank was fourteenth out of 22 states and 1 Union Territory. As Fig. 1 indicates, there has been very little growth of per-capita NSDP in Kerala since 1970.

Through the seventies and eighties, the compound annual rate of growth of NSDP per capita in Kerala was substantially lower than the compound annual rate of growth in Net Domestic Product (NDP) in India (Table 1). Significantly, however, over the most recent quinquennium for which official data are available, 1986–7 to 1991–2, the growth rate of NSDP per capita in Kerala was substantially *higher* than the corresponding growth rate of NDP per capita in India.

[7] On the current problems of Kerala's economy, and other issues relating to the sustainability of its development achievements, see Namboodiripad (1994), Gulati (1994), Raj (1994), K.K. George (1994), Isaac (1994), C.T. Kurien (1994), Krishnan (1992), Damodaran and Govindarajulu (1994), and other contributors to A.K.G. Centre for Research and Studies (1994a–e).

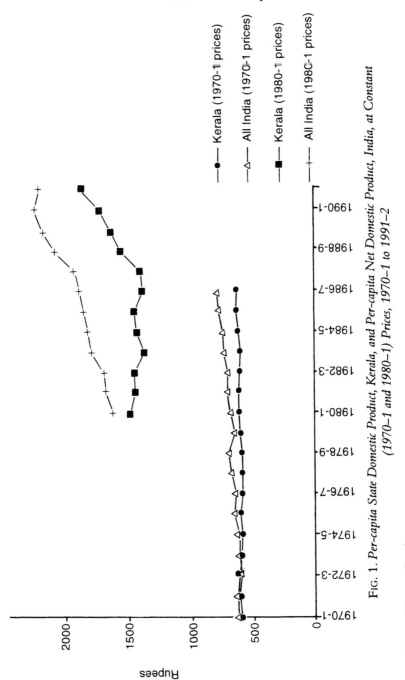

FIG. 1. Per-capita State Domestic Product, Kerala, and Per-capita Net Domestic Product, India, at Constant (1970–1 and 1980–1) Prices, 1970–1 to 1991–2

Notes and Sources: See Annexure.

TABLE 1. Compound Annual Rates of Growth of Per-capita
Net Domestic Product in Kerala and India, 1970–1 to 1991–2

(in per cent)

Time period	Kerala	India
1970–1 to 1980–1	0.06	1.39
1980–1 to 1990–1	1.40	3.25
1986–7 to 1991–2	6.16	3.79

Source. See Annexure.

According to estimates of the proportion of the population below the poverty line (or the head-count ratio), which are available until 1987–8 (see EPW Research Foundation, 1993), the head-count ratios for Kerala were higher than the corresponding all-India ratios through the nineteen sixties and seventies; in 1983 and 1987–8, however, the rural head-count ratio was marginally lower (ibid.; see Table 2).[8] Similarly, the Sen index for Kerala, which was much higher than the all-India index in the nineteen sixties and seventies, was marginally lower than the all-India index in 1986–7 (ibid.; see Table 3).

TABLE 2. Proportion of Persons Below the Poverty Line
(Minhas, Jain, and Tendulkar Estimates), Kerala and India

(in per cent)

Year	Rural		Urban		Rural + Urban	
	Kerala	India	Kerala	India	Kerala	India
1970–1	69.0	57.3	62.4	45.9	68.0	55.0
1983	47.2	49.0	47.8	38.3	47.3	46.5
1987–8	44.0	44.9	44.5	36.5	44.1	42.7

Source. EPW Research Foundation (1993).

[8] On issues related to the measurement of income-poverty in Kerala and its incidence, see Mohandas (1994).

TABLE 3.   *Sen Index, Kerala and India*

Year	Kerala	India
1960 1	0.25	0.14
1970–1	0.29	0.18
1977–8	0.16	0.14
1986–7	0.06	0.08

Source.   EPW Research Foundation (1993).

Kerala's agriculture is characterized by the existence of a series of agricultural micro-environments suited to different kinds of mixed farming, and by a substantial proportion of perennial crops in total agricultural output. In 1985–6, ten crops accounted for about 84 per cent of the gross cropped area: paddy, tapioca, banana, rubber, coffee, cardamom, areca nut, cashew, pepper, and coconut. Kerala's growth performance in agriculture has been very poor. The decade 1975–6 to 1985–6 was, according to Kannan and Push-pangadan (1990), a period of 'generalized stagnation', that is, it was characterized by stagnation or decline in the rates of growth of output of most crops (the exceptions were rubber and coffee). For all crops other than paddy, the stagnation in output reflected stagnant yields. The rate of growth of paddy production declined as a result of a fall in the area under cultivation.[9] In a review of the performance of the 1987 Communist government in Kerala, Isaac and Mohana Kumar (1991) note that there was a distinct improvement in agricultural production between 1986–7 and 1990–1 (on a review of changes in the eighties whose conclusions are consistent with the findings of Isaac and Mohanakumar, see Sathian, 1994). According to data on net state domestic product at constant prices, the annual compound rate of growth of agriculture was 7.5 per cent between 1986–7 and 1990–1.[10]

In 1950, the value of output per capita of the manufacturing sector in Travancore was Rs 48 against an all-India average of Rs 37 (Isaac and Tharakan, 1986a). In the same year, per-capita net domestic product in Travancore–Cochin was also a little higher than the Indian

[9] On Kerala's agricultural economy, see Narayana (1992); see also Mohan Das (1992).

[10] Government of Kerala (1992), Appendix 2.2, p. 140. On constraints on growth and growth alternatives in Kerala, see also Shyamasundaran Nair (1994).

average. After 1950, Kerala's industrial growth performance was worse than the all-India record, and worse than the other three south Indian states. The manufacturing sector grew at 2.8 per cent per annum between 1970–1 and 1986–7; the corresponding rates of growth in Tamil Nadu and Karnataka were 5.3 per cent and 6.0 per cent.[11] Again, Isaac and Mohana Kumar (1991) note an improvement in industrial growth between 1986–7 and 1990–1. The share of the manufacturing sector in net state domestic product increased from 13 per cent in 1986–7 to 16 per cent in 1990–1 (Government of Kerala, 1992, Appendix 2.2, p. 140). The compound rate of growth of the manufacturing sector in state domestic product at constant prices was 12 per cent per annum between 1986–7 and 1990–1 (ibid.).

Productive capital per capita in the factory sector has been consistently lower in Kerala than in the neighbouring states of Karnataka and Tamil Nadu, and much lower in Kerala than in India as a whole (Table 4). Similarly, gross per-capita output in the factory sector has been consistently lower in Kerala than in the neighbouring states and in India as a whole (Table 5). In respect of small industry, for which data are available for the years 1972–3 and 1987–8, the growth in Kerala in the number of working units, in fixed investment, in production, in net value-added, and in employment was also below the all-India average (Subrahmanian and Mohanan Pillai, 1993).

TABLE 4. *Total Productive Capital Per-capita at Constant (1970–1) Prices in the Factory Sector: Kerala, Neighbouring States, and India* [a]

(in rupees)

Years	India	Kerala	Karnataka	Tamil Nadu
1969–72	205 (100)	124 (100)	195 (100)	262 (100)
1973–6	187 (91)	158 (127)	157 (80)	215 (82)
1978–81	256 (125)	201 (162)	209 (107)	276 (105)
1983–6	322 (157)	228 (184)	254 (130)	451 (172)
1988–91	370 (180)	219 (177)	265 (136)	527 (201)

Note. [a] Index numbers in brackets, with 1969–72 as the base period.

Source. Calculated from Annual Survey of Industries data cited in Chandhok and the Policy Group (1990); also Annual Survey of Industries (1993, 1994). Each figure is a three-year average.

[11] Subrahmanian (1990). On industrial stagnation, see also Albin (1990, 1992).

TABLE 5. *Gross Output Per-capita at Constant (1970–1)*
Prices in the Factory Sector: Kerala, Neighbouring States, and India [a]

(in rupees)

Years	India	Kerala	Karnataka	Tamil Nadu
1969–72	240 (100)	172 (100)	184 (100)	316 (100)
1973–6	261 (109)	197 (114)	199 (108)	347 (110)
1978–81	358 (149)	308 (179)	293 (159)	531 (168)
1983–6	451 (188)	314 (182)	348 (189)	682 (216)
1988–91	586 (244)	418 (243)	489 (266)	876 (277)

Note. [a] Index numbers in brackets, with 1969–72 as the base period.
Source. Calculated from Annual Survey of Industries data cited in Chandhok and the Policy Group (1990); also Annual Survey of Industries (1993, 1994). Each figure is a three-year average.

Kerala's share in total industrial investments by the Government of India was 3.2 per cent in 1975, and fell to 1.5 per cent in 1990 (well below its population share, 3.4 per cent).[12] Kerala received 2.9 per cent of central investment in 1971–2 and 1.6 per cent in 1987–8 (Subrahmanian, 1990). The state government spread its investment thin; most units were small with low absolute levels of investment (Subrahmanian, 1990). Subrahmanian (1990) argues that their small size has made many of these enterprises 'financially and technologically unviable' (p. 2058). A study of the private manufacturing sector in Kerala between 1972 and 1985 showed that the financial performance of the corporate sector in Kerala was worse than the all-India average (Nirmala Padmanabhan, 1990).

Although Kerala has a largely literate, skilled labour force, capitalist industrial entrepreneurship in Kerala is ill-developed. According to K.N. Raj, 'one reason for the relatively slow development of large and medium-scale industries is perhaps the lack of entrepreneurs interested in their development. Kerala, it would seem, is still at the stage of capitalist development when projects which promise easy as well as quick money, and even speculative enterprises, seem to have appeal to those who have reasonable amounts of capital' (cited in Isaac and Tharakan, 1986a, p. 29). There is only

[12] Government of Kerala (1992), pp. 62–3.

one big capitalist industrial house from Kerala. Its main industrial production establishments are, however, based in Madras; its plantations are in Tamil Nadu and Kerala, and, not surprisingly, its newspaper group and publishing enterprises are in Kerala.

Kerala has the highest rate of unemployment in the country. This is so whatever the measure of unemployment used. The proportion of males 'usually unemployed' (unemployed for more than 183 days in a year), according to the 43rd round of the National Sample Survey (1987–8) was 14.1 per cent in urban areas and 12.5 per cent in rural areas. The corresponding proportions for females were 33.8 per cent in urban areas and 25.0 per cent in rural areas. The all-India rates of 'usual status' unemployment for the same year were 6.1 per cent (males, urban), 2.8 per cent (males, rural), 8.5 per cent (females, urban), and 3.5 per cent (females, rural). The comparative situation is similar when the employment data by 'current daily status' and 'current weekly status' are considered. By all three measures, 'Kerala has the highest incidence of unemployment for males and females in rural as well as urban areas among Indian states' (Oommen, 1992, p. 233).[13] The most recent annual survey of employment and unemployment by the National Sample Survey (NSS), conducted in 1992–3 (this annual survey covered a smaller sample than the quinquennial survey in 1987–8) confirms these basic findings.

Unemployment in Kerala is particularly high among educated persons.[14] According to NSS data for 1986–7, the unemployment rate among educated adults in urban Kerala was 18 per cent for males and 42 per cent for females (the corresponding all-India figures were 6 per cent and 22 per cent). The average waiting period for a first job for a job-seeker with a school leaving certificate was as high as 48 months for a permanent job and 35 months for a temporary job.[15] Data from the Census of 1981 show that 87.8 per

[13] It is possible, of course, that higher rates of employment partly reflect a consciousness factor, that people who do not consider themselves *gainfully* employed report themselves *un*employed; see also Mukherjee and Isaac (1994) on special features of data on disguised employment in a labour force whose members have relatively high levels of education.

[14] Oommen (1992), Table 3, p. 238; see also Mukherjee and Isaac (1994). On aspects of unemployment among women in Kerala, see E.T. Mathew (1994) and Rachel Kumar (1994).

[15] Isaac and Mukherjee, cited in Oommen (1992); see also Mukherjee and Isaac (1994). An interesting feature of the labour market in Kerala, noted by Mukherjee and Isaac, is that the 'spread of education and strong traditions of affirmative action

cent of all unemployed persons were in the age group 15–34 years. Another interesting pattern is the apparent decline over time in the availability of employment in rural areas. According to data from the Rural Labour Enquiry and the Government of Kerala, among rural labour households, a male worker gained employment for an average of 196 days in 1964–5, 168 days in 1974–5 and 146 days in 1983–4. The corresponding figures for female rural workers were 164 days, 126 days, and 112 days.[16]

Kerala has a history of labour migration, and remittances from outside the state influence disposable incomes significantly. In the early part of the century, there was large-scale migration of workers from Travancore and Malabar to the plantations. After the great depression, there were different streams of migration (discussed in Isaac, 1992). One was of peasants from Travancore to the hill regions of Malabar (Tharakan, 1977, 1981). Another was to Malaya, Ceylon, and Burma, and involved poor and oppressed-caste migrants from coastal Travancore. A third stream was to other parts of India, and involved educated persons, professionals, and workers. From the seventies, following the 1973 increase in petroleum prices, the migration of workers to countries of West Asia (particularly Kuwait, Qatar, Saudi Arabia, and the United Arab Emirates) and Libya, has been a major feature of social and economic life in Kerala. Thomas Isaac (1992) estimated the number of migrants in the mid-eighties from Kerala to this region to have been about 500,000.[17]

Calculations of net state domestic product do not, of course, include remittances from Kerala's emigrants. In an important recent paper, in which he has estimated Kerala's state income from a consumption function, T.N. Krishnan (1994) presents new estimates of the part played by remittance incomes in income change in Kerala. According to Krishnan, remittances were in the region of 15 to 22 per cent of the state domestic product after 1972–3. The peak levels were 30 per cent in 1978–9 and 26 per cent in 1986–7, and the lowest level was 15 per cent, in 1989–90 (Krishnan, 1994, p. 58). Earlier

---

in education and employment has significantly reduced inter-caste differentials in the probability of gaining employment' (Mukherjee and Isaac, 1994, p. 67).

[16] Government of Kerala (1985), Table 26, p. 22. For field-work based data that show a decline in the average number of full days of agricultural employment per worker, see Krishnakumari and George (1994) and Mencher (1994).

[17] The number of emigrants to the region from Kerala has recently been estimated as being between 700,000 and 800,000 persons (Gopinathan Nair, 1994).

estimates worked on the Gulati and Mody (1983) assumption that 50 per cent of the remittances from the countries of the Persian Gulf and 5 per cent of the remittances from the rest of the world were destined for Kerala; on this basis, Isaac (1992) estimated per-capita remittances to have been 18 per cent of SDP per capita in 1980–1, and 13 per cent of SDP in 1988–9.

As a result of remittances from outside the state, despite the crisis of production and employment, according to National Sample Survey data, Kerala's rank among states in respect of annual household per-capita consumer expenditure improved substantially, particularly in rural areas, between the early seventies and the eighties. According to Krishnan (1994), 'despite the stagnation in per-capita domestic income, per-capita consumption expenditure registered a steady increase, 1.61 per cent from 1960–1 to 1971–2 and 1.81 per cent from 1972–3 to 1989–90'. Krishnan estimated that if the same rate of growth was maintained after 1990, real per-capita consumption in Kerala in 1994 would be approximately double the per-capita consumption level of 1960–1.[18] Table 6 and Figs. 2–3 present two series of per-capita household consumer expenditure at constant prices (see the Annexure for an explanation of the methods used to derive the two series). By our Series 1, which is from 1970–1 to 1987–8, per-capita household consumer expenditure in rural Kerala has been higher than the Indian average after 1983, and per-capita household consumer expenditure in urban Kerala went above the all-India figure in 1987–8. These data show that annual per-capita household expenditure among rural households in Kerala was 11.6 per cent below the Indian average in 1970–1, but 9.5 per cent more than the Indian average in 1987–8. In urban areas, annual per-capita household consumer expenditure in Kerala was 13.8 per cent less than the all-India average in 1970–1, and 0.7 per cent more than the Indian average in 1987–8. By our Series 2, which is from 1970–1 to 1992, per-capita household consumer expenditure in rural Kerala has been higher than the Indian average after 1973–4; per-capita household consumer expenditure in urban Kerala crossed the Indian average in 1983, dipped below the Indian average in 1986–7, and has been above the Indian average since 1987–8. In our Series 2, annual per-capita household consumption expenditure in rural Kerala was 11.8 per cent

[18] Krishnaji (1994) notes the impact of remittances from the Gulf region on household incomes in Kerala, and also notes the contribution of remittances to increases in employment in the services sector of Kerala's economy.

below the Indian average in 1970–1 and 31.1 per cent above the Indian average in 1992. In urban Kerala, annual per-capita household consumption expenditure was 13.9 per cent lower than the Indian average in 1970–1 and 4.4 per cent higher in 1992.

TABLE 6. *Per-capita Annual Consumption Expenditure at Constant (1970–1) Prices, Adjusted for Inter-state Price Variations*

(in rupees)

	1970–1	1972–3	1973–4	1977–8	1983	1986–7	1987–8	1989–90	1990–1	1992
Series 1										
Rural										
Kerala	380	399	429	467	540	553	549			
India	430	423	435	475	482	498	501			
Urban										
Kerala	554	571	560	575	695	700	750			
India	643	647	612	674	708	732	745			
Series 2										
Rural										
Kerala	374	n/a	432	519	602	653	662	606	628	708
India	424	n/a	421	491	507	562	557	588	569	540
Urban										
Kerala	546	n/a	542	579	699	695	777	842	896	807
India	634	n/a	579	658	689	723	738	774	756	773

Notes. In Series 1, the price deflators for states and India are consumer prices for all items as given in Jain and Minhas (1991) and Tendulkar and Jain (1993). In Series 2, the price deflators for states and India are consumer price indices for agricultural labourers for rural areas, and consumer price indices for industrial workers for urban areas. In both series, inter-state variations in price levels are accounted for by using indices of price levels in different states relative to the all-India level (all items, with 1970–1 as base) as given in Minhas and Jain (1990) for rural areas and Minhas, Jain, and Saluja (1990) for urban areas.

Sources. See Annexure.

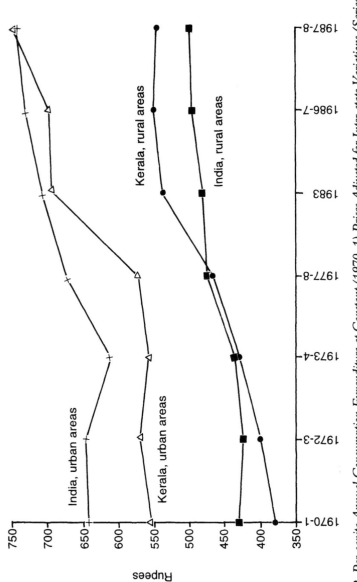

FIG. 2. Per-capita Annual Consumption Expenditure at Constant (1970–1) Prices Adjusted for Inter-state Variations (Series 1), Kerala and India, Rural and Urban Areas, 1970–1 to 1987–8

Note. The price deflators for states and India are consumer price indices for all items as given in Jain and Minhas (1991) and Tendulkar and Jain (1993). See Annexure for further notes.

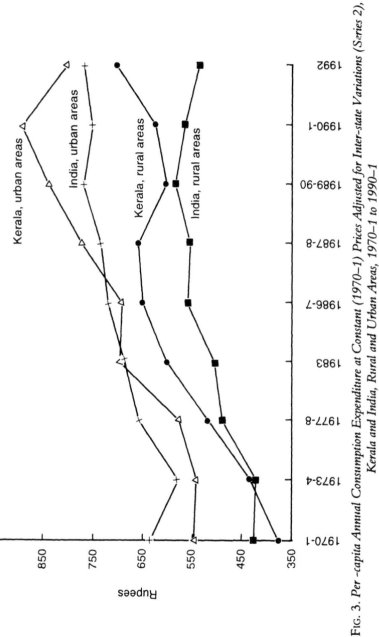

FIG. 3. *Per-capita Annual Consumption Expenditure at Constant (1970–1) Prices Adjusted for Inter-state Variations (Series 2), Kerala and India, Rural and Urban Areas, 1970–1 to 1990–1.*

Note. The price deflators for Kerala and India are consumer price indices for agricultural labourers for Kerala and India respectively. See Annexure for further notes.

Although it is not the objective of this paper to attempt a detailed analysis of the causes of industrial and agricultural stagnation in Kerala, or to work at some kind of blueprint for production and employment in the state, some general points can be made. First, market forces will not ensure that productive investment appears spontaneously; transformation in the spheres of production and employment requires public intervention. It requires the conscious policy attention of governments and intervention by political parties and mass organizations. Secondly, it is clear, and there is general scholarly consensus, that state-supported infrastructural investment is crucial for industrial and agricultural growth in Kerala. Thirdly, the potential for the expansion of skilled employment in Kerala is extraordinary. Unlike the rest of India, where schemes for mass employment are basically earth-work projects that involve unskilled work or work that requires low skills, Kerala is a region where even schemes for *mass* employment can draw on a labour force, rural and urban, whose members are literate, with high levels of political and social consciousness. Fourthly, any plan for rural economic growth in Kerala must consider the very promising opportunities for growth based on the mixed cultivation of diverse crops that require skilled crop management, with support (in respect for instance, of marketing) from public institutions and that involve new forms of production organization.

3. Kerala's Health Achievements

Historically, Kerala has done better than the rest of India in respect of literacy and key demographic indicators. In the eighties, Kerala's position in respect of some major health-transition and literacy indicators improved substantially, and Kerala began to achieve standards comparable with countries of the developing world that were medium-to-high achievers. In doing so, once again, it left the rest of India behind.[19]

3.1 Demographic Indicators

Kerala has been described as a 'unique' case among developing countries, a society where the 'health and demographic transitions

---

[19] See the comparative data in Shiva Kumar (1991).

have been achieved within a single generation', that is, after the formation of Kerala state (Krishnan, 1991, p. 1). Fertility and the birth rate have also fallen; the infant mortality rate, the mortality rate among children below the age of five years, and the death rate have declined; life expectancy at birth has risen; and the ratio of men to women in the population is characteristic of a society where there is not a systematic bias against the survival of girls and women in the population. Following Krishnan (1991), four indicators are taken here as representing the outcomes of the health and demographic transitions in Kerala: life expectancy at birth, the infant mortality rate, and the birth and death rates. Time series are available on these indicators from at least the early part of this century; caste-wise and class-wise data are difficult to come by, other than from micro-studies and from sources other than official ones, such as Zachariah et al. (1992).

TABLE 7. *Expectation of Life at Birth, Kerala and India*

(in years)

Row no.	Years	Males		Females	
		Kerala	India	Kerala	India
1.	1911–20	25.5	22.6	27.4	23.3
2.	1921–30	29.5	26.9	32.7	26.6
3.	1951–61	44.3	35.5	45.3	35.7
4.	1961–71	54.1	43.2	57.4	43.5
5.	1971–81	60.6	49.8	62.6	49.3
6.	1971–5	60.5	49.7	63.0	48.3
7.	1976–80	63.5	51.7	67.4	51.8
8.	1981–5	65.2	54.5	71.5	54.9
9.	1986–8	67.5	56.0	73.0	56.5
10.	1990–2	68.8	59.0	74.4	59.4

Sources. Rows 1–2: cited in Nag (1983), Table 3. Rows 3–5: Census of India, cited in Zachariah et al. (1992), ch. 3, Table 3. Rows 6–9: *Sample Registration System*, cited ibid. Row 10: Drèze and Sen (1995), Statistical Appendix, based on Sample Registration System data.

One of the key indicators of Kerala's health achievements is a high life expectancy at birth (Table 7). Life expectancy at birth in

Kerala is similar to the corresponding figures for developing countries classified as having achieved 'high human development' in *Human Development Report, 1993*. A man in Kerala can expect to live to be 69 years, or 10 years longer than the average Indian man, and a woman in Kerala can expect to live 74 years, or 15 years longer than the average Indian woman. Table 7 shows that life expectancy for men and women in Kerala has been higher than all-India life expectancy since at least the second decade of this century. In the post-independence period in Kerala, there was a sharp increase in life expectancy in the sixties over the previous decade, and again in the eighties compared with the seventies.[20]

TABLE 8. *Birth Rates, Kerala and India*

(per 1000)

Years	Kerala	India
1931–40	40.0	45.2
1941–50	39.8	39.9
1951–60	38.9	41.7
1970	31.6	36.8
1974	26.5	34.5
1977–9	25.7	33.1
1981–3	25.6	33.8
1983–5	23.7	33.6
1985–7	21.5	32.6
1987–9	20.7	31.5
1989–91	19.4	30.1
1990–2*	18.5	29.5

Note. * Provisional.

Sources. T.N. Krishnan (1976), Table 1; CMIE (1991), Table 2.11; *Sample Registration Bulletin*, January 1994, Table 11.

[20] With higher life expectancy, an issue that has important implications for the sustainability of Kerala's present path of development is the aging of its population and the need to provide health facilities and other kinds of social and economic support for senior citizens. On aging, and on the need for social provisioning for senior citizens and widows, see also Gulati (1992), P.K.B. Nayar (1994), Gulati and Gulati (1994), and Asari (1994).

The birth rate in Kerala is also much lower than the birth rate for all of India (see Table 8); it has been so for the whole period covered by our data (although the difference was marginal in the forties); the gap between the Kerala figure and the all-India figure was greater at the end-point in the time-series (1987–9) than at any time in the past; and the birth rate in Kerala declined substantially in the eighties.

Kerala's low birth rate is associated with comparatively high rates of birth control. The couple protection rate (CPR), which is the proportion of eligible couples that use long-term or temporary methods of birth control, increased sharply in Kerala over the eighties. Official data indicate that the CPR for the state rose from 36.8 per cent in 1981 to 60.9 per cent in 1990.[21] According to the National Sample Survey, the all-India CPR for rural areas was 24.9 per cent in 1986–7; rural Kerala (43.6 per cent) ranked third after Delhi (51.8 per cent) and Maharashtra (44.5 per cent). The all-India CPR for urban areas was 36.8 per cent; urban Kerala (48.4 per cent) ranked fourth after Delhi (52.7 per cent), Maharashtra (49.1 per cent), and Punjab (48.9 per cent) (National Sample Survey, 1992a). Low fertility rates in Kerala are also associated with a higher age at marriage among women in Kerala than elsewhere. The all-India average, which was 18.3 years in 1981, was substantially lower than the Kerala average, 21.8 years.[22] The average age of a woman at the time of first

[21] Official data cited in Zachariah et. al., 1992, ch. 5, Table 1. Results from a comparison of data from the NSS on the utilization of family planning services in 1986–7 with the 1990 Kerala data are also consistent with a record of a substantial increase in birth control in Kerala in the second half of the eighties (although comparisons of data sets from different sources must be made with caution).

[22] According to district-level primary data from three districts reported in Zachariah et al. (1992), the average age at marriage of women married in the period 1985–90 was 22.9 years in Ernakulam district (1975–80 average: 20.9 years); 20.9 years in Palakkad district (1975–80 average: 19.5 years); and 19 years in Malappuram district (Zachariah et al., 1992, ch. 6, p. 6, Table 3). The average age of marriage varied with the educational status of women and of men (women of higher formal educational status married later than others: Zachariah et al., 1992, ch. 6; Kannan et al., 1991, ch. 6). It varied with caste and religious status, and in the Zachariah et al. (1992) survey, Christian women and Nayar women had the highest age at marriage, followed by Izhava women and women of the scheduled castes and tribes. The lowest average age at marriage was among Muslim women (Zachariah et al., 1992, ch. 6, Table 6). Women from income and asset-poor families married, on average, at an earlier age than others (Kannan et al., 1991, ch. 6).

childbirth is also higher in Kerala than in any other state (Kannan et al., 1991, p. 87).

Improved child health and higher levels of education, particularly female education, are among the most important reasons for Kerala's low and declining birth rate and the general acceptance of a small family norm.[23] Caldwell and Caldwell (1985) conclude that parental education has a greater influence than income on fertility (p. 182). We shall return to these themes of the role of education and better child health.

The death rate in Kerala has declined steadily since the beginning of this century, and more rapidly than the Indian average (see Table 9). So has the infant mortality rate (Table 10). The infant mortality rate in Kerala in 1992 — 17 per thousand in rural areas and 13 per thousand in urban areas — put Kerala higher than the average for developing countries with 'high human development', among whom the average rate of infant mortality was 31 per thousand in 1991 (UNDP, 1993, p. 142). The decline in the infant mortality rate in Kerala has been associated with important improvements in pre-natal and post-natal health care and higher levels of institutional childbirth. As 1991 survey data from the Zachariah et al. (1992) study showed, for groups of people among whom there was immunization, hospitalization, and ante-natal and post-natal care, infant mortality rates of 6 to 7 per thousand were achieved in Kerala.[24]

T.N. Krishnan (1991) divides the post-1956 decline in infant mortality in Kerala into three periods: first, the decade after the formation of Kerala state, i.e. 1956 to 1966, when, according to Krishnan, 'infant mortality appears to have declined by about 43 per cent'; secondly, 1966 to 1975, when the decline 'appears to have slowed down'; and thirdly, from 1976 to 1988, when 'the decline again accelerated' (pp. 5–6). Krishnan associated changes in the first period with improvements in health care in Malabar and with greater control of infectious diseases; changes in the second period were associated with a levelling-off of the achievements of the first period; and the improvements in the third period were

---

[23] Caldwell (1986), Kannan et al. (1991), Zachariah and Patel (1982), and Raj (1994).

[24] For a comparative study of infant mortality in Tamil Nadu and Kerala, see Nagaraj (1986).

TABLE 9. *Death Rates, Kerala and India*

(per 1000)

Years	Kerala	India
1911–20	37	47
1921–30	32	36
1931–40	29	31
1941–50	18	27
1951–60	16	23
1961–70	11	18
1971–5	8.6	15.5
1976–80	7.3	13.9
1981–3	6.6	12.1
1983–5	6.5	12.1
1985–7	6.2	11.3
1987–9	6.2	10.7
1989–91	6.0	9.9
1990–2[*]	6.1	9.8

Note. [*] Provisional.
Sources. Nag (1983), Table 1; Zachariah et al. (1992), ch. 3, Table 2; *Sample Registration Bulletin*, January 1994, Table 11.

TABLE 10. *Infant Mortality Rates, Kerala and India*

(per 1000 live births)

Years	Kerala	India
1911–20	242	278
1921–30	210	228
1931–40	173	207
1941–50	153	192
1951–60	120	140
1961–70	66	114
1971	58	129

Table 10 cont'd

Years	Kerala	India
1972	63	139
1973	58	134
1974	54	126
1975	54	140
1976	56	129
1977	47	130
1978	42	127
1979	43	120
1980	40	114
1981	37	110
1982	30	105
1983	33	105
1984	29	104
1985	31	97
1986	27	96
1987	28	95
1988	28	94
1989	22	91
1990	17	80
1991[*]	16	80
1992[*]	17	79

Note. [*] Provisional; all–India data for 1991 and 1992 exclude Jammu and Kashmir.

Sources. 1911–20 to 1961–70: computed from Census of India volumes in Bhattacharjee and Shastri (1976), cited in Nag (1983), Table 4. 1971 to 1990: *Sample Registration System*, various issues, cited in Zachariah et al. (1992), ch. 3, Table 1. 1991 and 1992: *Sample Registration Bulletin*, January 1994, Table 8.

associated with improved ante-natal and post-natal care and more institutional childbirths.[25]

By the second half of the eighties, the pattern of infant mortality shifted away from the pattern characteristic of less-developed economies. Perinatal mortality (deaths in the first seven days) accounted for 67 per cent of all infant deaths, and deaths in the first twenty-eight days for 75 per cent of all infant deaths (data from Krishnan, 1991, pp. 6–7). Deaths after the first four weeks are attributed to what are considered 'exogenous' factors, which can, to a greater extent than deaths in the first four weeks, be controlled by appropriate medication (ibid.).[26]

According to NSS data from the 42nd round (1986–7), the proportion of 'domiciliary' births or births at home was lower in urban Kerala (7.6 per cent) than in any other region (the all-India proportion was 46.9 per cent); in respect of rural areas, Kerala (20 per cent) ranked second after Goa, Daman, and Diu (6.5 per cent). The all-India figure for rural areas was 80.5 per cent (National Sample Survey, 1991b). Citing more recent data from rural Kerala, T.N. Krishnan reports that institutional births and home births attended by trained professionals added up to 90 per cent of all births, up from 46 per cent in 1973 and 57 per cent in 1978 (Sample Registration Reports for rural Kerala, cited in Krishnan, 1991, p. 26, Table 6).

The proportion of infants and children who were vaccinated was much higher in Kerala than in India, immunization coverage improved substantially in the eighties, and all the data point to a noteworthy improvement in this respect in the last years of the eighties.[27] The survey of immunization in Kerala in 1989 and the

[25] Zachariah et al. (1992) provides more data on the decline of infant mortality in the second half of the eighties, and deals with the part played by state-sponsored programmes of infant and child immunization in this decline.

[26] On causes of infant death, Krishnan suggests that the proportion of 'death due to digestive disorders, disorders of the respiratory system, and fevers appears higher in Kerala. Secondly, the percentage of deaths due to prematurity appears lower in Kerala, and no deaths were recorded due to birth injury, malnutrition, cord infection, and malposition. Thirdly, Kerala does not report any deaths from typhoid, tetanus, and meningitis; these causes appear significant in India' (cited in Krishnan, 1991, p. 9).

[27] The main sources of data on immunization in Kerala in recent years are the National Sample Survey (1991b), from the 42nd round, conducted in 1986–7, a survey of immunization in 1989 that was part of a national review of the Universal

1991 survey in Ernakulam, Palakkad, and Malappuram reported in Zachariah et al., 1992 indicate rates of immunization that were high, substantially higher than the rates recorded by the NSS in 1986–7.

A noteworthy feature of studies of immunization of children in Kerala was that incomes were not the major determinant of immunization. From a study of child health in an urban slum and a more prosperous 'middle class' area in Thiruvananthapuram in 1987–8, Soman et al. (1990) concluded that although the morbidity load in the slum was greater, vaccine-preventable diseases against which immunization services were freely available did not pose a particular problem in either area. An all-Kerala study conducted by the Kerala Shastra Sahitya Parishad showed that the incidence of vaccine-preventable diseases was not significantly concentrated among families in low-income and low-asset categories (Kannan et al., 1991).

The Zachariah et al. (1992) study showed continuing differences in the infant mortality rate (IMR) between districts and sections of the population. The survey figures on IMR in 1985–9 were, per thousand, 9 for Ernakulam district, 34 for Palakkad district, and 28 for Malappuram district. The infant mortality rate was lowest among Christians (among Christians in Ernakulam district, according to the survey, the rate of infant mortality in 1980–9 was as low as 6 per thousand), and highest among Muslims; among Hindus, IMR was highest among people of the Izhava and scheduled castes (though it remains lower for those groups than for Muslims). With reference to these community-based data, it is worth making three points. First, health indicators among the worse-off in Kerala, though much lower than the Kerala average, are generally better than among their counterparts in other parts of the country. Secondly, performance indicators for groups such as scheduled castes and Muslims often pick up information that is, strictly speaking, relevant to *class* status, rather than exclusively to religious or caste status. Thirdly, there is some evidence that community-based differences have narrowed over time in recent years.[28]

Immunization Programme (cited in Krishnan, 1991), the survey of Zachariah et al. (1992), and the National Family Health Survey of 1992–3 (IIPS, 1994). The first and last sources have comparative data for individual states and for India.

[28] According to a study of households over the eighties by the Kerala Statistical Institute under its Development Monitoring System, disparities between people of different religions and castes in Kerala narrowed between 1981 and 1990 in respect of education, sanitation, housing, age structure, household size, the numbers of

Certain features of female empowerment in Kerala are vital to its achievements in respect of child health and health conditions in general; their importance really cannot be overemphasized.[29] Female literacy and girls' schooling are, of course, critical factors in Kerala's performance in this sphere. Caldwell and Caldwell (1985) identify girls' schooling as 'the single most important influence' on survivorship differentials (p. 183); they also note that the historical record does not show 'examples of economic development leading to low mortality levels where low levels of female education continue' (p. 184). Mari Bhat and Irudaya Rajan (1990) identify female literacy as the 'single most important factor explaining the demographic transition in Kerala' (p. 1979), and, in an earlier paper, P.G.K. Panikar wrote that 'the spread of education, especially among women in rural Kerala, was a crucial factor contributing to the high degree of awareness of health problems and fuller utilization of health facilities' (Panikar, 1979). Other factors associated with female empowerment and relevant to Kerala's better performance in child and general health than elsewhere that have been discussed in the literature include: a higher average age at marriage, higher rates of female employment in the organized sector, higher levels of health awareness and information among women, maternal utilization of the health system, and the greater decision-making roles of women in Kerala households. Of great importance also are social and cultural attitudes towards female survival: primary-data based studies in Kerala emphasize the absence of parental discrimination in providing health care to boys and girls.[30]

---

earners and dependents, electricity supply, and household and per-capita incomes (Somasekharan Nair, 1994).

[29] Caldwell (1986), Sen (1993), Caldwell and Caldwell (1985), Krishnan (1985, 1991), Moni Nag (1983, 1989), Raman Kutty (1987), Soman et al. (1990), Panikkar (1979), Mari Bhat and Irudaya Rajan (1990), Raman Kutty et al. (1993b), Kannan et al. (1991), are some of the contributors to the literature on women's agency and health in Kerala.

[30] Raman Kutty (1987), Soman et al. (1990). The absence of significant anti-female discrimination in child care is reflected in a female advantage in child survival in Kerala, which contrasts with the pronounced male advantage that can be found in many other parts of India (see e.g. *Sample Registration System 1991*, Table 7).

3.2 Morbidity

Recent trends in morbidity in Kerala have been the subject of some controversy. The controversy concerns three distinct issues, and I shall begin to discuss these issues by describing the position of one side with respect to each issue. First, some scholars hold that there has been no real reduction in the extent of illness in Kerala (Soman and Panikar, 1984; Kannan et al., 1991; Soman, 1993). Secondly, some scholars hold that there has been no real change in the pattern of disease in Kerala (Soman and Panikar, 1984; Kannan et al., 1991; Soman, 1993). Thirdly, some scholars hold that increased longevity does not indicate an improvement in the health of the population, that it represents the result of a trade-off between lower mortality and lower levels of illness (that Kerala has lower levels of mortality at the expense, as it were, of lower levels of morbidity) (Vaidyanathan, 1992; Gopalakrishna Kumar, 1993). The controversy has served the function of focusing attention on some crucial issues, in particular, the complex relationships between self-reported morbidity and some objective standard of illness, and between morbidity and mortality. Having said that, it is also true that the three arguments stated earlier lack convincing analytical and evidentiary bases.

In a book published by the Centre for Development Studies in 1984, P.G.K. Panikar and C.R. Soman (an economist and a medical doctor), noted that the annual compound rates of growth of in-patients and out-patients treated at government allopathic hospitals between 1956 and 1977 (6.62 per cent and 5.06 per cent) were higher than the rate of growth of population (2.34 per cent) during the same period, and concluded that there was no morbidity decline in Kerala during that period (Panikar and Soman, 1984, p. 145). Data across Indian states for the mid-seventies showed that reported illness was higher in Kerala than, say, Bihar (see Murray and Chen, 1992); this, too, was taken as evidence of higher illness in a state that had had conspicuous success in bringing down mortality rates and improving longevity (see, for example, Kumar, 1993). A similar point of view was expressed in the report of a major survey of health conditions in Kerala in the second half of the eighties: 'On the one hand the incidence of poverty and environment-related diseases has not been controlled, and on the other, the incidence of chronic degenerative diseases has increased' (Kannan et al., 1991, p. 68). Closely related to this proposition is the statement that the 'remarkable reduction in

mortality (in Kerala) was more due to medical interventions preventing death than by an effective reduction in the incidence of
preventable and communicable disease' (ibid.).

The argument is fundamentally flawed. Morbidity data such as
used by Panikar and Soman are based on reportage by patients
themselves (i.e. on a respondent's own assessment of his or her
medical status, rather than on medical examination), and higher
reportage in Kerala reflects a better health care system and higher
levels of health consciousness, as well as a greater awareness of
personal rights and of the demands that a citizen can legitimately
and successfully make of the health care system.[31] In the most
authoritative contemporary review of the issues involved, Christopher Murray and Lincoln Chen show that self-perceived morbidity rates in Kerala, while higher than the rest of India, are
substantially lower than in the United States, and they present data
on Cote d'Ivoire, Ghana, and Peru where rates of self-perceived
morbidity *rise* with income (Murray et al., 1992, cited in Murray
and Chen, 1992).[32] As the authors emphasize, studies that do not
distinguish adequately between self-perceived morbidity and the
objective illness-status of a society fail to recognize the possibility
that higher self-perceived morbidity may simply reflect 'more demanding health ideals and a social situation less willing to tolerate
illness' (ibid., p. 492). This situation does seem to apply in Kerala.
Indeed, there is no objective evidence of morbidity rates being
higher in Kerala than in other parts of India.

This paper argues that the provision of health facilities has an
outstanding effect on societies where social, economic, and political
conditions are such that people are ready to receive and make good
use of these facilities, and that Kerala in the eighties was such a
society (see Caldwell, 1986; Kannan et al., 1991). Literacy, political
awareness, and political action through political parties and mass

[31] See particularly Amartya Sen's (1984) discussion of self-perceived morbidity
among women during the Bengal famine, and Murray and Chen (1992).

[32] In his memoir of work with a Protestant medical mission in Travancore, the
medical missionary T.H. Somervell compares data in the first annual report of the
South Travancore Medical Mission in 1862 with the work done in a year in the late
thirties (Somervell, 1940), and notes that the number of patients treated rose from
2,629 in 1862 to 'over 200,000' in the late thirties. It would, of course, be pretty
much off the mark if these data were taken as evidence of an extraordinary increase
in morbidity in the region.

organizations were crucial for better health conditions because they helped make people sensitive to their rights and to the duties of the State to its citizens. People demanded more health facilities in Kerala than in the rest of India and they utilized them better.[33]

A question that remains open is whether the morbidity profile of Kerala is markedly different from that of other societies with similar levels of life expectancy and infant mortality. Although the conditions that existed in the early fifties, particularly in Malabar, have certainly improved, poor living environments are still an important cause of illness in Kerala, and income an important determinant of the kind of living environment that is available (this, too, must be qualified: the land reform that provided house sites has made better living environments available to a larger section of the rural population than elsewhere).[34] According to Soman (1993), infectious and parasitic diseases constitute a major share of the total illness of the population (p. 3). He writes that 'in-patient statistics from the SAT hospital, Thiruvananthapuram, indicate that in 1989, the five major causes for admission of children were acute respiratory illness, acute diarrhoeal disease, measles, bronchial asthma, and congenital heart disease.' This disease profile, according to him, is corroborated by statistics on out-patients and by material from community-based observations. Kabir and Krishnan (1991) also write that 'morbidity related to water and air-borne infections still dominate the health picture' (p. 25), and that 'a very high proportion of the morbidity in Kerala can be traced to the lack of protected water supply and the absence of proper toilet facilities within households' (ibid.). Has any other society achieved life-expectancy and

---

[33] Joan Mencher has written that 'in Kerala, if a Primary Health Centre were unmanned for a few days, there would be a massive demonstration at the nearest collectorate led by local leftists, who would demand to be given what they knew they were entitled to. . . . [T]he availability of doctors at a primary health facility, and public knowledge that something will be done at any time of the day or night if it is an emergency, has gone a long way to lowering child death' (Mencher, 1980,. pp. 1781–2; see the discussion in Caldwell, 1986, and also Antia, 1994).

[34] On the effect of the living environment on disease prevalence in village Malabar in the fifties, see Mayer (1952), pp. 13–14; on village-level health and sanitary conditions in a village in Ponnani taluk in the fifties and what he saw to be the 'progressive deterioration in the health of the villages', see Aiyappan (1965), pp. 100ff. and p. 104. On environmental factors as a cause of ill-health in Kerala, see Panikar and Soman (1984); also see Krishnan (1991) and Kabir and Krishnan (1991).

infant-mortality levels similar to Kerala while diseases such as these (diseases 'linked to underdevelopment and poverty') remained as prevalent as they are in Kerala? There is, at present, no scholarly work on this subject with reference to Kerala. In response to the question, T.N. Krishnan suggested to me that while changes have certainly occurred in the disease profile of the state, the pattern of diseases may well reflect the fact that the health transition in Kerala took place over a relatively short space of time.

3.3 Food Consumption and Nutrition

From the first half of the seventies, the National Nutrition Monitoring Bureau (NNMB, Hyderabad) has carried out nutrition surveys in different states. These include clinical and anthropometric studies as well as measurements of household food consumption. The food consumption data come from weighing the food consumed by a section of respondent households over a 24-hour period, as well as from recall by other respondent households of their food consumption over the 24 hours preceding the survey. The NNMB has now published comparative material, the results of surveys conducted in

TABLE 11. *Quantity of Monthly Consumption Per Person,*
Selected Food Items, Kerala and India, 1987–8

Item	Rural		Urban	
	Kerala	India	Kerala	India
Cereals, gram, cereal substitutes (kg)	12.43	14.64	10.29	11.29
Pulses and pulse products (kg)	0.40	0.84	0.55	0.96
Milk (l)	2.16	3.23	3.07	4.33
Edible oils (kg)	0.26	0.31	0.36	0.53
Meat (kg)	0.19	0.10	0.20	0.21
Eggs (nos.)	1.73	0.52	2.93	1.46
Fresh fish (kg)	1.06	0.15	1.59	0.17
Fresh fruit (kg)	4.48	0.68	5.12	1.28

Source. National Sample Survey (1991c), pp. S-105, S-127, S-136, S-158,

1975–9 and 1988–90. Data are presented for seven — and for some variables, eight — states separately, and for all states and respondents combined. The Kerala studies covered households in 7 districts, 979 households in 106 villages in 1975–9, and 835 households in 91 villages in 1988–90. The other source of data on food consumption is, of course, the National Sample Survey (NSS). The main features of the NSS data are presented in Tables 6, 11, and 18.

According to the NNMB data, food consumption per consumption unit in Kerala in 1975–9 was the lowest among all the states surveyed, and in 1988–90 was the lowest among all states but one, Tamil Nadu. Kerala was also well below the recommended daily intake in respect of protein consumption, energy consumption, and the consumption of micronutrients (see Tables 12, 13, and 14). At the same time, according to the NNMB data, Kerala was the *only* state in which consumption improved over the two periods in terms of *both* anthropometric and intake indicators. The 1983 NSS data also suggested that Kerala was at the bottom of the table in respect of food intake (Soman, 1993, p. 7), and the reported gap in energy intake was, according to Soman, 20 per cent in adults and over 30 per cent in children (ibid.).

TABLE 12. *Average Consumption of Selected Food Items, Kerala and Combined Data for Seven States, 1975–9 and 1988–90*

(in grams per consumption unit per diem)

Item	RDI	Years	Kerala	Combined states
Cereals	460	1975–9	341	504
		1988–90	369	490
Pulses	40	1975–9	14	36
		1988–90	18	32
Green leafy vegetables	40	1975–9	4	8
		1988–90	9	11
Other vegetables	60	1975–9	81	51
		1988–90	65	49
Roots and tubers	50	1975–9	135	48
		1988–90	63	40

Table 12 cont'd

Item	RDI	Years	Kerala	Combined states
Milk and milk products	150	1975–9	47	100
		1988–90	87	96
Fats and oils	20	1975–9	4	12
		1988–90	14	13
Sugar and jaggery	30	1975–9	19	23
		1988–90	32	29

Notes. 1. The seven states in which surveys were conducted in both periods and for which we have the data which are pooled here are: Andhra Pradesh, Gujarat, Karnataka, Kerala, Madhya Pradesh, Maharashtra, and Tamil Nadu.
  2. The surveys covered only rural areas.
  3. RDI = recommended daily intake.
Source. National Nutrition Monitoring Bureau (1991), Table 3.1, p. 49.

TABLE 13. *Households for which Protein and Energy Consumption were Adequate as a Proportion of all Surveyed Households: Kerala and Combined Data for Seven States, 1975–9 and 1988–90*

(in per cent)

Status	1975–9		1988–90	
	Kerala	Combined states	Kerala	Combined states
Protein-adequate	69.7	88.2	71.5	83.5
Energy-adequate	39.0	58.0	39.7	53.5

Notes. 1. The seven states in which surveys were conducted in both periods and for which we have the data which are pooled here are: Andhra Pradesh, Gujarat, Karnataka, Kerala, Madhya Pradesh, Maharashtra, and Tamil Nadu.
  2. The surveys covered only rural areas.
Source. National Nutrition Monitoring Bureau (1991), Table 4, p. 50.

TABLE 14. *Average Daily Consumption of Nutrients per Consumption Unit: Kerala and Combined Data for Seven States, 1975–9 and 1988–90*

Nutrient (units)	RDI	Years	Kerala	Combined states
Protein (grams)	60.0	1975–9	46.4	62.9
		1988–90	52.9	82.5
Energy (kcal)	2350	1975–9	1978	2340
		1988–90	2140	2283
Calcium (mg)	400	1975–9	507	590
		1988–90	608	556
Iron (mg)	28.0	1975–9	20.8	30.9
		1988–90	22.0	28.4
Vitamin A (µg)	600	1975–9	176	257
		1988–90	297	294
Vitamin C (mg)	40	1975–9	67	37
		1988–90	47	37
Thiamine (mg)	1.20	1975–9	0.72	1.60
		1988–90	0.72	1.53
Riboflavin (mg)	1.40	1975–9	0.72	0.97
		1988–90	0.74	0.94
Niacin (mg)	16.0	1975–9	11.5	15.7
		1988–90	11.8	15.5

Notes. 1. The seven states in which surveys were conducted in both periods and for which we have data which are pooled here are: Andhra Pradesh, Gujarat, Karnataka, Kerala, Madhya Pradesh, Maharashtra, and Tamil Nadu.

2. The surveys covered only rural areas.

3. RDI = recommended daily intake.

Source. National Nutrition Monitoring Bureau (1991), Table 4, p. 50.

Those were the intake data; the NNMB results on nutritional outcomes showed Kerala in a better light. In terms of (i) age-wise mean anthropometric evidence (height, weight, arm circumference, fat-fold at triceps); (ii) clinical signs of nutritional deficiency in children; and (iii) the classification of children according to nutritional grades in 1988–90, Kerala does markedly better than the other states (see Tables 15 and 16). The low incidence of 'severe' child undernourishment in Kerala by the end of the eighties (see Table 15) is particularly noteworthy.

TABLE 15. *Distribution of Children aged One Year to Five Years by Nutritional Grades: Kerala and Combined Data for Seven States, 1975–9 and 1988–90*

(in per cent)

Group/ Year	Region	Nutritional grade			
		Normal	Mild	Moderate	Severe
Children					
1975–9	Kerala	7.5	35.7	46.5	10.3
	Combined states	5.9	31.6	47.5	15.0
1988–90	Kerala	17.7	47.4	32.9	2.0
	Combined states	9.9	37.6	43.8	8.7
Boys					
1975–9	Kerala	7.5	32.4	49.9	10.2
	Combined states	5.3	30.3	49.8	14.6
1988–90	Kerala	16.6	47.7	33.3	2.4
	Combined states	8.9	37.8	44.3	9.0
Girls					
1975–9	Kerala	7.4	39.0	43.2	10.4
	Combined states	6.7	33.1	44.9	15.3
1988–90	Kerala	18.8	47.1	32.5	1.6
	Combined states	10.9	37.3	42.8	9.0

Notes. 1. The seven states in which surveys were conducted in both periods and for which we have data which are pooled here are: Andhra Pradesh, Gujarat, Karnataka, Kerala, Madhya Pradesh, Maharashtra, and Tamil Nadu.

2. The surveys covered only rural areas.

Source. National Nutrition Monitoring Bureau (1991), Tables 9.1, 9.2, 9.3, pp. 55–7.

TABLE 16. *Prevalence of Signs of Nutritional Deficiency in Pre-school Children: Kerala and Combined Data for Seven States, 1975–9 and 1988–90*

(in per cent)

Nutritional deficiency signs	Survey period	Kerala	Combined states
Oedema	1975–9	–	0.4
	1988–90	–	0.1
Marasmus	1975–9	0.2	1.3
	1988–90	0.1	0.6
Two or more signs of PEM	1975–9	0.2	1.2
	1988–90	–	0.2
Bitot's spots	1975–9	0.1	1.8
	1988–90	0.5	0.7
Angular stomatitis	1975–9	1.6	5.7
	1988–90	–	5.7
No apparent deficiency	1975–9	91.7	80.7
	1988–90	94.5	83.5

Notes. 1. The seven states in which surveys were conducted in both periods and for which we have data which are pooled here are: Andhra Pradesh, Gujarat, Karnataka, Kerala, Madhya Pradesh, Maharashtra, and Tamil Nadu.

2. The surveys covered only rural areas.

3. PEM = protein energy malnutrition.

Source. National Nutrition Monitoring Bureau (1991), Table 10, p. 59.

One attempt to resolve this apparent paradox of comparatively low intake and comparatively high nutrition (not to speak of better health outcomes as measured by other indicators) has been by C.R. Soman. According to him, 'the only possible explanation is that [in Kerala] the nutrients are better utilized, quite possibly because of the positive interaction between health care and nutrition.'

The part played by the health care system and the health environment in Kerala is, no doubt, of enormous importance in determining the nutritional status of Kerala's people. There are, however, some issues that Soman's explanation does not consider.

First, there could well be problems with the data on consumption. The NNMB data, for instance, are problem-ridden in terms of the stratification of the sample at the village level. There is nothing in the survey method that ensures the appropriate representation of different socio-economic strata in the villages surveyed. The NNMB account of its sampling design deals with this (crucial) issue thus: 'The selection of households will be done by the team on the spot by random sampling after consultation with the village head' (NNMB, 1991, p. 65).

There may also be important problems of measurement with the NSS data. In the seventies, scholars of the Centre for Development Studies showed that consumption in Kerala was underestimated because the National Sample Surveys did not capture the consumption of cereal substitutes — in particular, tapioca — by people in Kerala (see Centre for Development Studies, 1977). That problem may well persist in some form or other: there are problems of capturing, by means of standard all-India questionnaires, every item in a diet in a region where diets can be very different from other regions (is, for instance, the specific range of vegetables, fruit, and tubers that is to be found in a Kerala diet represented adequately in the questionnaire; is the consumption of dried fish measured accurately?). There is likely to be another data problem: people eat outside the household and in eating-houses a great deal in Kerala (large numbers of agricultural labourers, men and women, for instance, eat a morning meal in tea-shops or small restaurants), and this consumption may not adequately be recorded in questionnaire-based data on aggregate household consumption.[35] In my opinion, given these problems of measurement, it has not conclusively been established that intakes (and particularly intakes among the poor), are significantly lower in Kerala than in the rest of the country.

Secondly, the quantitative data may hide some important features of the composition of diets in Kerala. There are marked differences in the component parts of household consumption in Kerala and India.[36] According to data from the 43rd round of the National Sample Survey, the average household diet in Kerala was lower in

---

[35] Thomas Isaac, personal communication. Robin Jeffrey (1992) cites material from the literature on working people eating out in tea-shops; he also reports that, in 1971, there were four times more tea-shops per head in Kerala than other states (pp. 210–11).

[36] According to one assessment, 'food and nutrition security in Kerala depends on two factors: the public distribution system and the diversity of its people's diets' (M.S. Swaminathan, interview, May 1992).

cereals and cereal substitutes, pulses, milk and milk products, and edible oil, and higher in meat, fish, eggs, and fruit than the average household diet in India (see Table 11). The NNMB data suggest a decline in the intake of cereals and cereal substitutes (consistent with the decline in tapioca production), and an increase in the consumption of milk (a non-traditional item), edible oils, and pulses.[37]

Thirdly, per-capita consumption data presented by the NSS and the NNMB are, respectively, household per-capita consumption (and consumer expenditure) and total household consumption divided by the number of consumption units in the household. In other words, in both cases, the data collected are for whole households, and the figures for individuals ignore intra-household inequalities in distribution. If intra-household distribution in respect of consumption in Kerala is better than elsewhere (and, from the information on female survival, that seems reasonable to assume), a consequence is likely to be better nutritional outcomes for given average intakes.

3.4   The Public Distribution System

Kerala is a food deficit state; more than fifty per cent of the cereals consumed by the people of Kerala comes from outside the state.[38] It also has the best public distribution system of India's states, and the availability of food from the public distribution system has been, as can be expected, a major factor in providing nutrition to the income-poor.

Kerala's network of ration and fair-price shops is widespread, covering towns and villages. A substantial proportion (relative to the rest of India) of the essential consumer purchases of the people are made in fair-price and ration shops. Ration shops provide rice, whole wheat flour, cooking oil, and kerosene at about half the market rate. There are bonus issues at festival times, at Christmas, Onam, Easter,

[37] Panikar and Soman (1984) reported a 'mild' qualitative improvement in diets in Kerala, particularly with respect to the consumption of fish (p. 26); data from a village survey in the late eighties showed that 96 per cent of households in the village ate fish 'regularly' (Raman Kutty, 1987, p. 77, Table 3.10). It is not clear, though, whether the increase in fish consumption has been sustained in recent years.

[38] In 1985, of the total amount of rice and wheat available for consumption in Kerala, 62 per cent came from outside the state (Koshy et al., 1989, Table 2.7).

ld, and so on. Shops of the state-run Maveli Stores chain sell pulses, spices, and condiments and a wide range of other consumer goods.

The public distribution system in Kerala was first established during World War II, in response to the food crisis of 1942–3 (Isaac and Ramachandran, forthcoming). The food crisis of 1942–3 in Malabar can, I think, be characterized as a famine (in any case, there were mass deaths during this period). If the figure for all deaths (in particular, cholera-related deaths in 1943) that I have put together from news reports of the time is correct, almost one per cent of the population died from hunger and epidemic disease. Data from the distinguished medical surveys of the Servants of India Society for Cochin and from the same surveys and the Coir Workers Union in Alleppey district suggest that there were local, taluk-wide food crises leading to mass deaths in Shertallai taluk in Travancore and Cochin–Kanayannur taluk in Cochin.[39]

In Malabar and Travancore, the public distribution system was directly the consequence of mass action and government response to such action during the period of food crisis. In Malabar, after 1942, peasant organizations, trade unions, and other mass organizations fought for compulsory procurement from landlords and for distribution through fair-price shops. People's Food Committees, which drew on wide sections of the population, were set up in most localities, and women in large numbers joined the struggle for food. Because of this pressure, and because of the administrative need of the British government itself, ration shops were set up; they were subsequently converted into producers' and consumers' cooperative societies.[40] The governments of Travancore and Cochin brought the distribution of foodgrain under government control in 1943.[41]

[39] See Sivaswamy et al. (1946a, b, and c). There were reported to have been 30,000 cholera deaths in Malabar alone in June–August 1943, about 1 per cent of the population (Namboodiripad, 1943). The Servants of India Society reported 90,000 excess deaths in Travancore during the food crisis. In respect of Cochin, the Society concluded that 'there was famine in Cochin–Kanayannur taluk in 1943–4, severe malnutrition in many places, and food distress in many others in the state of Cochin' (Sivaswamy et al., 1946a, p. v).

[40] E.M.S. Namboodiripad, interview, April 1992. On activism on the food front during this period, see the despatches from Kerala in *People's War* between 1942 and 1945, Nayanar (1982), Gopalan (1974), and Karat (1977).

[41] See Famine Inquiry Commission (1945). See also the Namboodiripad despatches in *People's War* (Namboodiripad, 1942, 1943, 1944 are a selection); Jeffrey (1992), pp. 83ff.

In Travancore, the coir workers' union was active in the struggle for rationing (see Isaac, 1984); the struggle for food was also an important factor in the formation of agricultural labour unions in Travancore (Jose George, 1980, p. 56). A very significant feature of the food crisis in Cochin was the establishment of rural rationing in February 1943, described by K.G. Sivaswamy of the Servants of India Society as the first of its kind in India.

The system of public distribution of food and rationing survived the war. In most parts of the Madras Presidency, the public distribution system was dismantled after the war and in the early years of independence. In Malabar (and the rest of Kerala), people's organizations fought to ensure that the system was not abolished.

A widespread, effective public distribution network in Kerala is, however, a post-1957 phenomenon. Among the most important spheres of activity of the first Communist Ministry was the food economy: the Government of Kerala negotiated the supply of foodgrain to Kerala with the Government of India, and established locality-based food committees to supervise the system of food distribution (see Namboodiripad, 1994b). An important change in the system came in 1964, during an extended period of President's Rule in Kerala, when the government abolished the southern food zone. Food all but ceased to come into Kerala, there was a sharp rise in food prices, and the Congress Party could not control the state-wide people's protest movement. Chief Ministers of the states of India met in New Delhi on 26 October 1964. At that meeting, it was decided to begin what was called 'informal rationing' in Kerala from 1 November 1964, 'so as to ensure an equitable distribution of the available supplies at a specified price' (Government of Kerala, 1989a, p. 10). The Government of India undertook to supply grain to the public distribution system in the state, and it was agreed that it 'would not be generally necessary for the State Government to procure any quota directly from other States'.[42] There was a major expansion of the rationing system after 1964 (Koshy et al., 1989); this expansion continued in the eighties (see Table 17).[43]

---

[42] Government of Kerala (1989a), p. 10; see also Koshy et al. (1989), p. 9.

[43] An important legal measure in respect of the public food-distribution system in Kerala was the Kerala Rationing Order of 1966, which specified procedures for running the system (for discussion, see Mooij, 1994).

TABLE 17. Classification of Ration Shops by
Year of Establishment: Kerala State, 1987

(in per cent)

Years	Proportion of ration shops established in the specified period
Pre-independence	1.6
1956–60	7.9
1961–7	27.6
1968–73	13.4
1974–9	25.2
1980–5	16.5
1985–7	4.7
Not known	3.1
All shops	100.0

Source. Survey of 127 ration shops from all districts, in Koshy et al. (1989), p. 136, Table 5.3.

There is a two-level system of public distribution of essential commodities in Kerala. The Civil Supplies Department of the Government of Kerala administers public distribution activity in the state. It runs a network of authorized ration shops; and rice, wheat, sugar, cooking oil, and kerosene are the main commodities distributed through the ration system. The state depends on central allotments for the items distributed through the ration system. The Kerala State Civil Supplies Corporation, a statutory state-run body established in 1974, operates the second level of the public distribution system. It procures rice, wheat products, sugar, pulses, vegetables, and a wide range of consumer goods independently from the open market, and sells it through its own network of 'Maveli' stores and supermarkets (Koshy et al., 1989, pp. 7–8).

The state government recovers the operating costs of the public distribution system (P.S. George, 1979, 1985; Narayana, 1992). The central government, however, provides a subsidy to cover the difference between the issue price and the total cost of procurement. Food subsidies accounted for around 5 per cent of central government expenditures on the revenue account in most years, and around 20–30 per cent of central government subsidies (Narayana, 1992). P.S. George's assessment of the functioning of the public distribution system is that the gains to producers and consumers from the public distribution system in Kerala 'exceeded the direct cost of government subsidy' (P.S. George, 1979, p. 61).

Kerala is the only state that has near-universal rationing; all families that do not have land holdings big enough to meet household requirements have the right to a ration card (and a ration card is an important document of household identification in Kerala). About 90 per cent of households had ration cards in 1991 (Kannan, 1993, p. 28).[44] In January 1992, there were 13,028 authorized retail outlets, one for every 389 households (Government of Kerala, 1992).

Commodities distributed through the public distribution system form a major part of the consumption basket of households in Kerala.[45] As Table 18 indicates, food purchases from the public distribution system in Kerala account for a high share of total purchases (e.g. around 50 per cent for rice, and more than 90 per cent in the case of wheat); these purchases are large, in comparison with the corresponding all-India figures, in all expenditure groups; and the pattern of purchases from the public distribution system in Kerala is distinctly progressive, much more so than in India as a whole.

In 1986–7, fair-price shops in Kerala sold 59.4 kilograms of rice per capita (Koshy et al., 1989). By 1991, according to one calculation, the average amount of rice and wheat bought per consumer from the ration system was 69.6 kg (Kannan, 1993). By way of comparison, in 1989, the quantity of foodgrain per person per year distributed through the public distribution system was calculated to be 5 kg in Haryana, 6 kg in Uttar Pradesh, 8 kg in Bihar, 9 kg in Madhya Pradesh, 23 kg in West Bengal, and 52 kg in Kerala (Geetha and Suryanarayana, 1993).

---

[44] According to Koshy et al. (1989), more than 97 per cent of households in Kerala were covered by the rationing system in 1986–7 (p. 9).

[45] Households with ration cards were entitled to the following food items in 1987 (per adult, with lower entitlements — about half as large — for children): wheat, 240 grams per day; rice, 220 grams per day (with an additional entitlement of 5 kilograms per month per card, subject to availability); sugar, 450 grams per month; and palmolein (edible oil), 3 kilograms per month. See Koshy et al. (1989), p. 9.

TABLE 18. *Share of Purchases from the Public Distribution System, by Household Monthly Per-capita Consumption Expenditure Category, Selected Commodities: Kerala and India, 1986–7*

(in per cent)

Area/ fractile group	Rice		Wheat		Edible oil		Sugar		Kerosene	
	Kerala	India	Kerala	India	Kerala	India	Kerala	India	Kerala	India
Rural										
0–10	64.9	16.9	94.7	9.5	8.9	11.0	69.7	54.6	95.8	51.7
10–20	58.6	15.3	93.8	9.7	9.1	11.2	64.9	56.2	96.0	4.9
20–40	51.6	17.6	94.8	14.0	7.5	12.7	63.0	51.7	93.4	47.7
40–60	51.9	15.5	94.3	12.8	6.7	10.9	56.2	47.9	95.2	47.6
60–80	47.1	17.9	95.3	14.1	8.4	12.1	51.3	77.2	90.4	47.0
80–90	40.7	17.8	91.9	13.4	9.4	9.6	41.6	37.3	87.1	47.4
90–100	38.8	16.3	76.5	13.6	15.3	8.4	40.0	32.8	83.6	47.4
All	51.4	16.8	92.0	12.6	8.9	11.0	55.5	61.2	92.1	25.9
Urban										
0–10	54.4	21.5	96.1	12.3	10.6	17.4	60.8	58.4	96.6	55.4
10–20	54.1	21.0	100.0	16.6	15.8	16.3	66.3	54.5	84.7	58.3
20–40	51.5	18.5	97.8	18.1	18.8	16.1	56.9	51.3	91.1	57.3
40–60	45.2	19.6	87.3	23.6	9.4	16.0	47.4	45.9	76.6	60.9
60–80	38.9	18.2	90.3	20.0	10.6	14.0	43.0	42.9	87.2	60.1
80–90	37.5	16.7	93.6	22.1	12.9	12.8	44.3	40.7	55.0	60.7
90–100	23.6	14.7	72.2	19.5	21.6	8.3	27.4	36.3	80.3	60.7
All	46.2	19.0	91.5	19.3	13.6	14.5	50.4	46.8	83.0	59.3

Source. National Sample Survey (1990).

Data from the 1987 survey of 806 beneficiaries of the public distribution system (Koshy et al., 1989) provide useful information on the utilization of the system, and highlight the fact that the poor use the system more than the rich. About 85 per cent of consumers met all or part of their rice requirements from fair-price shops. Beneficiaries with monthly incomes of less than Rs 100 bought 71 per cent of the amount of rice for which they were eligible; the corresponding figure for beneficiaries with monthly incomes of more than Rs 3000 was 6 per cent. In general, low-income consumers did not have serious complaints regarding rice quality and did not complain that ration shops were overcrowded; 70 per cent of respondents did not have serious complaints about the weights and measures used in the shops, and 96 per cent said that there was no problem of availability with respect to rice and wheat. All respondents wanted the range of commodities available through the system to be extended. Transferring ration cards was not, in the assessment of the researchers, a serious problem; in fact, most transfers were from high-income beneficiaries who loaned their cards to beneficiaries with lower incomes.[46]

The system of comprehensive food subsidy in Kerala, which provides crucial income and nutrition support to its people, has been, by all accounts, highly successful. An important feature of the food system in Kerala has been public awareness of matters relating to the food-distribution system (see Mooij, 1994), and any attempt to restrict the public distribution system is likely to meet with strong political resistance, though that is certainly the policy of the present central government.[47]

3.5 Sex Ratios

A key indicator — and perhaps the most illustrative summary measure — of the historical status of women in Kerala, and of the influence

---

[46] See Koshy et al. (1989), pp. 74, 78–9, 81, 84–5, 103. The data in the preceding paragraph refer to purchases in fair-price, or ration, shops. They do not include grain and other commodities bought at the Maveli outlets of the Civil Supplies Corporation. As mentioned, a very wide range of commodities is sold in these shops, and they have had a very important influence on the general price level in the state.

[47] See, in this context, Kannan (1993) and Krishnaji (1994); on current policy statements in respect of the public food-distribution system, see Swaminathan (1994). Those proposing restrictions on the public distribution system have, of course, focused on targeting, on excluding a section of households from the benefits of a public distribution system. In a recent paper on food security in Kerala, Krishnaji (1994) warned that 'no matter what the Centre decides, whether to wholly dismantle the public distribution system or severely curtail its scope and coverage, it will pose serious problems of financial and economic management for Kerala'. On welfare losses caused by shifts from universal schemes to targeted schemes, see Cornia and Stewart (1993).

of what Robin Jeffrey calls the 'culture of old Kerala' on socio-economic development in Kerala, is the sex ratio, measured here as females per thousand males in the population (see Table 19).

TABLE 19. *Females Per Thousand Males:*
Kerala and Constituent Regions, 1820–1991

Year	Travancore	Cochin	Malabar	Kerala
1820	983	1033		
1836	962	992		
1849		1003		
1851–2			983	
1856–7			974	
1858		1000		
1861–2			994	
1866–7			994	
1871			992	
1875	1010	988		
1881	1006	—	1014	
1891	982	989	1018	
1901	981	1004	—	
1911	980	—	1037	
1921	971	1027	—	
1931	987	1043	1059	
1941	993	1042	1067	
1951	996	1046	1056	
1961	998	1039	1039	1021
1971	1003	1024	1024	1016
1981	1022	1046	1035	1032
1991	1035	1043	1043	1040

Notes. 1. — indicates years for which I was not able to get the data.
2. Blanks indicate years in which censuses were not held in the administrative divisions, or years in which the administrative division did not exist.
3. On the modern districts that constitute the regions of Malabar, Cochin, and Travancore, see footnote 3 in the text.

Source. Censuses of Cochin, Travancore, Madras Presidency, and India. Data for Travancore in 1820 from Ward and Conner (1816–20), p. 111. Data for Travancore in 1836 from Horsley (1860), p. 11.

We know that although more males are born than females, if the living environment is not hostile to female survival, more females survive in a population than males. The sex ratio in Japan was 1030 in 1990 and the average for industrial countries in 1990 was 1060. The sex ratio in Kerala was 1040 in 1991, and has been more than 1000 at every census after the formation of the state. For two component parts of Kerala, Cochin and Malabar, sex ratios have been greater than 1000 all of this century, and possibly also for much of the nineteenth century.[48]

With respect to the three regions that were brought together into the single state of Kerala in 1957, it is noteworthy that Malabar does best with respect to the sex ratio; the sex ratio in Malabar was higher than the ratios in Cochin and Travancore at every census but one since 1881. The case of Travancore, commonly thought to be the high-flier on socio-cultural indicators, is interesting and needs further investigation. In the modern period, the sex ratio in Travancore was the lowest of the three component regions of the state, and the sex ratio in the districts that comprised old Travancore crossed 1000 only at the Census of 1971 (and continued to be lower in 1991 than in the districts that comprised Cochin and Malabar).

Nineteenth-century observers of population didn't fail to see that the relatively high proportion of females to males in the population was a distinguishing feature of Kerala's demography and of local society. Ward and Conner noted this in the report of their well-known survey, which was carried out from 1816 to 1820. Their point of reference, and the standard that they perceived as representative of the usual order of things was, unsurprisingly, early nineteenth-century Europe. They wrote that 'among the Nairs, particularly in Cochin, the females are most numerous, and the circumstance can only be ascribed to the singular economy of the people; the difference varies with locality; the excess is in some instances considerable and on the whole almost inverts the usual order' (Ward and Conner, 1816–20, p. 109). There is a footnote at this point that seeks to explain the 'usual order'; it reads: 'In

---

[48] The nineteenth-century data are not unproblematic; the important problem with regard to the calculation of sex ratios is that there may have been gaps in enumeration. C. Achyuta Menon, the Superintendent of Census Operations in Cochin in 1891, for instance, noted that 'the persons left uncounted in an Indian Census are chiefly to be found among the females and the low castes' (see Census of Cochin 1891 (1893), pp. 45ff., on the nature of omissions in the Census).

Europe the males are to females as one hundred to ninety-seven, with the Nair here in the proportion of one hundred and ten, to one hundred and twelve.'

The Census Superintendent of Travancore at the Census of 1875 also sought to explain the preponderance of females in the population at the Census:

More boys are born [in Travancore] than girls, though it would appear that mortality is greater among boys than girls, a circumstance which changes the relative proportion of the sexes when they survive to attain an adult age. The causes of this disparity in the relative positions of the sexes when viewed in connection with their ages, it is difficult to discover, while to ascribe it to the partiality of parents in bestowing greater care on their *female* issues, will be hazarding an opinion based on insufficient data, though it is a fact that among [matrilineal] people a female child is prized more highly than a male one (Census of Travancore, 1875 (1876), pp. 139–40).

Although the idea that there was a marked preference for girls and that girls were much better taken care of than boys in matrilineal families is, I think, overstated (relatively high levels of female *survival*, can appear to be female *preference* when the observer's outlook and social background were patriarchal), it is of note that the explanation for the preponderance of females in Travancore in 1875 is sought in the fact that the marriage and inheritance system of a significant section of the people was matrilineal (more on that issue further down).

3.6 Sectional Deprivation

Public provisioning in the spheres of health and education has been more effective in Kerala than elsewhere, and better distributed between men and women, between social groups, and between regions of the state. This does not mean that traditional patterns of inequality and deprivation have been eliminated. Important differences between traditionally disadvantaged social groups and regions — people of the scheduled castes and tribes and the less developed regions of old Malabar — and the rest of the population persist.[49]

[49] See also Gulati (1992) and Kerala State Women's Development Corporation (KSWDC) (1990) on deprivation among women workers, particularly of the scheduled castes and tribes, and in low-technology occupations (e.g. coir, cashew, and bamboo work, and stone-crushing).

There are at least three distinct pockets of deprivation in contemporary Kerala, three social groups that are substantially behind
the rest of the state in respect of living standards.

The first group consists of traditional coastal fishing communities.[50] According to a study by John Kurien, the rate of infant mortality among fishing communities in Thiruvananthapuram district in
1981 was 85 per thousand (John Kurien, 1993b, p. 40; see also Jessy
Thomas, 1981). The sex ratio among traditional fishing communities
was 972 women per 1000 men (ibid., p. 41). This study also presents
evidence of environmental deprivation in coastal villages, including
'overcrowding, lack of facilities for faeces disposal and scarcity of
drinking water', contributing to a high prevalence of respiratory
diseases, skin infections, diarrhoeal disorders, and hookworm infes-
tations (p. 40). A 1985 study of a fishing community in Vizhinjam
in Thiruvananthapuram district (Vimala Kumary, 1991) has evidence
of infant mortality rates that are, by any standard, very high. The
study reports that the infant mortality was 123 per 1000 live births
(129 among Muslim families and 116 among Christian families).
The deaths were related to the lack of 'timely medical help to infants',
to 'food prejudices' during pregnancy and lactation (p. 159), and to
conditions of poor hygiene. Of the deaths, 50 to 60 per cent were in
families that had had more than 5 live births. The infant mortality
rate among illiterate families was double the rate among literates.

The second such deprived social group is made up of the people
of the scheduled tribes of the north Kerala highlands. There is much
less information on this social group than on the fishing communities. As the subsequent section shows, rates of literacy among
some tribal groups were lower than in the state as a whole (on
deprivation, particularly educational deprivation, among people of
the scheduled tribes of north Kerala, see S.S. Sreekumar, 1994 and
Sebastian, 1994). In 1993, a series of articles in the daily Malayalam
newspaper *Deshabhimani* pointed to an appalling situation in Wayanad district. Noolpuzha panchayat, Wayanad district, has 70 tribal
'colonies' or settlements. In the six settlements for which the *Deshabhimani* correspondent had information, 28 people died of hunger-
related causes between July 1993 and 6 December 1993. Most of
the dead were young men.

The third such group is the new underclass of Tamil migrant

---

[50] See particularly John Kurien (1993a, 1993b, 1993c, 1994).

workers in Kerala (this does not include Tamil plantation workers, who have worked in Kerala for generations). The workers come in search of unskilled or low-skill manual jobs, particularly non-agricultural jobs (which the educated unemployed in Kerala do not do), or are self-employed at low-income occupations. Their numbers include child workers, particularly young boys. Many such workers are homeless, and many live in exceptionally deprived and unhygienic conditions in new slums in Kerala's towns and villages. There is little research on this group, and, indeed, little recognition that they are a part of the community in Kerala.[51]

Although it may be said that, in numerical terms, these three groups are relatively small (the tribal population in Kerala, for instance, represents about one per cent of the total population), the persistence of acute deprivation among these three groups is, nevertheless, an important social failure, and calls for greater attention and concern from state authorities and political movements.

4. LITERACY IN KERALA

4.1 Educational Achievements

A cardinal feature of culture and society in Kerala, and of Kerala's political and economic development, is the high proportion of literate and educated persons in the population. Literacy — and, in particular, female literacy — is an essential (and is often regarded as *the* essential) facilitator of Kerala's achievements in the spheres of health and of demographic change. Literacy is a foundational feature of Kerala's political culture, crucial in the creation of public opinion and essential to that consciousness of individual and political rights that is so conspicuous a feature of social and political life in Kerala. Robin Jeffrey, writing in the context of Kerala, calls literacy 'the basic personal skill that underlies the whole modernizing sequence'.[52]

---

[51] On conditions of life and work, and the absence of strong trade unions among construction workers from Tamil Nadu in Kerala, see Anand (1994). For a description of migrants to Kerala from a dry-land village in Dindigul taluk in Tamil Nadu, see Swaminathan (1985).

[52] Jeffrey (1976); see also Caldwell and Caldwell (1985) and Weiner (1991). On the personal and social importance of literacy and basic education, see chapter 2 in

TABLE 20. *Proportion of Literate Persons in the Population:*
Kerala and India, 1961–91

(in per cent)

Year	Persons		Males		Females	
	Kerala	India	Kerala	India	Kerala	India
1961	46.8	24.0	55.0	34.3	38.9	12.9
1971	60.4	29.5	66.6	39.5	54.3	18.7
1981	69.2	36.2	74.0	46.7	64.5	24.9
1991	78.1	42.9	80.9	52.6	75.4	32.4
1981	*81.6*	*43.6*	*87.7*	*56.4*	*75.7*	*29.8*
1991	*90.6*	*52.1*	*94.5*	*63.9*	*87.0*	*39.4*

Notes. 1. The state of Kerala was formed in 1956.
2. Numbers in italics represent the number of literate persons above the age of seven as a proportion of all persons above the age of seven.
Source. Censuses of India.

With regard to the proportions of persons in the population who are literate, Kerala and the other states of India are in different leagues (see Table 20). Kerala has, historically, been ahead of other states in this respect, and today it is the only state that has achieved what UNESCO calls 'total literacy', or a state of society in which more than 85 per cent of the adult population is literate. In 1991, there was mass literacy among men as well as among women. Although the proportion of literates in the population of the northern districts (Kasargod, Kannur, Wayanad, Kozhikode, Malappuram, and Palakkad, approximately the old Malabar) at the Census of 1991 was lower than in the rest of the state, the gap was smaller than before (see Table 21). National Sample Survey data from the 42nd round (1986–7) on age-specific literacy show very high rates of literacy in the younger age-groups, over 97 per cent each among males and females in each age group between 6 years and 24 years,

---

the companion volume (Drèze and Sen, 1995). In a post-revolution formulation that set tough standards, Lenin wrote: 'I can say that so long as there is such a thing as illiteracy in our country, it is too much to talk about political education. . . . An illiterate person stands outside politics, he must first learn his ABC. Without that, there can be no politics, without that there are rumours, gossip, fairy-tales and prejudices, but not politics' (Lenin, 1921, p. 78).

TABLE 21. *Literate Persons as a Proportion of the Population:*
Constituent Regions of Present-day Kerala and India, Persons, Males and Females, 1871 to 1991

(in per cent)

Year	Persons				Males				Females			
	T	C	M	I	T	C	M	I	T	C	M	I
1871	n/a	n/a	5.3[a]	—	n/a	n/a	9.7[a]	—	n/a	n/a	0.8[a]	—
1875	5.7	4.4	n/a	n/a	11.1	8.4	n/a	n/a	0.5	0.4	n/a	n/a
1881	n/a	—	10.0[a]	—	n/a	—	17.6[a]	6.6	n/a	—	2.5[a]	0.4
1891	13.4	n/a	12.9	5.8	23.1	30.5	22.0	8.7	3.5	5.6	3.9	0.5
1901	12.4	13.4	—	5.3	21.5	21.5	17.2	9.8	3.1	3.1	3.0	0.7
1911	15.0	15.1	11.1	5.9	24.8	24.3	19.0	10.6	5.0	6.1	3.5	1.1
1921	24.2	18.5	12.7	7.1	33.1	27.3	20.9	13.9[b]	15.0	9.9	4.9	1.9
1931	23.9	28.2	14.4	9.5	33.8	38.3	22.9	15.6[b]	13.9	18.5	6.4	2.4
1941	47.2	43.7[c]	n/a	15.1	58.2	55.5[c]	n/a	—	36.1	32.5[c]	n/a	6.9

Table 21 cont'd

Year	Persons				Males				Females			
	T	C	M	I	T	C	M	I	T	C	M	I
1951[d]	46.7	43.3	31.3	16.6	55.6	52.2	41.3	25.0	37.7	34.7	21.7	12.9
1961	52.3	49.6	38.9	24.0	59.3	56.6	48.8	34.3	45.3	42.8	29.4	12.9
1971	66.3	63.6	52.1	29.5	71.4	68.5	60.3	39.5	61.3	58.7	44.2	18.7
1981	74.8	75.2	63.5	36.2	78.7	79.1	69.8	46.7	71.0	71.5	57.4	24.9
1991	80.9	80.7	74.2	42.9	83.2	83.2	77.8	52.6	78.8	78.3	70.8	32.4

Notes. 1. T = Travancore; C = Cochin; M = Malabar; I = India; n/a = not available; — = I have not been able to get the data.
   [a] Proportion of persons who are 'able to read and write' or 'learning' in the total population.
   [b] The reference population consists of persons aged 5 and above.
   [c] The reference population consists of persons aged 7 and above.
   [d] Figures for Travancore, Cochin, and Malabar are based on sample data.

Source.   Censuses of Cochin, Travancore, Madras Presidency, and India. On the modern districts that constitute the regions of Malabar, Cochin, and Travancore, see footnote 3 in the text.

in rural areas and urban areas. In every age group below 34, even the *rural female* literacy rate in Kerala is higher than the *urban male* literacy rate in India as a whole (Table 22). According to data from the Census of India 1901, child labour was lower in Kerala than any other state (see Table 23).

TABLE 22. *Proportion of Literate Persons in the Population, by Age Group: India and Kerala, 1986–7*

(in per cent)

Age group (years)	Rural				Urban			
	Male		Female		Male		Female	
	India	Kerala	India	Kerala	India	Kerala	India	Kerala
6–11	64.7	97.4	48.9	97.4	81.5	97.0	77.3	97.9
12–14	75.3	99.5	54.5	99.1	89.2	98.6	81.7	99.7
15–24	69.3	98.4	45.3	97.2	88.6	99.1	76.0	97.2
25–34	60.6	96.1	32.5	91.3	86.2	98.8	66.4	95.2
35–44	54.7	92.1	24.9	80.9	81.3	97.8	57.6	86.5
45–59	46.0	86.7	18.7	69.3	76.0	92.5	47.8	78.5
60 & above	38.5	81.0	14.9	53.1	71.2	90.5	33.9	70.2
All[a]	52.4	84.1	31.6	79.6	74.0	88.7	59.0	84.8

Note. [a] Including persons in the 0–5 age group.
Source. National Sample Survey (1993).

TABLE 23. *Working Children as a Proportion of All Children: India and Kerala, 1981*

(in per cent)

Age group (in years)	Boys		Girls		All children	
	India	Kerala	India	Kerala	India	Kerala
5–9	0.89	0.06	0.76	0.06	0.83	0.06
10–14	16.97	2.86	12.74	2.73	14.97	2.80
5–14	8.67	1.53	6.42	1.47	7.58	1.50

Source. Census of India 1981, cited in B.A.N. Sharma (1994).

Owing to the prevalent levels of literacy, the dissemination of information by means of the written word goes much deeper in Kerala than elsewhere in India; this has important implications for the quality and depth of public opinion, and of participatory democracy in the state.[53] There are data on the circulation of daily newspapers from the Registrar of Newspapers; following the basic paper on this subject (Jeffrey, 1987), I have used calculations from census data on the number of speakers of different languages to calculate dailies-to-persons ratios (see Table 24). Kerala, predictably, has always done better than the rest of India in this respect: the circulation of newspapers in Malayalam per thousand speakers of Malayalam in 1989 was 61, and the corresponding figure for all newspapers in all languages and speakers of all languages in India was 28.[54] There are also data from an all-India readership survey conducted in 1989 by the Operations Research Group that deals with adult readers of dailies, weeklies, fortnightlies, and monthlies in India. The data are given separately for men and women, and rural and urban areas, and by categories of income, age, occupation, and formal educational achievement. Some of the data for Kerala and the whole of India are recomputed in Tables 25 and 26. The differences between the Kerala results and the all-India results are very striking.[55]

TABLE 24. *Circulation of Daily Newspapers: India, 1961–89*

Language	Circulation of daily newspapers per thousand speakers			
	1961	*1971*	*1981*	*1989*
Assamese	1	2	6	15
Bengali	6	13	21	19
Gujarati	18	26	35	33
Hindi	5	7	14	25
Kannada	8	14	22	23

[53] For descriptions of the spread of information through newspapers, see Jeffrey (1987, 1992) and Aiyappan (1965), pp. 95–6.

[54] Kerala is still far behind the developing countries in UNDP's 'high human development' category, among whom the figure was 200 in 1988–90 (UNDP, 1993, p. 166).

[55] I must add, however, that I was surprised to see that the readership figures for women agricultural labourers, although much higher than elsewhere, were less than 12 per cent, and markedly lower than the figure for men.

Table 24 cont'd

Language	Circulation of daily newspapers per thousand speakers			
	1961	1971	1981	1989
Malayalam	32	51	54	61
Marathi	12	22	28	29
Oriya	4	4	8	22
Punjabi	2	5	12	16
Sindhi	–	–	–	20
Tamil	20	24	21	26
Telugu	4	5	9	12
Urdu	10	13	21	34
All languages	11	16	22	28

Notes. 1. 'Speakers' are persons whose mother tongues are specified in the first column.

2. The data on persons in 1981 whose mother tongue was Tamil were lost 'due to flood' (*Census of India 1981*, 1991, p. ix) and were not reported. Data on Tamil in column 5 are from *Census of India 1981* (1987), pp. 38–9.

3. The increase in the population of the speakers of a specific language between 1981 and 1989 was calculated by using the compound rate of growth of the population between 1981 and 1991 of the state in which that language is the principal language. For Hindi the increase was calculated by using the compound rate of growth of the combined populations of Bihar, Haryana, Himachal Pradesh, Madhya Pradesh, Rajasthan, and Uttar Pradesh. For Urdu and Sindhi, the increase was calculated by using the compound rate of growth of the population of India between 1981 and 1991.

4. Census operations did not take place in Assam in 1981. The data in columns 5 and 6 for Assamese are projections from the 1971 mother-tongue data, 1981 population estimates, and the 1991 final population totals for Assam.

5. The calculations of population growth rates mentioned in note 3 are based on population totals given in *Census of India 1981* (1983), *Census of India 1991* (1993), and Bose (1991).

6. The data on circulation of newspapers in Assamese in 1971 are, in fact, data for 1970 (Jeffrey, 1987, Table 1, p. 607).

Sources. Censuses of India; Registrar of Newspapers (1962, 1991); *Press in India*, cited in Jeffrey (1987a), Table 1, p. 607. See the detailed notes in Ram (forthcoming).

TABLE 25. *Proportion of Readers in the Estimated Adult Population: India and Kerala, 1989*

(in per cent)

Readers		Any daily		Any publication	
		India	Kerala	India	Kerala
	Persons	17.7	44.3	21.1	58.6
Total	Men	23.6	53.4	26.6	63.3
	Women	11.5	35.8	15.4	54.2
	Persons	6.8	37.5	9.0	53.1
Rural	Men	10.0	45.6	12.0	57.2
	Women	3.6	29.7	5.9	49.1
	Persons	49.4	72.2	56.4	81.1
Urban	Men	61.2	84.8	66.8	87.7
	Women	35.8	60.2	44.6	74.9

Notes. 1. The survey covered persons above 15 years of age.
2. The category 'any publication' is made up of all the dailies, weeklies, fortnightlies, and monthlies in the survey schedule.
3. The reference period for each publication was the frequency of publication of the individual publication (a day for dailies, a week for weeklies, and so on).

Source. Operations Research Group (1990a, 1990b).

TABLE 26. *Proportion of Readers in the Estimated Adult Population, by Occupation Group: India and Kerala, 1989*

(in per cent)

Occupational Category		Any daily		Any publication	
		India	Kerala	India	Kerala
	Persons	75.2	92.9	84.6	100.0
Professional/Executive	Men	79.2	94.2	87.7	100.0
	Women	51.8	89.0	66.5	100.0
	Persons	64.6	84.5	71.3	97.9
Clerk/Salesperson	Men	64.3	80.7	70.5	97.8
	Women	66.6	97.8	77.5	98.5

Table 26 cont'd

Occupational Category		Any daily		Any publication	
		India	Kerala	India	Kerala
Industrialist/Trader	Persons	45.6	76.4	49.2	78.1
	Men	46.8	77.1	50.4	78.7
	Women	15.5	17.3	19.2	31.3
Worker	Persons	16.1	30.0	18.9	43.6
	Men	17.4	33.8	20.0	44.5
	Women	6.1	12.7	10.7	39.3
Student	Persons	49.8	74.5	59.7	94.0
	Men	52.4	84.8	60.1	96.5
	Women	45.5	65.0	59.2	91.7
Housewife/Non-worker	Persons	11.7	40.5	15.3	56.1
	Men	27.3	62.0	31.6	68.3
	Women	9.7	34.4	13.1	52.6
Agriculturist	Persons	7.8	37.9	8.9	50.6
	Men	8.0	36.8	9.1	49.6
	Women	3.4	67.6	4.6	77.5
Agricultural Labourer	Persons	1.9	23.5	2.6	32.9
	Men	2.4	36.4	3.1	45.9
	Women	0.3	2.7	0.7	11.9
Artisan	Persons	15.2	100.0	18.0	100.0
	Men	18.2	100.0	20.6	100.0
	Women	3.1	100.0	5.8	100.0
Other	Persons	12.8	29.9	15.7	41.1
	Men	17.3	41.4	20.5	56.6
	Women	5.7	7.5	8.1	11.0

Notes. See Table 25.

Source. Operations Research Group (1990a, 1990b).

Among castes, literacy traditionally matched a caste's position in the ritual hierarchy. In descending order of literacy, the position was, in general, Brahman, Kshatriya, and Ambalavasi, followed by

Nayars and then Izhavas and the so-called agrarian slave castes. Christians were ahead of Muslims and, in fact, right behind the Nayars. If we were to separate Syrian Christians from missionary converts, the pattern would be different. While on this theme, it is worth dispelling the notion that, because the traditional system of inheritance among the Nayars was matrilineal, Nayar women in traditional society were mainly literate. In the area for which we have data, Travancore, the literacy rate among Nayar females in 1875 was 1.2 per cent.

TABLE 27. *Proportion of Literate Persons among Scheduled Castes and Scheduled Tribes: Kerala and India*

(in per cent)

	Scheduled castes		Scheduled tribes		Total population	
	Kerala	India	Kerala	India	Kerala	India
1961						
Female	17.4	3.3	11.9	3.2	38.9	12.9
Male	31.6	17.0	22.6	13.8	55.0	34.3
1991[a]						
Female	74.3	23.8	51.1	18.2	86.2	39.3
Male	85.2	49.9	63.4	40.7	93.6	64.1

Note. [a] Age 7 and above.
Source. *Census of India 1961*; Tyagi (1993), Tables 10–13, based on 1991 Census data.

Disaggregated data on literacy among different classes and social groups in the nineties are still not available (other than in the report of the Total Literacy Campaign in Ernakulam district). From the data in the Census of 1981 and other studies in the eighties, including the surveys that were undertaken by the literacy campaigns prior to the campaign in each place, it was clear that although, from an all-India perspective, Kerala's achievements were impressive, some traditional differences persisted. The 1991 Census data showed literacy among people of the scheduled castes and tribes to be below the general level (see Table 27). According to the studies by John Kurien and others of living standards among the fisherpeople of

Kerala's coasts, the rate of male literacy among fishing workers was 67 per cent, and the rate of female literacy was 44 per cent (John Kurien, 1991). In Nadur village, near Shoranur, in 1987, Richard Franke found that while literacy improved over the seventies and eighties, the general pattern of literacy followed the pattern of traditional hierarchy in the village. Michael Tharakan's evaluation of the total literacy campaign showed the persistence of illiteracy among scheduled castes and scheduled tribes, among the poorest section of agricultural labourers and fishing communities, and among Muslims, particularly women (he documents one case of family resistance to a young Muslim woman becoming an instructor in the campaign).[56]

4.2 Literacy Expansion in the Nineteenth Century

The progress of literacy is the achievement whose history has been written about in the greatest detail. This history has been documented, in particular, for Travancore. Conditions in Cochin are relatively understudied.

Mass literacy requires mass schooling, and the history of literacy in Kerala is closely linked with the history of modern schooling, introduced in the region in the first part of the nineteenth century.[57]

In her pioneering work on literacy in Kerala, Kathleen Gough argued that widespread literacy was an important feature of pre-British society in Kerala (Gough, 1968). She contended that before British rule, almost all Nayar men and most Nayar women were literate and that more than 50 per cent of men in general and more

---

[56] Tharakan (1990). Tharakan also discusses the specific problems during the literacy campaign of fisherpeople and dock-workers in Mattanchery and Cochin (ibid., p. 74). The literacy profile and the differences that still remain between identifiable social groups in respect of literacy will need to be reassessed in the light of the achievements of the Total Literacy Campaign, which ended in April 1991. The discussion of educational disparities in the eighties is subject to the qualification that the studies that identified these differences preceded the mass literacy campaign.

[57] See, for instance, Jeffrey (1987, 1992), Tharakan (1984), Gopinathan Nair (1974). See also the Census volumes by Nagam Aiya, Velu Pillai, Achyuta Menon, and Kerala's District Gazetteers. On the history of literacy and other features of Kerala's achievements in education, see the contributions to National Institute of Educational Planning and Administration (1986).

than 25 per cent of women in the early eighteenth century were literate. Gough argued that there was a massive decline in literacy in the early part of British rule.[58] The wars of the late eighteenth century and the neglect of Sanskrit and vernacular learning by the British were, according to Gough, responsible for the decline. There is, however, little evidence to substantiate this argument.

Michael Tharakan, a more recent historian of literacy in Kerala, argues that the sixteenth to eighteenth centuries were a period of growth of literacy in Kerala, and that during this period education spread beyond the Brahmans and 'came within reach of almost all the socially and economically privileged sections of society' (Tharakan, 1984, p. 1915).[59] Nevertheless, he considers Gough's estimates to be based on inadequate information and 'exaggerated': in his view, it is unlikely that literacy among caste Hindus went too much beyond Brahmans and aristocratic Nayars, or that literacy among Christians and Muslims went beyond traders within the communities, or that literacy among Izhavas went beyond the ayurveda practitioners and astrologers among them. He also writes that 'there is no reason to believe that there was any significant spread of literacy' among the agrarian Pulaya and Cherumar slave castes (ibid., p. 1916). To this must be added the fact that female literacy was very low.

Modern schools were first established by Christian missionaries and, later, by the state. There were two streams of missionary activity, Roman Catholic and Protestant. Protestant missionaries, and not Roman Catholic, were the pioneers of modern school education. Roman Catholic missionaries opened seminaries, and they also established schools among fishing communities. Michael Tharakan cites the historian H. Hoster, who wrote that these schools were 'essentially catechism classes', and is doubtful that they made any real contribution to literacy in that period (ibid., p. 1919).

A key nineteenth-century event in the history of literacy in Kerala was the missionary activity of the London Missionary Society (LMS) and the Christian Mission Society (CMS). The objective of these organizations was, of course, to evangelize among the people of

---

[58] She cites, with approval, A.S. Menon, who wrote that there was an 'alarming increase in illiteracy' in the early British period (Gough, 1968, p. 155).

[59] This was also the period of emergence of an independent Malayalam alphabet; the Malayalam alphabet was introduced in the seventeenth century (Zograph, 1960, p. 141).

Travancore; in practice, their activity also took on the character of movements for educational and social reform.[60]

Although Syrian Christian schools outnumbered Protestant schools by the early twentieth century, Protestant missionary influence on education was very important, and its importance lay in its leading role in giving a new direction to schooling in the early nineteenth century. These are some of the main features of missionary education in Travancore as they emerge in the writings of historians of nineteenth-century Travancore. First, the mass base of the Protestant missionaries, such as it was, came from the oppressed castes: the Shanars, Pulayas, and Izhavas. Secondly, as Tharakan writes, 'there was a clear perception among early Protestant missionaries that educational work was a necessary pre-requisite for their religious work' (Tharakan, 1984, p. 1920). Thirdly, it followed that missionaries asserted the right of people of oppressed castes to modern education, and mission schools were the only new-style schools to which the people of oppressed castes had access. This was part of a conscious effort by Protestant missionaries, and, on this subject, Samuel Mateer, the nineteenth-century missionary and missionary historian, wrote:

Let (the educated classes of Travancore) take a decided stand against the social evils of caste. Let them make an attempt in real earnest to raise the masses by primary education and by a few firm and resolute measures against the cruel oppression of the poor and helpless; and a solid and general advance in national prosperity, power, and happiness will speedily be evident to the world.

(Mateer, 1883, p. 352).

Mateer also wrote that 'the lowest classes are . . . without the means of obtaining instruction, except in Mission Schools; their children being refused admission to all respectable schools, and, with rare and recent exceptions, to all Government Schools' (Mateer, 1871, p. 156).[61] By 1883, he was able to write that there were 'some ten or twelve thousand (Pulayar people) under the instruction of the Church and London Missionary Societies' (Mateer, 1883, p. 33).

[60] See, in this context, Tharakan (1984), Kooiman (1989), Mateer (1871), and Agur (1903).

[61] Michael Tharakan writes that the 'education of the lower castes — Izhava and Shanar as well as "slave" castes — was the exclusive preserve of missionary schools until the government came into the field at the end of the nineteenth century' (Tharakan, 1984, p. 1920).

Fourthly, conversion and primary education were linked with missionary-led movements against other features of Hindu society: against untouchability and distance pollution, against agrarian slavery, against the upper-caste prohibition on women of ritually 'impure' castes wearing clothes above the waist, and against other caste-based taboos. Fifthly, missionary education brought girls from oppressed castes to schools.[62] Sixthly, although school courses were biased towards the teaching of Christian theology, there was also a secular component to school studies. Geography and arithmetic, for instance, were part of the primary school curriculum (Tharakan, 1984). Seventhly, instruction in missionary schools was in the vernacular, i.e. in Tamil and Malayalam. Eighthly, missionary schools were the first institutions of elementary technical training, or craft schools. Missionary activity in education was also linked to their activities in the development of health facilities. They established dispensaries and hospitals and provided instruction in hygiene and public health.

The missionary effort had, in important matters and in spite of ruling class opposition to the oppressed castes, the support of state power in Travancore, particularly during the period that James Munro was in Travancore. Munro was Resident in Travancore from 1810 to 1819, and was actually Dewan as well from 1811 to 1814. He was also Resident in Cochin. During this period, the LMS and CMS received grants of land and the patronage of the state in other forms. Francis Maltby, Resident from 1860, was a member of the Madras committee of the CMS (Jeffrey, 1976).

In 1817 in Travancore the remarkable Royal Rescript, addressed to the Dewan Peishkar at Quilon, was issued. The Rescript was, in all likelihood, written by James Munro,[63] and its best-known section read:

The state should defray the entire cost of the education of its people in order that there might be no backwardness in the spread of enlightenment among them, that by diffusion of education they might become better subjects and public servants and that the reputation of the state might be enhanced thereby.

---

[62] The missionaries began efforts at female education from the start; see Mateer (1871), p. 156.

[63] Gopinathan Nair (1974); A. Sreedhara Menon, cited in K. Francis (1985), p. 156.

The Rescript was remarkable because it declared universal educa-tion, paid for by the state, to be an objective of state policy. It was also remarkable for the fact that it was issued as early as 1817,[64] in a princely state (no comparable statement was made, in the nine-teenth century or the twentieth, by any government in British India, since universal education was never British policy), and by a young — fifteen-year old — woman ruler.

In the first half of the nineteenth century, despite the Royal Rescript, there was little state activity in Travancore in the sphere of modern school education beyond the establishment of some schools in which instruction was in English, and support to mission schools (Tharakan, 1984). In the second half of the nineteenth century, primary education in Travancore 'expanded, and . . . acquired the characteristics of a "modern" system'.[65] During this period, and par-ticularly when T. Madhava Rao was Dewan of Travancore (1862–74), the government opened new schools (including for girls), and gave substantial grants-in-aid to private organizations and individuals to start schools.[66] Instruction in schools was mainly in Malayalam or Tamil, and primary education was largely in the vernacular (Francis, 1985, pp. 166ff.). The first English school was established in 1834 in Thiruvananthapuram during the rule of Maharaja Swati Tirunal. The school was free until 1863–4, and was subsequently fee-based (Fran-cis, 1985, p. 159). Education was linked to employment, and school-ing was a pre-requisite for a government job; a proclamation of 1844 gave preference in government employment to persons with an English education (Jeffrey, 1976, pp. 75ff.; Francis, 1985, p. 159). The government also established a text-book committee, which worked on translations and commissioned the writing of text-books (Jeffrey, 1976, p. 79). In 1881, the Maharaja declared that

No civilized government can be oblivious to the great advantages of popular education . . . for . . . a government which has to deal with an educated

[64] The Rescript was issued 55 years before the Meiji Educational Law of 1872 in Japan. The Meiji law said: 'People have made a mistake of thinking that learning is a matter for those above samurai rank. . . . It is intended that henceforth universally (without any distinction of class or sex) in a village there shall be no house without learning and in a house no individual without learning' (Beasley, 1972, p. 360).

[65] Tharakan, 1984, p. 1921. On education policy in nineteenth-century Travan-core, see also Jeffrey (1976, 1992); Gopinathan Nair (1981), K. Francis (1985).

[66] Jeffrey (1976, 1992); Tharakan (1983); Gopinathan Nair (1974); K. Francis (1985).

population is by far stronger than one which has to control ignorant and disorderly masses. Hence education is a twice-blessed thing — it benefits those who give it and those who receive it.

(cited in Jeffrey, 1992, p. 55).

Traditional systems of learning were disrupted and dislodged in the eighteenth and nineteenth centuries. They were disrupted by war and changing political conditions in the eighteenth century and the early nineteenth century, and supplanted by new systems of education in the second half of the nineteenth century (and in the twentieth century). Some of the main types of traditional schools were the *ezhuttuppalli*, the *kalari* (schools of martial arts) and Vedic schools. There was also the *madrasa* (information cited in Francis, 1985, p. 156). These were pre-modern non-secular schools in terms of what was taught, and socially exclusionary; many of them appear to have been based on rote learning; and even in the second half of the nineteenth century, books and paper were not used in these schools and children wrote on sand, rice grains or, when they were better at writing, on palm leaves.[67] Although socially exclusive, the system of traditional schools was extensive, and traditional, caste-based schools existed in villages across the region. Traditional schools did not entirely disappear, and in fact showed remarkable resilience. In the nineteenth and twentieth centuries, they also functioned as pre-primary schools in which educationally privileged children were educated before they went to non-traditional schools (Tharakan, 1984; Krishna Menon, 1949). They appear to have survived longer in Travancore than elsewhere in the state.

For all the progress that was made in terms of educational policy during that period, there was no mass literacy at the end of the nineteenth-century (see Table 21). Even in Travancore — where Christian missionaries were most active and where the nineteenth-century state was most interventionist — less than a quarter of all males and less than five per cent of all females were literate. Although Kerala's performance was outstanding compared to other parts of India, it was a century and three-quarters after the Rani of Travancore's proclamation that Kerala achieved mass literacy.

---

[67] See, in this connection, Jeffrey (1976).

4.3   Overcoming Social Divisions

Mass education cannot be that without overcoming the great barriers to mass education in Indian society — gender and caste discrimination and class oppression. Although official policy in Travancore and Cochin created what Richard Franke calls an 'official environment of support for education', it required female education, organized movements of people of the oppressed castes and, later, the left movement to establish comprehensive schooling and mass literacy.

To take the caste question first. Some of the worst forms of untouchability and distance pollution were practised in Kerala, and one of the most important reasons for Travancore pulling decisively ahead of Malabar in respect of literacy in the twenties was the spread of education among people of the Izhava caste, the upper tier of Kerala's (roughly speaking) two-tier system of untouchability. The change in literacy levels on a social scale came in the thirties, with higher levels of education among people of the Izhava caste, and the change occurred when the Izhava social reform movement became a large-scale mass movement, more than four decades after Sree Narayana Guru began his public mission. In the nineteen twenties and thirties, there was a rapid expansion in enrolment, in educational investment, and in affirmative action (in the form of scholarships, fee concessions, and unrestricted access to primary schools), that consolidated the basis of mass education.[68]

The argument that female literacy was the key factor in the high levels of literacy achieved by Kerala (that 'women made Kerala literate') has been made most forcefully by Robin Jeffrey.[69] Female literacy leads to mass literacy; Jeffrey refers to the old wisdom that 'literate men have literate sons; literate women have literate children'. Jeffrey illustrates his argument on the role of female literacy in achieving mass literacy using Baroda as a control; Baroda was another princely state with similar levels of male literacy at the beginning of the century, and where the princely government declared a policy of mass primary education. Kerala got ahead because Kerala's culture fostered female literacy. Kerala

[68] Jose George (1980) writes of the enthusiasm for literacy among agricultural workers in Travancore in the thirties and forties.
[69] Jeffrey (1987b, 1992).

has a history of matriliny among a significant section of the population, and it did not have a tradition of female seclusion, except among Namboodiris and a section of Muslims (and, among these groups, Namboodiri women were more literate than other women). There was never organised social opposition to women's literacy in Kerala.[70]

For all the favourable conditions, however, *mass* literacy among women in Kerala is recent. It was only from the sixties that a majority of adult women in Kerala were able to read and write. This was also the period when literacy spread decisively to the backward districts and to the rural poor. The gap between Malabar and Cochin and Travancore in respect of literacy widened during the period of British rule in Malabar. Mass schooling in Malabar was established after the formation of Kerala. The extension of mass literacy to the rural poor, and particularly the rural poor in Malabar, also took place in the sixties and subsequently.

4.4   Towards Total Literacy

The transition from a stage in which literacy is achieved by social elites and by some sections of the skilled labour force (but not by all people and, in particular, not by rural workers and women) to mass literacy has, historically, been the achievement of mass social movements for schooling and literacy. The transition, in other words, is not a matter merely of the passage of time, but requires public action for literacy on a societal scale. Kerala was the first, and remains the only, state for which every district was declared wholly literate by the National Literacy Mission. This followed the state-wide Total Literacy Campaign (TLC) of 1989 to 1991. On 18 April 1991, Aysha Chelakkodan, a 55-year-old neoliterate Muslim woman from Malappuram district, lit a lamp at a public ceremony at Kozhikode to mark the successful end of the first phase of the Total Literacy Campaign in Kerala. She lit the lamp and said: 'I pray that

---

[70] This was a feature of society that Protestant missionaries did not fail to notice. 'There has never been any decided objection on the part of Sudras or Ilavars to the elementary instruction of females,' Samuel Mateer wrote, 'probably in consequence of their singular system of inheritance by the female line. One or two thousand girls of these castes attend the ordinary village schools' (Mateer, 1871, p. 156).

the lamp that has been lit will carry the light of literacy to all corners of the world. May it drive away the darkness of evil and ignorance' (see Ramakrishnan, 1991).

The Ernakulam District Total Literacy Campaign was the first district-wide movement of its kind in Kerala and India. It established a method for literacy campaigns in the districts of the state, and, although the Ernakulam method could not be reproduced in every other TLC district in the country, it was a major influence on the design of total literacy campaigns all over India. The organization whose activists were the main inspirers and organizers of the movement was the Kerala Shastra Sahitya Parishad (KSSP), and KSSP activists have been important organizers of total literacy campaigns in different parts of India.[71]

The Ernakulam campaign was conducted by a Literacy Society in which representatives of the district administration, different mass organizations and other non-government organizations, and concerned citizens were members. The target-group of the campaign were illiterates in the age group 6 years to 60 years (a bigger group than the target-group of persons between the ages of 15 years to 35 years recommended by the National Literacy Mission). The campaign sought to eliminate illiteracy through a single, sustained campaign, and to do so by using unpaid volunteers as instructors (more than 350,000 volunteers participated in the literacy campaign). The organizers surveyed the illiterate population of each district, and they made careful efforts to actually identify every illiterate person in the district, and to identify groups and areas where illiteracy was disproportionately high (Tharakan, 1990, pp. 7–8, *passim*).[72] The campaign primer, called *Aksharam*, included lessons on food, work, the dignity of labour, disease-prevention, drinking water, oral rehydration therapy, India's freedom struggle,

[71] Michael Tharakan evaluated the Ernakulam Total Literacy Campaign for the National Literacy Mission. His report (Tharakan, 1990) is the basic source of information on the campaign.

[72] The Ernakulam campaign formulated an interesting criterion for literacy. The objective of the campaign was to teach a learner, first, to read without difficulty a description of something that was within his or her experience at a rate of at least 30 words a minute; and, secondly, to copy out a description of something at a rate of seven words a minute. Numeracy was defined as the ability to count and write from 1 to 100, to add and subtract 3-digit numbers, and to divide and multiply 2-digit numbers (Tharakan, 1990, p. 44).

panchayats, post offices, the equality of the sexes, fair-price shops, and immunization (ibid., p. 60, *passim*). The literacy campaign was also linked to the Universal Immunization Programme and with a wide range of cultural activities (ibid., p. 64, *passim*).[73]

All enlightened societies, developed and less-developed, have instituted laws of compulsory school education. India has not,[74] and, although Kerala has achieved mass literacy, it, too, has no law of compulsory education. It has been pointed out that such a legislation is necessary and still of relevance (Ram, 1994). First, a law of compulsory education would provide a legal basis for ensuring that not a single child in Kerala (including the children, for instance, of migrant workers) is out of school; secondly, it would help ensure that mass literacy and mass education are irreversible;[75] and, thirdly, it would serve as an example to other states of a state that has a law of compulsory education and has achieved mass literacy.

5. Aspects of Caste and Gender Relations in Kerala

In Kerala, as elsewhere in India, the caste system was an enemy of social progress. The traditional caste system in Kerala had special features, as did traditional systems of marriage, inheritance, and succession.[76]

Among the worst forms of untouchability in the country were practised in Kerala, and the persecution of people of the oppressed castes took savage forms. The rules of the caste system also included complex rules on distance pollution ('unapproachability') and

---

[73] After the government led by the Congress (I) came to power in June 1991, the post-literacy phase of the campaign ran into serious trouble. The committee that organized the campaign, the Kerala Saksharata Samiti, was disbanded, funds were withdrawn from the campaign, and there have been reports of neo-literates regressing into illiteracy (Ramakrishnan, 1991; Venugopal, 1992).

[74] Only the Tamil Nadu legislature has passed a Bill on compulsory primary education.

[75] See, in this context, Tharakan and Navaneetham (1994).

[76] There is a vast literature on castes and caste hierarchy in Kerala; see, for instance, Namboodiripad (1976, 1984), L.A. Krishna Iyer (1968, 1970), L.K. Anantha Krishna Iyer (1912). For descriptions of castes and caste functions in early post-independence Kerala, see Mayer (1952), Aiyappan (1965), and Gough (1970). On matriliny and on the oppressed castes, see references below. On caste status and customs, a useful reference is Jeffrey (1976), p. 9, *passim*.

included, against some castes, rules of 'unseeability'. The people of the 'slave castes' (for instance, the Pulayar, Parayar, and Cherumar castes) and the people of the aboriginal tribes of Kerala, as well as those born into the Izhava caste did not have access to public places, temples, bathing tanks, public paths and roads, and educational institutions. The employment of people born into these castes in occupations outside their traditional caste callings was also prohibited. Persons of oppressed castes were not permitted to wear clean clothes, or cloth other than coarse cloth, nor any clothes at all above the waist; they were not permitted to keep milch cattle or use the services of oil-presses, to use metal pots and pans, or carry umbrellas, or wear slippers on their feet. They were not permitted to take Sanskrit given names, and there were rules that governed the words that could be used in conversation with persons of status-superior castes: for example, the use of the first person singular was not permitted (it had to be 'this slave' or 'this inferior'); a person of an oppressed caste could not refer to 'my money' but to 'copper'.[77]

At the top of the traditional caste hierarchy were the Namboodiris, Malayalam-speaking Brahmans who read the Vedas and were patrilineal. Kathleen Gough, in her seminal analysis of matrilineal kinship in Kerala, points out that in Kerala, 'the higher the caste, the wider the field of social relationships' (Gough, 1962, p. 319). Of Namboodiris in the traditional order she writes: 'the field of social relations of the Namboodiris was the whole of Kerala. . . . Alone of all the castes, they moved unmolested between enemy kingdoms' (ibid., p. 305). At the bottom of the caste-Hindu

---

[77] The early missionary literature has detailed descriptions of the conditions of life of people of the oppressed castes and of slavery: see, for instance, Cox (1857); 'A.H.' (1860); Agur (1903); Mateer (1871, 1883); and the writings of Claudius Buchanan, cited in Yesudas (1978). See also, in this context, Jeffrey (1976) and Kooiman (1989). A memorial of 19 March 1847, signed by 13 missionaries, said there were 164,864 slaves in Travancore, and called on the Raja to pass a law against slavery (Cox, 1857, p. xii). Ward and Conner (1816–20) described vividly the contrast between the houses of the upper castes and the living spaces of the oppressed (pp. 7–8). Chandramohan (1981) and Peter (1987) have detailed descriptions of forms of oppression of the Izhava people. For a summary of descriptions of the literature on hierarchy, see Jeffrey (1992), p. 19, *passim*, and for forms of caste discrimination in a Malabar village, see Aiyappan (1965). See also Saradamoni (1980, 1981) and Kusuman (1973). On social discrimination against scheduled caste agricultural labourers, see Jose George (1980), pp. 50ff.

scale were the Nayars, who did not read the Vedas as part of their traditional caste duties and who were matrilineal. Below the Nayar caste in terms of ritual status was the Izhava caste. The people of the Izhava and equivalent castes were considered outcaste by caste Hindus, who practised untouchability against the Izhava people. The people of the Izhava caste, however, occupied an intermediate position between caste Hindus and castes that were traditionally subjected to chattel slavery and people of Kerala's aboriginal tribes. The people of Izhava and equivalent castes considered the slave castes and the aboriginal tribes of Kerala to be polluting castes. The main traditional occupation of the people of the Izhava caste was agricultural labour. There were also tenants and (mainly small) peasant proprietors among them, and toddy tappers and coconut workers. A striking feature of the Izhava caste is that there were within it, in different parts of the state, men of learning in Sanskrit as well as ayurvedists and astrologers. This diversity in the traditional caste calling of the people of the Izhava caste was to have important consequences for the Izhava social reform movement.

Rules of female seclusion in Kerala were less widespread than elsewhere in India. Female seclusion was practised among Namboodiris and among Muslims. Female seclusion was not practised by others and was not a mark of status or social advance among other castes.[78]

In traditional Kerala, matrilineal systems of inheritance were followed by an important section of the people.[79] The Nayars were matrilineal and, traditionally, matrilocal as well (the system of matrilineal family organization and inheritance was called the *marumakkattayam* system).[80] Nayars lived in joint families in which family

[78] Of the status of Namboodiri women, E.M.S. Namboodiripad wrote in 1942: 'The absence of free marriage and of the right of divorce, the existence of polygamy and compulsory purdah, the lack of economic rights and backward educational and cultural standards — all these social disabilities of Hindu womanhood was the lot of Namboodiri women alone among the women of Kerala' (Namboodiripad, 1942).

[79] There is an extensive literature on matriliny in Kerala. For an introduction, see Gough (1962), Fawcett (1901), Fuller (1976), which proposes a very useful framework for the study of social change among Nayars; also Jeffrey (1976), Puthenkulam (1977), Balakrishnan (1981), and the references in the first footnote in this section.

[80] We shall not deal here with sub-castes; the main Nayar caste organization, the Nair Service Society, brought together more than a hundred (notional) sub-castes into the organization.

property was inherited by female descendants. Male members of a joint family had rights in the family property only during their lifetimes; when they died, land was inherited by their sisters, sisters' children, and by other members of the family female bloodline. This system was practised not only by Nayars, but by sections of the Ambalavasi castes (castes of temple servants, who had traditional temple duties), and by sections of the Izhava caste (different sections of the Izhava caste followed patrilineal and matrilineal systems of inheritance; some followed a combination of the two).[81] A significant section of the Muslim population in Malabar was, by tradition, matrilineal.[82]

Matrilineal did not, of course, mean matriarchal.[83] The heads of joint families were males. Among Nayars, the *karanavar* was the head of the joint family; he was the eldest male of the *taravad* or Nayar house. A feature of the social system in Kerala was that this system of succession was followed by the caste of Kshatriyas, to which the ruling families of Travancore and Cochin belonged, and whose system of inheritance was not wholly matrilineal. The Maharajas of Travancore and Cochin were chosen in this way: on the death of a Maharaja, his younger brother succeeded him; when he had no brother, his sister's son succeeded him (the sister's son was the successor also in cases where the deceased Maharaja's brother was younger than him, i.e. when a person was older than his maternal uncle). When there were no females in the bloodline to provide successors, women were adopted into the royal families.

A distinguishing feature of the marriage system among caste Hindus was that Nayar women entered into marriage relations with men of all castes equivalent to or above them in the caste Hindu hierarchy. The means for this was the form of marriage called *sambandham*. A stylized version is as follows: first, when the sambandham involved Nayar men, men of the Nayar caste visited Nayar women and had sexual relations with them; the men continued to live in their taravads; the children of the marriages became children of the women's families. Men of upper castes — including Namboodiris and Kshatriyas — visited Nayar women and had sexual

[81] On systems of inheritance among people of the Izhava caste, see Chandramohan (1981); on Izhava family structure, see Jeffrey (1992), pp. 49ff.

[82] On matriliny among Mappila Muslims, see Miller (1992), pp. 251–2.

[83] Matriliny, Robin Jeffrey writes, 'gave women . . . a unique importance, though this stopped far short of equality with men (Jeffrey, 1992, p. 25).

relations with Nayar women. This relationship was not considered an illicit one by the upper castes; it had social legitimacy.[84] The difference between the sambandham and what is conventionally understood by the term marriage is that children of the unions did not become members of their fathers' family. For the Nayar woman, the sambandham was recognized socially as a marriage, and her children became members of her joint family and took her family name. The sambandham was not polyandrous in the conventional sense: a woman did not share a household with many men. Traditionally, a Nayar woman could have sexual relations with more than one man. Later — and this was particularly true of aristocratic Nayar families — women either stopped having multiple relations with men or, indeed, became monogamous in practice (although continuing matrilocal practices). A sambandham relationship could be broken by a man; more significantly, it could be broken unilaterally by a woman.

Among Namboodiris, only the eldest son married within the caste; Namboodiris have also been described as the only caste in south India that followed the principle of primogeniture.[85] Younger sons entered sambandham relationships with women from matrilineal castes. For Namboodiri men, such unions were 'socially acceptable concubinage' (Gough, 1962, p. 320) in which a union was not initiated with Vedic rites and the children of which were not accepted as Brahmans or kinfolk. On the other hand, 'matrilineal castes considered the same unions as marriages', that 'fulfilled the recognized rules of Nayar marriage and served to legitimise the children' of the unions (ibid.).

A further feature of the system was that there occurred — particularly in the case of Nayars who belonged to the landed aristocracy — certain disjunctures between ritual status and other aspects of social and cultural status. Gough writes that hypergamy 'inextricably linked the secular and religious hierarchies' and that it permitted office-bearing lineages 'to sidestep the awkward question of their precise rank in the hierarchy as a whole' (p. 322). As an illustration, there is an example that Namboodiripad discusses in his autobiography:

---

[84] Kerala, Professor Aiyappan wrote, was 'the only area in India where the Brahmans could legally mate with Sudra women' (Aiyappan, 1965, p. 5).

[85] See Suresh Kumar (1979), p. 50.

Very close relations existed between the royalty of Valluvanad [a landed Nayar family] and the Namboodiri families. The women of the former were given in marriage only to Namboodiris, so much so that the members of their families could be called semi-Namboodiris. Except in learning the Vedas and performing Vedic rites, in social and cultural fields there was no difference between them. However, it was acknowledged that they were of a lower caste than the Namboodiris.

(Namboodiripad, 1976).

In a very important discussion, E.M.S. Namboodiripad has written that a feature of Kerala society 'which marked Kerala off from the rest of (northern and southern) India is the continuity of the patriarchal and the matriarchal joint family system' (Namboodiripad, 1984, p. 31). As we have seen, an aspect of this 'continuity' was the fact that there was marriage and sexual relations between women of matrilineal families and men of patrilineal families. Much has been written on the rigidity of the caste system and the inflexibility of the caste environment in Kerala. At one end, the caste system was characterized by the crime of untouchability and by detailed gradations of distance pollution. Among caste Hindus, however, the caste system permitted forms of marriage between Nayar women and men at different levels of the caste hierarchy; sexual intermingling among caste Hindus was a special feature of the caste system in Kerala.

In Nayar families, the ultimate positions of control were held by men. Female literacy among Nayars, even at the turn of the century and later, was a fraction of male literacy. At the same time, Nayar women had greater personal freedom than most women to take decisions regarding marital and sexual relations. Nayar women played a crucial role in making household decisions, the decision-making role being invested with greater authority for the fact that inheritance was through them, and it was they who were the bearers of the family name. The birth of a girl in a Nayar household was welcomed; it was far from being considered a disaster as in other parts of India.

The matrilineal system was an enormous influence on social and cultural development in Kerala. It contributed to changing social attitudes and it contributed to creating social conditions in which women made real progress in health and education. The lesson to be had here is not that the achievement of Kerala-style outcomes requires a history of matriliny — that would be absurd — but that a precondition for the health and demographic transition are progressive social attitudes towards female survival and female education. In the case of Kerala, a unique set of historical and sociological conditions — including systems of marriage and matrilineal inheritance that were specific to the region — contributed to the establishment of such attitudes.

6. AGRARIAN CHANGE

6.1 Agrarian Relations

The progressive transformation of agrarian relations is intrinsically important, since such transformation undermines pre-capitalist relations of unfreedom in the countryside. It is important instrumentally as well: societies dominated by pre-capitalist landlordism suppress the forces of production in rural society and they have little stake in improving the conditions of health and education of the masses of their people. In a recent study published by the Inter-American Development Bank, a group of scholars present the results of a comparative study of two sets of countries. They took one group of countries that were small and resource-rich and distinctly less-developed in the middle of the last century and are at the top of the table today (the Nordic countries: Denmark, Norway, Sweden, and Finland) and compared them with four medium-sized Latin American countries (Colombia, Ecuador, Chile, and Uruguay). 'It is no surprise,' a reviewer of this research writes, 'that two points emerge strongly that are just what also emerge from East Asian comparisons: the role of early agrarian reform . . . and the role of education.'[86] The significance of education and changes in archaic agrarian relations are lessons from Kerala's experience as well. A foundational feature of Kerala's development experience, and of social and economic progress in Kerala, is the transformation of agrarian relations in the state. A more radical transformation of agrarian relations has been brought about by the people of Kerala after independence than of any other state of India. The history of this change is a history of public action — which took the form of mass struggle and of legislative action — against some of the most complex, exploitative, and oppressive rural social formations in the country.

[86] Thorp (1993).

Landlordism dominated social and economic arrangements in villages throughout Kerala; there were also important differences between regions in agrarian relations and land tenures, associated, *inter alia*, with differences in administration, administrative policy, and the nature of government, and in the development of the productive forces (which includes differences in farming practices, irrigation, land use, and land colonization, and the development of agricultural entrepreneurship).[87]

Malabar

In Malabar, the agrarian population was divided into four main categories.[88] The first category was that of *janmi* landlords, holders of *janmam* rights. All agricultural land, forest land, and cultivable waste land in Malabar was owned by janmi landlords.[89] The second category was that of the *kanakkaran*, holders of *kanam* rights. Kanam was a superior tenancy right and the kanakkaran (a heterogeneous category) was often an intermediary. The third main category, also internally differentiated, was that of *verumpattakkaran*, or tenant (non-owner) cultivator. The fourth main category was made up of unfree landless agricultural labourers, descendants of the members of the 'slave castes', subject to the worst forms of untouchability and class oppression.

After the seizure of Malabar from Tipu's rule and its annexation in 1792, the East India Company began to codify land tenure and to create a new system of land rights from the old.[90] The objectives of the new system were to extract as much revenue as possible from the people and to create, in the janmi, a bulwark for British rule in Malabar. To these ends, British administrators crammed local agrarian relationships into the conceptual categories available to English

---

[87] The earliest attempt to characterize pre-capitalist agrarian relations in Kerala theoretically was by E.M.S. Namboodiripad in the thirties and forties; he described feudalism in Kerala as being characterized by *janmi–savarna*–chieftain (landlord–upper caste–chieftain) domination of agrarian society (see Namboodiripad, 1994 for a discussion).

[88] For simplicity, only the four main categories are presented here.

[89] Varghese (1970).

[90] On the traditional functions and rights in land of the janmi, kanakkaran, verumpattakkaran, and others, see Namboodiripad (1943), Karat (1973), Panikkar (1989), Radhakrishnan (1989), and the original work of William Logan.

and Roman law.[91] The janmam right was considered equivalent to the Roman *plenum dominium*; in practice, all land in Malabar (except in Wayanad taluk) was recognized as being on private janmam tenure. Janmam was declared to be 'a right as absolute as can be had in property', one that gave the proprietor 'the right to alienate [property] in every possible way and to oust all the occupants of it at pleasure, all such at least as have not a lease from the proprietor.[92] The archetypal janmi was the head of a Namboodiri Brahman family or the head of a matrilineal Nayar or cognate caste-Hindu chieftain family.[93] Legislation, government policy, and judgements of civil courts under the Company and the crown reinforced the dominant legal status of the janmi.[94] The kanakkaran, whose traditional role was that of 'supervisor' and 'protector' of the inhabitants of the territory and traditionally of Nayar or cognate caste, was given the legal status of a mortgagee, and the kanam right was deemed a usufructuary mortgage, in which the period of mortgage, unless specified otherwise, was twelve years. The verumpattakkaran had the insecure legal status of a tenant-at-will.

Statutory janmi landlordism was disastrous for production and for the people. It was a ruinous combination of large-scale ownership and small-scale, primitive production, with one level or more of sub-leasing in between. Although the ryotwari system was formally extended to all non-zamindari parts of the Madras Presidency, janmam tenure was, in fact, not ryotwari at all, it was far more oppressive.

Land ownership was vested in the janmi, and was concentrated in the hands of the most powerful of them. The degree of concentration of ownership was extraordinary. For instance, Panikkar's calculations show that, in 1920–1, just 32 janmi landlords held 628,921 out of 1,229,217 acres, or 51 per cent of all cultivated land. Their land was spread over whole taluks; the Samutiri of Kozhikode, for example, owned land in 6 taluks and 520 villages. Prakash Karat

[91] As they did elsewhere in India: 'The zamindari and the ryotwari were both . . . effected by British ukases . . . the one a caricature of English landlordism, and the other of French peasant proprietorship' (Marx, 1853, p. 78).

[92] Cited in Varghese (1970), p. 26.

[93] There were some Muslim janmi landlords, and a very small number of Izhava families acquired janmam rights as well.

[94] British rule did not recognize the allodial right claimed by holders of janmam rights; all land was, of course, taxed.

studied land records in 20 villages (*desam*) that were among the first Karshaka Sangham (Peasant Union) villages. Title deeds on which the assessment was more than 100 rupees comprised 3 per cent of all title deeds, and covered 53 per cent of all agricultural land. In 10 of these villages, just 5 landlords and the temples controlled 43 per cent of the cultivated land.[95]

Under the janmi system, peasants were subjected to an uncommon degree of rack-renting. In the eighteen-eighties, William Logan reported that the rates of assessment were about 86 per cent of the net produce of wet lands and 63 per cent of the produce of garden lands; in 1917, F.B. Evans, Collector of Malabar, reported that rents were invariably between 75 and 85 per cent of the net produce. In his well-known report of 1916, Charles Innes, Evans' predecessor, reported that actual rents on wet land varied between 10 and 12 times the assessments; basing himself on Innes' observations, Karat calculated that '10 to 12 times the assessment would consume the whole net produce and leave the producer with nothing but the straw in most cases'.[96]

Rates of assessment were not only high, they were also regressive, laying 'a heavier burden of land revenue on the weaker rather than on the better-off sections of the agricultural population' (Panikkar, 1989, p. 7). Of the early years of the nineteenth century, Panikkar writes that 'as many as fifty different taxes were realized from the people', including taxes on houses, shops, cattle, looms, ferries, fishing nets, tapping knives, toddy, and arrack. 'Nothing,' in Panikkar's words, 'fell outside the exacting grasp of the state' (ibid.). There were also many other exactions from tenants and landless workers, in kind and in the form of free labour, and often associated with festivals and life-cycle events and rituals in landlord households.[97]

In general, where a kanakkaran intervened between the tenant and the janmi, the kanakkaran appropriated the largest share of the rent paid by the tenant, and, indeed, of the produce. However, although the kanakkaran received the largest share of the individual tenant's produce, the kanakkaran had to pay burdensome renewal-

---

[95] Panikkar (1989), p. 25; Karat (1973), pp. 28–9. See also Radhakrishnan (1989) for evidence on the concentration of ownership of land in a north Malabar village prior to the land reform of the nineteen-seventies.

[96] Karat (1973), p. 32. See also Panikkar (1989), pp. 18ff. and *passim*, and Namboodiripad (1943).

[97] See Panikkar (1989), Namboodiripad (1943).

fees at the end of 12 years (or the end of the contract-period) to the janmi (who, of course, collected rents from many more producers than a kanakkaran did). Punishing renewal-fees were also demanded of the verumpattakkaran. With rents, taxes, and other exactions as high as they were, it is not surprising that indebtedness among the peasantry was widespread as well.[98]

In 1819, Malabar had, in the reckoning of revenue officials of the Company, more slaves than other districts of the Madras Presidency. These slaves belonged to the lowest levels of the caste hierarchy — from, for example, the Cherumar, Pulayar, and Vettuvan castes — and were transferred with landed property. Revenue officials considered them tangible property, and entered them as such in accounts submitted to the Collector, and it is recorded that only in Malabar were slaves sold for arrears of revenue.[99] Although slavery was formally abolished in 1843 in Madras, unfree and bonded labour remained. The important point is that the decline in patron–client relations was asymmetric: the landlord rid himself of the obligations of the patron, while he continued to demand the services and material benefits that derived from the client status of the status-inferior.

Landlords could extract very high rents from tenants-at-will, and eviction was a major janmi weapon against tenants-at-will and intermediaries. Janmi landlords could evict tenants without compensation from wet-land leases and for very little when a tenant had made improvements on other-than-wet land.[100] Intermediaries who could afford to challenged evictions in court, and the number of eviction suits in Malabar courts was enormous: about 4,700 a year between 1916 and 1926, and about 5,300 a year between 1940 and 1946 (which was *after* the Malabar Tenancy Act was passed in 1930).[101] Evictions were also from homestead land, on which tenants had established dwellings. In their efforts to evict kanakkaran intermediaries, landlords concluded contracts to overlease land (the

[98] Karat (1973), pp. 34ff. 'One of the chief characteristics of holding *verumpattam* land was that the peasant could not escape debt' (ibid.).

[99] Proceedings of the Board of Revenue, Madras, 25 November 1819, p. 349. Officials of the Company estimated the number of slaves in the district, excluding Wayanad taluk, at 100,000.

[100] Varghese (1970), p. 41. Wet land: a term in revenue administration in south India that refers to crop land under surface irrigation (and not to all irrigated land). The main crop on wet land was generally paddy.

[101] Karat (1973), p. 32.

contracts were called *melchart*) with persons who became new intermediaries. Again, examples from the literature indicate that the
number of such contracts was huge: more than 40,000 overleases
were concluded between 1916 and 1926.[102]

Travancore

Travancore was the largest of the three constituent parts of Kerala.
Its territory was consolidated under a single kingdom by its most
important eighteenth century ruler, Martanda Varma (1729–58)
with the help of the Company. Its treaty with the Company was
concluded in 1788. After Martanda Varma's armies suppressed the
forces of scattered feudal Nayar chieftains, new forms of agrarian
relations emerged in the state. Land under the control of the chieftains came under the control of the Travancore state (and was
formally consecrated to the main deity of the Travancore family),
while the land held by the Brahmans, major temples, and the Travancore royal family and its hangers-on remained under the old
forms of control.[103]

In the mid-nineteenth century, there were three main legal categories of land. The first was State or *sirkar* land, which had two main
sub-categories. The first sub-category was land for which persons
deemed to be tenants of the State paid revenue to the State (*pandaravaka* land). The second sub-category was land held by the royal
family and its accomplices: it included land of the royal palace
(*kandukrishi*), land that belonged to the Padmanabha temple in Thiruvananthapuram (*Sree Pandaravaka*) and land that belonged to the
women of the royal family (*Sree Padam*). The second main category
was non-sirkar or janmam land, controlled mainly by Namboodiri
and status-superior Nayar and other chieftain families and wealthy
temples. The third category of land was granted to certain families
for no rent or very low payments (similar to *inam* tenures).

The most dynamic component of the agrarian economy in the
mid-nineteenth century was the pandaravaka category of land holding. In the eighteen-fifties, between 60 and 70 per cent of all cultivated

[102] On forms of land ownership, tenancy, and employer–employee relations,
and on tied and 'free' labour in early post-independence Malabar, see Mayer (1952).
For descriptions of land tenures and castes and rural occupations in a Malabar village
before land reform, see Aiyappan (1965).

[103] Varghese (1970), pp. 20ff.

land was pandaravaka, and all uncultivated waste land was deemed pandaravaka.[104] In 1865, a Royal Proclamation was issued that was to make a dramatic difference to land relations in Travancore. The terms of the proclamation began a process that unfettered the productive forces on pandaravaka land in a way that did not occur on any other tenure-category of land in Travancore, Cochin, or Malabar. The Travancore government conferred full ownership rights on tenant-cultivators of pandaravaka lands and allowed the new owners of pandaravaka land to transfer property without restriction. Revenue incentives were given for the cultivation of cultivable waste and for starting plantations (plantation agriculture in the hill tracts of Travancore dated from 1834). In 1891, an Agricultural Loans Act provided possibilities for new rural investment. There was a significant increase in the area of land under field crops and plantation crops, and, by the turn of the century, large investments were made to convert extensive reaches of swamp-land in the Kuttanad region (the region of backwaters, or *kayal*) to a type of reclaimed agricultural land.[105] Pandaravaka and kayal lands were the most important components of the land holdings of the Syrian Christian agrarian elite that rose to prominence and wealth in the nineteenth century.[106] The rise in prices of agricultural commodities and plantation crops that occurred in the nineteenth century, and the coconut and coir boom of the late nineteenth century served as price incentives for the expansion of cultivation in a way that did not happen in Malabar, where agrarian relations stifled advances in production.

Cochin

Agrarian relations in Cochin represented something in between conditions in Malabar and Travancore, though they were closer to Malabar than to Travancore. In the eighteen-fifties, 60 per cent of cultivated land was on forms of janmam tenure, and 40 per cent was sirkar land. Janmam land was owned by Namboodiris, temples, Nayar and other leading families, and by families close

---

[104] Varghese (1970), p. 45, *passim*.

[105] On state investment in land reclamation, see Jose George (1980), p. 48.

[106] On social and economic change among Syrian Christians in the second half of the nineteenth century, see Jeffrey (1976), especially ch. 4; and for a diagrammatic representation of caste and agrarian hierarchies in nineteenth-century Travancore, see Tharakan (1991), p. 4.

to the royal family.[107] The rates of assessment imposed on tenants on sirkar land were very high (the tribute paid by the Cochin state to the Company and later the crown was also exceptionally high) and continued to be high after ownership rights were conferred, which was only after the Cochin land settlement of 1905–9. Conditions were not as detrimental to the expansion of cultivation as in Malabar; since the control of unassigned waste land was not in the hands of janmi landlords, area under field crop cultivation expanded.

Overview

As is evident, the land system and the caste system were closely connected, and, consequently, there were close links between agrarian relations and the marriage and family systems. Hierarchies of land ownership and hierarchies of caste and ritual purity overlapped substantially. Worst-off in the system were, of course, people of the ritually inferior castes, who bore the double burden of class and caste oppression in rural Kerala. Most severe was the oppression of the people of the lowest tier of 'untouchable' castes, who were subject to slavery and different forms of bondage and unfreedom even after the formal abolition of slavery.[108]

Large joint families were poor agents of accumulation and of social and economic change. The joint family property of patrilineal Namboodiri families and of families of matrilineal Nayar and cognate castes was impartible. In the late nineteenth century and the early twentieth century, new laws allowed the partition of joint family property; first came laws that permitted lineages to split from the main family, and, later, laws that permitted property to be partitioned and acquired by smaller units of joint families (including nuclear families). Family properties were partitioned faster in Travancore than in Cochin and, of course, than in Malabar (Varghese, 1970, ch. 6). In central and northern Kerala, it was also noted that aristocratic Nayar lineages kept their property together longer (Gough, 1962, p. 373).

---

[107] Varghese (1970), pp. 32–3, 48–50, 69–74, *passim*. On agrarian slavery and civil disabilities in rural Cochin, see Achyuta Menon (1923), pp. 144ff.

[108] Laws against slavery were passed in Malabar in 1843, in Cochin in 1854 and 1855, and in Travancore in 1853 and 1855.

In Travancore, a formally free market in pandaravaka land was created after 1865. Land that was brought under new cultivation — crop land and plantation land — was also deemed pandaravaka, and was, *ipso facto*, part of the land market. The persons who were most active in taking advantage of the new market in land were, above all, from the Syrian Christian elite (although there were also persons of the Izhava elite, relatively few in number though important in terms of their social significance and impact). Syrian Christian entrepreneurs were typically less burdened by huge joint families and traditions of impartible property, and they made substantial gains in agricultural and trading activity in the nineteenth century. When joint-family households of traditional Hindu landlords weakened and when their land began to be partitioned and sold, Syrian Christian entrepreneurs were the major beneficiaries. The two processes identified by Varghese — of undermining the landed power of landlord families under the old system and of the emergence of communities that could 'fill the void' — went furthest in Travancore. The processes were weak in Cochin, and least advanced in Malabar.[109]

It is worth noting that the difference between Malabar and Travancore was not between an area characterized by the economic dominance of landlordism and another by peasant proprietorship (as has been suggested in the literature). Travancore was *not* a region where 'peasant proprietorship' was dominant. First, janmam land and sirkar and inam land directly under the control of the royal family, its temples and persons favoured by it continued to exist. Secondly, even on pandaravaka land, the dominant class of landowners were not *peasants*, they did not touch the plough or participate directly in the major manual operations on the land. The dominant class on pandaravaka land was made up of capitalist landlords (and corresponded roughly to ryotwari landlords in some parts of the Madras Presidency). They were vastly more advanced entrepreneurs than old-style landlords, but were landlords nevertheless. The difference between Malabar and Travancore was between a region where the janmi system was almost total, and another where a circumscribed janmi system existed with a growing, and more dynamic, sector that was dominated by new forms of capitalist landlordism.

---

[109] See Varghese (1970), especially ch. 6.

6.2 Agrarian Movements

Agrarian rebellion in the nineteenth century and until 1921 was fiercest in Malabar, and the organized peasant and agricultural worker movement in Kerala began there. The foremost modern historian of the Mappila revolts of the nineteenth and twentieth centuries, K.N. Panikkar, writes that 'rural society in Malabar was in a state of perpetual ferment during the nineteenth and early twentieth centuries. The revolts, dacoities, thefts, and social banditry that occurred almost regularly were essentially an expression of the protest of the rural poor against oppression and exploitation.'[110]

The literature identifies three main currents in the movement to transform agrarian relations in Malabar.[111] The first was the movement of Mappila tenants and agricultural labourers 'against lord and state',[112] from the first of what the British called 'Moplah outrages' in 1836 to the Malabar rebellion of 1921, which lasted eight months and in which thousands of persons were killed. The Mappila Muslims of Malabar were converts from Hinduism (often from oppressed castes, such as the so-called slave castes, and the fisherfolk castes), and also included descendants of Arab traders. They became a predominantly rural community in Malabar from the sixteenth to the nineteenth centuries, concentrated in the south Malabar taluks of Eranad, Valluvanad, and Ponnani.[113] The Mappila masses were mainly tenants, agricultural workers, workers in petty trade, and fisherpeople, owning little land and with low educational levels.[114] From 1834, united by their status as a class exploited by the janmi system and the colonial power, and united as well by religious identity, the Mappila rebels fought landlords and government furiously, and often mercilessly. The social background of the rebels was overwhelmingly peasant and labour and their targets were janmi landlords and their accomplices and government revenue officials.

The colonial government saw the struggles of the rural Mappila

---

[110] Panikkar (1989), p. 49. See also Panikkar (1990), a collection of documents on agrarian revolt and peasant struggles in nineteenth and twentieth-century Malabar.

[111] Namboodiripad (1943), Radhakrishnan (1989), Panikkar (1989).

[112] The term is the title of Panikkar's book. Most of the information in this paragraph is from chapter 2 of the book.

[113] For the leading account of social organization among Mappila Muslims, and a history of the community, see Miller (1992).

[114] On mass conversions of fisherfolk to Islam, see Aiyappan (1965).

poor as 'outrages' committed by a fanatical, less-than-civilized section of the population, and the basic administrative response of the government was repression. By the end of the nineteenth century, administrators, particularly William Logan, perceived, and attempted to analyse the agrarian roots of Mappila rebellion.[115] In practice, however, the thrust of late nineteenth-century and twentieth-century British policy in this sphere was to make some concessions to the more powerful and status-superior sections of Hindu kanakkaran intermediaries, while preserving the basic power of janmi landlords (and their status as bulwarks of British rule). It was not to concede the demands of the working poor of Malabar's villages.

The second major current in the movement for agrarian change in Malabar was the organized effort of kanakkaran intermediaries to acquire occupancy rights on land over which they had kanam rights. Most kanakkar did not touch the plough, the land over which they had kanam rights was cultivated by sub-tenants, and often there was more than a single layer of sub-leasing between them and the actual cultivators of the soil.

The most powerful of the kanakkar intermediaries were from Nayar and related castes.[116] These families acquired status and rights to land on kanam tenure through hypergamous sambandham arrangements with Namboodiri families. More than any other social group, they took advantage of opportunities for English education and entered professions such as the law, journalism, politics, and the bureaucracy. From the late nineteenth century, some prominent Nayars began to write and speak against Namboodiri domination and against sambandham relationships between Nayar women and Namboodiri men.[117] Over the same period, rich intermediaries — with Nayar intermediaries the most prominent among them — began a movement for occupancy rights, for security of tenure, for regulated rents and renewal fees, against overleases, and against other janmi exactions. Although sections of working tenants were mobilized during this movement — which can be said to have lasted

---

[115] See Panikkar (1989); on Logan's investigations of agrarian relations in Malabar, see also Kurup (1981), Radhakrishnan (1989), Nambiar (1982).

[116] On the rise of the kanakkaran, see Namboodiripad (1943), Panikkar (1989), Radhakrishnan (1989).

[117] The first novel in Malayalam, *Indulekha*, written by O. Chandu Menon, a judge of a subordinate court, dealt with this theme. On sambandham, see section 7.3 below.

until the Malabar Tenancy Act was passed in 1930 — it represented the interests of privileged intermediaries, and was a struggle for a greater share of the surplus between two non-labouring groups, one more privileged than the other.[118]

The kanakkaran demands were agitated in the courts, in the restricted-franchise legislatures, in departments of government in Calicut, Madras, New Delhi, and Simla, in the newspapers, and through public meetings — and not in the fields and streets and in battle against the armed strength of the janmi and state.[119] From 1912 through 1929, different versions of tenancy legislations were discussed, and despite the machinations of the landlords and of those in government who supported them, the essential demands of the intermediaries were made law in the Malabar Tenancy Act of 1930.

Thus, the long history of tenant–landlord *legislative* conflict (as distinct from the class struggle outside) in Malabar in the late nineteenth-century, and before 1930, represented conflicts between janmi landlord oppressors, on the one hand, and representatives of non-cultivating tenants — many of whom were actual or potential rent-collecting landlords, capitalist landlords, or upper-stratum peasants themselves — on the other, rather than conflicts between feudal janmi landlords and representatives of the toiling peasantry. The first significant and explicit statement of the socio-economic interests of the actual tenant-cultivators on official record was E.M.S. Namboodiripad's note of dissent to the Report on Malabar Tenancy Reform in 1939, and the first piece of tenancy-reform legislation that unambiguously took the part of, and ensured rights in land to, working tenants — tenant families whose members participated in the major manual tasks on the land — was the Kerala Agrarian Relations Bill of 1959.

The conditions of life of the rural poor worsened during the great depression. In Malabar, the combination of high rents and renewal fees, illegal exactions, new and higher levels of land revenue assessment after the land resettlement of 1929, and indebtedness

[118] In his 1943 history of the peasant movement in Malabar, E.M.S. Namboodiripad described this aspect of the kanakkaran perspective thus: 'The educated and professional man with a wide outlook and a sturdy sense of self-respect has to humiliate himself before the narrow-minded and conceited ignoramus who is his landlord' (Namboodiripad, 1943, p. 174).

[119] The most useful modern description of this phase is in Radhakrishnan (1989), ch. 3. See also Gopalankutty (n.d.).

became more than many peasants could bear, and evictions took place on a very large scale.[120] In these conditions, the third current in the movement for agrarian change in Malabar gained strength. This was the most radical current, the movement of peasants and working tenants that culminated in the land reform of contemporary Kerala.[121] The movement was led by persons who were active in the freedom movement and the Congress in the early thirties, who formed the Congress Socialist Party in Malabar later in the decade, and who were the core of the Communist Party in Malabar when it was established in the late thirties.

Politics in Malabar in the thirties and forties had many special qualities. The political movement brought together the struggle against British imperialism and the struggle against landlordism, and, by the forties, its main leaders were Communists. The Communist movement spread over an extraordinary range of sociopolitical activities. Communists led the peasants' and workers' movements, and the Communist Party and Communist-Party-led organizations were the strongest contingent of the national movement. Persons who became Communists were the leading activists in the struggle for progressive social reform, against untouchability and in the temple-entry movement. Communist organizers and school-teachers organized village schools and study-classes and were active in the *granthasala* or public library movement. Communists led the struggle for food in 1942–3, and Communist volunteers were the most active in relief work during the epidemic diseases of that period. Communist agit-prop theatre and journalism became well known. The first serious modern social-theoretical work on Malabar was by a Communist social theorist and political leader, E.M.S. Namboodiripad.

From the days of the *khilafat* movement, the emphasis in Malabar political organization was on *village*-level organization. After Congress activists were released from jail after the Civil Disobedience movement, and after E.M.S. Namboodiripad became the Secretary of the District Congress Committee, the Congress organization attempted to set up, in every village, a village Congress committee, a reading room, and a night school (from Namboodiripad interview,

---

[120] See Karat (1973), Radhakrishnan (1989), Nambiar (1982).

[121] See Prakash Karat (1973), Namboodiripad (1943), Radhakrishnan (1989), Gopalankutty (1981), and Nambiar (1982) for analyses of this period. Radhakrishnan's summary is particularly useful.

1992). This organizational practice of village-level organization, unique to Malabar, was taken over and extended by the Communists of Malabar in the late thirties and forties.

The Kerala *Karshaka Sangham* (Peasants' Union) was established in 1933. By 1937, it became an organization with village and taluk-level committees as well as an all-Malabar committee. By the forties, it was a major mass organization in the district. Its demands were against the janmi system, against social disabilities of people of the oppressed castes, and for the amendment of the Malabar Tenancy Act and its extension to the Hosdurg taluk of the South Canara district. The 'hunger marches' of 1936 — including the landmark Kannur-to-Madras march led by A.K. Gopalan — were organized by the Peasants' Union. The unions organized the procurement of grain and its distribution through fair-price shops and campaigns of de-hoarding grain during the food crisis of 1942–3.

At the turn of the century, agricultural workers were a larger proportion of rural workers in Travancore than in Malabar or Cochin. Powerful independent organizations of agricultural workers emerged in Travancore, where the first *Thiruvithamkur Karshaka Thozhilali Union* (Travancore Agricultural Workers' Union) was formed in 1939, in Kainakiri village in the Kuttanad region.[122] Scholars have pointed out that it was no accident that such a union was formed in Kuttanad. Reclaimed kayal land was cultivated in blocks of hundreds of acres on which thousands of workers were employed for the cultivation of wet-land rice. Big landlords dominated land ownership in Kuttanad, and wage labour was more prevalent here than in other parts of Kerala. The agricultural labour movement, which was led by Communists, was deeply influenced by (and, in time, influenced) the social-reform movement among people of the oppressed castes, by the freedom struggle and the struggle for democratic rule in Travancore, and by the movement for literacy, schooling, and education in Travancore. There were close links between the agricultural workers' movement and the unions of coir workers in the Kuttanad region.

The independent class demands of agricultural workers involved the right to organize, and demands against social oppression, for higher wages, for payment in standard measures and against arbitrary exactions from landlords. Later, particularly from the fifties, there

[122] See Jose (1980), Kannan (1988), Jose George (1980).

were struggles around the issue of the length of the working day. In the sixties and seventies, agricultural workers were active in the struggle for agricultural and house-site land. Agricultural workers' organizations were important participants, from the forties, in the movement to establish a public food-distribution system.[123]

6.3   Land Reform

Land reform, or passing and implementing new laws to alter or abolish old land tenures and to create new ones, was crucial to the transformation of agrarian relations in Kerala. The first Communist Ministry represented a turning point in that transformation; a few days after it took office in 1957, the legislative process for land reform began.

Land reform in Kerala had three major components.[124] The first involved that burdensome, complex, and widespread affliction of Kerala agriculture, tenancy. Tenancy legislation had four main features. First, it sought to provide security of tenure to tenants. It is noteworthy that action on this front began less than a week after the Namboodiripad ministry was sworn in. By an Ordinance of 11 April 1957 (the Ministry was formed on 5 April), evictions were prohibited and land holdings restored to tenants who were evicted after the formation of the state of Kerala. Secondly, arrears of rent were cancelled. Thirdly, the rights of janmi landlords and intermediaries on tenanted land were taken over by the government. Where land rights vested in the government, all rent payments were

---

[123] See Jose (1980) and Kannan (1988) for useful accounts of the agricultural labour movement and its demands, on new features of the movement after the introduction of new varieties of rice in the seventies and on the spread of the movement in other regions of Kerala. On living conditions among agricultural workers in Travancore, on the politicization of the agricultural workers' movement in the region, and for an account of workers' demands, see Jose George (1980). On the peasant movement in Cochin, see Balan (1994).

[124] There is an extensive scholarly literature on this subject, from which this summary derives. Raj and Tharakan (1983) and Radhakrishnan (1989) have the best analytical summaries; the latter has a very useful full-length study of land reform and before-and-after data that include data from a village study. See also Namboodiripad (1985), Raj (1992), Herring (1983), Saradamoni (1981, 1982), Franke and Chasin (1992), Franke (1993). On the Communists and agricultural labour after 1957, see Kannan (1988) and Jose George (1980).

stopped. Fourthly, tenancy legislation sought to give land to the tiller. Communist Party policy was, of course, to expropriate land-lords without compensation. However, legal requirements related to the constitutional 'right' to property made some sort of compensation necessary; the solution taken on was to make the purchase price of land a multiple of rent, to set a statutory rent, and to set that rent low (at between one-fourth and one-twelfth of the gross produce). The terms of payment were favourable to the tenant, and the purchase price was treated as a debt to the government, with no forfeiture of ownership rights in case of default.

The second main component of land reform involved homestead land (*kudikidappu*) occupied by the rural poor. Occupants of such land were to be given ownership rights. The size of the plot to be allotted varied from 0.03 acres in a town or city to 0.10 acres in a village, and could be purchased at 25 per cent of the market rate, and half that if the owner had land above the ceiling. Government subsidized half the purchase price, and the rest was due in instalments. There were subsidiary provisions in respect of kudikidappu regarding, first, security of tenure; secondly, making occupancy rights heritable; thirdly, discharging arrears of rent; and, fourthly, rent control.

The third component of land reform concerned the imposition of limits on land ownership and the distribution of land identified as surplus to the landless. The land ceiling in Kerala, which was imposed on household land-holdings, varied with the size of household; it did not exceed 25 standard acres.

Radical land reform laws with the foregoing features were drafted by the ministries (1957–9 and 1967–9) led by E.M.S. Namboo-diripad. Soon after the Kerala Agrarian Relations Bill was passed by the Kerala Legislative Assembly in 1959, a coalition of right-wing opposition groups, made up of reactionary landed interests, representatives of the private sector in higher education, the Church, caste organizations such as the Nair Service Society led by Mannath Padmanabhan, and other anti-Communist individuals and organizations in the state, in league with the Congress Party, began a violent campaign of social disruption in Kerala. The Congress Party (of which Indira Gandhi was then President) and the Government of India organized the dismissal of the Government of Kerala by the President of India.

The next Congress government introduced a new land-reform

bill. This could not completely and explicitly undo the Communist law, but it attempted to enfeeble it by introducing new exemptions regarding land transfers. A new Act was passed, the Kerala Agrarian Relations Act of 1960. The courts declared even this unconstitutional, and another Act, the Kerala Agrarian Relations Act of 1964 was passed and entered in the Ninth Schedule of the Constitution, that is, it was placed outside the purview of the courts. In 1967, the second E.M.S. Namboodiripad ministry, a coalition government led by the CPI(M), introduced the Kerala Land Reforms Bill, and the Act that ensued provided the basis for the land reforms that took place in the seventies.

Land reform was a struggle until the end. From 1 January 1970, peasant unions and other mass organizations of the CPI(M) — which was no longer in government — began intensive state-wide campaigns to ensure that land reforms were implemented. The government of which C. Achutha Menon was Chief Minister called in the paramilitary Central Reserve Police to put down the mass struggle in the state. The first years of the seventies were years of demonstrations and land-occupation campaigns, and of attacks on the people's movement by police, paramilitary forces, and landlords' henchmen. Repression took the form of arrests, tear-gas, and *lathi* attacks, shooting down demonstrators, and burning down the huts of peasants and agricultural workers. During the eighty-day mobilization of agricultural workers and peasants in June–August 1972 alone, 1,60,000 demonstrators were arrested, and 10,000 sentenced to jail terms (Nayanar, 1982, pp. 149–50). Despite state and landlord-sponsored repression that organizations of the left had to face, the writing was on the wall, and state power could not prevent the implementation of certain aspects of land reform.

Put very briefly, the implementation of the first two sets of land reform (concerned with tenancy and homestead land) was relatively successful; the implementation of reforms relating to the identification of land above the ceiling and its redistribution was not. Using official data, Radhakrishnan reported that the first set of reforms resulted in the transfer of 1,970,000 acres to 1,270,000 households, the second set of reforms resulted in the transfer of 20,000 acres of homestead land to 270,000 households, and the third led to the transfer of 50,000 acres to 90,000 households (Radhakrishnan, 1989, p. 185).

Radhakrishnan (1989) discusses the reasons for the poor performance in respect of the third set of land reforms. Landlords transferred land on a large scale in order to escape ceiling laws. There were bogus transfers as well as transfers validated by the Acts of 1964 and 1969, and their combined effect was to make a lot of surplus land disappear. In 1979, in order to validate transfers in the form of gifts made by certain classes of landlords so as to circumvent ceiling laws, the Congress government passed the Kerala Land Reforms Amendment Act (known as the Gift Deeds Act) and, although rejected earlier the same year because its provisions 'defeated the very purpose of land reforms' (Radhakrishnan, 1989, pp. 184–5), it was approved by the President of India in October 1979.[125]

Two important studies provide village-level information on the implementation of land reform. Of Kodakkad in north Malabar, P. Radhakrishnan writes that the 'land system now is strikingly different from . . . the pre-reforms period', 'the land system is no longer characterized by the extreme concentration of land in a single group', and old forms of class–caste correspondence in land ownership in the village no longer exist (Radhakrishnan, 1989, p. 229). In Nadur, Richard Franke reports, 'the land reform redistributed substantial amounts of land from the biggest owners to small holders and the landless' (Franke, 1993, p. 148). Land reform 'reduced both land and income inequality', and the 'land reform undermined the material basis of caste and class inequality' (ibid.).[126]

The Kerala Agricultural Workers' Act came into effect on 2 October 1975. It has been described as a trade union act for agricultural workers, and is the only one of its kind in the country. The Act legislated minimum wages, job security, and retirement benefits (in the form of a Provident Fund to which workers and employers contribute), it limited the length of the working day,

---

[125] See the very useful account of the Gift Deeds Act controversy in Tharakan (n.d.). The area involved was not trivial: it amounted to 14,164 acres or 9 per cent of the area ordered for surrender (Ronald Herring, 1981, cited in Radhakrishnan, 1989, p. 185). Radhakrishnan writes: 'The enactment of the Bill was undoubtedly a defeat for the CPI(M) and other progressive forces in Kerala as much as it was a victory for the Kerala Congress and the Muslim League. The real losers were . . . the thousands of landless labourers, especially Harijans and persons from other socially and economically backward sections of society who . . . [hoped] to get a piece of land as their own through the surplus land redistribution' (p. 185).

[126] See the accounts in Radhakrishnan (1989), ch. 6, and Franke (1993), ch. 7.

and it created arbitration boards for settling disputes between workers and employers. It required local bodies to prepare lists of agricultural workers (Franke and Chasin, 1992, pp. 65ff.; Jose George, 1980, pp. 111ff.). According to Franke and Chasin, the highest real wage gains for agricultural workers since the mid-sixties occurred immediately after the Act was passed. Legislation for unemployment insurance for agricultural workers was enacted in 1980–1 and agricultural labour pensions were started in 1982. Franke and Chasin calculated that, at 1986 prices, the pension was enough to buy rice for an adult for about 10 days in a month (Franke and Chasin, 1992, op. cit.).

According to data from the Government of Kerala, the proportion of rural labour households to all households was 50 per cent in 1983–4 (Government of Kerala, 1985, p. 1, Table 1). Of all rural labour households, no less than 93 per cent owned land (ibid., p. 7), and 93 per cent owned the houses in which they lived (ibid., p. 34). A.V. Jose (1994) shows that, between 1970–1 and 1988–9, the highest percentage increase in real daily agricultural wages paid to men (63 per cent) was in Kerala, and that the trends in wage rates for women workers were similar. In 1988–9, the daily money wage rates paid to men were highest in Punjab (Rs 28.90), Kerala (Rs 27.70), and Haryana (Rs 26.40) (ibid.). Jose writes that 'social policy . . . and redistributive transfers effectively complemented labour market interventions' which together 'conditioned improved terms of wage employment in Kerala' (ibid.). Despite these measures, given the stagnation of agricultural production in Kerala and the stagnation in the number of days of employment available in agriculture, there is no evidence of radical change in the income status of agricultural workers in Kerala in the contemporary period.

The phase of large-scale mass struggles for land reform ended with the seventies. Until the end of the seventies in Kerala, a party's or a person's political position was defined by where they stood on the land question. Today agrarian change is a fact, and there is no political challenge to land reform or movement for its reversal.[127]

---

[127] On this issue, see Jose George (1980), p. 19, Jeffrey (1992), p. 185, Herring (1992), p. 5. While the history of Kerala's agrarian relations and the implementation of land reform have been studied by scholars in some detail, I am not aware of any scholarly primary-data based study that attempts to characterize, in a convincing way, agrarian relations and class structure in the countryside in contemporary Kerala.

The gains of land reform should not, of course, be exaggerated. The scope of land reforms in any single region is circumscribed by the class character of the Indian state and the government in power in New Delhi. Land reform in Kerala did not transfer agrarian power to agricultural labourers and poor peasants, and it did not end capitalist landlordism.[128] It did not lead to the establishment of production cooperatives or collectives or to other post-capitalist forms of agrarian production organization (or, for that matter, to the creation of a panchayat system as democratic as the one in West Bengal).[129] Land reform in Kerala was not followed by substantial increases in crop production, as was the case in West Bengal, nor were there substantial increases in rural employment.

Despite these limitations, the achievements of land reform in Kerala are far from negligible. Land reform abolished statutory landlordism and ended the janmi system. It reduced the concentration of ownership of land holdings (see Table 28). It broke the back of Namboodiri landlordism and weakened Nayar landlordism. It protected tenants, and ended systems of rack-renting and those illegal exactions from the poor that characterized the old system. It provided house sites to tens of thousands of families. Further, agricultural workers' wage struggles and the achievements of the people in gaining agricultural and house-site land contributed to raising rural daily wage rates in Kerala significantly,[130] and to the introduction of social security schemes for agricultural labourers.[131]

There is also no detailed study or informed survey of the rights in land of women in the contemporary period, particularly after the land reform.

[128] In an interview recently, E.M.S. Namboodiripad characterized landlordism in contemporary Kerala in the following way. In his opinion, although 'the old type of *janmi* ceased to exist', there is still 'landlordism of another type', that is, of landlords 'who get their lands cultivated through wage labour and those who live on usury and are also the dominant section in rural trade' (interview, April 1992).

[129] The programmes of group farming that were introduced in the late eighties during the 1987–91 Nayanar ministry were very interesting experiments, and indicate areas of possible public action in the future, but they did not survive or spread.

[130] Total agricultural wage earnings are, of course, another matter, since earnings depend also on the number of days of employment.

[131] On social security schemes for agricultural labourers, see Gulati (1993).

TABLE 28. *Distribution of Household Ownership Holdings:*
Kerala, 1961–2 and 1982

(in per cent)

Size category of ownership holding (acres)	1961–2		1982	
	Number of households	Area	Number of households	Area
Landless	30.9	0.0	12.8	0.0
0.01–0.99	41.5	12.3	63.5	21.0
1.00–2.49	14.8	18.1	14.4	24.8
2.50–4.99	7.4	20.2	6.1	23.5
5.00–14.99	4.6	27.5	3.0	25.8
≥ 15.00	0.8	21.9	0.2	4.9

Source. National Sample Survey, 17th and 37th rounds, cited in H.R. Sharma (1992).

The role must be emphasized of land reform not only as a process that helped to transform agrarian relations in the state, but also as a facilitator of social change in Kerala. Land reform and the larger achievement of change in agrarian relations were not, as is clear, achieved 'from above'. They were achieved after decades of struggle by people's organizations that were based on powerful village-level organizational units and led by the Communist Party. Their struggles influenced and changed the lives of the rural poor in many spheres. For decades, the agrarian movement mobilized the rural poor for economic and social (including educational) change. The agrarian movement has played a crucial role in creating an awareness of people's rights, in democratizing rural life, and in creating conditions favourable to the spread of mass education and facilities for improved conditions of public health.

7. AGENTS OF CHANGE

7.1 Travancore and Cochin

The establishment of the kingdom of Travancore in the eighteenth century was accompanied by a strengthening of the centralized power of the State. An important feature of the consolidation of state power was the destruction, by Martanda Varma and his successors, of small feudatories and of independent centres of feudal power. Land was brought under state control, and the ceremonial consecration of the state of Travancore to Anantapadmanabha, the family deity of the royal family of Travancore, was symbolic of Travancore's unification and of the conquest of scattered sources of military–feudal power.

From the beginning of the nineteenth century, British suzerainty was well established. The revolts of Velu Thampi in Travancore and of Paliyath Achan in Cochin had been crushed. The state in Travancore and Cochin functioned within the bounds set by the British power, and by its immediate representative, the British Resident in Thiruvananthapuram. The Resident from 1810 to 1819 was Sir James Munro, who was, among other things, influenced by the activity of the London Missionary Society (LMS) and its work (particularly in south Travancore) in the spheres of education and health, for the elimination of slavery, and against other forms of oppression of the lower castes. Although they practised untouchability themselves, the rulers of Travancore accommodated the activity of the LMS, and absorbed important features of missionary activity into state policy.

In a recent interview, E.M.S. Namboodiripad said that, in his opinion, the royal administrations of Travancore and Cochin were sensitive to the aspirations of the local bourgeoisie and upper-caste elites, and 'closer to the people' than the rulers in other Indian princely states.[132] We have seen that men of the royal families of Travancore and Cochin, who belonged to the Kshatriya caste, married Nayar women (the men of the Cochin royal family had to cast their nets wider among Nayar families for wives than those of the Travancore family, for the reason that there were more of them). The characteristics of the royal families of which Namboodiripad speaks, and the so-called 'middle-classness' of the extended royal family, had to do, undoubtedly, with the broad-based (for royalty) system of marriage and the system of succession that the royal families followed.

The administrative history of nineteenth-century Travancore was marked by an extraordinary series of state-sponsored reforms

[132] Interview, April 1992.

and declarations of intent.[133] Free and universal education was declared to be an objective of public policy. Schools were opened and instruction was introduced in Malayalam. The first public library in India was established in Thiruvananthapuram and the state sponsored a remarkable programme of translations. Legislation against chattel slavery was passed. Civil and criminal laws and laws of legal procedure were codified. A system of public health was introduced and hospitals were built. Land tenure legislation brought Travancore closer to a system of ryotwari, investing proprietary rights in new sections of persons who were actually responsible for farming the soil. There was an important programme of agricultural colonization. Public works became an important sphere of state activity. There was progress in road transport in Travancore. Travancore was the first princely state to constitute some sort of council for the work of legislation.[134] There is an interesting comparison to be had here with the Meiji, another example of a regime which, in a general context of foreign intervention, brought the decentralized power of scattered military–feudal lords to an end and initiated a programme of social, educational, and economic reform under a centralized monarchy.[135]

It is useful to remember, though, that the monarchy and the upper-caste elite remained an autocratic and undemocratic ruling stratum. Its members practised untouchability and were hostile to the demands of the outcaste and the oppressed. State power under Dewan C.P. Ramaswamy Aiyar discriminated openly against the Christians in Travancore's population, and attacked the state's people's movements and the movement of peasants, agricultural workers, and coir workers.

Are Kerala's achievements today the 'consequence' of the policies of the royal administrations of the princely states? Certainly not.

133 On the changes brought about by the Travancore administration in the second half of the nineteenth century, the best account is in Jeffrey (1976), especially ch. 3.

134 See All-Travancore Joint Political Congress (1934), pp. 2ff.

135 According to the historian K.N. Ganesh, the state-formation process in eighteenth-century Travancore took place in circumstances in which the centralized monarchy derived direct support from the lower echelons of the agrarian population as well as from merchants, and, consequently, acted in favour of those groups (Ganesh, 1990, cited and discussed in Tharakan, 1991), p. 2; in this context, see also Washbrook (1994).

The policies of the princely states did create what has been called an 'environment of official support' for primary education, and Travancore and Cochin did better than Malabar or other princely states in respect of the public administration of, broadly speaking, social services.[136] Nevertheless, Kerala's achievements today required radical changes in the status of people of the oppressed castes and land reform, and policies that closed the gap between different regions of the state — changes well outside the class and caste calling of the ruling elites of the princely states of Travancore and Cochin.

7.2   Missionary Activity

By one account, Travancore had a higher density of Protestant missionaries in the mid-nineteenth century than any other part of India (Jeffrey, 1992, p. 97); one of the reasons for Travancore having become a major field of Protestant evangelical effort was certainly the extraordinary state of unfreedom of the people of the oppressed castes. They came as agents of the colonial power, and to evangelize; the Protestant missionaries in Travancore in the late eighteenth and first half of the nineteenth centuries also constituted the first modern organized group opposed to untouchability and caste discrimination as they found it in Travancore.[137] They put their social outlook into practice in many ways: they opened the first modern schools in the state, and they opened them to the children of the outcastes, boys and girls.[138] They opened rural

---

[136] In 1868, Lord Salisbury, the Secretary of State for India, said that 'if all Native States were governed as were Travancore by Madhava Rau and Cochin by Sankunni Menon, the British Government would have to look for their laurels' (cited in Achyuta Menon, 1922, p. 9).

[137] See, for instance, Kooiman (1989), Agur (1903), Somervell (1940), and Hardgrave (1969). On Protestant missionary initiatives in advocating social reform in the eighteenth and nineteenth centuries, and on changes in missionary activity after 1850, see Oddie (1978); see also Potts (1967). Of Protestant missionary activity in the nineteenth century, the church historian C.M. Agur wrote: 'It has always been the method of the Gospel, first to find its home among the humbler classes, the despised and rejected ones. . . . It was so and is so in India; and it is remarkably so in Travancore' (Agur, 1903, vol. 1, p. 13).

[138] On the part played by Protestant missionaries in the history of schooling in Kerala in the nineteenth century, see section 4.2.

hospitals and dispensaries (the establishment of the South Travancore Medical Mission in Neyyoor in 1838 by the missionary Archibald Ramsay was a landmark event in the history of health care in Kerala).[139] They played a major role in medical education in south India and in propagating principles of hygiene and public health. They encouraged the breaking of caste taboos, and were the main support of the people who fought for women of oppressed castes to be allowed to clothe themselves above the waist.[140] They began literacy and anti-slavery campaigns among the Shanar people of south Travancore and among the Pulayar people, and pressed for legislation against slavery and against forms of torture. In a society in which social sanctions against the ritually 'impure' castes and outcastes were as severe as they were in Travancore, the systematic spread of education among the people of such groups could not but be profoundly destabilizing.

Because Protestant missionaries were representatives of the colonial power, they were also able to influence public policy. Two Residents, James Munro and Francis Maltby, had direct links with Protestant missions. As written earlier, the statement of Gowri Parvathi Bai on education was undoubtedly influenced directly by — in all likelihood written by — the Dewan and Resident, James Munro, a person described as 'a devout Christian with evangelical convictions, who wanted to convert all Christians and non-Christians to the Protestant faith' (Yesudas, 1978, pp. 99 and 100; see also Yesudas, 1980).[141]

There is no question that missionary activity and influence helped prepare the ground for the social movements of the second half of the nineteenth century, and in the twentieth century.[142]

[139] For a description of the mission ('At first it was only a small medicine chest . . . '), see Somervell (1940).

[140] Samuel Mateer introduced his description of the 'Upper Cloth Riots' thus: 'Towards the close of 1858 the powers of darkness, error and paganism again came into direct collision with Christian truth and social freedom' (Mateer, 1871, p. 295).

[141] It is another matter that the missionaries were also racist and social-exclusionary themselves. The punishment when an LMS missionary married a local person was expulsion from the society.

[142] Professor Aiyappan accorded the missionaries a formative role in the history of social relations in Kerala: 'The social legislation against untouchability, the temple entry act and the tenancy acts were the culmination of a long process which really started with the beginnings of westernization of India and the impact of Protestant Christianity' (Aiyappan, 1965, pp. 8–9).

7.3   Caste-based Reform Movements

There were caste-based movements among many castes in Kerala. Among the most well-known of these were the reform movements among the people of the Izhava caste and the Pulaya caste and among Nayars and Namboodiris. The Nadars of south Travancore — particularly in Kanniyakumari and Tirunelveli — were also organized into a caste-based movement; the centre of activity and organization of the Nadar caste organization was in Tamil Nadu. Something of the heterogeneity of the caste-based reform movements is apparent even from this list — it consisted of oppressed castes as well as oppressor castes. Caste movements were active in the movement for social reform and for changes in social practices, particularly the practice of untouchability; they also made efforts to reform internal caste rules and to alter, by means of state intervention through legislation, inheritance laws and rules of family organization.

The Izhava Movement

The Izhava social reform movement of the late nineteenth and early twentieth century was one of the most important caste-based social-reform movements of the modern period in India.[143] The Izhava social-reform movement, one scholar writes, was 'the most radical aspect of the social awakening that accompanied the rise of capitalism (in Travancore) and was the most sweeping mass movement that Travancore had known' (Isaac, 1985). Its early leaders — persons such as Sree Narayana Guru, Kumaran Asan, Dr Palpu — and the chief caste organization of the Izhava people — the Sree Narayana Dharma Paripalana Yogam, or SNDP Yogam — have been described as being the first organizers and inspirers of the mass democratic movement of cultivating peasants and the landless in Kerala (Namboodiripad, 1984, p. 99). Although the Izhava social-reform movement became widespread and was active in Malabar and Cochin, its origins were in Travancore, as was its real organizational strength.

In Kerala's caste hierarchy, the Izhava caste was the upper tier of the two levels of untouchability. Considered outcaste and untouchable by caste Hindus, Izhavas were also considered ritually superior

[143] On the movement led by Narayana Guru and on social change among the Izhava people in the late nineteenth and early twentieth centuries, see Chandramohan (1981, 1987).

to the Pulaya and other slave castes.[144] A salient feature of social change among the Izhavas is a kind of discrepancy between ritual status and economic opportunity that emerged in the last decades of the nineteenth century and in the early part of the twentieth. This was a period in Travancore of commercialization and the capitalist development of agriculture, a period of agricultural colonization and the development of plantations in the hill regions, of agrarian legislation in the direction of 'peasant proprietorship', and of the beginning of the break-up of the old Nayar and Namboodiri estates. Travancore also benefited from the late-century boom in the coconut trade, when the demand for coconut and for coir-matting in Britain and the United States became an important stimulus for growth in coconut cultivation and coir-making in Travancore.[145]

The traditional occupations of the people of Izhava caste involved agricultural labour and peasant cultivation, the cultivation and processing of coconut and coconut-palm products, and the production and sale of toddy and arrack. The Izhava people were not completely excluded from traditional learning: there were ayurvedists and astrologers among them, and men of learning in Sanskrit. The traditional occupations of the caste became, in the context of changes in Travancore's economy, a springboard for the economic advancement of some members of the caste during this period. They obtained contracts for the production of arrack and for tapping toddy, and they entered the coconut trade and coir manufacture and trade. The occupations that were characteristic of their low ritual status provided the basis, in a sense, for economic advancement among an Izhava elite in the twentieth century. By 1875, there was a higher proportion of traders in the Izhava caste than in any other Malayalam-speaking Hindu caste. Izhava workers were more mobile than others, and an Izhava working class grew in non-agricultural occupations (by the end of the nineteen-thirties, 80 per cent of coir

---

[144] This latter demarcation was one that conservative mainstream Izhava leaders insisted on at one stage of the movement in the twentieth century. When the Izhava leader Sahodaran Aiyappan attempted, in the twentieth century, to introduce inter-caste eating, leaders of the SNDP Yogam said no to the presence of people from the slave castes.

[145] On economic status and social change among people of the Izhava caste in the second half of the nineteenth century, see Jeffrey (1976), especially ch. 4; for information on the transition from caste to class factors in social change among the Izhava people, see ibid., especially ch. 6.

workers were of the Izhava caste: Isaac, 1985), on plantations, in public works (public works were an important sphere of activity of the Travancore government in the nineteenth century), and in land reclamation and agriculture. Their exclusion from government salaried employment influenced the search by persons of the caste for employment elsewhere.

Social change was also helped by the greater flexibility of the marriage and inheritance systems among Izhava families, and the tendency to form nuclear families was more marked among Izhava families than, say, among Nayar or Namboodiri families (Varghese, 1970). Social consciousness was influenced by missionary activity in the field of education and against caste discrimination (Chandramohan, 1981).

For all these advances, the Izhava people continued to be victims of different forms of caste discrimination. A vivid example of the disjuncture between caste and economic status, and one often referred to, is the case of Alamoottil Channar, one of the two owners in Travancore of private automobiles in the nineteen- twenties. When the car got to public roads on which persons of the caste were not permitted, he got out of the car and ran along to a point where he could get back in, to which his Nayar chauffeur drove the car. He also had roads built on his private estate on which to drive his car.[146] Izhava representation was disproportionately low in government employment. In 1891, people of the caste were 16 per cent of the population; in 1881, persons of the caste had less than 1 per cent of government jobs. The best-known example of government discrimination was against Dr Palpu, who was ranked second in the entrance examinations to the medical college but was refused admission because he was an Izhava. He qualified in medicine at Madras, was refused employment in Travancore, and found employment in the princely state of Mysore. In 1932, people of the Izhava caste were 17 per cent of the population and had less than 4 per cent of government jobs. By comparison, Nayar persons were 17 per cent of the population and had 52 per cent of jobs; Brahmans were 0.8 per cent of the population and had 18 per cent of government jobs.[147]

The emerging Izhava elite demanded the right to be full participants in the modernization that began in the nineteenth century.

---

[146] Chandramohan (1981); interview with P. Govinda Pillai.
[147] Data from Chandramohan (1981).

The SNDP Yogam was established in 1903. The main demands of the Izhava social-reform movement were against untouchability and against caste-Hindu prohibitions on access by members of the caste to roads, bathing-places, water sources and other public places, for free entry into Hindu temples, for literacy and education, for employment in government jobs, and for greater representation in the restricted-franchise legislature of the Travancore state (an issue on which the Izhava social-reform movement made common cause for a time with representatives of the Christian and Muslim communities in Travancore).

The emphasis on education was remarkable. At the first meeting of the Yogam, Dr Palpu declared: 'We are the largest Hindu community in Kerala. . . . Without education no community has attained permanent civilized prosperity. In our community there must be no man or woman without primary education.'[148] The most striking feature of the early history of the Izhava social-reform movement is the movement to gain access to primary education for all boys and girls, and to higher education as well. Caste Hindu Nayars opposed mass education among the Izhava people with violence, as during the attacks on Izhava people in Quilon.

The movement also organized against backward customs and primitive practices associated with Hinduism. Its demands regarding the reform of inheritance laws led to the promulgation of the Izhava Regulation of 1925. The demand for temple-entry received broad support. The famous *satyagraha* of 1924–5 at Vaikkam in Travancore was not, in fact, for temple entry, but demanded the right of people of the oppressed castes to travel on roads near the temple. The struggle was called off in 1925 on Gandhi's advice, when the government permitted public access to all roads near the temple but one, the eastern road. The Vaikkam satyagraha was, however, a landmark event, and the movement for temple-entry gained in strength. The government issued a temple-entry proclamation in 1936.[149]

---

[148] Cited in Isaac and Tharakan (1986b). On education and social mobility in Travancore at the turn of the century, see Tharakan (1991), pp. 10–11.

[149] See Isaac and Tharakan (1986b) on the impatience of activists of the movement with the strategy and tactics of upper-caste Congressmen and Gandhi on the issue of temple-entry. For a village-level description of the Izhava social-reform movement, see Aiyappan (1965).

The late eighteen-eighties and early eighteen-nineties were a crucial period in the formation of modern Kerala.[150] In the seventies and eighties, newspapers emerged and the language of the people was used in print.[151] In the eighties and nineties, translating texts into Malayalam became a movement. In 1889, the first full-fledged Malayalam novel, Indulekha, which had a social-reform theme, was published. In 1889, literary criticism first appeared as a modern literary form in Malayalam. In 1888, Sree Narayana Guru, who was the son of a middle peasant from a matrilineal Izhava family, and was deeply influenced by Vedanta and by ideas of social equality and social and religious reform, began his public mission. He proclaimed the teaching with which his personal philosophy was to be identified: 'One Caste, One Religion, One God for Man.' In 1891, the Malayalee Memorial was presented to the court of Travancore. Although it reflected the demands of the Nayars against non-Malayalam speaking Brahmans, the third signatory was Dr Palpu, and the Memorial referred to the fact that not a single Tiyya (Izhava) was employed in any government job that carried a salary of more than five rupees a month.[152]

An outstanding — and perhaps unique — feature of the Malayalam renaissance of the nineteenth and early twentieth centuries was that people from a caste that was considered outcaste and whose members were considered untouchable by caste Hindus, that is, people of the Izhava caste, played a distinguished part in the renaissance.[153] Kumaran Asan, educated in Calcutta, was the first Secretary of the SNDP Yogam, and the first lyrical poet in modern Malayalam.

Political and ideological trends within the Izhava social-reform movement, and the relationship between this movement on the one hand and the workers' movement on the other, have been discussed in a few contributions to the scholarly literature.[154] In the nineteen-

---

[150] Interview, P. Govinda Pillai.

[151] The first Malayalam daily, *Deepika*, began in 1887, and *Malayala Manorama* was founded as a weekly in 1890 (Kesavan, 1988, p. 657).

[152] The Memorial said also that this was worse than in Malabar, where persons of the Izhava caste could rise to high positions in the uncovenanted civil services. The reply of the Dewan of Travancore referred to the position of Izhavas as that of 'confirmed social inferiors' (Chandramohan, 1981). On the Malayalee Memorial, see Jeffrey (1978); on class aspects of the Memorial, see Prabhash (1994).

[153] P. Govinda Pillai, interview. See also Govinda Pillai (1994), in which he discusses the contrast between Kerala and Bengal in this regard.

[154] On this phase, see Isaac and Tharakan (1986b) and Isaac (1985).

thirties and forties, social and economic differentiation within the caste led to a clear demarcation of conservative and radical trends in the social-reform movement (Isaac and Tharakan, 1986b). With the economic advance of an Izhava elite, the conservative section of the Izhava leadership turned against the national movement, the movement against princely rule, and the coir-workers' movement in Travancore.[155] Another section moved to secular, radical positions (turning, for instance, the old Narayana Guru precept of 'One Caste, One Religion, One God for Man' to 'No Caste, No Religion and No God for Man') and identified with and participated in the agricultural workers' and coir-workers' movements, with the movement against autocracy, and, later, with the left movement (see Isaac, 1985 and Isaac and Tharakan, 1986b). The turning point, in Isaac's (1985) analysis, was the general strike of workers in the Alleppey area in 1938, when the pro-government positions of the conservative leadership isolated it and undermined its hold on working Izhava people. In later years, peasants and agricultural labourers and coir-workers of the Izhava caste joined the Communist Party and mass organizations led by the Communists in large numbers.[156]

Other Caste-based Reform Movements

The Pulaya social reform movement had to confront more formidable obstacles to social progress than the Izhava social reform movement.[157] 'The nature of upper-class opposition,' according to a historian of the Pulaya movement, 'can be described today by no word other than barbaric' (Saradamoni, 1980). This movement did

[155] In a memorandum to the Simon Commission in 1928, the General Secretary of the SNDP Yogam said, of the Izhava people and people of other oppressed castes, that 'their own self-interest demands them to cast their lot with the British Government and not with a caste Hindu oligarchy under whom they suffered untold miseries for thousands of years. The presence of these classes in the Council will be a source of strength to Government and will have a sobering effect on the political visionary and the nationalist enthusiast crying himself hoarse at the top of his voice for the expulsion of the Englishman from India' (Kunjuraman, 1928, p. 255).

[156] Isaac (1985). On the influence of the movement of the people of the oppressed castes and of the temple-entry movement on agricultural workers' movements and consciousness, see Jose George (1980).

[157] On the social-reform movement among the Pulaya people, see Saradamoni (1980) and Alex George (1990). On obstacles before Pulaya liberation, see also Tharakan (1991).

not have the same windows of opportunity, even for an elite within the caste.

From the eighteen-nineties, Ayyankali of Travancore (1863–1911), the great leader of the Pulaya masses of Travancore, organized movements for access to public roads near his village south of Thiruvananthapuram. The demands for education and against caste discrimination and civil disabilities were important items on the movement's agenda. One of the first (it has been suggested that it was *the* first) strike of agricultural labourers in Kerala was organized by Ayyankali in 1914.[158] Ayyankali attempted to gain admission for a Pulaya girl in a government school in Ooroottambalam village in Neyyatinkara taluk near Thiruvananthapuram. The Nayars of the area began a campaign of violence against the Pulayas for this act and, after violent clashes, burned the school down. Ayyankali organized a strike of agricultural labourers, and work stopped in the fields of the upper castes. Government intervened, and after a magistrate's inquiry, the strike ended in success for the workers.[159]

Among Nayars, by the nineteenth century it was clear that the Nayar joint family system was singularly unsuited to modern society.[160] With Nayar militias disbanded by the late eighteenth and early nineteenth centuries, men hung around the taravad with little to do, and were subject to the petty tyranny of the karanavar (the male head of the Nayar joint family).[161] There were new developments in agrarian relations — including the growth of capitalist relations of production in agriculture, new agrarian legislation, and the growth of the land market — and Nayar joint families began to partition and sell taravad property.

The situation was specially oppressive for women. Fathers took no responsibility for bringing up their children; men crowded the

[158] Scholars' accounts differ on whether it took place in 1914 or 1915; the correct year appears to be 1914.

[159] On village-level organizations of people of oppressed castes and their role in the struggle for civil liberties and education, see Joseph (1992). On the role of education in social mobility among the oppressed castes, see Leela Kumari (1994), Kusalakumari (1994), and Ashley Mathew (1994).

[160] On the political and social history of the Nayars in the nineteenth century, focused on Travancore, the standard work is Jeffrey (1976).

[161] Reviewing events in Travancore, a British administrator wrote in 1812 that 'many of the Nairs are now reduced to the necessity of working for their subsistence, a circumstance which they regard as an intolerable hardship . . . ' (Fort St. George, 1812).

taravad, living off family property and contributing nothing to it; women did not work outside the taravad; levels of female literacy, though higher than among the excluded castes, were still much lower than literacy rates among men. It is little surprise that the impulse to transform the matrilineal joint family in the direction of monogamy and nuclear families came largely from the women of these families.

Nayar caste movements in the nineteenth and early twentieth centuries aimed at increased Nayar access to higher education and at large-scale Nayar entry into the professions and the bureaucracy.[162] Given the ability of the Nayars to influence and manipulate court affairs, a Nayar elite soon began to fill up government positions, and to gain positions of dominance in the bureaucracy. Needless to say, Nayar achievement was not as investors of capital or, in general, in the sphere of material production.

Two important features of reform among Nayars were the reform of marriage law and the reform of property law. The first was against the practice of sambandham marriages. The other important demand of the Nayars was for legislation permitting the partition of taravad property. The passing of the *Marumakkatayam* Acts in Malabar, Cochin, and Travancore played a decisive role in the break-up of the old matrilineal, matrilocal joint-family system of the Nayars.

Among Namboodiris, there were reform movements against reactionary marriage practices within the caste and for the right to modern education. There were close links between these movements in Malabar and the freedom movement. There were also social-reform movements among Christian communities in Kerala. A distinction is to be made here between Christian missionaries and the Syrian Christians. Christian missionaries, as we have seen, came with the colonial powers. They played an important role in the spheres of education and health and against traditional forms of slavery. The Syrian Christians were, by contrast, non-evangelical; theirs was not a missionary church, and caste distinctions existed within the Syrian church. There were also movements among the Nadar people of south Travancore.[163]

162 In order to gain clout from numbers, Nayar organizations attempted to unify 116 castes identified in the 1901 Census into a single caste category (Tharakan, 1991, p. 7).

163 On caste-like observances among Syrian Christians, see Tharakan (1991) and Jeffrey (1976), ch. 2; see also Jeffrey (1976), ch. 7 on Syrian Christian efforts against

It is clear that the real area of activity of caste organizations of the oppressed castes and of the Nayars and of religion-based Christian organizations was Travancore and not Malabar. To take an example, the membership of the SNDP Yogam in 1929 was 63,674, of whom only 121 were from Malabar (Chandramohan, 1981). In Malabar, movements against caste oppression became part of the freedom movement and the left movement. Travancore's politics in the nineteen-twenties and thirties has been described as consisting of court intrigues above, and caste and communal politics below.[164] It took the formation of the State's People's Congress and the entry of Communist political organizers to reorient the political scene in Travancore and to win the people of the oppressed castes over to the freedom movement and the class struggle. A leading scholar of the left movement in Kerala considers the attitude of the Communists towards caste reform movements as being 'perhaps the most important contribution of the Communists in Kerala' (Isaac, 1994):

> While supporting and actively participating in the social reform movements in various communities, particularly the anti-*savarna* movements of the oppressed castes, the Communists (also) sought to build class and mass organizations . . . irrespective of caste, and raised caste-reform slogans as part of their anti-feudal democratic struggle. The Communists carried forward the radical legacy of the social reform movement and won over a large part of the masses in these movements, while the elites within these castes began to confine themselves to sectarian demands and withdraw into casteist organizational shells. (ibid.)

7.4   The Role of the Left

The Communist Party and the organizations of workers, peasants, agricultural labourers, students, teachers, youth, and women under its leadership have been the major organizers and leaders of mass political movements in Kerala since the end of the nineteen-thirties

---

discrimination in employment and on Syrian Christian community organizations in the late nineteenth century. On Nadar social reform, see Hardgrave (1969); on socio-religious reform movements among Muslims in Kerala and their distinct features, see Kabir (1994).

[164] Robin Jeffrey's descriptions of caste factionalism and palace intrigues provide a flavour of events in this regard in the second half of the nineteenth century (Jeffrey, 1976).

and have been the major agents of the politicization of the mass of Kerala's people. Kerala is one part of India where the Communist Party assimilated the most progressive features of diverse local socio-political movements and gave them a new philosophical and political direction. These different movements in Kerala included the freedom movement, the radical and anti-caste sections of the social-reform movement, the movement against landlordism, the movement against autocracy and monarchy, the movement for the linguistic reorganization of the region and for the establishment of a unified Kerala, and, of course, the modern movement of workers, peasants, and radical intellectuals.[165] Communists were among the early organizers of mass political organizations of women in the state.[166] Communists played a leading part in the literary movement and in the cultural movement (including the theatre movement) in Kerala. School teachers were key activists and mass organizers of the national movement and the Communist Party; they were the first organizers of the *granthashala* (library) movement and the movement for literacy in Malabar.[167] In the nineteen-seventies and eighties, Communists were the main activists in the popular science movement led by the Kerala Shastra Sahitya Parishad, and in the Total Literacy Campaign of 1989 to 1991.

The modern state of Kerala was formed in 1956, and elections were held to the first Legislative Assembly in 1957. Of all the political forces in the state, only the Communists had a coherent vision for Kerala's future; they knew what they were going to do and how they would go about it. In June 1956, the Communist Party in Kerala met in Thrissur to discuss a policy framework for Party activity in Kerala, and the document that emerged from the meeting, 'Communist Proposal for Building a Democratic and Prosperous Kerala', provided the basis for the communist election manifesto of 1957 and, indeed, for future public policy in the

[165] See Namboodiripad (1984), p. 207.

[166] See Meera Velayudhan's (1992) interview with Kalikutty Asatty, a proletarian and social and political activist who went from the SNDP Yogam to the Communist Party and worked in the trade union and women's movements.

[167] On school teachers as organizers of the Malabar movement, see Namboodiripad (1984, 1994b), Gopalan (1974), Karat (1977), Nayanar (1982), Nambiar (1982), pp. 102ff.; Jeffrey (1992), pp. 69ff. On the radical student movement, its role in fighting caste, its role in the freedom movement and against autocracy, see Jeffrey (1992), pp. 59ff.; see also Bhaskaran (1992).

state.[168] The first Government of Kerala was a Communist government, and the major features of its agenda and of later Communist ministries in the state were, among other things, land reform, health, education, and strengthening the system of public distribution of food and other essential commodities. It has been noted in the scholarly literature that, brief though the periods of Communist rule in the state have been, each was decisive in consolidating the basic agenda for Kerala's transformation.[169] Land reform and the public distribution system are recognized as unmistakably Communist projects; Communist governments also worked on policies that helped bridge the gap between regions, they drafted early legislation on local self-government, and the ministry of 1987–91 provided administrative and institutional support to the Total Literacy Campaign. Kerala's electorate has kept the Communists on a tight leash (Isaac and Mohana Kumar, 1992); at the same time, the left has made many parts of its agenda part of the broad social consensus in the state. Put another way, even when the left loses the elections, it does not mean that the electorate rejects the socio-economic programme of the left *in toto*; it is not, for instance, a vote against the literacy programme, or for agrarian counter-reform, or against the system of public distribution of foodgrain (see Herring, 1992).

Radical individuals in Travancore began to make an impact on intellectual life in Kerala from the early part of the century; the Communist movement, however, began in Malabar. There is a stimulating scholarly literature and memoirs by leading participants, and novels as well, on the left movement in Malabar in the thirties and forties, which deals with the events of the time and with the people who lived and died in its cause.[170] The number and quality of the extraordinary mass organizers and leaders for which the Communist movement in Malabar is famous — of whom E.M.S. Namboodiripad, A.K. Gopalan, and P. Krishna Pillai are the best-known — are remarkable. Selfless, enlightened, and acutely sensitive

[168] See Namboodiripad (1994b), Nossiter (1982), pp. 121–2.

[169] Isaac and Mohana Kumar (1991). See also Namboodiripad (1984) and, for an assessment of Kerala's development that highlights the role of the left and of public policy in the modern period, Franke and Chasin (1992).

[170] See, for instance, Namboodiripad (1976, 1984, 1994b); Nayanar (1982); Gopalan (1974); T.V. Krishnan (1971); K.C. George (1975); Karat (1973, 1977); Gopalankutty (1978).

to injustice, the Communist organizers of Malabar faced extraordinary repression by the ruling classes in order to achieve a better future for the people of Kerala and of India. E.M.S. Namboodiripad himself is Kerala's leading social theorist. No person has played as important a part in the socio-political and cultural life of a region of India for as long a period in the twentieth century as has EMS in Kerala.

In the literature on regional issues in Kerala's development, the dynamism of Travancore is often contrasted with stagnation in Malabar; it is often assumed that while the waves of change beat on Travancore and (to a lesser extent) Cochin, Malabar was, in Kerala terms, a backwater; that, in regional terms, Kerala's development involved taking the lessons of Travancore and applying them to Malabar. This perception of Malabar as an area of unrelieved backwardness and no change, which underlies many discussions of the regional factor in Kerala's development, must be recognized for what it is — a partial and ill-informed view. Malabar made a distinct and, in the historical balance, crucial contribution to Kerala's development. It was the people of Malabar who faced the most archaic and reactionary system of agrarian relations; it was the people of Malabar who confronted the British colonial power directly. In Malabar emerged a mass-based movement — later led by the left in the Congress and still later by the Communists — against landlord oppression and against British rule.

An anti-imperialist, anti-feudal political movement, based on mass organizations of workers, peasants, agricultural workers, teachers, and youth, and led by the left-wing (and later Communist) contingent of the freedom movement was Malabar's specific contribution to Kerala's development.[171] The stimulus to organize the freedom movement in the princely states of Travancore and Cochin came from the north. An important aspect of the movement in Malabar was the struggle against caste discrimination and for entry into Hindu temples by the people of all castes. In this context, the fact is often overlooked that the political movement of the left infused new content into the movement of the people of oppressed castes — particularly of the slave castes and of the Izhavas — in Kerala as a whole, and gave these movements a new direction. In an interview in April

---

[171] See, in this context, Nambiar (1982) on socio-political movements in North Malabar after 1934, and Gopalankutty (1978, 1981, 1989, n.d.).

1992, E.M.S. Namboodiripad summarized his views on this point in the following way:

As a matter of fact, the anti-imperialist freedom movement and the left in that movement came from Malabar to the States part, while educational and socio-cultural developments went from the States part to Malabar.

In short, Malabar was the birthplace of the left movement in Kerala and, as such, it played a crucial role in Kerala's development history.

7.5 Women's Agency

At the risk of some repetition, two issues regarding the place and role of women in Kerala's development achievements are worth emphasizing. First, Kerala's women have made outstanding gains in the fields of education and health and are more equal participants with men in education and health achievements than in any other part of India. Kerala is the only state where mass literacy has been achieved among women as well as among men. Literacy among adolescent girls was almost universal in 1986–7. Women's literacy is supported by society and the state, and there has never been any organized opposition to female literacy and education in Kerala. At 74 years, female life expectancy at birth in Kerala is 15 years higher than the Indian average and almost 6 years above the corresponding figure for men in Kerala. Girls and women have access to the health care system in Kerala and primary-data based surveys show that, in general, the rates of immunization of girls are as high as those of boys. As a result of progressive social attitudes in Kerala towards the survival of girls and towards female survival in general, the proportion of females in the population was 1040 per thousand males in 1991; the all-India average was 927.

Secondly, Kerala's experience is a dramatic example of the role of women's agency in advancing the social and economic development of a society. Female literacy and education are crucial determinants of child survival, general health, and hygiene. These, in turn, determine progress in other demographic and health indicators: the expectancy of life at birth, the birth and death rates, the infant mortality rate, and general morbidity. Kerala's achievements in the sphere of health would have been impossible without female literacy and without an enlightened social attitude towards the survival of girl children and women. Female literacy ensures next-generation literacy; literate mothers generally have literate children. Women in Kerala have been, historically, important participants in the trade union movement (and particularly in the coir and cashew industries and in the plantations), in the peasant and agricultural labour movements and the movement for land reform, and in the movement for food.[172]

While the extraordinary historic gains of women in Kerala cannot be underestimated — and it is simply incorrect to dismiss the achievements of Kerala's women as superficial — there are still important spheres in which women's equality has not been achieved, and in which discrimination persists. Representatives and supporters of the women's movement in Kerala express the opinion that socio-political and economic advance among women in recent years is not commensurate with the historic achievements of women in the spheres of education and health. Work participation rates among women are low, rates of unemployment are very high, and gender differentials in the labour market persist across caste, income, and education categories. A substantial section of the women's labour force is concentrated in traditional occupations — coir-work, cashew-processing, bamboo-work, for example — that are now stagnant or in decline. The representation of women is very low in elected bodies — Parliament, the Legislative Assembly, and local bodies — and in trade union executives, even in trade unions in occupations where most workers are women. The women's movement in Kerala has drawn attention to dowry-related deaths in Kerala and to sexual harassment and other crimes against women.[173]

7.6 State Governments

It remains to review certain features of action by state governments in Kerala. The areas of state government intervention in Kerala that

[172] For a summary of the range of activities of the left women's movement in Kerala, see AIDWA (1994), pp. 44–86.

[173] On these issues, see AIDWA (1994), Duvvury (1994a), Karat (1994), Mukherjee and Isaac (1994), Franke and Chasin (1989), ch. 11, Surendran (1993), Roy (1994), Saradamoni (1994a and b), Rachel Kumar (1994), and contributions to A.K.G. Centre for Research and Studies (1994a–f). See also the reports and analyses (e.g. Leela Menon, 1992 and Parvathi Menon, 1992) at the time of the appalling *putrakameshti yaga*, or mass Hindu ritual for the birth of male children, held in Cochin in 1992.

have been most significant for the people have been land reform, health, and education, and the public distribution system. The state has also introduced a series of measures that are intended to provide protective social security to persons outside the 'organized' sector, who are not usually covered by such schemes. Government policies have also attempted to reduce disparities in major development achievements between the north and the south. Government action in these spheres has been in response to political action by political parties and mass organizations of the people.[174] Government action on land reform, for instance, began a few days after the first Government of Kerala took office (see section 6.3).

There is no question that government policy after the formation of Kerala has played a key role in raising health standards and in demographic change.[175] Throughout the post-independence period, health expenditure as proportion of total expenditure has been higher in Kerala than in any other state. Although the economic history of health care in Kerala is yet to be written, the data indicate high levels of expenditure in the princely states of Travancore and Cochin (particularly the former) on health and education (although a greater proportion was spent on education than health) from the nineteen-twenties (see Table 29; see also Jeffrey, 1992, pp. 188ff.). In terms of hospitals and dispensaries, the health infrastructure in Kerala is far better developed than in India as a whole: in 1989, there were 106 hospitals and dispensaries per 1000 sq km in Kerala against 12 in India, and 254 hospital and dispensary beds in Kerala per 100,000 persons against 77 in India (Centre for Monitoring the Indian Economy, 1991). While per-capita expenditure on health was only marginally higher in Kerala than in other states in the late nineteen-eighties (Krishnan,

---

[174] 'The demands of class organizations were not confined to issues of land and wages alone . . . they were also concerned with the social provisioning of many basic needs as well as with a variety of social and cultural issues. Left-led governments in Kerala set new paradigms of radical redistributive state policies. Class organizations succeeded in implementing land reform, improving the level of wages and conditions of work, and strengthening a radical sense of self-respect and awareness among the people' (Isaac, 1994, p. 58).

[175] See Krishnan (1991), Zachariah (1994). Zachariah writes that 'much of Kerala's success in moderating fertility and mortality in such a short span . . . was due to the policies which successive governments in Kerala followed since independence' (p. 94).

1991), an important feature of health expenditure in Kerala has been the emphasis on mother and child care and immunization as well as on curative medicine (Krishnan, 1991; Kabir and Krishnan, 1991; Panikar, 1979).[176]

TABLE 29. *Share of Education and Health Expenditure in Total Government Expenditure: Travancore and Cochin*

(in per cent)

Year	Share of Education		Share of Health	
	Travancore	Cochin	Travancore	Cochin
1867–8 to 1869–70	1.9	0.9	n/a	n/a
1870–9	2.7	1.5	1.8[a]	n/a
1880–9	3.4	2.8	1.5	1.7[b]
1890–9	4.6	4.2	3.2	2.6
1900–9	6.3	4.2	4.1	3.4
1910–19	11.1	10.9	4.0	7.9
1920–9	18.3	16.5	4.5	5.4
1930–9	19.8	18.1	5.3	6.3
1940–1 to 1942–3	16.1	17.3[c]	4.6	6.9[c]

Notes. [a] 1873–9. [b] 1887–9. [c] 1940–1 to 1941–2.
  1. Each figure is an unweighted average of the corresponding figures for the relevant individual years.
  2. For Cochin, expenditure on 'health' represents annual disbursements under the head 'Medical, vaccination, sanitation and conservancy' (this first appeared as a separate category in the Cochin reports in 1887–8). For Travancore, expenditure on 'health' has been obtained by aggregation over the relevant heads.
  3. For Travancore, expenditures on education from 1864–5 to 1902–3 were presented under the heading 'Education, Science, and Art'; these are the figures in the table. In subsequent years, disbursements on education are given separately.

Source. Calculated from Government of Travancore, Reports of the Administration of Travancore, various issues; and Government of Cochin, Reports of the Administration of Cochin, various issues.

[176] Health expenditure has risen steadily from the early sixties, and Krishnan's estimates indicate that an important feature of the health system in Kerala is the rise in private medical expenditure since the mid-seventies (see Table 30). Remittances from emigrant Malayalees are likely to have played a key role in this development, and in the general expansion of health expenditures (Krishnan, 1991, pp. 33ff.).

TABLE 30.   *Rate of Growth of Per-capita Health Expenditure in Kerala*

(in per cent)

Year	Government	Private	Total
1961–2 to 1973–4	1.4	1.9	1.9
1973–4 to 1986–7	2.5	4.9	4.1

Source. Krishnan (1991), p. 32, Table 8.

With regard to the structure of the public health system, every district has an apex district hospital where specialized curative care is provided (the information here is from Kannan et al., 1991, pp. 108ff.). In rural areas, the Primary Health Centre (PHC) is the basic medical institution.[177] PHCs were first established in 1952 as part of the Community Development Programme. They are intended to cover a rural population of 30,000 (or 20,000 in hill and tribal areas). Each PHC is to have 2 to 3 physicians, a female health assistant, a male health assistant, and supporting technical and administrative personnel. The female health assistant deals with maternal and child health — ante-natal and post-natal care — and birth control matters. The male assistant's functions include recording vital events, immunization, house-to-house malaria surveillance, and so on. Although the basic structure of public health facilities is quite similar in Kerala and other states, an important difference is that health programmes in Kerala have been far better implemented, largely due to the vigilance of an educated and politically conscious public.

Education was also an early concern (see section 4). The proportion of total government expenditure spent on education in Kerala is much higher than the corresponding proportion spent by all states (see Table 31), and it is of note that the proportion of total expenditure spent on education by the states of Travancore and Cochin crossed 15 per cent in the twenties (see Table 29). Most primary school children go to state-run or state-supported schools. In the

---

[177] There are sub-centres below the PHC, serving populations of 5,000 each (2,500 in hill regions); the personnel here are one female and one male multipurpose health worker. The Sixth Plan envisaged establishing one Community Health Centre (CHC) for every 100,000 persons in the population. A CHC is a 30-bed hospital with specialized medical services in gynaecology, paediatrics, and general surgery and medicine.

late eighties, Kerala's non-plan expenditure per capita on primary education was the highest among 14 states (see Table 32).[178]

TABLE 31. *Expenditure on Education as a Proportion
of Development and Non-development Expenditure
(Revenue Account): All States and Kerala*

(in per cent)

Year	Kerala	All states
1959–60	37.0	19.6
1960–1	35.1	19.5
1962–3	32.1	19.9
1964–5	33.8	20.2
1965–6	35.4	19.7
1966–7	36.0	19.1
1971–2	36.4	21.9
1981–2	32.2	21.4
1990–1	27.8	18.4
1991–2	25.3	17.4
1992–3	26.9	17.4

Note. The figures for 1960–1 and 1991–2 are based on revised budget estimates; the figures for 1992–3 are based on budget estimates; all other figures are based on final accounts.

Source. *Reserve Bank of India Bulletin*, successive issues.

The two-tier public distribution system was established and strengthened in the seventies and eighties; early attempts to establish an extensive public food-distribution system of a permanent nature in the state began with the 1957 ministry (see the sub-section on the public distribution system in section 3). As with land reform, the establishment of ration shops and other state-run stores to sell food and some basic articles of consumption to the people has been described as a 'Communist project' (Herring, 1992).

[178] 'Government education has particularly directed its efforts towards the education of children in the first four standards. . . . The [Catholic] Church's activity, on the contrary, is concentrated more on higher and secondary education' (Houtart and Lemercinier, 1974, pp. 150–1). The authors point out that that was also the case with respect to private non-Catholic organizations.

TABLE 32. *Non-plan Government Expenditure
on Education in Fourteen States, 1986–7*

(in rupees per capita)

State	Non-plan expenditure		
	Primary Education	*Secondary Education*	*Higher Education*
Andhra Pradesh	39	26	21
Bihar	43	13	12
Gujarat	61	38	15
Haryana	38	42	17
Karnataka	54	23	20
Kerala	*83*	*48*	*27*
Madhya Pradesh	43	27	10
Maharashtra	58	49	18
Orissa	33	29	11
Punjab	44	62	21
Rajasthan	42	28	11
Tamil Nadu	51	29	21
Uttar Pradesh	33	23	7
West Bengal	34	43	14
Fourteen states	45	31	15

Source. Report of the Ninth Finance Commission, December 1989, cited in
Government of West Bengal (1992), pp. 17–19.

Kerala has social security measures that cover most sections of
rural workers (Duvvury, 1994; Isaac and Mohana Kumar, 1991;
Kannan, 1993). These are mainly contributory welfare funds in
which government, employers, and workers participate. Nata Duvvury (1994) lists twenty-five such programmes, including welfare
funds for agricultural workers, toddy workers, head-load workers,
artisans, fishermen, cashew workers, coir workers, handloom and
khadi workers, and construction workers. There are also pension

schemes for destitutes and for physically handicapped persons and for assisting the unemployed. Duvvury notes that welfare funds are intended to cover 'not only (workers') pensions, gratuity, provident funds, and other retirement benefits, but also medical, educational, marriage and housing assistance' (ibid., p. 2). She notes, however, that 'most schemes today are pension schemes' (ibid.).

Seventeen of twenty-five such social security measures listed by Nata Duvvury were begun in the nineteen-eighties (ibid.). In an assessment of the agricultural workers pension scheme, Leela Gulati (1992, p. 44 and 1993) indicates that although the amount received by individual pensioners appears low, the entitlement is enough to pay for half the foodgrain requirements of an adult, and that pension entitlements make an appreciable difference to the status and acceptability of older persons in the households to which they belong. The gamut of such social security measures in Kerala are the subject of research in progress (see Duvvury, 1994); while their effectiveness is still to be assessed, their important feature is their coverage, which extends to most rural workers. In the seventies, 57,000 low-cost houses for working people were built under a mass housing scheme (see Jeffrey, 1992, pp. 204ff).

A highlight of Kerala's development experience is that public action after 1957 helped close the gap in important respects between Malabar and the southern districts of Kerala. The disparities in health and education facilities in Travancore and Malabar have been usefully discussed in Kabir and Krishnan (1991). In respect of literacy, it is clear that the literacy gap between Malabar and the princely states widened substantially during the period that Malabar was part of British India, and it narrowed only after mass schooling was established in Malabar after 1957. The reduction of differences between the north and south in respect of literacy, medical facilities, infant mortality, immunization, and fertility and death rates, and in infrastructural and general cultural development is a standing example of the achievement of people and governments in *recent* decades.[179]

---

[179] On the relative backwardness of Malabar in respect of medical facilities, see Kabir and Krishnan (1991) and Jeffrey (1992), pp. 25ff. On changes in health achievements in Malabar, see Krishnan (1985) and Kabir and Krishnan (1991); see also Caldwell (1986).

8. CONCLUSIONS

This paper attempted to review and analyse the most important social and economic development achievements of the people of Kerala. The achievements of the people of Kerala are the result of major social, economic, and political transformations. These changes have roots in Kerala's history, but they were also, in an important sense, achievements of public action in post-1957 Kerala. They were possible because there was mass literacy; because agrarian relations were transformed; because there were important changes in the conditions of unfreedom of the people of the oppressed castes; because of enlightened social attitudes towards girls' and women's survival and education, and because of the public policy interventions of governments in Kerala. All these conditions are replicable.

There has been a progressive transformation in Kerala of the health and demographic conditions characteristic of less-developed societies, and the state is far ahead of the rest of India in respect of these conditions. In 1990–2, the expectation of life at birth of males was 68.8 years against an Indian average of 59.0 years, and the expectation of life at birth of females was 74.4 years against an Indian average of 59.4 years. The birth rate in Kerala was 18.5 per thousand against an Indian average of 29.5 per thousand. The death rate was 6.1 per thousand against an Indian average of 9.8 per thousand. The infant mortality rate was 17 per thousand against an Indian average of 79 per thousand. There were 1040 females per thousand males in Kerala's population, against an Indian average of 927.

Kerala was the only state of India where the socio-economic arrangements were in place to absorb international advances in the last three decades in epidemiology and public health. The ratio of medical establishments to population is substantially higher in Kerala than the rest of India. In an area of mass literacy and where social and political consciousness are high, people demand more health facilities, use the health system more, and use it better. Recent data indicate that the rate of immunization of boys and girls is higher than elsewhere and that immunization is not determined by the level of income. While the evidence is of progressive change in the pattern of morbidity and of improved facilities to deal with illness, medical evidence also indicates that much remains to be done to control the incidence of water-borne and air-borne infections in Kerala.

Nutrition levels have improved in Kerala after the seventies and, according to official data, household consumption levels were higher than the Indian average by the late eighties. The public food-distribution system, the best among India's states, gives basic nutritional support to the people of Kerala. There is a two-tier system of public distribution of essential commodities. The system was extended and consolidated from the second half of the seventies. Of the population of the state, 90 per cent held ration cards (which entitle households to buy subsidized rice, wheat, sugar, cooking oil, and kerosene), and the average amount of foodgrain bought from ration shops by an individual in Kerala was 69.6 kg in 1991. The corresponding figures for Uttar Pradesh and Bihar in 1989 were 6 kg and 8 kg.

The people of Kerala have altered radically a system of agrarian relations that was among the most complex, burdensome, and exploitative in India, and have won important victories against some of the most monstrous forms of caste oppression. Public action in recent decades has narrowed the gap in health and educational facilities and achievements between the districts of the north and the districts of the south, a gap that widened during the period of colonial rule. The modern state of Kerala has also introduced a series of interesting protective social security measures that attempt to provide pensions and other payments to working people in the so-called 'informal' sector, and to destitute and physically handicapped persons. Kerala is the only state in India where there is mass literacy (and near-total literacy among adolescents and youth), and is also the state with the lowest proportion of child workers in the population.

The case of Kerala is an outstanding example of the importance of literacy for social and economic progress. Widespread literacy was a precondition of Kerala's major health and demographic achievements. The achievement of mass literacy in Kerala required — just as the achievement of mass literacy in India will require — mass schooling. Mass literacy was not achieved in Kerala until basic caste, gender, and class obstacles to literacy were overcome; that is, until literacy was gained by people of the oppressed castes, by women, by the working people, and by the rural and urban poor. The case of Kerala is also an important example of women's achievement in health and education and of women's agency in development.

It is necessary also to remember that there are many people in Kerala's population among whom conditions of education and health remain unacceptably poor, and are far behind the rest of the population: among them are sections of the people of the scheduled tribes (particularly in north Malabar), of the fishing communities, and of the scheduled castes. Among them are also the members of the new underclass of migrant workers, mainly from Tamil Nadu, who work at a wide range of manual tasks in contemporary Kerala.

With regard to specific features of Kerala's modern history, in nineteenth-century Kerala, missionary activity and government policy in the princely states (particularly Travancore) played a foundational role in establishing a climate of official support for education and public health. The pervasive influence of the matrilineal system was important in determining social attitudes towards women's survival, women's education, and women's health. In the late nineteenth and early twentieth centuries, social-reform organizations of people of the oppressed castes emerged as pioneers of anti-caste social reform and as the first organizers of democratic socio-political movements among rural working people. The mass political movements led by the Communist Party from the thirties and the communist governments that came to power in 1957, 1967, 1980, and 1987 were crucial agents of socio-political change. When the state of Kerala was established in 1956, the Communist Party was the only political organization in the state with a programme for socio-economic and political change. Despite its relatively short periods in the leadership of government in the state, it is the Communist Party that has set the basic legislative agenda of the people of Kerala.

The crises in the spheres of employment and material production are perhaps the most pressing economic problems in Kerala at present. The present situation of a low to no-growth economy is neither desirable nor politically viable (and it is no surprise that transforming the conditions of production in the economy is the task that senior representatives of the left in Kerala's polity see today as its most important task). Kerala's development experience and Kerala's development future are matters of great importance for the left in India and internationally. Working within the constraints imposed by the Constitution of India and by hostile central governments, the left in Kerala has mobilized the people for kinds of social change unprecedented in the rest of the country. It is now clear that the tasks of increasing employment and production (and transforming production conditions) have to be principal components of the next phase of Kerala's development. This transformation, however, must build on, consolidate, and extend the achievements of the past, and not undermine (or liquidate) the gains of a long history of public action in order to impose a capitalist-market-driven, income-growth-alone strategy of development on the people. Such a new phase of economic development has special resources on which to draw. Kerala has extraordinary natural resources, a basic land reform, an educated, skilled, and politically conscious work-force, and unique achievements in the spheres of health and education. It has a strong left political movement that is sensitive to issues of development and growth, that has set itself the task of building social alliances for economic development and socio-political change, and is active in the movement to create new institutions of local government in the state.

To reiterate the major conclusion of this paper, Kerala's achievements were possible because of mass literacy and because traditional patterns of gender, caste, and class dominance were transformed radically. In the conditions of contemporary India, it is worth remembering that public action, and not policies of globalization and liberalization, was the locomotive of Kerala's progress.

Annexure

Note on Income and Expenditure Data

Income

The data on per-capita domestic product used in this paper (see particularly Fig. 1 on p. 214) are based on publications of the Central Statistical Organisation (CSO). Fig. 1 presents two separate series: one for per-capita domestic product at constant 1970–1 prices for the period 1970–1 to 1986–7, and one for per-capita domestic product at constant 1980–1 prices for the period 1980–1 to 1991–2. Owing to data limitations, we were unable to merge the two series.

In recent years, data on state domestic products have become more difficult to get. The CSO does not currently publish the data, because of problems with the comparability of data generated by different State Bureaus of Statistics. We also learn that the CSO does not, at present, authenticate data on state domestic products, which is considered the responsibility of State Bureaus.

Consumer Expenditure

Two series on per-capita household consumption expenditure at constant prices are used in the paper (see Table 5, and Figs. 2–5).

The data on per-capita household consumer expenditure at current prices for both series come from various rounds of the National Sample Survey (NSS). The most detailed data are from the quinquennial surveys of the NSS; the last such survey from which data have been published was part of the 43rd round of 1987–8 (data from the 1992–3 survey were not published at the time of writing). Data from the 45th, 46th, and 48th rounds, when annual surveys of consumer expenditure were conducted, have been published and are used in the paper. The annual surveys cover a smaller sample than the quinquennial surveys, and the material published at present does not include data on quantities consumed (kilograms of cereals and pulses, etc.). The most recent survey from which such data are published is the quinquennial survey (43rd round, 1987–8).

We got the data on consumer expenditure at current prices from Roy Choudhury (1993), and from reports of the NSS and *Sarvek-shana* (see under National Sample Survey in the bibliography). The data in Roy Choudhury (1993) represents expenditure for 360 days; in our statistical tables, all annual data are for a 365-day year.

In our Series 1, the price deflators for states are consumer price indices for states and India as given in Jain and Minhas (1991) and Tendulkar and Jain (1993). These price indices are available for NSS rounds until the 43rd round (1987–8), and we have presented data for the states for which the sources cited in this paragraph provide data.

Inter-state variations in prices were accounted for by using state-wise consumer price indices adjusted to an all-India base for 1970–1 for all items as given in Jain and Minhas (1991) and Tendulkar and Jain (1993).

In our Series 2, the price deflators are the Consumer Price Index for Agricultural Labourers (CPIAL) for Kerala and the CPIAL for India for rural areas, and the Consumer Price Index for Industrial Workers (CPIIW) for Aluva (formerly Alwaye) and CPIIW for India for urban areas. We took CPIAL and CPIIW data from different volumes of *Indian Labour Statistics, Indian Labour Year Book*, the *Reserve Bank of India Bulletin* and from the *Index Numbers of Wholesale Prices and Consumer Prices* published by the Centre for Monitoring the Indian Economy.

The price deflators were the average value of the relevant monthly price indices for the months covered by the particular round of the NSS. The price data for certain months covered by the 27th round (1972–3) were not available to us; for that reason, the statistical table does not present data for that year. All price indices were converted to a 1970–1 (July 1970 to June 1971) base.

The variation between prices in Kerala and India were accounted for by the procedure used for Series 1, that is, by using consumer price indices for Kerala adjusted to an all-India base for 1970–1 for all items as given in Jain and Minhas (1991) and Tendulkar and Jain (1993).

Since the CPIAL and CPIIW are up-to-date, Series 2 includes data from the 45th (1989–90), 46th (1990–1), and 48th (1992) rounds. These data are presented with a reminder that the sample covered in the 45th, 46th, and 48th rounds were smaller samples than in the quinquennial surveys.

REFERENCES

'A.H.' (1860), *Day Dawn in Travancore: A Brief Account of the Manners and Customs of the People and the Efforts That Are Being Made for Their Improvement* (Kottayam: C.M. Press).

A.K.G. Centre for Research and Studies (1994a), International Congress on Kerala Studies, Abstracts, volume 1, Thiruvananthapuram.

—— (1994b), International Congress on Kerala Studies, Abstracts, volume 2, Thiruvananthapuram.

—— (1994c), International Congress on Kerala Studies, Abstracts, volume 3, Thiruvananthapuram.

—— (1994d), International Congress on Kerala Studies, Abstracts, volume 4, Thiruvananthapuram.

—— (1994e), International Congress on Kerala Studies, Abstracts, Supplementary volumes, Thiruvananthapuram.

Aberle, Kathleen Gough, see Gough, Kathleen.

Agur, C.M. (1903), *Church History of Travancore* (Madras: SPS Press).

Aiyappan, A. (1965), *Social Revolution in a Kerala Village*, Bombay.

Albin, Alice (1990), 'Manufacturing Sector in Kerala: Comparative Study of its Growth and Structure', *Economic and Political Weekly*, 25, 37, 15 September.

—— (1992), 'Kerala Economy at Crossroads', *Economic and Political Weekly*, 27, 12, 21 March.

All-India Democratic Women's Association (AIDWA) (1994), Fourth National Conference, *State Reports*, Coimbatore.

All-Travancore Joint Political Congress (1934), Executive Committee, *Travancore: The Present Political Problem*, submitted to His Highness the Maharaja of Travancore, published by M.M. Varkey, Thiruvananthapuram, and printed at the Empire Press, Calicut.

Anand, S. (1994), 'Migrant Construction Workers: A Case Study of Tamil Workers in Kerala', in A.K.G. Centre for Research and Studies (1994b).

Annual Survey of Industries (1993), *Summary Results for Factory Sector 1989–90*, New Delhi.

—— (1994), *Summary Results for Factory Sector 1990–91*, New Delhi.

Antia, N.H. (1994), 'Kerala Shows the Way to Health', in A.K.G. Centre for Research and Studies (1994b).

Arnove, Robert F. and Harvey J. Graff (eds.) (1987), *National Literacy Campaigns: Historical and Comparative Perspectives* (New York and London: Plenum Press).

Arthur, Lieutenant (Engineers) (1810), *Report on the Countries of Travancore and Cochin*, addressed to the Resident, Colonel John Munro, Selections from the Records of Travancore, No. II, in Drury (1860).

Asari, V. Gopalakrishnan (1994), 'Population Change in Kerala and its Socio-Economic Implications', in A.K.G. Centre for Research and Studies (1994a).

Bahauddin, K.M. (1986), 'Socio-Political Developments and Education in Kerala', in National Institute of Educational Planning and Administration (1986).

Balakrishnan, P.V. (1981), *Matrilineal System in Malabar* (Cannanore: Satyavani Prakashan).

Balakrishnan, V. and R. Leela Devi (1982), *Mannathu Padmanabhan and the Revival of Nairs in Kerala* (New Delhi: Vikas).

Balan, C. (1994), 'Peasant Consciousness and Mobilisation: A Case Study of Peasant Movement in Cochin', in A.K.G. Centre for Research and Studies (1994c).

Beasley, W.G. (1972), *The Meiji Transformation* (Stanford: Stanford University Press).

Bhaskaran, C. (1992), *Student Movement in Kerala* (Thiruvananthapuram: Chintha Publishers).

Bhat, P.N. Mari and S. Irudaya Rajan (1990), 'Demographic Transition in Kerala Revisited', *Economic and Political Weekly*, 25, 35 and 36, 1–8 September.

Bhattacharjee, P.J. and G.N. Shastri (1976), *Population in India: A Study of Inter-State Variations* (New Delhi: Vikas).

Bose, Ashish (1991), *Population of India: 1991 Census Results and Methodology* (New Delhi: D.K. Publishing Corporation).

Buchanan, Claudius (n.d.), *Christian Researches in Asia*, cited in Yesudas (1978).

Caldwell, J.C. (1986), 'Routes to Low Mortality in Poor Countries', *Population and Development Review*, 12, 2, June.

Caldwell, J.C. and Pat Caldwell (1985), 'Education and Literacy as Factors in Health', in Halstead et al. (1985).

Casinader, Rex (1994), 'Enigma of Kerala Spatial Formations: *Gragara* as an Invalidation/Recovery of the Desakota Hypothesis', in A.K.G. Centre for Research and Studies (1994b).

Centre for Development Studies (1977), *Poverty, Unemployment and Development Policy: A Case Study of Selected Issues with Reference to Kerala* (Madras: Orient Longman).

Central Statistical Organisation (CSO) (1989), *Estimates of State Domestic Product 1970–71 to 1987–88*, New Delhi.

Central Statistical Organisation (CSO) (1991a), *Estimates of State Domestic Product and Gross Fixed Capital Formation*, New Delhi.

—— (1991b), *National Accounts Statistics*, New Delhi.

—— (1994), *National Accounts Statistics*, New Delhi.

Centre for Monitoring the Indian Economy (CMIE) (1991), Economic Intelligence Service, *Basic Statistics Relating to the Indian Economy*, volume II: States, Bombay, September.

—— (1992), Economic Intelligence Service, *Basic Statistics Relating to the Indian Economy*, volume II: States, Bombay, September.

—— (1994a), Economic Intelligence Service, *Basic Statistics Relating to the Indian Economy*, August.

—— (1994b), Economic Intelligence Service, *Basic Statistics Relating to the States of India*, September.

Chandhok, H.L. and the Policy Group (1990), *India Database: The Economy: Annual Time Series Data*, in two volumes (New Delhi: LM Books).

Chandramohan, P. (1981), 'Social and Political Protest in Travancore: A Study of the Sree Narayana Dharma Paripalana Yogam (1900–1938)', M.Phil. Dissertation, Jawaharlal Nehru University.

—— (1987), 'Popular Culture and Socio-Religious Reform: Narayana Guru and the Ezhavas of Travancore', *Studies in History*, 3, 1, new series.

Chattopadhyaya, Srikumar (1994), 'Spatial Organisation of Settlement System in Kerala', in A.K.G. Centre for Research and Studies (1994b).

Chen, Lincoln C. and Claire van Schaik (1986), Review of Panikar and Soman (1985), *Population and Development Review*, 12, 4, December.

Cornia, G.A. and Frances Stewart (1993), 'Two Errors of Targeting', *Journal of International Development*, 5, 5.

Cox, Reverend John (1857), Missionary, L.M.S., *Travancore: Its Present Ruin Shown and the Remedy Sought in a Correspondence with the Government of Madras in the Years 1855–1857*, printed for the author at the London Mission Press, Nagercoil.

Damodaran, A.D. and V. Govindarajulu (1994), 'Ecstasy and Agony of Kerala Development Model', in A.K.G. Centre for Research and Studies (1994b).

Dantwala, M.L. (1967), 'Incentives and Disincentives in Indian Agriculture', *Indian Journal of Agricultural Economics*, 17, 2, April–June.

—— (1993), 'Agricultural Policy: Prices and Public Distribution System: A Review', *Indian Journal of Agricultural Economics*, XLVIII, 2, April–June.

da San Bartholomeo, Fra Paolino, *Voyage to the East Indies*, cited in Yesudas (1978).

Dev, S. Mahendra and M.H. Suryanarayana (1991), 'Is PDS Urban Biased and Pro-Rich: An Evaluation', *Economic and Political Weekly*, 26, 4, 12 October.

Drèze, Jean and Amartya Sen (1989), *Hunger and Public Action* (Oxford: Clarendon Press).

—— (1995), *India: Economic Development and Social Opportunity* (Oxford and Delhi: Oxford University Press).

Drury, Major Heber (ed.) (1860), *Selections from the Records of Travancore*, edited by Major Drury at the request of Francis Newcombe Maltby, Esq., Resident at the Courts of Travancore and Cochin, Printed at the Press of His Highness the Rajah of Travancore, Thiruvananthapuram.

Duggal, Ravi, Sunil Nandraj, and Sahana Shetty (1992), *State Sector Health Expenditures: A Data Base: All-India and States, 1961–1985* (Bombay: Foundation for Research in Community Health).

Duvvury, Nata (1994a), Report on the Discussions on the Status of Women, International Congress on Kerala Studies, Thiruvananthapuram.

—— (1994b), 'Social Security in the Unorganised Sector: A Study of Labour Welfare Funds', Thiruvananthapuram.

EPW Research Foundation (1993), 'Poverty Levels in India: Norms, Estimates and Trends', *Economic and Political Weekly*, 28, 34, 21 August.

Famine Inquiry Commission (1945), *Final Report* (Madras: Government Press).

Fawcett, F. (1901), *Nayars of Malabar*, reprinted by Asian Educational Services, New Delhi, 1990.

Feachem, R.G. (1985), 'The Role of Water Supply and Sanitation in Reducing Mortality in China, Costa Rica, Kerala State (India) and Sri Lanka', in Halstead et al. (1985).

Fort St. George (1812), 'Affairs of Travancore', Political Letter, 29 February.

Francis, K. (1985), 'Politics of Education in Kerala', Ph.D. thesis, Jawaharlal Nehru University, New Delhi.

Franke, Richard W. (1993), *Life is a Little Better: Redistribution as a Development Strategy in Nadur Village, Kerala*, Conflict and Social Change Series (Boulder and Oxford: Westview Press).

Franke, Richard W. and Barbara H. Chasin (1992), *Kerala: Development through Radical Reform* (New Delhi: Promilla and Co. Publishers), in collaboration with The Institute for Food and Development Policy, San Francisco.

Fuller, C.J. (1976), *The Nayars Today* (Cambridge: Cambridge University Press).

Ganesh, K.N. (1990), 'The Process of State Formation in Travancore', *Studies in History*, 6, 1, new series.

Gazetteer of India (1986), *Kerala State Gazetteer*, volume I (by Adoor K.K. Ramachandran Nair), published by the State Editor, Kerala Gazetteers, Thiruvananthapuram.

—— (1989), *Kerala State Gazetteer, Volume III: Economic Affairs*, published by the State Editor, Kerala Gazetteers, Thiruvananthapuram.

Geetha, S. and M.H. Suryanarayana (1993), 'Revamping PDS: Some Issues and Implications', *Economic and Political Weekly*, 28, 41, 9 October.

George, Alex (1990), 'The Militant Phase of Pulaya Movement of South Travancore: 1884–1914', Werkdocument nr. 22, CASA, Amsterdam.

George, Jose (1980), 'Politicisation of Agricultural Workers in Kerala: A Study of Kuttanad', M.Phil. Dissertation, Jawaharlal Nehru University.

George, K.C. (1975), *Immortal Punnapra-Vayalar*, Communist Party Publication, No. 16, Communist Party of India, New Delhi, June.

George, K.K. (1994), 'Whither Kerala Model?', in A.K.G. Centre for Research and Studies (1994e).

George, P.S. (1979), 'Public Distribution of Foodgrains in Kerala', IFPRI.

—— (1985), 'Aspects of Public Sector Procurement and Distribution of Foodgrains in India', IFPRI.

Goody, Jack (ed.) (1968), *Literacy in Traditional Societies* (Cambridge: Cambridge University Press).

Gopalan, A.K. (1974), *In the Cause of the People* (Madras: Orient Longman).

Gopalankutty, K. (n.d.), 'Movement for Tenancy Reform in Malabar: A Comparative Study of Two Movements, 1920–1939', in D.N. Panigrahi, *Economy, Society and Politics in Modern India* (New Delhi: Vikas Publishing House).

—— (1978), 'The Rise and Growth of the Communist Party in Malabar, 1934–47', M.Phil. Dissertation, Centre for Historical Studies, Jawaharlal Nehru University, New Delhi.

—— (1981), 'The Integration of the Anti-Landlord Movement with the

Movement Against Imperialism — The Case of Malabar, 1935–39', *Studies in History*, III, 1 & 2.

Gopalankutty, K. (1989), 'The Task of Transforming the Congress: Malabar, 1934–40', *Studies in History*, 5, 2, new series.

Gough, Kathleen (1962), 'Nayar: Central Kerala' and 'Nayar: North Kerala', in Schneider and Gough (1962).

—— (1968), 'Literacy in Kerala', in Goody (1968).

—— (1970), 'Palakkara: Social and Religious Change in Central Kerala', in Ishwaran (1970).

Government of Cochin, *Report on the Administration of Cochin State*, and *Administration Reports and Budget Estimates for the Cochin State*, Cochin, successive volumes.

Government of India (1944), Foodgrains Policy Committee, 'Conclusions and Recommendations', chapter 2, 'Statistical Position', in Government of India, Department of Food, *Food Situation in India* (Delhi: Manager of Publications).

—— (1946), Department of Food, *The Food Statistics of India*, prepared under the direction of V.K.R.V. Rao, Manager of Publications, Delhi.

Government of Kerala (1964), Kerala District Gazetteers, *Quilon* (by A. Sreedhara Menon), Government of Kerala, Thiruvananthapuram.

—— (1968), Bureau of Economics and Statistics, *Socio-Economic Survey on Caste/Communities in Kerala*, Thiruvananthapuram.

—— (1976), Department of Public Relations, *Kerala Through the Ages*, Thiruvananthapuram, reprinted in 1988.

—— (1985), Department of Economics and Statistics, *Report of the Survey on Socio-Economic Conditions of Agricultural and Other Rural Labourers in Kerala — 1983–84*, Thiruvananthapuram.

—— (1988a), Department of Public Relations, *Ahead of Other States in Education*, Thiruvananthapuram.

—— (1988b), Department of Economics and Statistics, *Statistics for Planning 1988*, Thiruvananthapuram.

—— (1989a), Department of Public Relations, *Where There Is A Will . . .* , Thiruvananthapuram.

—— (1989b), Department of Economics and Statistics, *Women in Kerala — 1989*, Thiruvananthapuram.

—— (1991a), State Planning Board, *Economic Review, 1990*, Thiruvananthapuram.

—— (1991b), Department of Economics and Statistics, *Kerala at a Glance*, Thiruvananthapuram.

Government of Kerala (1992), State Planning Board, *Economic Review, 1991*, Thiruvananthapuram.

Government of Travancore, *Report on the Administration of Travancore*, Thiruvananthapuram, successive volumes.

Government of West Bengal (1992), *Report of the Education Commission*, Calcutta, August.

Gulati, I.S. (1994), Speech at the Inaugural Session of the International Congress on Kerala Studies, in A.K.G. Centre for Research and Studies (1994a).

Gulati, I.S. and Ashoka Mody (1983), 'Remittances of Indian Migrants to the Middle East: An Assessment with Special Reference to Migrants from Kerala', Centre for Development Studies, Working Paper No. 182, Thiruvananthapuram.

Gulati, Leela (1982), *Profiles in Female Poverty: A Study of Five Working Women in Kerala* (New York: Pergamon Press and Delhi: Hindustan Publishers).

—— (1992), 'Economic and Social Aspects of Population Ageing in Kerala, India', Department of Economic and Social Development, United Nations, New York.

—— (1993), 'Agricultural Workers Pension in Kerala — An Experiment in Social Assistance', paper presented at the conference of the Indian Association of Women's Studies, Manasagangotri.

Gulati, Leela and I.S. Gulati (1994), 'Social Security Coverage of Widows in Kerala', in A.K.G. Centre for Research and Studies (1994e).

Gulati, Leela and S. Irudaya Rajan (1988), 'Aging of Population in Kerala', Working Paper, Centre for Development Studies, Thiruvananthapuram.

Gundert, Hermann (1872), *A Malayalam–English Dictionary*, reprinted 1992 (Kottayam: DC Books).

Halstead, Scott B., Julia A. Walsh, and Kenneth S. Warren (eds.) (1985), *Good Health at Low Cost*, Proceedings of a Conference Held at the Bellagio Conference Center, Bellagio, Italy, 29 April–2 May 1985 (New York: The Rockefeller Foundation).

Hardgrave, Robert L., Jr. (1969), *The Nadars of Tamilnad* (Berkeley and Los Angeles: University of California Press).

Herring, Ronald J. (1980), 'Abolition of Landlordism in Kerala: A Redistribution of Privilege', *Economic and Political Weekly*, 15, 26.

—— (1983), *Land to the Tiller: The Political Economy of Land Reform in South Asia* (New Haven: Yale University Press).

—— (1992), 'Contesting the "Great Transformation": Land and Labour in South India', Government Department, Cornell University, Ithaca.

Horsley, Lieutenant W.H. (1860), Engineers, *Memoir of Travancore: Historical and Statistical: Compiled from Various Authentic Records and Personal Observation*, at the request of Major-General J.S. Fraser, British Resident, in Drury (1860).

Houtart, Francois and Genevieve Lemercinier (1978), 'Socio-Religious Movements in Kerala: A Reaction to the Capitalist Mode of Production', *Social Scientist*, 6, 7, June.

Isaac, T.M. Thomas (1984), 'Class Struggle and Industrial Structure: A Case Study of Coir Weaving Industry at Alleppey', Ph.D. thesis submitted to the Jawaharlal Nehru University, Centre for Development Studies, Thiruvananthapuram.

—— (1985), 'From Caste Consciousness to Class Consciousness: Alleppey Coir Workers during Inter-War Period', Review of Political Economy, *Economic and Political Weekly*, xx, 4, 26 January.

—— (1986), 'The National Movement and Communist Party in Kerala', *Social Scientist*, 159–60, August–September.

—— (1992), unpublished MS on the impact of the Gulf War on migration from Kerala to the Gulf states, Thiruvananthapuram, April.

—— (1994), 'The Left Movement in Kerala: Lessons of the Past and Challenges of the Present', in A.K.G. Centre for Research and Studies (1994a).

Isaac, T.M. Thomas and P.K. Michael Tharakan (1986a), 'An Enquiry into the Historical Roots of Backwardness of Kerala — A Study of Travancore Region', Centre for Development Studies, Working Paper no. 215, Thiruvananthapuram.

—— (1986b), 'Sree Narayana Movement in Travancore, 1888–1939: A Study of Social Basis and Ideological Reproduction', Centre for Development Studies, Working Paper no. 214, Thiruvananthapuram.

Isaac, T.M. Thomas and S. Mohana Kumar (1991), 'Kerala Elections, 1991: Lessons and Non-Lessons', *Economic and Political Weekly*, 26, 47, 23 November.

Isaac, T.M. Thomas and Nata Duvvury (1993), 'Workers' Remittances to India: A Country Report', Centre for Development Studies, Thiruvananthapuram.

Isaac, T.M. Thomas and V.K. Ramachandran (forthcoming), 'A Note on the Origin of the Public Food-Distribution System in Kerala'.

Ishwaran, K. (ed.) (1970), *Change and Continuity in India's Villages* (New York: Columbia University Press).

Iyer, L.A. Krishna (1968), *Social History of Kerala*, volume I (Madras: Book Centre Publications).

—— (1970), *Social History of Kerala*, volume II (Madras: Book Centre Publications).

Iyer, L.K. Anantha Krishna (1912), *The Tribes and Castes of Cochin* (New Delhi: Cosmo Publications, reprinted in 1981).

Jain, L.R. and B.S. Minhas (1991), 'Rural and Urban Consumer Price Indices by Commodity Groups (States and All-India: 1970–1 to 1983)', *Sarvekshana*, 15, 1, July–September.

Jeffrey, Robin (1974), 'The Social Origins of a Caste Association 1875–1905: The Founding of the SNDP Yogam', *South Asia*, 4, October.

—— (1976a), 'Temple Entry Movement in Travancore, 1860–1940', *Social Scientist*, March.

—— (1976b), *The Decline of Nayar Dominance: Society and Politics in Travancore, 1847–1908* (Delhi: Vikas Publishing House).

—— (1977), 'A Note on the Malayali Origins of Anti-Brahmanism in South India', *Indian Economic and Social History Review*, XIV, 2, April–June.

—— (1978), 'Travancore: Status, Class and the Growth of Radical Politics, 1860–1940 — The Temple-Entry Movement', in Jeffrey (1978).

—— (1987a), 'Culture of Daily Newspapers in India: How Its Grown, What It Means', *Economic and Political Weekly*, 22, 14.

—— (1987b), 'Culture and Governments: How Women Made Kerala Literate', *Pacific Affairs*, 60, 4, Fall.

—— (1992), *Politics, Women and Well-Being: How Kerala became 'a Model'* (Basingstoke and London: Macmillan).

Jeffrey, Robin (ed.) (1978), *People, Princes and Paramount Power: Society and Politics in the Indian Princely States* (Delhi: Oxford University Press).

Jose, A.V. (1980), 'Agricultural Labourers in Kerala: An Historical and Statistical Analysis', Ph.D. thesis, Centre for Development Studies, Thiruvananthapuram.

—— (1994), 'Social Policy Towards Wage Determination: Some Lessons from the Indian States', in A.K.G. Centre for Research and Studies (1994b).

Joseph, S.V. (1992), 'Educational Growth Among the Depressed Classes in Kerala: Formulating a Hypothesis', *Journal of Education and Social Change*, 6, 1, April–June.

Kabir, M. (1994), 'Socio-Religious Reform Movements among the Muslims of Kerala: *c.* 1900–1930', in A.K.G. Centre for Research and Studies (1994a).

Kabir, M. and T.N. Krishnan (1991), 'Social Intermediation and Health Transition: Lessons from Kerala', paper prepared for a seminar on 'Health and Development in India', jointly sponsored by the National Council of Applied Economic Research and Harvard University Center for Population and Development Studies, held in New Delhi from 2 to 4 January, 1992, Thiruvananthapuram, December.

Kannan, K.P. (1988), *Of Rural Proletarian Struggles: Mobilisation and Organisation of Rural Workers in Southwest India* (Delhi: Oxford University Press).

—— (1990), 'Kerala Economy at the Crossroads?' *Economic and Political Weekly*, 25, 35 and 36, 1–8 September.

—— (1993), 'Public Intervention and Poverty Alleviation: A Study of the Declining Incidence of Poverty in Kerala', Centre for Development Studies, Thiruvananthapuram.

Kannan, K.P. and K. Pushpangadan (1988), 'Agricultural Stagnation and Economic Growth in Kerala: An Exploratory Analysis', Centre for Development Studies, Working Paper No. 227, June.

—— (1990), 'Dissecting Agricultural Stagnation in Kerala: An Analysis across Crops, Seasons and Regions', *Economic and Political Weekly*, 25, 35 and 36, 1–8 September.

Kannan, K.P., K.R. Thankappan, V. Ramankutty, and K.P. Aravindan (1991), *Health and Development in Rural Kerala: A Study of the Linkages between Socioeconomic Status and Health Status* (Palakkad: Integrated Rural Technology Centre of the KSSP).

Karat, Prakash (1973), 'Agrarian Relations in Malabar — 1925–1948', *Social Scientist*, 2, 2 & 3, September and October, 24–37 and 30–43.

—— (1977), 'Organised Struggles of the Malabar Peasantry, 1934–40', *Social Scientist*, March.

—— (1994), Valedictory address, International Congress on Kerala Studies, Thiruvananthapuram.

Kerala Shastra Sahitya Parishad (KSSP) (1991), *Lead Kindly Light: Operation Literacy Eradication* (Kozhikode: KSSP).

Kerala State Women's Development Corporation (KSWDC) (1990), 'Some Proposals submitted to DANIDA following a Workshop on Women Workers in Coir, Cashew, Bamboo and Stone Crushing Industries in Kerala', Thiruvananthapuram.

Kesavan, B.S. (1988), *History of Printing and Publishing in India: A Story of Cultural Re-awakening*, volume II, *Origins of Printing and Publishing in Karnataka, Andhra and Kerala* (New Delhi: National Book Trust).

Kooiman, Dick (1989), *Conversion and Social Equality in India: The London Missionary Society in South Travancore in the 19th Century* (Delhi: Manohar).

Koshy, Abraham, A.A. Gopalakrishnan, V. Vijayachandran, and N.K. Jayakumar (1989), *Report of the Study on the Evaluation of the Public Distribution System in Kerala*, Department of Civil Supplies, Ministry of Food and Civil Supplies, Government of India, Centre for Management Development, Thiruvananthapuram.

Krishnaji, N. (1994), 'Food Security', in A.K.G. Centre for Research and Studies (1994a).

Krishnakumari, R.R. and Alexander George (1994), 'Occupational Structure of Labour Force with Special Reference to the Role of Women in the Agrarian Economy of Kuttanad', in A.K.G. Centre for Research and Studies (1994b).

Krishnan, T.N. (1976), 'Demographic Transition in Kerala: Facts and Factors', *Economic and Political Weekly*, 11, 31–3.

—— (1991), 'Kerala's Health Transition: Facts and Factors', Harvard Center for Population and Development Studies and Centre for Development Studies, Thiruvananthapuram, September.

—— (1992), 'EMS on Kerala's Planning and Development: A Comment', Thiruvananthapuram.

—— (1994), 'Foreign Remittance, Consumption and Income', in A.K.G. Centre for Research and Studies (1994b).

Krishnan, T.V. (1971), *Kerala's First Communist: The Life of 'Sakhavu' Krishna Pillai* (New Delhi: Communist Party Publication).

Kumar, B. Gopalakrishna (1993), 'Low Mortality and High Morbidity in Kerala Reconsidered', *Population and Development Review*, 19, 1, March.

Kumar, Rachel (1994), 'Emerging Trends in Female Unemployment in Kerala', in A.K.G. Centre for Research and Studies (1994b).

Kunjuraman, C.V. (1928), Memorandum Submitted to the Indian Statutory Commission (Simon Commission), 26 May.

Kurien, C.T. (1994), 'Kerala's Development Experience: Random Comments about the Past and Some Considerations for the Future', in A.K.G. Centre for Research and Studies (1994a).

Kurien, John (1991), 'Kerala's Marine Fisheries: The Socio-Economic Profile', Centre for Development Studies, Thiruvananthapuram.

—— (1993a), 'Kerala's Marine Fisheries: A Historical Perspective of the Development Process', Centre for Development Studies, Thiruvananthapuram.

Kurien, John (1993b), 'Kerala's Marine Fisheries: The Socio-Economic Profile', Centre for Development Studies, Thiruvananthapuram.

—— (1993c), 'Kerala's Marine Fisheries: The Ecological Crisis', Centre for Development Studies, Thiruvananthapuram.

—— (1994), 'The Kerala Model: The Central Tendency and the Outlier', in A.K.G. Centre for Research and Studies (1994b).

Kurup, K.K.N. (1981), *William Logan: A Study in the Agrarian Relations of Malabar* (Calicut: Sandhya Publications).

Kusalakumari, P. (1994), 'Education and Social Changes among Pulayas of Travancore', in A.K.G. Centre for Research and Studies (1994c).

Kusuman, K.K. (1973), *Slavery in Travancore* (Thiruvananthapuram: Kerala Historical Society).

Lach, Donald F. (1968), *India in the Eyes of Europe: The Sixteenth Century*, Phoenix Books (Chicago: The University of Chicago Press).

Leela Kumari, P. (1994), 'Social Mobility among Scheduled Caste Women in Kerala', in A.K.G. Centre for Research and Studies (1994c).

Lenin, V.I. (1921), 'The New Economic Policy and the Tasks of the Political Education Departments: Report to the Second All-Russia Congress of Political Education Departments', 17 October 1921, in *Collected Works*, 1966 (Moscow: Progress Publishers).

Lieten, Georges Kristoffel (1982), *The First Communist Ministry in Kerala, 1957–9* (Calcutta: K.P. Bagchi).

Logan, William (1887), *Malabar*, in two volumes (Madras: Government Press), reprinted by Asian Educational Services, New Delhi and Madras, 1989.

Marx, Karl (1853), 'India', reprinted in K. Marx and F. Engels, *On Colonialism* (Moscow: Progress Publishers), 1959.

Mateer, Samuel (1871), *'The Land of Charity': A Descriptive Account of Travancore and its People, With Especial Reference to Missionary Labour* (London: John Snow and Co.).

—— (1883), *Native Life in Travancore* (London: John Snow).

Mathew, A. (1986), 'Educational Policies and State Efforts at Reorganisation in Kerala, 1900–1958', in National Institute of Educational Planning and Administration (1986).

—— (1994), 'Education: The Key to Occupational Mobility among Women', in A.K.G. Centre for Research and Studies (1994c).

Mathew, E.T. (1994), 'Some Socio-Economic Aspects of Educated

Unemployment in Kerala', in A.K.G. Centre for Research and Studies (1994b).

Mayer, Adrian (1952), *Land and Society in Malabar* (London: Oxford University Press).

Mencher, Joan (1966), 'Kerala and Madras: A Comparative Study of Ecology and Social Structure', *Ethnology*, 5, 2.

—— (1980), 'The Lessons and Non-Lessons of Kerala: Agricultural Labourers and Poverty', *Economic and Political Weekly*, Special Number, xv, 41–3.

—— (1994), 'The Kerala Model of Development: The Excluded Ones', in A.K.G. Centre for Research and Studies (1994b).

Menon, A. Sreedhara (1988), *A Survey of Kerala History* (Madras: S. Viswanathan Printers and Publishers).

—— (1990), *Kerala History and Its Makers*, second revised edition (Madras: S. Viswanathan Printers and Publishers).

Menon, C. Achyuta (1922), *Diwan Sankara Variyar of Cochin: A Biographical Sketch* (Trichur: V. Sundra Iyer and Sons).

—— (1923), *T. Sankunni Menon: Diwan of Cochin* (Trichur: V. Sundra Iyer and Sons).

Menon, Leela (1992), 'Kerala's Mythical Yagas', *Indian Express*, 28 April.

Menon, Parvathi (1992), 'The Putrakameshti Yaga: All for a Son', *Frontline*, 6–19 June.

Menon, T.K. Krishna (1932), *Progress of Cochin* (Ernakulam: Cochin Government Press).

—— (1949), *The Days That Were (Memoirs)* (Ernakulam: Industrial School Press).

Miller, Roland E. (1992), *Mappila Muslims of Kerala: A Study in Islamic Trends*, revised edition (Madras: Orient Longman).

Minhas, B.S. and L.R. Jain (1990), 'Incidence of Rural Poverty in Different States and All-India: 1970–1 to 1983', in *Indian Society of Agricultural Economics*, reprinted in *Agricultural Development Policy: Adjustments and Reorientation* (New Delhi: Oxford and IBH).

Minhas, B.S., L.R. Jain, and M.R. Saluja (1990), 'State Specific Urban Consumer Price Differentials Relative to All-India for Middle Fractiles and Total Population: 1961–1983', *Indian Economic Review*, 25, 2.

Mohandas, M. (1994), 'Paradox of High Poverty and High PQLI in Kerala: Facts and Fallacies', in A.K.G. Centre for Research and Studies (1994b).

Mohan Das, R. (1992), 'Growth and Spatial Distribution of Agriculture in Kerala', *Agricultural Situation in India*, December.

Mooij, Jos (1994), 'Food, Law and Politics: The Essential Commodities Act and PDS in Kerala', paper presented at the International Congress on Kerala Studies in Thiruvananthapuram, 27–9 August 1994, Centre for Asian Studies, Amsterdam.

Mukherjee, Chandan and T.M. Thomas Isaac (1994), 'Nine Observations on Educated Unemployment in Kerala', in A.K.G. Centre for Research and Studies (1994b).

Munro, Colonel James (1817), Report Respecting the District of Malabar, Letter from the First Commissioner to the Chief Secretary, Madras Revenue Department, 4 July.

Murray, Christopher J.L. and Lincoln C. Chen (1992), 'Understanding Morbidity Change', *Population and Development Review*, 18, 3, September.

Nag, Moni (1983), 'Impact of Social and Economic Development on Morbidity: Comparative Study of Kerala and West Bengal', *Economic and Political Weekly*, 18, 19–21.

—— (1989), 'Political Awareness as a Factor in Accessibility of Health Services: A Case Study of Rural Kerala and West Bengal', *Economic and Political Weekly*, 24, 8.

Nagaraj, K. (1985), 'Towns in Tamil Nadu, Karnataka and Andhra Pradesh: A Study of Population and Spatial Configurations, 1961–1981', Madras Institute of Development Studies, Working Paper No. 54, Madras.

—— (1986), 'Infant Mortality in Tamil Nadu', *Madras Institute of Development Studies Bulletin*, January.

Nair, G. Somasekharan (1994), 'Demographic and Community-Wise Changes in Kerala: Community-Wise Analysis', in A.K.G. Centre for Research and Studies (1994a).

Nair, K.N. Shyamasundaran (1994), 'Constraints to Kerala's Development, or What Ails Kerala's Agriculture?', in A.K.G. Centre for Research and Studies (1994b).

Nair, P.R. Gopinathan (1974), 'Decline in Birth Rate in Kerala: A Hypothesis About the Inter-Relationship Between Demographic Variables, Health Services and Education', *Economic and Political Weekly*, 9.

—— (1976), 'Education and Social Change in Travancore', *Social Scientist*, March.

—— (1981), *Primary Education, Population Growth and Socio-Economic Change: A Comparative Study with Particular Reference to Kerala* (New Delhi: Allied Publishers).

—— (1986), 'Educational Developments in Kerala: An Overview', in

National Institute of Educational Planning and Administration (1986).

Nair, P.R. Gopinathan (1994), 'Broad Trends in Migration to the Middle East. A Note', in A.K.G. Centre for Research and Studies (1994b).

Nambiar, T.K. Gangadharan (1982), 'Growth of Class Consciousness Among the Peasantry of North Malabar, Kerala, 1934–42', M.Phil. Dissertation, Jawaharlal Nehru University, New Delhi.

Namboodiripad, E.M.S. (1942), 'In Kerala: Our Sisters Make History', *People's War*, 20 December.

—— (1943), 'Must Kerala Go the Bengal Way?', *People's War*, 26 December.

—— (1943), 'A Short History of the Peasant Movement in Malabar', reprinted in Namboodiripad (1985).

—— (1944), 'A Year and a Half of Famine and Misery', *People's War*, 9 July.

—— (1976a), *How I Became a Communist*, translation P.K. Nair (Thiruvananthapuram: Chinta Publishers).

—— (1976b), Comment on P. Sivanandan, 'Economic Backwardness of Harijans in Kerala', *Social Scientist*, 4, 12, July.

—— (1984), *Kerala: Society and Politics: An Historical Survey* (New Delhi: National Book Centre).

—— (1985), *Selected Writings*, volume 2 (Calcutta: National Book Agency).

—— (1994a), Presidential Address, International Congress on Kerala Studies, in A.K.G. Centre for Research and Studies (1994a).

—— (1994b), *The Communist Party in Kerala: Six Decades of Advance and Struggle* (New Delhi: National Book Centre).

Narayana, D. (1992), 'Interaction of Price and Technology in the Presence of Structural Specificities: An Analysis of Crop Production in Kerala', Ph.D. thesis submitted to the Indian Statistical Institute, Calcutta.

Narayanan, M.G.S. (1986), 'Educational Traditions of Kerala: Persuasions from the Past', in National Institute of Educational Planning and Administration (1986).

National Institute of Educational Planning and Administration (NIEPA) (1986), 'Workshop-cum-Seminar on Educational Developments in Kerala: October 27–8, 1986: Report', NIEPA.

National Nutrition Monitoring Bureau (1991), *Report of Repeat Surveys (1988–90)* (Hyderabad: National Institute of Nutrition).

National Sample Survey (1977), Consumer expenditure, NSS 28th round (1973–4), *Sarvekshana*, 1, 1, July.

National Sample Survey (1978), NSS 25th round: July 1970–June 1971, No. 231, Tables with notes on consumer expenditure, Delhi.

—— (1979), Consumer expenditure: NSS 27th round (October 1972–September 1973), *Sarvekshana*, 2, 3, January.

—— (1986a), Some results on the second quinquennial survey on consumer expenditure: NSS 32nd round, *Sarvekshana*, 9, 3, January.

—— (1986b), Results on the third quinquennial survey on consumer expenditure: NSS 38th round, *Sarvekshana*, 9, 4, April.

—— (1989), Results on consumer expenditure: NSS 42nd round (1986–7), *Sarvekshana*, 12, 4, April–June.

—— (1990), 42nd round, July 1986 to June 1987, Results on utilisation of public distribution system, *Sarvekshana*, April–June.

—— (1991a), 42nd round, July 1986 to June 1987, Results on Participation in Education (All-India), *Sarvekshana*, 14, 3, January–March.

—— (1991b), 42nd round, July 1986 to June 1987, Child and Maternity Care, *Sarvekshana*, 14, 4, April–June.

—— (1991c), 43rd round, July 1987 to June 1988, Fourth quinquennial survey on consumer expenditure, *Sarvekshana*, 15, 1, July–September.

—— (1992), 42nd round, July 1986 to June 1987, Use of Family Planning, *Sarvekshana*, 16, 1, July–September.

—— (1993), 42nd round, July 1986 to June 1987, Results on Participation in Education for 8 Major States, *Sarvekshana*, 16, 4, April–June.

Nayanar, E.K. (1982), *My Struggles: An Autobiography* (New Delhi: Vikas).

Nayar, P.K.B. (1994), 'Social and Economic Implications of Ageing in Kerala', in A.K.G. Centre for Research and Studies (1994a).

Nossiter, T.J. (1982), *Communism in Kerala: A Study in Political Adaptation*, University of California Press for the Royal Institute of International Affairs, London, Berkeley.

Oddie, G.A. (1978), *Social Protest in India: British Protestant Missionaries and Social Reforms, 1850–1900* (Columbia: South Asia Books and New Delhi: Manohar).

Oommen, M.A. (1992), *The Kerala Economy* (New Delhi: Oxford and IBH).

Operations Research Group (1990a), *National Readership Survey, 1989, Kerala* (Baroda: Operations Research Group).

—— (1990b), *National Readership Survey, 1989–90, All-India*, in three parts (Baroda: Operations Research Group).

Padmanabhan, Nirmala (1990), 'Poor Performance of Private Corporate Sector in Kerala', *Economic and Political Weekly*, 25, 37, 15 September.

Panikar, P.G.K. (1975), 'Fall in Mortality Rates in Kerala: An Explanatory Hypothesis', *Economic and Political Weekly*, x, 47, 22 November.

—— (1979), 'Resources Not the Constraint on Health Improvement: A Case Study of Kerala', *Economic and Political Weekly*, xiv, 44, 3 November.

Panikar, P.G.K. and C.R. Soman (1985), *Health Status of Kerala: The Paradox of Economic Backwardness and Health Development* (Thiruvananthapuram: Centre for Development Studies).

Panikkar, K.N. (1989), *Against Lord and State: Religion and Peasant Uprisings in Malabar, 1836–1921* (New Delhi: Oxford University Press).

Panikkar, K.N. (ed.) (1990), *Peasant Protests and Revolts in Malabar* (New Delhi: Indian Council of Historical Research and People's Publishing House).

Peter, Ivy (1987), 'History of the Ezhavas of Kerala', Ph.D. thesis, Madurai Kamaraj University.

Pillai, P. Govinda, 'Art and Literature in the Second Stage of Kerala Renaissance', in A.K.G. Centre for Research and Studies (1994a).

Potts, E. Daniel (1967), *British Baptist Missionaries in India, 1793–1837* (Cambridge: Cambridge University Press).

Prabhash, J. (1994), 'Malayali Memorial: Class Interest through Caste and Community Interaction', in A.K.G. Centre for Research and Studies (1994a).

Puthenkulam, Fr. J. (1977), *Marriage and the Family in Kerala with Special Reference to Matrilineal Castes* (Calgary: Journal of Comparative Family Studies Monograph Series).

Radhakrishnan, P. (1989), *Peasant Struggles, Land Reforms and Social Change: Malabar 1936–82* (New Delhi: Sage Publications).

Raj, K.N. (1992), 'Land Reform and Complementary Measures in Kerala', *IASSI Quarterly*, 10, 3.

—— (1994), 'Has There Been a "Kerala Model"?', in A.K.G. Centre for Research and Studies (1994a).

Raj, K.N. and P.K. Michael Tharakan (1983), 'Agrarian Reform in Kerala and its Impact on the Rural Economy — A Preliminary Assessment', in Ajit Kumar Ghose (ed.), *Agrarian Reform in Contemporary Developing Countries* (London and New York: Croom Helm and St. Martin's Press).

Rajeev, P.I. (1993), 'Modern Day Slaves', *Indian Express*, Bombay, 13 October.

Ram, N. (1994), Valedictory Address, International Congress on Kerala Studies, Thiruvananthapuram.

Ram, N. (forthcoming), *The Press, Politics and Society in India*, ms., Madras.

Ramakrishnan, Venkitesh (1991), 'Politics of Literacy: Threats to an Ambitious Scheme in Kerala', *Frontline*, 17–30 August.

Raman Kutty, V. (1987), 'Socioeconomic Factors in Child Health Status: A Kerala Village Study', M.Phil. Dissertation (unpublished), Centre for Development Studies, Thiruvananthapuram.

—— (1989), 'Women's Education and Its Influence on Attitudes to Aspects of Child Care in a Village Community in Kerala', *Social Science and Medicine*, 29, 11.

Raman Kutty, V. and Malati Damodaran (1989), 'Health Status of Children in Two Villages of Kerala', unpublished, Thiruvananthapuram.

Raman Kutty, V., K.G. Balakrishnan, A.K. Jayasree, and, Jessy Thomas (1993a), 'Prevalence of Coronary Heart Disease in the Rural Population of Thiruvananthapuram District, Kerala, India', *International Journal of Cardiology*, 39, 59–70.

Raman Kutty, V., K.R. Thankappan, K.P. Kannan, and K.P. Aravindan (1993b), 'How Socio-Economic Status Affects Birth and Death Rates in Rural Kerala, India: Results of a Health Study', *The International Journal of Health Services*, 23, 93.

Rao, N. Bhaskara (1990), 'Media Scene in India: Highlights from ORG-NRS, 1989–90', Centre for Media Studies, New Delhi.

Registrar of Newspapers (1957), *Annual Report*, Ministry of Information and Broadcasting (New Delhi: Government of India).

—— (1962), *Annual Report*, Ministry of Information and Broadcasting (New Delhi: Government of India).

—— (1991), *Press in India 1990*, Ministry of Information and Broadcasting (New Delhi: Government of India).

Roy, Mary (1994), 'A New Bill which Proposes to Protect the Rights of Christian Women in Kerala', in A.K.G. Centre for Research and Studies (1994b).

Roy Choudhury, Uma Datta (1993), 'Inter-State and Intra-State Variations in Economic Development and Standards of Living', *Journal of Indian School of Political Economy*, 5, 1, January–March.

Sanoo, M.K. (1978), *Narayana Guru* (Bombay: Bharatiya Vidya Bhavan).

Saradamoni, K. (1980), *Emergence of a Slave Caste: Pulayas of Kerala* (New Delhi: People's Publishing House).

Saradamoni, K. (1981), *Divided Poor: Study of a Kerala Village* (Delhi: Ajanta Publications).

—— (1994a), 'Kerala Society and Politics', in A.K.G. Centre for Research and Studies (1994a).

—— (1994b), 'Women, Kerala and Some Development Issues', *Economic and Political Weekly*, 29, 9, 26 February.

Sathian, Lelithabai (1994), 'Analysis of Agricultural Growth in Kerala', in A.K.G. Centre for Research and Studies (1994b).

Schneider, David M. and Kathleen Gough (eds.) (1961), *Matrilineal Kinship* (Berkeley: University of California Press).

Sebastian, M. (1994), 'Tribal Situation in Kerala', in A.K.G. Centre for Research and Studies (1994d).

Sen, Amartya (1984), 'Rights and Capabilities', in Amartya Sen, *Resources, Values and Development* (Oxford: Basil Blackwell).

—— (1993), 'The Economics of Life and Death', *Scientific American*, 268, 5, May.

Sharma, B.A.N. (1994), 'Child Labour: A Grim Reality', Indira Gandhi Institute of Development Research, Bombay.

Sharma, H.R. (1992), 'Agrarian Relations in India Since Independence', *Journal of Indian School of Political Economy*, 4, 2, April–June.

Shiva Kumar, A.K. (1991), 'UNDP's Human Development Index: A Computation for Indian States', *Economic and Political Weekly*, 26, 41, October.

Sivanandan, P. (1976), 'Economic Backwardness of Harijans in Kerala', *Social Scientist*, 4, 10.

—— (1979), 'Caste, Class and Economic Opportunity in Kerala: An Empirical Analysis', *Economic and Political Weekly*, 14, 7–8.

Sivaswamy, K.G., et al. (1946a), *Famine Rationing and Food Policy in Cochin*, with Medical Surveys by T.S. Shastry and J.A. Bhat, Servindia Kerala Relief Board, Madras.

—— (1946b), *Food Control and Nutrition Surveys, Malabar and South Kanara* (Madras: Servindia Kerala Relief Centre).

—— (1946c), *Food, Famines, and Nutritional Diseases in Travancore* (Coimbatore: Servindia Kerala Relief Centre).

Soman, C.R. (1993), 'Health and Fertility Transition: Lessons From Kerala', K.S. Sanjeevi Lecture, Madras, April.

Soman, C.R., Malati Damodaran, S. Rajasree, V. Ramankutty, and K. Vijayakumar (1990), 'High Morbidity and Low Mortality: The Experience of Urban Pre-School Children in Kerala', *Journal of Tropical Paediatrics*, 37, 17–141.

Somervell, T. Howard (1940), *Knife and Life in India: The Story of a*

Surgical Missionary at Neyyoor, Travancore, revised edition, 1955 (London: The Livingstone Press).

Sreekumar, S.S. (1994), 'Adult Education in Tribal Areas: The Problem of Dropouts', in A.K.G. Centre for Research and Studies (1994d).

Sreekumar, T.T. (1990), 'Neither Rural Nor Urban: Spatial Formation and the Development Process', *Economic and Political Weekly*, 25, 35 and 36, 1–8 September.

Subrahmanian, K.K. (1990), 'Development Paradox in Kerala: Analysis of Industrial Stagnation', *Economic and Political Weekly*, 25, 37, 15 September.

Subrahmanian, K.K. and P. Mohanan Pillai (1993), 'Modern Small Industry in Kerala: A Review of Structural Change and Growth Performance', Working Paper, Centre for Development Studies, Thiruvananthapuram.

Surendran, P.K. (1993), 'Women Empowerment Below Par in Kerala', *Times of India*, Bombay, 22 October.

Suresh Kumar, P.M. (1979), 'A Sociological Study of the Brahmins of Kerala With Special Reference To Their Downward Mobility', M.Phil. Dissertation, Jawaharlal Nehru University, New Delhi.

Swaminathan, Madhura (1985), 'On to Pastures New: A Study of Migration, *Frontline*, 7–20 September.

—— (1994), 'Economic Development, Structural Adjustment and Anti-Poverty Programmes in India', background paper for the UNDP Conference on Sustainable Human Development, UNDP Office, New Delhi, September.

Tendulkar, S.D. and L.R. Jain (1993), 'An Analysis of Inter-State and Inter-Commodity Group Rural–Urban Consumer Prices in India; 1983 to 1988–89', *Journal of Indian School of Political Economy*, 5, 2, April–June.

Thankappan, K.R. and V. Ramankutty (1990), 'Immunisation Coverage in Kerala and the Role of the Integrated Child Services Programme', *Health Policy and Planning*, 5, 3.

Tharakan, P.K. Michael (1977), 'Migration of Farmers from Travancore to Malabar from 1930 to 1960: An Analysis of Its Economic Causes', M.Phil. Dissertation, Jawaharlal Nehru University, Centre for Development Studies, Thiruvananthapuram.

—— (1981), 'Intra-Regional Differences in Agrarian Systems and Internal Migration: A Case Study of the Migration of Farmers from Travancore to Malabar, 1930 to 1950', Centre for Development Studies, Thiruvananthapuram.

Tharakan, P.K. Michael (n.d.), 'The Kerala Land Reforms (Amendment) Bill, 1979: A Note', Thiruvananthapuram.

—— (1984), 'Socio-Economic Factors in Educational Development: Case of Nineteenth Century Travancore', *Economic and Political Weekly*, XIX, 45 and 46, 10 and 17 November.

—— (1986), 'Divergent Effects of Similar Policies: A Study of Educational Policies of Travancore and British India', in National Institute of Educational Planning and Administration (1986).

—— (1990), 'The Ernakulam Total Literacy Programme', mimeo, Centre for Development Studies, Thiruvananthapuram.

—— (1991), 'Socio-Religious Reform Movements and Demand for Indicators of Development: Thiruvithamkoor, 1860–1930,' paper presented to the 11th European Conference on Modern South Asian Studies, Amsterdam.

Tharakan, P.K. Michael and K. Navaneetham (1994), 'Demographic Trends and Implications for Policy in the Primary Education Sector: Discussion with Reference to Kerala', in A.K.G. Centre for Research and Studies (1994e).

Thomas, Jessy (1981), 'Socio-Economic Factors Influencing Educational Standards in a Marginalised Community: A Case Study on the Marine Fisherfolk of Kerala', M.Phil. Thesis in Applied Economics, Centre for Development Studies, Thiruvananthapuram.

Thorp, Rosemary (1993), review of Magnus Blomstrom and Patricio Meller (eds.), *Diverging Paths: Comparing a Century of Scandinavian and Latin American Economic Development* (Washington: Inter American Development Bank, 1991), in *The Economic Journal*, 103, 420, September.

United Nations Development Programme (UNDP) (1990, 1991, 1992, 1993), *Human Development Report* (New York: Oxford University Press).

Vaidyanathan, A. (1992), 'On Assessment of Nutritional and Health Status', Harvard Center for Population and Development Studies, Cambridge, MA.

Varghese, T.C. (1970), *Agrarian Change and Economic Consequences: Land Tenures in Kerala 1850–1960* (Bombay: Allied Publishers).

Velayudhan, Meera (1992), 'A Voice from the Women's Movement in Kerala: Meera Velayudhan in Conversation with Kalikutty Asatty', *Women's Equality*, 5, 1, January–March, 34–7.

Venugopal, K. (1992), 'Undoing a Cultural Revolution', *The Independent*, Bombay, 17 June.

Vimala Kumary, T.K. (1991), *Infant Mortality Among Fishermen* (New Delhi: Discovery Publishing House).

Ward, Lt. B.S. and Lt. P.E. Conner (1816–20), *Geographical and Statistical Memoir of the Survey of Travancore and Cochin States*, Executed under the Superintendence of Lts. Ward and Conner, From July 1816 to the end of the Year 1820, vol. 1, Surveyor General's Office, Madras, 1827, Travancore Sircar Press, 1863.

Washbrook, David (1994), 'Kerala in Eighteenth-Century Perspective', in A.K.G. Centre for Research and Studies (1994e).

Weiner, Myron (1991), *The Child and the State in India*, Princeton University Press, reprinted by Oxford University Press, Delhi, 1992.

Yesudas, R.N. (1978), 'The English and the Christians of Kerala, 1800–1836', *Journal of Kerala Studies*, v, i, March.

—— (1980), *The History of the London Missionary Society in Travancore 1806–1908* (Thiruvananthapuram: Kerala Historical Society).

Zachariah, K.C. (1992), *Demographic Transition in Kerala in the 1980s: Results of a Survey in Three Districts*, with contributions by S. Irudaya Rajan, K. Navaneetham, P.S. Sarma, U.S. Mishra, and P.S. Gopinathan Nair, Centre for Development Studies, Thiruvananthapuram, and Gujarat Institute of Area Planning, Ahmedabad, April.

—— (1994), 'Demographic Transition in Kerala: A Response to Official Policies and Programmes', in A.K.G. Centre for Research and Studies (1994a).

Zachariah, K.C. and Sulekha Patel (1982), 'Trends and Determinants of Infant and Child Morbidity in Kerala', Discussion Paper 82–3, Population and Human Resources Division, Washington, DC.

Zograph, G.A. (1960), *The Languages of India: A Guide*, reprinted, 1982, translated from the original Russian edition of 1960 (London: Routledge and Kegan Paul).

Census Volumes

Census of Cochin 1875 (1877), *Report on the Census of Native Cochin*, taken on the 6th Karkatam 1050/20th July 1875, together with Statistical Tables and a Manual of Geography, by A. Sankariah, BA, Dewan Peishkar, Cochin, printed in Madras.

Census of Cochin 1891 (1893), *Report on the Census of Cochin 1891 AD 1066 ME: Part i — The Review*, by C. Achyuta Menon, BA, Superintendent of Census Operations, Cochin Government Press.

Census of India 1891 (1893a), volume xiii, Madras, *The Report on the Census*, by H.A. Stuart, ICS, FRSS, Member RAS, Superintendent of Census Operations, Madras, Government Press, Madras.

Census of India 1891 (1893b), volume XIV, Madras, *Tables I–XVII C*, *British Territory*, Madras.

—— (1893c), volume XIV, Madras, *Tables A to E, British Territory, Tables for Feudatory States and a Caste Index*, Madras.

Census of India 1901 (1902), volume XX-A, Cochin, Part II, *Imperial Tables*, by M. Sankara Menon, BA, Superintendent of Census Operations, Ernakulam.

—— (1903a), volume XX, Cochin, Part I, *Report*, by M. Sankara Menon, BA, Superintendent of Census Operations, Cochin Government Press, Ernakulam.

—— (1903b), volume XXVI, Travancore, Part I, *Report*, by N. Subrahmanya Aiyar, MA, MB, CM, Dewan Peishcar, Census Commissioner, Thiruvananthapuram.

—— (1903c), volume XXVI-A, Travancore, Part II, *Imperial Tables*, by N. Subrahmanya Aiyar, MA, MB, CM, Dewan Peishcar, Census Commissioner, Thiruvananthapuram.

Census of India 1911 (1912a), volume XII, Part I, *Report*, by J. Chartres Molony, ICS, Superintendent of Census Operations, Madras, and Alfred Chatterton, CIE, Madras.

—— (1912b), volume XII, Part II, Imperial and Provincial Tables, by J. Chartres Molony, ICS, Superintendent of Census Operations, Madras, Madras.

—— (1912c), volume XVIII, Cochin, Part I, *Report*; Part II, *Imperial Tables*, by C. Achyuta Menon, BA, Superintendent of Census Operations, Cochin State, Ernakulam.

—— (1912d), volume XXIII, Travancore, Part I, *Report*, by N. Subrahmanya Aiyar, MA, Dewan Peishcar, Census Commissioner, Thiruvananthapuram.

—— (1912e), volume XXIII, Travancore, Part II, *Imperial Tables*, by N. Subrahmanya Aiyar, MA, Dewan Peishcar, Census Commissioner, Thiruvananthapuram.

—— (1912f), volume XXIII, Travancore, Part III, *Provincial Tables*, by N. Subrahmanya Aiyar, MA, Dewan Peishcar, Census Commissioner, Thiruvananthapuram.

Census of India 1921 (1922a), volume XIX, Cochin, Part I, *Report*; Part II, *Imperial Tables*, by P. Govinda Menon, BA, Superintendent of Census Operations, Cochin State, Government Press, Ernakulam.

—— (1922b), volume XXV, Travancore, Part I, *Report*; Part II, *Imperial Tables*, by Murari S. Krishnamurthi Ayyar, MB and CM, Fellow of the Royal Statistical Society, Census Commissioner, Travancore, Thiruvananthapuram.

Census of India 1921 (1922c), volume XIII, Madras, Part I, *Report*, by G.T. Boag, MA, of the Indian Civil Service, Superintendent of Census Operations, Madras, Madras.

Census of India 1931 (1932a), volume XIV, Madras, Part I, *Report*, by M.W.M. Yeatts, of the Indian Civil Service, Superintendent of Census Operations, Madras, Madras.

—— (1932b), volume XIV, Madras, Part II, *Imperial and Provincial Tables*, by M.W.M. Yeatts, ICS, Superintendent of Census Operations, Madras, Government of India Special Publications Branch, Calcutta.

—— (1932c), volume XXVIII, Travancore, Part I, *Report*, by N. Kunjan Pillai, Thiruvananthapuram.

—— (1932d), volume XXVIII, Travancore, Part II, *Tables*, by N. Kunjan Pillai, Thiruvananthapuram.

—— (1933), volume XXI, Cochin, Part I; *Report* and Part II, *A & B — Tables*, by T.K. Sankara Menon, Ernakulam.

Census of India 1941 (1942a), volume II, Madras, *Tables*, by D.H. Elwin, OBE, ICS, Superintendent of Census Operations, Madras, Manager of Publications, Delhi.

—— (1942b), volume XXV, Travancore, Part III, *State Tables*, by A. Narayanan Tampi, Thiruvananthapuram.

—— (1944), volume XIX, Cochin, Part I; *Report*, Part II, *Tables*, by B.V.K. Menon, Ernakulam.

Census of India 1951 (1953a), *District Census Handbook, Malabar District* (Delhi: Manager of Publications).

—— (1953b), volume XIII, Travancore–Cochin, Part I-A, *Report*, by U. Sivaraman Nair (Delhi: Manager of Publications).

—— (1953c), volume XIII, Travancore–Cochin, Part II, *Tables*, by U. Sivaraman Nair, Manager of Publications, Delhi.

—— (1957), Paper No. 1 of 1957, *General Population Tables and Summary Figures by Districts of Reorganised States — 1951 Census*, Delhi.

Census of India 1961 (1962), Paper No. 1 of 1962, *Final Population Totals*, Delhi.

—— (1964), volume VII, Kerala, Part II-A, *General Population Tables*, by M.K. Devassy, IAS, Manager of Publications, Delhi.

—— (1965), volume I, India, Part II-C(ii), *Language Tables*, Delhi.

—— (1966a), volume I, India, Part V-A(i), *Special Tables for Scheduled Castes* (Delhi: Controller of Publications).

—— (1966b), volume I, India, Part V-A(ii), *Special Tables for Scheduled Tribes* (Delhi: Controller of Publications).

Census of India 1961 (1967), volume VII, Kerala, Part V-A, *Special Tables for Scheduled Castes and Tribes* (Delhi: Manager of Publications).

Census of India 1971 (1972a), Series 1, India, Paper 1 of 1972, *Final Population*, Delhi.

—— (1972b), Series 9, Kerala, *General Population Tables*, by K. Narayanan, IAS (Delhi: Manager of Publications).

—— (1976), Series 9, Kerala, *Social and Cultural Tables* (Delhi: Controller of Publications).

—— (1977), Series 1, India, Part II-C(i), *Social and Cultural Tables* (Delhi: Controller of Publications).

—— (1981), Series 1, India, Part V-A(ii), *Special Tables for Scheduled Tribes* (Delhi: Controller of Publications).

Census of India 1981 (1983), Series 1, India, Paper 1 of 1982, *Final Population Totals* (Delhi: Controller of Publications).

—— (1985), Series 1, India, Part II-A(i), *General Population Tables (Tables A-1 to A-3)* (New Delhi: Controller of Publications).

—— (1987), Series 1, India, Paper 1 of 1987, *Households and Household Population by Language Mainly Spoken in the Household* (Delhi: Controller of Publications).

—— (1991), Series 1, India, Part IV-B(i), *Population by Language/Mother-Tongue (Table C-7)* (Delhi: Controller of Publications).

Census of India 1991 (1991), Series 1, India, Paper 2 of 1991, *Provisional Population Totals: Rural–Urban Distribution*, Ministry of Home Affairs (New Delhi: Government of India).

—— (1993), Series 1, India, Paper 1 of 1992, *Final Population Tables*, in two volumes (Delhi: Controller of Publications).

—— (1993a), Series 1, India, Paper 2 of 1991, *Final Population Totals: Brief Analysis of Primary Census Abstract*, Delhi.

Census of the Madras Presidency 1871 (1874), *Report on the Census of the Madras Presidency, 1871* (with Appendix containing the results of the Census arranged in standard forms prescribed by the Government of India), by W.R. Cornish, FRCS, Surgeon Major, Sanitary Commissioner for Madras, volume 1, Madras.

Census of Travancore 1875 (1876), *Report on the Census of Travancore*, (taken on the 18th May 1875 AD — 6th Vycausy 1050 ME), Census Superintendent: V. Nagam Aiya, Travancore Government Press, Thiruvananthapuram.

Census of Travancore 1881 (1884), *Report on the Census of Travancore*, taken on the 17th February 1881 AD — 7th Mausy 1056 ME along with the Imperial Census of India, by V. Nagamaiya, Thiruvananthapuram.

Census of Travancore 1891 (1892a), *Report on Census*, Part I, Thiru-vananthapuram.

—— (1892b), *Report on Census*, Part II, Thiruvananthapuram.

Imperial Census of 1881 (1883), *Operations and Results in the Presidency of Madras: Volume I: The Report*, by Lewis McIver, Barrister-at-Law, Madras Civil Service, The Government Press, Madras.

Other Serial Publications

Centre for Monitoring the Indian Economy, Economic Intelligence Service, *Index Numbers of Wholesale Prices and Consumer Prices*, Bombay.

Government of India, Ministry of Labour, Labour Bureau, *Indian Labour Statistics*, Chandigarh/Shimla.

—— Ministry of Labour, Labour Bureau, *Indian Labour Year Book*, Chandigarh/Shimla.

5

MORTALITY, FERTILITY AND GENDER BIAS IN INDIA: A District-Level Analysis[*]

Mamta Murthi
Anne-Catherine Guio
Jean Drèze

1. INTRODUCTION

India is a country of striking demographic diversity. Even broad comparisons between its states bring out enormous variations in basic demographic indicators. At one end of the scale, Kerala has demographic features that are more typical of a middle-income country than of a poor developing economy, including a life expectancy at birth of 72 years, an infant mortality rate of 17 per 1,000 live births, a total fertility rate below the replacement level (1.8 births per woman), and a ratio of females to males in the population well above unity (1.04). At the other end, the large north Indian states find themselves in the same league as the world's least developed countries of the world in terms of the same indicators. In Uttar Pradesh, for instance, the infant mortality rate is six times as high as in Kerala, the total fertility rate is 5.1, and the female–male ratio (0.88) is lower than that of any country in the world.[1]

* We are most grateful to Satish Agnihotri, Sudhir Anand, Peter Boone, Jean-Marie Baland, Monica Das Gupta, Angus Deaton, Tim Dyson, Michel Garenne, Haris Gazdar, Stuti Khemani, Sunita Kishor, P.N. Mari Bhat, Jean-Philippe Platteau, Rohini Somanathan, and P.V. Srinivasan for helpful discussions and comments.

[1] The figures cited in this paragraph (with 1991 as the reference year in each case) are taken from Drèze and Sen (1995), Statistical Appendix, and are based on data from the Census and the Sample Registration System. A few countries of West Asia (e.g. Kuwait and the United Arab Emirates) actually have a lower female–male ratio than Uttar Pradesh, but this is due to exceptionally high levels of male in-migration.

India is also, increasingly, a country of rapid demographic change. As in many other developing countries, mortality rates in India have significantly declined in recent decades; the infant mortality rate, for example, has decreased by about 50 per cent between 1961 and 1991. The same period has seen a sustained decline in fertility, particularly in the south Indian states (in Tamil Nadu, for instance, the total fertility rate declined from 3.5 to 2.2 during the eighties). There have also been significant changes in the relative survival chances of men and women.[2]

Apart from being of much interest in themselves, these inter-regional and intertemporal variations provide useful opportunities to study the determinants of demographic outcomes in India. This article examines some of the relevant relationships based on a cross-section analysis of district-level data from the 1981 Census of India.[3]

Our sample consists of 296 districts for which detailed information is available. The demographic outcomes under study are the child mortality rate, the total fertility rate, and the relative survival chances of male and female children. The choice of explanatory variables is partly guided by recent analyses of the determinants of demographic behaviour, but also reflects the limitations of available statistical sources. Particular attention is paid to the influence of per-capita income, male and female literacy, female labour-force participation rates, levels of urbanization, availability of health-care facilities, and related socio-economic variables. We begin with a brief discussion of the possible relevance of different explanatory variables, before turning to the presentation and interpretation of our results.

2. ISSUES AND HYPOTHESES

This section discusses some plausible relationships between demographic outcomes and basic personal and social characteristics and

[2] On this point, see e.g. I. Sen (1986), Karkal (1987), Dyson (1988), Miller (1989), Kundu and Sahu (1991), Srinivas (1991), Nanda (1992), Rajan et al. (1991, 1992) and Raju and Premi (1992).

[3] Earlier investigations of this type, for India, have often been based on state-level data, involving a much smaller number of observations; see e.g. Jain (1985), Bourne and Walker (1991), Reddy and Selvaraju (1993), and Tulasidhar and Sarma (1993). Analyses based on district-level data include Rosenzweig and Schultz (1982), Gulati (1992), Kishor (1993), Guio (1994), and Khemani (1994).

demographic outcomes. We focus, to start with, on mortality and fertility, before taking up the issue of gender bias.

2.1 Economic Development and the Demographic Transition

Demographic change (in particular, the 'demographic transition' from high to low levels of mortality and fertility) is sometimes thought of as a by-product of economic growth and rising incomes. It is certainly the case that a broad inverse association can be observed, at the international level, between per-capita GNP, on the one hand, and mortality and fertility levels, on the other. There is also much evidence of a causal relationship being involved, with rising incomes typically leading to some reduction of mortality and fertility. But recent research suggests that the 'income effect' can be quite slow and weak, and that other personal and social characteristics, such as female literacy, often have a more powerful influence on demographic outcomes.

The limited explanatory power of per-capita income and related variables can be illustrated by considering the relationship between child mortality and the incidence of poverty (as measured by the 'head-count ratio') in different states of India. The relevant information is presented in Fig. 1.[4] The association between the two variables is clearly weak. Some aspects of this weakness of association are rather striking; for instance, rates of child mortality are more than six times higher in Uttar Pradesh than in Kerala, even though the head-count ratios are very similar, and close to the all-India average, in both states. This need not be taken to mean that income or expenditure have no effect on child mortality and related demographic outcomes. There is plenty of evidence, for India as for many other countries, that mortality does decline with higher incomes (this elementary relationship also emerges in the empirical analysis presented below). The point is that many *other* factors, not all of which are themselves strongly correlated with income, also have a strong influence on demographic outcomes.

---

[4] The head-count ratio on which Fig. 1 is based measures the proportion of the population living in households with per-capita expenditure below a pre-specified poverty line. The reference year is 1987–8, the latest year for which state-specific estimates of the head-count ratio are available.

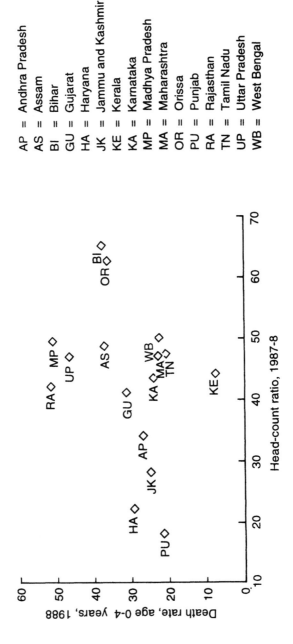

FIG. 1. *Poverty and Child Mortality in Indian States*

Source. Minhas, Jain, and Tendulkar, 1991; Government of India, 1990, Statement 39, p. 48.

2.2   The Role of Literacy

Among the factors other than private income that have a strong influence on fertility and mortality, basic education — especially female education — is now widely considered as one of the most powerful. The close relationship between education and demographic change has clearly emerged in recent empirical studies.[5] A wide range of theoretical analyses from different disciplines point in the same direction.[6]

Considering fertility first, economic, demographic, and anthropological studies suggest specific ways in which female education contributes to fertility reduction. At a general level, it is useful to distinguish between the influences of female education on (1) desired family size, (2) the relationship between desired family size and planned number of births, and (3) ability to achieve the planned number of births.

Female education can be expected to reduce desired family size for several reasons. First, educated women are more likely to voice resentment against the burden of repeated pregnancies and to take action to lighten that burden. This may be the case because they have other sources of prestige and fulfilment than reproductive performance, more control over household resources and personal behaviour, and greater involvement in reproductive decisions (Dyson and Moore, 1983; Cain, 1984). Second, educated women are likely to be less dependent on their sons as a source of social status and old-age security, and this too may lead to some reduction in desired family size. Third, educated women often have higher aspirations for their children, combined with lower expectations from them in terms of labour services provided (United Nations, 1993). This may reduce desired family size if there is a perceived tradeoff between the number of children and their personal achievements. Fourth, the

[5] On the international evidence, see Caldwell (1979, 1986), Behrman and Wolfe (1984, 1987), Ware (1984), Cleland and van Ginneken (1987, 1988), United Nations (1987), Cleland (1990), Bhuiya and Streatfield (1991), Thomas et al. (1991), Barro and Lee (1993a, 1993b), and Subbarao and Raney (1994). For studies relating to India, see Vlassoff (1980), Jain (1985), Jain and Nag (1985, 1986), Nag (1989), Beenstock and Sturdy (1990), Bourne and Walker (1991), Satia and Jejeebhoy (1991), United Nations (1993), International Institute for Population Sciences (1994), and Basu and Jeffery (forthcoming).

[6] See e.g. Dasgupta (1993) and the literature cited there.

opportunity cost of time tends to be comparatively high for educated women, and this creates an incentive to minimize such time-intensive activities as child-bearing and child-rearing.[7] Further links of this kind have been found to have empirical relevance, usually implying a negative association between female education and desired family size.

Female education also affects the relationship between desired family size and the planned number of births. Specifically, since better maternal education reduces infant and child mortality (as discussed below), educated mothers need to plan fewer births in order to achieve a particular family size. Maternal education also helps in achieving the planned number of births, by facilitating knowledge and command of modern contraceptive methods. This reduction of unplanned pregnancies is another basis of the negative relationship between female education and fertility.[8]

Some of the effects described in the preceding paragraphs, for example, the reduction of fertility through lower child mortality, also suggest a negative link between *paternal* education and fertility. But it is clear that many of the links between education and fertility are likely to be much weaker for male than for female education.[9] In the statistical analysis below, we attempt to identify the separate contributions of male and female education to fertility reduction.

The relationship between maternal education and child mortality

[7] Some formal economic models in the neoclassical tradition have analysed the relationship between education and fertility in terms of standard income and substitution effects (see e.g. Becker, 1960 and Olsen, 1994 for a review). If children are 'normal goods' intensive in the use of the mother's time, then the income effect of a rise in female education (implying a rise in the mother's 'shadow wage') raises the demand for children while the substitution effect lowers it. If the analysis is extended so that parents derive utility from both the number of children and child 'quality' (also likely to be intensive in the use of time), the income effect on the demand for children is attenuated and the substitution effect strengthened.

[8] There are some effects in the other direction, too. For instance, the duration of breastfeeding often declines with maternal education, lowering the duration of post-partum amenorrhoea, and post-partum abstinence taboos tend to be less influential among educated women. But these effects are unlikely to be strong enough to dominate the negative links between maternal education and fertility.

[9] In the neoclassical framework mentioned in footnote 7, male education has an income effect only (assuming that fathers have little involvement in child care). The direction of the income effect is ambiguous, as it depends on the relative strengths of the demands for child 'quantity' and 'quality'.

requires comparatively little elaboration. At the most obvious level, educated women are likely to be more knowledgeable about nutrition, hygiene, and health care. This aspect of maternal education may be particularly significant given the remarkably uninformed and deficient nature of child-care practices in large parts of rural India. In addition, basic education can be important in helping mothers to demand adequate attention to children's needs from others within the household, to take advantage of public health-care services, and generally to achieve a more informed and effective pursuit of their aspirations (including the well-being of children) in the family and society.

In assessing the relationship between education, mortality, and fertility, it is important to remember that mortality and fertility tend to be positively related, in the sense that, other things being equal, mortality is likely to have a positive effect on fertility and vice versa. High fertility rates, for instance, are typically associated with short birth spacing, which is often quite detrimental to child health. Similarly, high child mortality rates raise the number of births required to achieve a given desired family size (in terms of surviving children), and this has the effect of elevating fertility. These interaction effects are also relevant in assessing the influence of other explanatory variables on mortality and fertility. We return below to their implications for estimation procedures and interpretation.

2.3   Other Influences

Aside from the demographic impact of income and education, discussed earlier, the influences of several other variables on mortality and fertility can be usefully investigated on the basis of district-level data for India.

One relationship of interest is that between female labour-force participation and child mortality. It is difficult to determine a priori whether the effect of higher female labour-force participation on child survival is likely to be positive or negative.[10] In the case of

[10] The variable we use to measure female labour-force participation is the ratio of female 'main workers' (women engaged in 'economically productive work' for at least 183 days in the year) to the total female population. The instructions to census investigators state that unpaid 'household duties' are not to be counted as economically productive work. The census definition of 'economically productive

boys, there are two important effects to consider, working in opposite directions. First, involvement in gainful employment often enhances the effectiveness of women's agency roles in society and family, including those connected with child care. Second, the 'double burden' of household work and outside employment can impair women's ability to ensure the good health of their children, if only by reducing the time available for child-care activities (since men typically show great reluctance to share the domestic chores).[11] In the case of girls, a third consideration is that higher levels of female labour-force participation may enhance the importance attached to the survival of a female child. The net result of these different effects is a matter of empirical investigation.

The effect of female labour-force participation on fertility is more predictable. Generally, we expect higher female labour-force participation to have a negative impact on fertility, since the double burden of household work and gainful employment makes repeated child-bearing particularly stressful. It is, of course, also possible that fertility affects female labour-force participation, since having many children makes it more difficult for women to take up gainful employment. This effect may not be important in India, where other social and economic factors are likely to be far more crucial determinants of female labour-force participation. If the effect is important, however, some bias will be involved in using female labour-force participation as an exogenous explanatory variable in analysing the determinants of fertility (and also of mortality, given the interaction effects mentioned earlier). We therefore also present results based on treating female labour-force participation as an endogenous variable (this essentially involves dropping female labour-force participation from the set of explanatory variables in the 'reduced form' equations.)

The availability of health-care services can reasonably be expected to have a negative impact (if any) on child mortality. However, it should be remembered that the *functioning* of health services

---

work', while questionable, serves our purpose since we are interested in the relationship between child survival and women's independent income-earning opportunities (rather than their economic contribution generally — whether or not rewarded).

[11] For useful empirical analyses of this 'maternal dilemma' in the Indian context, see Basu (1992) and Gillespie and McNeill (1992). On the international evidence, see Leslie (1988), Leslie and Paolisso (1989), and the literature cited there.

can be as important as their availability. Many studies have demonstrated the poor functioning of health services in large parts of India, especially the large north Indian states.[12] A particular aspect of this problem, noted in a large number of empirical studies, is the massive diversion of rural health-care services to family planning campaigns.[13] In the absence of statistical information on these and other qualitative aspects of health-care provision, quantitative indicators of available health facilities are likely to provide imprecise measures of the services actually supplied, and the relationship between health-care provision and child mortality may be hard to identify. Similar caveats apply in the case of fertility. The fact that rural health services have given overwhelming priority to family planning in many Indian states may suggest a strong negative relationship between the availability of health services and fertility levels. But the validity of this inference is far from obvious, given the ineffective and even counterproductive nature of the top-heavy methods that have often been used in rural India to promote family planning.

Another issue of interest is whether the identified relationships between demographic and socio-economic variables are roughly the same in urban and rural areas. It is quite possible for urbanization to influence fertility and mortality independently of the other variables included in the analysis, due to better access to various types of relevant information in urban areas.[14] Similarly, it is worth investigating whether the identified relationships vary significantly between social groups. In India, the contrast between 'scheduled castes', 'scheduled tribes', and other sections of the population is of particular interest.

Finally, the relationship between poverty, on the one hand, and mortality and fertility, on the other, deserves careful examination.

[12] See particularly the evaluations carried out by the Operations Research Group (including Khan and Prasad, 1983; Khan et al., 1980, 1983, 1986, 1988, 1989) and by the Public Systems Group (Indian Institute of Management, 1985; Shah, 1989); for some fairly damning case studies see Budakoti (1988), Prakasamma (1989), Indian Council of Medical Research (1989).

[13] See e.g. Iyengar and Bhargava (1987), Jeffery et al. (1989), Prakasamma (1989), Priya (1990), Jesani (1990), Gupta et al. (1992), and the studies cited in footnote 12.

[14] Analyses of fertility in the neoclassical tradition also point to the lower costs of children in rural compared with urban areas, given the opportunities for rural children to contribute to household production and to acquire training and skills cheaply within the household. See Schultz (1981, 1994).

We have already noted that the bivariate association between poverty and child mortality appears to be rather weak in India, judging from broad interstate comparisons (Fig. 1). The question remains whether poverty has a strong effect on mortality or fertility after controlling for the other explanatory variables mentioned so far. Also, quantitative estimates of that effect are of interest, especially in comparison with the effects of other variables. These estimates give us an idea of the relative effectiveness of different means of intervention aimed at more rapid reductions of mortality and fertility. Some tentative results of this type will be presented below.

2.4 Gender Bias

Basic Issues

Relatively little is known about the antecedents of gender bias in child survival in India. The existence of a female disadvantage in large parts of the country has been clearly identified, and the regional patterns (see Map 1) are quite well known.[15] But the factors underlying these sharp regional contrasts remain a matter of some speculation, and much also remains to be learned about the social, economic, and cultural factors that influence gender bias in one direction or another.

In fact, the literature contains a number of contradictory claims and findings on this subject.[16] It has been suggested, for instance, that the extent of gender bias tends to go down with higher female literacy (Bourne and Walker, 1991) as well as lower female literacy (Basu, 1992); with higher levels of poverty (Krishnaji, 1987; Dasgupta, 1993; Miller, 1993) as well as lower levels of poverty (Agarwal, 1991); with higher levels of fertility (Das Gupta, 1993, 1994) as well as lower levels of fertility (Basu, 1995).

---

[15] In 1991, the death rate in the 0–4 year age group (per thousand population) was 25.6 for males and 27.5 for females at the all-India level. The female mortality rate in this age group was lower than the male rate in the southern states of Andhra Pradesh, Kerala, and Tamil Nadu, but higher in all other major states except Assam and Himachal Pradesh. The female mortality disadvantage was most pronounced in the north-central and north-western states of Bihar, Madhya Pradesh, Punjab, Rajasthan, and Uttar Pradesh. See Government of India (1993), Table 7.

[16] For recent reviews of this literature, see Guio (1994) and Kishor (1995).

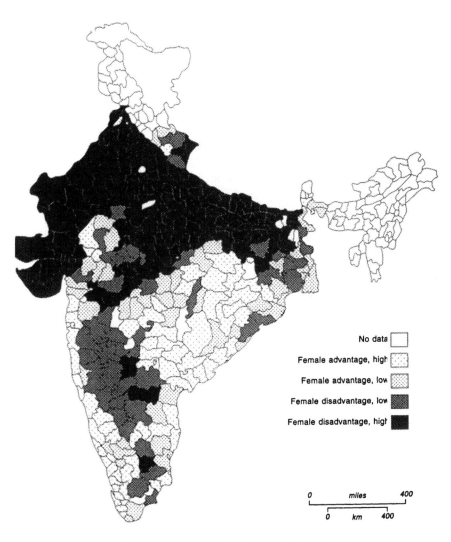

MAP 1.   *Gender Bias in Child Mortality Rates, 1981*

Notes. Female disadvantage, high: FD > 5;
Female advantage, high: FD < –5;
Female disadvantage, low: 0 < FD < 5;
Female advantage, low: –5 < FD < 0.
For the definition of FD, see Table 1.

There are at least two reasons for this confusion. First, as far as theoretical analysis is concerned, it is often difficult to predict whether the effect of a particular variable on the extent of gender bias in child survival is likely to be positive or negative, and plausible arguments can often be presented in both directions. Consider, for instance, what happens to the relative survival chances of boys and girls as a household's access to medical facilities improves. It has often been argued that, in a situation of widespread boy preference, this improved access to medical facilities is likely to enhance the survival chances of boys more than those of girls (because of an anti-female bias in the use of additional health-care facilities), and therefore to accentuate gender inequality in child survival. However, it has also been argued — sometimes by the same authors — that greater *scarcity* of medical facilities exacerbates gender bias, because boys are given priority in the use of limited resources. Both lines of reasoning are plausible but, in any particular context, only one can be correct. Similarly, when other constraints on household opportunities are relaxed (e.g. through higher parental literacy or higher per-capita income), it is difficult to predict whether the improved opportunities are likely to be used to the advantage of boys, and therefore to accentuate gender bias, or whether they will reduce the force of discriminatory practices that were initially due to the limited nature of available opportunities. Different authors have tended to emphasize one or the other of these two plausible effects.

Second, when it comes to empirical investigation, the findings often depend on which variables are included in the analysis. It has been observed, for instance, that gender bias in child survival tends to be relatively low among poor households, among disadvantaged castes, and among households with high levels of female labour-force participation.[17] But we also know that there is a good deal of colinearity between these three variables; only multivariate analysis can tell us whether, say, poverty has a positive or negative effect on gender bias *independently* of the influence of caste or female labour-force participation. Similarly, an examination of the relationship between parental literacy and gender bias in child survival can be misleading if it fails to take into account other relevant variables.

[17] See e.g. Miller (1981) on the caste factor, Krishnaji (1987) on the poverty factor, and Bardhan (1974) on the female labour-force participation factor.

Indeed, if gender bias is lower among poorer households, it would be quite possible, in principle, to find a positive *bivariate* association between parental literacy and gender bias (given the positive cor-relation between poverty and illiteracy), even if literacy reduces gender bias at any given level of poverty.

Clearly, then, empirical investigation in a multivariate framework has much to contribute to the identification and quantification of relevant relationships. Two earlier studies have taken that route. In a pioneering study, Rosenzweig and Schultz (1982) examined the relationship between differential adult employment opportunities and intrafamily resource allocation between girls and boys. Based on a multivariate statistical analysis of district-level census data for India in 1961 (supplemented with a similar analysis of household survey data collected by the National Council of Applied Economic Research), they found that improved employment opportunities for adult women tended to raise the relative survival chances of girls. This is in line with the predictions of the human capital approach adopted in that study. Most of the other variables included in the analysis did not have a statistically significant effect on relative survival chances.

A more recent study by Sunita Kishor (1993, 1995) investigates the determinants of gender bias in child survival using district-level data from the 1981 Census of India. The author attempts to examine the relevance of two different hypotheses, respectively stressing the influence of daughters' 'economic worth' and 'cultural worth' on their relative survival chances *vis-à-vis* male children. Economic worth is measured by female labour-force participation. The incidence of patrilocal exogamy (measured, roughly speaking, as the proportion of women not born in their village of enumeration) is taken as an inverse indicator of cultural worth, which essentially refers to the influence of kinship systems on the valuation of female survival. The author finds that the relative survival chances of girls strongly depend on *both* economic and cultural worth (i.e. they tend to be higher in districts where female labour-force participation is higher, and where the incidence of patrilocal exogamy is lower).

The soundness of this dichotomy between economic worth and cultural worth (and of the identification of these notions with female labour-force participation and patrilocal exogamy, respectively) is not entirely clear. It can be argued that *both* female labour-force participation and patrilocal exogamy (or, more generally, kinship systems) have an economic as well as a cultural basis.[18] Similarly, both variables may influence the relative survival chances of girls through economic as well as cultural links.[19] Be that as it may, Kishor's study represents a major achievement in terms of bringing out the respective influences of female labour-force participation and kinship systems on relative female survival chances. It also yields a wealth of insights into the relationship between gender bias in child survival and a whole range of other variables such as mortality and fertility levels, development indicators, and geographical location.

Many of these relationships also emerge in the analysis presented further in this paper. Although there are important differences of approach between Kishor's analysis of gender bias and our own, the results are broadly consistent, and the two studies can usefully be treated as complementary. Some of the important similarities and differences will be mentioned as we go along.

Claims and Counter-claims

Before presenting our own results, it may be worth commenting a little more on the tensions that have emerged from earlier studies of the relationship between gender bias in child survival and particular economic and social variables. The following discussion concentrates on the possible influence of four variables: female labour-force participation, female literacy, poverty, and fertility.

Perhaps the only uncontroversial finding of earlier studies is that *female labour-force participation* tends to go with lower levels of female disadvantage in child survival. The empirical studies of Rosenzweig and Schultz (1982) and Kishor (1993) both confirm this hypothesis. What remains somewhat unclear, however, is the precise mechanism underlying that relationship. There are a number of possibilities,

---

[18] It has been suggested, for instance, that patrilocal exogamy in rural India can be usefully interpreted as an insurance mechanism, which facilitates risk-sharing between households living in diverse agro-climatic zones (Rosenzweig, 1988, 1993; Rosenzweig and Stark, 1989). On the other side, female labour-force participation is closely linked with the practice of female seclusion, which may be a cultural phenomenon as much as an economic one.

[19] To illustrate: patrilocal exogamy can reduce the returns to parental investment in female child survival (an economic link), and female labour-force participation can raise the general perception of women's role and value in society (which is part of the local culture).

including that female labour-force participation: (i) raises the returns to 'investment' in girls; (ii) raises the status of women in society, and therefore the value attached to young girls; (iii) lowers dowry levels, and therefore reduces the costs of rearing daughters; (iv) makes women less dependent on adult sons for security in old age, and therefore reduces son preference; and (v) raises the bargaining power of adult women, and their ability to resist male pressure to discriminate in favour of boys. There is, as things stand, little evidence to discriminate between these alternative hypotheses.

The link between adult *female literacy* and gender bias in child survival is far from clear. In her analysis of data from the Khanna study in Punjab, Das Gupta (1987) found a positive bivariate association between anti-female bias and maternal education, and she suggested that educated women are in a better position to 'keep the mortality of undesired children high by withholding the requisite care' (p. 84). It is a little hard to believe, however, that it takes good education to discriminate between boys and girls. A different line of explanation, pursued in greater depth in Das Gupta and Mari Bhat (1995), is that educated mothers have lower fertility, and that low fertility tends to go with higher gender bias (more on the last point further in this section).

Other studies have yielded a wide range of results. Different empirical investigations have suggested that the relationship between maternal education and gender bias in child survival may be: (i) positive, as originally argued by Das Gupta (Bhuiya and Streatfield, 1991); (ii) generally positive, but possibly negative in south India (Basu, 1992); (iii) positive in north India but negative in south India (Bourne and Walker, 1991); (iv) negative in the case of first daughters but positive for higher-parity daughters (Amin, 1990); (v) negative (Simmons et al., 1982).[20] Another group of studies find, or suggest, that no simple relationship between the two can be firmly established (Chen et al., 1981; Sen and Sengupta, 1983; Caldwell, Reddy, and Caldwell, 1989). The debate continues.

As far as the influence of *poverty* is concerned, there is a widespread hunch that discrimination against female children is less intense among poorer households. Arguments along those lines

[20] Kishor (1993), unfortunately, does not include female education in her analysis. Rosenzweig and Schultz (1982) find no statistically significant relationship between female education and the relative survival chances of female children.

have been advanced by Miller (1981, 1993), Krishnaji (1987), Das-gupta (1993), among others. Some authors have distanced themselves from this hypothesis (Agarwal, 1986), or suggested that poverty may not be a major determinant of gender bias in child survival (Chen, Huq, and D'Souza, 1981; Harris, 1990; Das Gupta, 1987). Unfortunately, detailed empirical investigations of this issue are few and far between.[21]

One noteworthy exception is Krishnaji's (1987) discussion of the relationship between female–male ratio and per-capita expenditure, based on National Sample Survey data. Krishnaji observed that the female–male ratio is higher at lower levels of the per-capita expenditure scale, suggesting that anti-female discrimination is less intense in poorer households. But the author qualified this possible conclusion, pointing out that households with a high female–male ratio may be concentrated at the lower end of the per-capita expenditure scale simply because females have more restricted earning opportunities than males.

In short, there is some evidence of gender bias in child survival being lower among poorer households, and no sound evidence of the opposite pattern. But the empirical basis of these observations remains quite limited as things stand. On the whole, we concur with Kishor's (1995) judgement that 'we do not as yet have any conclusive evidence that poorer households are necessarily less discriminatory'.

The relationship between *fertility* and gender bias in child survival is a complex issue. One major insight on this subject comes from Das Gupta's (1987) finding that, in rural Punjab, the female disadvantage in child survival is particularly pronounced among children of higher birth parity.[22] From this 'parity effect', it is tempting to conclude that fertility decline would generally be a factor in reducing gender bias in child survival.

---

[21] Poverty is not among the explanatory variables included in the multivariate statistical analyses of Rosenzweig and Schultz (1982) and Kishor (1993). Rosenzweig and Schultz (1982) found a positive association between landlessness and the relative survival chances of female children based on district data, but the *reverse* relationship based on household data. In Kishor's (1993) study, the variable most closely related to poverty is the proportion of agricultural labourers in the population, but this variable is not statistically significant.

[22] This finding is based on data from the Khanna study. For similar findings in rural Uttar Pradesh, see Khan et al. (1989).

This conclusion receives further support from another argument, namely that high fertility and excess female mortality in childhood derive from a common root, i.e. the economic and other advantages of having male children (Basu, 1991, 1992). A similar argument is advanced by Dyson and Moore (1983), who see the low status of women in society as a common cause of high fertility and gender bias in child survival. Here again, one might expect fertility and gender bias to move in the same direction.

In a recent study, however, Das Gupta and Mari Bhat (1995) argue that the recent intensification of gender bias in India (specifically, the decline in juvenile female–male ratios between 1981 and 1991) is 'a consequence of fertility decline'. The basic argument is that the 'parity effect' is outweighed by an 'intensification effect' which takes the form of parity-specific gender bias being more pronounced at lower levels of fertility. That pattern, according to the authors, can be observed in the Khanna study. The explanation proposed for the intensification effect is that, in many situations, the desired number of sons declines less rapidly than the desired number of children.

The general validity of this argument, however, calls for further empirical investigation. There is, for instance, some evidence that one force in the direction of fertility decline in India is the gradual displacement of 'two sons, one daughter' by 'one son, one daughter' as the most widely-preferred family pattern.[23] This is a case where the desired number of sons declines *more* rapidly than the desired number of children, contrary to Das Gupta and Mari Bhat's hypothesis.

The authors refer to the recent spread of sex-selective abortion in China, South Korea, and India as further evidence of the strength of the intensification effect. Selective abortion of female foetuses, however, has a direct and obvious effect on the female–male ratio in the population, *whether or not* it also contributes to the reduction of fertility, and there is no great advantage in seeing that direct effect through the prism of fertility decline. One difficulty in this whole discussion is that fertility decline can have many causes, not all of which would have the same influence on gender bias. While it is

---

[23] For some relevant evidence, see the studies cited in Basu (1991), and the more recent information made available by the National Family Health Survey (International Institute for Population Sciences, 1994).

easy to see that sex-selective abortion would often lead simultaneously to fertility decline and lower female–male ratios, the same pattern need not apply in the case of a reduction of fertility due to, say, more widespread literacy or a more equal valuation of boys and girls (fertility decline, for instance, has not 'caused' any intensification of gender bias in Kerala — on the contrary). To put it another way, there is some danger in treating 'fertility' as an exogenous variable in any analysis of gender bias in child survival.

2.5   Interpretation of the Estimates

As discussed earlier, mortality and fertility influence each other. This complicates the analysis if, for example, we are interested in estimating the effect of fertility on mortality, or the effect of female education on mortality *other* than through reduced fertility. Thinking in terms of a simple linear framework, if we include fertility as an explanatory variable when estimating the equation for mortality, the estimated coefficient is not easily interpretable (does it measure the effect of fertility on mortality or that of mortality on fertility?). Moreover, the use of an endogenous variable as a regressor induces a correlation between the error term and the explanatory variables. Under these circumstances, the ordinary least squares estimates will be inconsistent, the estimated coefficients will not approach their true values even in very large samples. In principle, if we can find suitable instruments (variables that are correlated with the endogenous variable but uncorrelated with the error term), we can estimate the relevant coefficients consistently. In practice, finding suitable instruments may not be an easy task for reasons both of theory and data availability.

We therefore concentrate, in this analysis, on the *reduced forms* that relate the dependent variables of interest (child mortality, fertility, and gender bias in child survival) to exogenous variables alone.[24] The estimated coefficients thus measure the *total* effect of each explanatory variable on each endogenous variable, without determining the relative importance of the endogenous mechanisms through which this

---

[24] Given the possibility that female labour-force participation is endogenous we also treat it as a fourth endogenous variable in some of the regressions presented further on.

effect operates.[25] For instance, the estimated coefficient on female education in the equation for mortality measures the total effect of female education, *including* its effect on child mortality through fertility reduction.

3. DATA AND ESTIMATION

The analysis that follows is based on a sample of 296 districts for which adequately detailed information is available. These 296 districts are located in 14 of India's 15 most populated states. These 14 states contained 326 districts in 1981 and accounted for 94 per cent of the total population of India. The missing state is Assam, where the 1981 Census was not conducted.

Fertility is measured by the total fertility rate (TFR), which represents the number of children that would be born to a woman if she were to live to the end of her child-bearing years and bear children at each age in accordance with the prevailing age-specific fertility rates. The age-specific fertility rates are derived from responses to the census question on births during the last year.[26] For our purposes, the total fertility rate is a more useful measure of the fertility level than, say, the crude birth rate, since it is independent of the age structure of the population. The child mortality variable (Q5) is the probability that a child will die before attaining the age of five years. It is based on census questions on the number of children ever born and the number of children surviving.[27] Gender bias in child mortality is measured as FD = (Q5F – Q5M)/Q5F, where Q5F is mortality among female children and Q5M is mortality among male children. For convenience, we shall refer to this

---

[25] Formally, the model can be written as $Y = AY + BX$, where Y_{ij} is the value of the ith endogenous variable in the jth district and X_{kj} is the value of the kth exogenous variable in the jth district (A is a square matrix with as many rows and columns as there are endogenous variables). Provided that the matrix $[I - A]$ is invertible, Y can be written as $y = [I - A]^{-1}BX$, which is the 'reduced form'.

[26] Estimates of birth rates obtained in this way are normally adjusted upwards to compensate for potential underestimation (see Government of India, 1989). In this analysis we use the adjusted series given in Sharma and Retherford (1990).

[27] Estimates of Q5 are 'graduated' to remove inconsistencies between the estimated probabilities of death at different ages. We use graduated estimates from Government of India (1988).

measure of gender bias as 'female disadvantage' (or FD for short). TFR, Q5, and FD are the three endogenous variables of interest.

Turning to the exogenous variables, our indicator of female literacy is the crude female literacy rate, defined as the proportion of literate females in the total population, and similarly with male literacy.[28] Female labour-force participation, where included, is defined as the proportion of female 'main workers' in the total female population (on the definition of 'main workers' see footnote 10). Urbanization is measured by the proportion of the total population living in urban areas.[29] We use the distributionally sensitive Sen index as an indicator of poverty.[30] The availability of health-care services is measured by the proportion of villages with medical facilities. In addition to these, we include two variables relating to the composition of the population: the proportion of 'scheduled castes' in the population, and the proportion of 'scheduled tribes'. Finally, three dummy variables are used to identify regional patterns: EAST, for districts in Bihar, Orissa, and West Bengal; WEST, for Gujarat and Maharashtra; and SOUTH, for Andhra Pradesh, Karnataka, Kerala, and Tamil Nadu.[31] A list of the variables, their definitions, and sources is given in Table 1, which also presents summary statistics for our sample. Table 2 gives the mean values of these variables in the 14 Indian states and for all of India.

---

[28] Literacy is defined in the Census of India as the ability to read and write with understanding in any language.

[29] Settlements counted as urban areas in the 1981 census were those with a population of over 5,000; those with a municipality, corporation, or cantonment board; those with a population density greater than 1,000 per square mile; and those with at least 75 per cent of the male labour-force in the non-agricultural sector.

[30] On the definition and properties of the Sen index, see Sen (1976). Another possible measure of economic status is average per-capita expenditure. The Sen index has the advantage of being more sensitive to what happens at the lower end of the per-capita expenditure scale (where child mortality tends to be heavily concentrated). In any case, the results obtained by replacing the Sen index with average per-capita expenditure are very similar to those we present here.

[31] The control region thus consists of Haryana, Punjab, Madhya Pradesh, Rajasthan, and Uttar Pradesh. The regional partition used here is essentially the same as that used in the Sample Registration System (see e.g. Government of India, 1993, p. 39), except that we have merged the SRS's 'Central' and 'North' regions and have taken this merged unit as the control region.

TABLE 1. *Variable Definitions and Sample Summary Statistics*

Variable name	Definition	Mean	Standard Deviation
TFR	Total fertility rate, 1981	5.0	1.0
Q5	Under-five mortality rate, 1981: probability that a child will die before the fifth birthday (× 1,000)	156.9	42.8
FD	Female disadvantage in child survival, 1981, defined as FD = (Q5F – Q5M)/Q5F (%)	5.4	10.7
Female literacy	Crude female literacy rate, 1981 (%)	22.0	13.7
Male literacy	Crude male literacy rate, 1981 (%)	44.8	12.2
Female labour force participation	Proportion of 'main workers' in the female population, 1981 (%)	14.5	10.5
Urbanization	Proportion of the population living in urban areas, 1981 (%)	19.8	12.0
Poverty	Sen index of rural poverty, 1972–3, for the 'region' in which the district is situated (× 100)	17.6	8.5
Medical facilities	Proportion of villages with some medical facilities (%)	21.4	20.5
Scheduled castes	Proportion of scheduled-caste persons in the population, 1981 (%)	16.0	6.9
Scheduled tribes	Proportion of scheduled-tribe persons in the population, 1981 (%)	8.0	13.5
SOUTH	Dummy variable, with value 1 for districts in Andhra Pradesh, Karnataka, Kerala, and Tamil Nadu	0.23	0.42
EAST	Dummy variable, with value 1 for districts in Bihar, Orissa, and West Bengal	0.16	0.37
WEST	Dummy variable, with value 1 for districts in Gujarat and Maharashtra	0.14	0.35

Sources. TFR: Sharma and Retherford (1990); Q5, Q5F, and Q5M (FD is calculated from the last two): Government of India (1988); Female literacy, Male literacy, Female labour-force participation: Government of India (1981); Urbanization: Government of India (1982); Poverty: Jain, Sundaram, and Tendulkar (1988); Medical facilities: Government of India (1986); Scheduled Castes and Scheduled Tribes: Government of India (1984).

TABLE 2. State-level Averages of the Regression Variables

	TFR	Q5	FD	Female literacy	Male literacy	Female labour-force participation	Urban-ization	Medical facilities	Poverty	SC	ST
Andhra Pradesh	4.35	138.6	-6.2	19.4	38.4	27.5	22.8	25.9	15.8	15.0	6.4
Bihar	5.24	141.1	14.4	13.4	37.6	8.6	11.6	18.1	24.8	14.9	1.8
Gujarat	4.80	126.1	6.2	30.9	53.1	10.7	28.2	28.2	15.5	7.4	11.0
Haryana	5.40	139.0	17.5	21.5	48.0	4.5	21.4	58.2	3.7	18.9	0.0
Karnataka	4.68	142.3	-3.4	27.1	48.0	19.9	24.5	13.4	14.5	14.2	5.1
Kerala	3.40	81.2	-10.5	66.0	75.4	13.1	17.9	95.8	20.9	10.4	0.9
Madhya Pradesh	5.57	202.9	4.4	14.5	38.5	20.3	19.6	5.8	19.3	14.9	21.1
Maharashtra	4.34	155.7	-2.0	31.8	56.4	26.2	26.2	18.3	25.1	7.3	10.1
Orissa	4.81	175.7	-4.2	18.9	44.9	11.8	11.6	10.8	37.8	14.2	24.9
Punjab	3.26	110.6	10.6	33.4	47.4	2.4	26.7	26.8	3.8	26.7	0.0
Rajasthan	6.05	174.6	9.8	10.5	34.4	9.6	19.2	16.7	13.2	16.7	14.2
Tamil Nadu	3.92	126.8	-2.8	35.7	58.5	22.7	32.3	32.6	17.6	17.6	1.1
Uttar Pradesh	5.89	185.6	15.3	14.7	50.2	8.0	17.3	11.8	13.0	20.8	0.5
West Bengal	4.57	123.0	1.0	28.2	46.6	7.1	23.3	15.2	28.4	22.9	7.2
India	5.02	156.5	5.3	22.1	44.7	14.3	20.7	21.4	17.9	15.9	8.0

Source. See Table 1. The state-level averages presented here are calculated by aggregation of the relevant district-level figures.

Most of the information used in this analysis is derived from the 1981 Census and available in published census reports (see Table 1 for sources). The main exception concerns the Sen index, which requires further comment.

District-specific indicators of income or expenditure are not available in India. The standard source of information on per-capita expenditure, the National Sample Survey (hereafter NSS), does not generate district-specific estimates, because the sample size is too small for many districts. Instead, the NSS sample divides the country into a number of 'regions', based on agro-climatic and socio-economic criteria, and permits reasonably reliable region-specific estimates of average per-capita expenditure and related indicators. The NSS region is essentially an intermediate unit between the district and the state, with each region consisting of several districts within a particular state, and each of the major states being divided into several regions. The 14 states included in this study contain 51 regions. For these regions, estimates of average per-capita expenditure, the head-count ratio, and the Sen index are available for 1972–3 (rural areas only) from Jain, Sundaram, and Tendulkar (1988), based on the 27th round of the National Sample Survey. The poverty indicator used here for each district is the Sen index of rural poverty for the *region* in which the district is situated. For want of information on the level of poverty in rural and urban areas combined, we have used these rural estimates and have also included a separate variable indicating the level of urbanization.

Two caveats are in order. First, the reference year for this poverty variable is 1972–3, rather than 1981 (as with the other variables). The justification for using 1972–3 as the reference year for the poverty variable is that the 1981 mortality estimates are based on birth and death information pertaining to the late seventies, and that poverty levels during that period must have been quite close to those observed in 1972–3. Fortunately, the relative position of different regions in terms of poverty levels seems to be fairly stable over time. In fact, replacing the Sen index for 1972–3 with the Sen index for 1987–8 (also available for NSS regions) has little effect on the results presented here.[32]

[32] To our knowledge, 1972–3 and 1987–8 are the only two years for which poverty indicators have been calculated for the NSS regions. The 1987–8 estimates are available from unpublished tabulations of the National Sample Survey performed by P.V. Srinivasan (Indira Gandhi Institute of Development Research, Bombay).

Second, the use of the regional poverty estimate for each district within a region involves the implicit assumption that intraregional variations in poverty are small. This is not implausible, since the NSS regions are meant to be relatively homogeneous in terms of agro-climatic and socio-economic features. However, some loss of information is certainly involved here, and the results presented below have to be interpreted bearing in mind the imprecise nature of the district poverty indicators.

One way of dealing with this second limitation of the poverty variable is to carry out the entire analysis at the level of 'regions' rather than of districts. Although this approach has the advantage of generating a more accurate poverty indicator for each observation, reducing the number of observations from 296 to 51 also entails a major loss of information. As it turns out, the broad conclusions of this alternative approach are similar to those obtained on the basis of district-level analysis. In the following, we focus primarily on the district-level results, but the region-level results are also presented.

Cross-section analysis is standardly based on the assumption that the error terms are independently and identically distributed. In this case, there is a possibility of spatial correlation in the error terms. Spatial correlation refers to the positive or negative correlation of a variable between neighbouring regions of a surface, such as contiguous districts of a map.[33] Spatial correlation in the errors may arise because of unobserved (or unobservable) variables that may themselves be spatially correlated. In this particular context, for instance, spatial correlation may result from the influence of unobserved cultural factors on mortality or fertility.[34] If the regression errors are spatially correlated, then the standard assumption of a diagonal error covariance matrix fails to hold. We therefore adopt a standard technique of spatial econometrics, which consists of modelling the spatial structure of the errors by parametrizing the error covariance matrix as a function of a spatial dependence parameter, λ, and estimating the model using maximum likelihood estimation. We test whether $\lambda = 0$, i.e. whether spatial correlation

---

[33] The analogy with time-series data is that of serial correlation. The main difference is that time provides an ordering to the data so that earlier disturbances can affect later disturbances but not vice versa; space provides no such ordering, so that a disturbance at one point affects neighbours in all directions.

[34] On cultural influences on demographic behaviour in India, see Sopher (1980a, 1980b), Dyson and Moore (1983), and Basu (1992).

in the errors is negligible (in which case the properties of the ordinary least squares estimator are restored). The test fails in all cases, confirming the need to take spatial correlation into account. For further details of the estimation procedure, and diagnostics, see Murthi, Drèze, and Guio (1995).

4. BASIC RESULTS

Table 3 presents the main results. Apart from indicating the signs of the coefficients and whether they are statistically significant, Table 3 makes it possible to assess the quantitative effects of different variables on fertility, child mortality, and gender bias by combining the given information with the mean values presented in Table 1.

In arriving at the estimates in Table 3, we began with general specifications that included quadratic terms (for nonlinearities) and cross-products. We found no evidence of nonlinearities, except in the equation for female disadvantage. Visual inspection and non-parametric estimation suggested that the relationship between this variable and the individual explanatory variables follows a logistic pattern, so we used a logistic transform of this variable as our dependent variable in Table 3. We present no cross-product terms at this stage, in order to keep the discussion relatively straightforward, but will discuss some results relating to cross-product terms later.

The estimates in Table 3 treat female labour-force participation as an exogenous variable, but, as discussed earlier, that variable may both influence and be influenced by the fertility rate and is therefore potentially endogenous. In Table 4, we exclude female labour-force participation as an explanatory variable in recognition of its endogeneity. In general, the conclusions that follow from Table 3 are upheld by Table 4.

We shall first comment on the influence of different explanatory variables on child mortality and female disadvantage, before turning to fertility.

4.1 Child Mortality and Female Disadvantage

With respect to child mortality and female disadvantage, the following observations are particularly noteworthy:

TABLE 3. *Determinants of Fertility,*
Child Mortality and Female Disadvantage
Maximum likelihood estimates of reduced forms

Independent Variables	Dependent Variables		
	TFR	Q5	FD [a]
Constant	6.60	205.82	0.86
	(23.10)*	(14.37)*	(3.00)*
Female literacy	–0.03	–0.87	–0.04
	(–4.28)*	(–2.45)*	(–4.46)*
Male literacy	–0.005	–0.49	0.01
	(–0.70)	(–1.40)	(1.97)*
Female labour-force participation	–0.02	0.44	–0.02
	(–3.57)*	(1.82)**	(–3.85)*
Urbanization	–3.9E–04	–0.31	0.005
	(–0.15)	(–2.40)*	(1.73)**
Medical facilities	–0.002	–0.25	0.005
	(–1.04)	(–2.23)*	(1.84)**
Poverty	0.007	0.53	–0.02
	(1.14)	(1.76)**	(–3.13)*
Scheduled tribe	–0.01	–0.60	–0.01
	(–3.40)*	(–3.57)*	(–3.96)*
Scheduled caste	–0.007	0.55	–0.007
	(–1.23)	(1.89)**	(–1.13)
South	–0.55	–41.50	–0.82
	(2.60)*	(–3.85)*	(–4.91)*
East	–0.25	–38.08	0.15
	(–0.99)	(–2.91)*	(0.81)
West	–0.38	–12.24	–0.15
	(–2.06)*	(–1.32)	(–0.87)
λ	0.82	0.84	0.61
	(25.95)*	(28.07)*	(11.00)*
Mean squared error	0.31	15.15	0.39
Adjusted R^2	0.89	0.87	0.81
Log likelihood	–155.95	–1310.26	–190.80
Sample size	296	296	296

Notes. Asymptotic t-ratios in brackets.

   * significant at 5%

  ** significant at 10%

  [a] The dependent variable is a logistic transform of FD.

TABLE 4. *Determinants of Fertility, Child Mortality and Female Disadvantage Excluding Female Labour Force Participation* Maximum likelihood estimates of reduced forms

Independent Variables	Dependent Variables		
	TFR	Q5	FD [a]
Constant	6.38	210.72	0.66
	(21.90)*	(14.09)*	(2.21)*
Female literacy	−0.02	−1.01	−0.03
	(−3.52)*	(−2.88)*	(−3.46)*
Male literacy	−0.01	−0.35	0.01
	(−1.49)	(−1.03)	(1.01)
Female labour-force participation	−	−	−
Urbanization	1.7E−04	−0.32	0.01
	(−0.06)	(−2.46)*	(1.88)**
Medical facilities	−0.002	−0.24	0.005
	(−1.07)	(−2.21)*	(1.92)**
Poverty	0.007	0.53	−0.02
	(1.14)	(1.73)**	(−3.05)*
Scheduled tribe	−0.01	−0.56	−0.01
	(−3.68)*	(−3.37)*	(−4.11)*
Scheduled caste	−0.005	0.50	−0.004
	(−0.82)	(1.72)**	(−0.54)
South	−0.66	−37.91	−1.02
	(−3.01)*	(−3.58)*	(−5.77)*
East	−0.11	−40.42	0.26
	(−0.42)	(−3.10)*	(1.21)
West	−0.41	−11.09	−0.23
	(−2.17)*	(−1.19)	(−1.26)
λ	0.84	0.83	0.68
	(28.43)*	(27.66)*	(14.05)*
Mean squared error	0.31	15.26	0.39
Adjusted R^2	0.89	0.87	0.81
Log likelihood	−162.05	−1311.91	−197.24
Sample size	296	296	296

Notes. Asymptotic t-ratios in brackets.
   * significant at 5%
  ** significant at 10%
   [a] The dependent variable is a logistic transform of FD.

Female literacy has a negative and statistically significant effect on child mortality. Female literacy has a negative effect on both male and female child mortality, but the effect on female child mortality is larger. This is why female literacy also has a negative (and statistically significant) effect on FD, the extent of female disadvantage in child survival. The last result contrasts with the hypothesis, advanced by several other researchers, according to which higher female literacy is often a tool of intensified discrimination against female children.

It is worth noting that higher female literacy reduces child mortality and anti-female bias in child survival independently of male literacy. Male literacy also has a negative effect on child mortality (independently of female literacy), but the effect of male literacy is much smaller than that of female literacy, and is not statistically significant. Male literacy has a significant effect on the extent of gender bias in child survival, in the direction of *enhancing* female disadvantage (because male literacy reduces male child mortality more than female child mortality). Interestingly, the last statement remains true even if female literacy is dropped from the regression.

We tested the hypothesis that the effect of female literacy on gender bias varies between different regions by introducing additional interaction terms involving the female literacy variables and regional dummies. None of the coefficients of these interaction terms are statistically significant. In particular, we find no support for the notion that the effect of female literacy on gender bias is positive in the north but negative in the south, or vice versa.

Higher *female labour-force participation* reduces the extent of gender bias in child survival, and this effect is statistically significant. This result is in keeping with the findings of earlier studies.

Although higher levels of female labour-force participation are clearly associated with reduced anti-female bias in child survival, the relationship between female labour-force participation and absolute levels of male and female child mortality is a little more complex. The results presented in Table 3 suggest that higher female labour-force participation is associated with higher levels of male and female child mortality, though the effect is significant only in the case of males. When examining the effects of female labour-force participation on child mortality, however, it is important to control carefully for the economic and social disadvantages that motivate many women to seek gainful employment.

In particular, it is important to control for the level of poverty; given the aforementioned limitations of our measure of poverty, the effect of female labour-force participation on absolute levels of child mortality requires further scrutiny. We return to this issue below.

Urbanization has a negative and statistically significant effect on child mortality (both sexes combined). The effect on male mortality is larger than that on female mortality, and correspondingly, urbanization is associated with higher levels of female disadvantage in child survival. The last effect is statistically significant at the 10 per cent level, but not at the 5 per cent level.

Medical facilities have essentially the same effects as urbanization: they reduce child mortality, but amplify the female disadvantage in child survival. Here again, the last effect is statistically significant at the 10 per cent level, but not at 5 per cent.

As expected, higher levels of *poverty* are associated with higher levels of child mortality. This variable is not significant at the 5 per cent level, although it is significant at 10 per cent.[35] Less evidently, there is a negative and statistically significant relationship between poverty and FD, higher levels of poverty are associated with lower levels of female disadvantage in child survival. This is consistent with the hypothesis, discussed earlier, that anti-female discrimination is particularly strong among privileged classes.[36]

A higher proportion of *scheduled tribes* in the population reduces the extent of anti-female bias in child survival, and this effect is statistically significant. It is interesting that this variable has a significant effect even after controlling for female labour-force participation which is generally higher among scheduled tribes than in the population as a whole. This suggests that tribal societies have other features that enhance the relative survival chances of female children. Examples of possibly relevant features are kinship systems and property rights.[37]

It is also worth noting that the absolute levels of male and (particularly) female child mortality seem to be relatively low in districts

[35] The absence of statistical significance at the 5 per cent level may reflect the lack of precision of the poverty variable, discussed above.

[36] On this, see earlier discussion, and also Drèze and Sen (1995), chapter 7.

[37] Kishor (1993) finds that the statistically significant association between gender bias in child survival and the proportion of tribals in the population disappears after her 'patrilocal exogamy' variable is included in the regression.

with a high proportion of scheduled tribes, after controlling for poverty and literacy. This is consistent with the common notion that tribal lifestyles have some healthy aspects (e.g. relatively low levels of crowding and pollution). But the precise basis of this statistical association requires further investigation.

There is no significant association between the proportion of *scheduled castes* in the population and the extent of female disadvantage in child survival. This is consistent with recent research on gender inequality among scheduled castes, particularly relating to trends in sex ratios. Until quite recently, the female–male ratio in the population was considerably higher than average among disadvantaged castes, including castes now classified as 'scheduled'. Many observers have attributed this contrast to the relatively egalitarian character of gender relations among these castes. In recent decades, however, there has been a striking decline of the female–male ratio among scheduled castes, so that by 1991 this ratio (0.922) was very close to the ratio in the population as a whole (0.927).[38] In other words, differences in gender relations between the scheduled castes and the rest of the population appear to have narrowed in recent years, and have even disappeared altogether as measured by the female–male ratio, a basic indicator of gender inequality. The fact that we find no difference between scheduled castes and the rest of the population in terms of the extent of female disadvantage in child survival is in line with these recent findings.[39]

Finally, with regard to *regional 'dummies'*, even after controlling for the other variables, the southern region has considerably lower levels of child mortality. This is particularly the case for girls, indeed, female children have a survival advantage over boys in that region

---

[38] On this, see Agnihotri (1994), and Drèze and Sen (1995), ch. 7.

[39] The 'Sanskritization' process, involving the emulation of high-caste practices by members of the lower castes as a means of improving their social status, provides a possible explanation for the recent convergence of female–male ratios in the two groups. Indeed, restrictions on the lifestyle and freedom of women have often played a prominent part in this process. However, there are other possible lines of explanation. For instance, the sharp decline of female–male ratios among scheduled castes may simply reflect the combination of (i) upward economic mobility among the scheduled castes, and (ii) a positive link between economic affluence and gender inequality (due to economic or other factors that may have little to do with caste as such). This alternative line of explanation need not invoke 'Sanskritization' as an important influence.

(see Table 2). With respect to both child mortality and gender bias, the contrast between the southern region and the rest of the country is statistically significant.

The demographic features of south India, including the relatively favourable survival chances of female children, have been much discussed in the literature.[40] The findings presented in Table 3 suggest that the demographic contrast between south India and the rest of the country cannot be explained entirely in terms of female literacy, female labour-force participation, and other variables included in the regression.[41] This is consistent with the view that differences in kinship systems, property rights, and related features of the economy and society not captured in this analysis (for lack of adequate statistical information) play an important role in this North–South contrast.[42]

4.2   Fertility

Tables 3 and 4 include further results relating to the determinants of the total fertility rate. Female literacy and female labour-force participation have a negative and statistically significant effect on TFR. Fertility is also significantly lower in the southern and western regions and in districts with a high proportion of scheduled tribes. None of the other variables is statistically significant.

5.   FURTHER RESULTS AND EXTENSIONS

5.1   Poverty and Female Labour-Force Participation

Earlier we commented on some limitations of the variable we have used to measure poverty. We noted, in particular, that the reference

[40] See e.g. Karve (1965), Bardhan (1974, 1984, 1988), Sopher (1980a, 1980b), Miller (1981), Dyson and Moore (1983), Mandelbaum (1988), Basu (1992), Gupta et al. (1993), and Kishor (1993).

[41] For a similar finding (even after including 'patrilocal exogamy' as an additional explanatory variable), and further discussion, see Kishor (1993).

[42] On these and related influences, see Basu (1992), Kishor (1993), and Agarwal (1994), among other recent contributions, and the studies cited in Drèze and Sen (1989, 1995), Gupta et al. (1993), and Dasgupta (1993).

year for this variable is 1972–3, rather than 1981 (as with the other variables), and also that the available poverty indicators relate to NSS 'regions' rather than to individual districts.

These limitations may lead to inaccurate estimates of the effect of poverty on demographic outcomes. They may also lead to bias in the estimated coefficients of variables that are strongly correlated with poverty. One important example of this concerns female labour-force participation, in particular the relationship between that variable and child mortality. As was discussed earlier, in estimating the effect of female labour-force participation on child mortality and other demographic outcomes, it is important to control for the incidence of poverty. Indeed, female labour-force participation in India is often a reflection of economic hardship, and failure to control for this factor may lead, for instance, to a spurious positive relationship between female labour-force participation and child mortality (implicitly reflecting, in fact, the positive association between *poverty* and child mortality).[43]

In view of these considerations, we have explored alternative ways of dealing with the poverty variable. As for the reference year, we have examined the effects of replacing the 1972–3 poverty estimates with the corresponding 1987–8 estimates. The basic results presented above continue to hold; hence the choice of reference year for the poverty variable does not seem to be a major issue.

Regarding the use of region-level poverty estimates (as opposed to district-level estimates) in the regressions, one way of investigating whether this procedure leads to serious bias is to re-estimate the regression equations using region-level estimates for *all* the variables listed in Table 1. Region-level estimates can easily be obtained by aggregation, as weighted averages of the district-level values. While this method leads to a sharp reduction in the number of observations (from 296 to 51), it eliminates any possible bias arising from the fact that the poverty variable and other variables relate to different levels of territorial aggregation. The corresponding results are presented in Table 5.

The results of the region-level analysis (Table 5) are very similar to those of the district-level analysis (Table 3). One difference is that the t-ratios tend to be lower in the region-level regressions than

---

[43] This argument holds whether or not female labour-force participation is exogenous.

TABLE 5.   *Determinants of Fertility,*
Child Mortality and Female Disadvantage: NSS Regions
Maximum likelihood estimates of reduced forms

Independent Variables	Dependent Variables		
	TFR	*Q5*	*FD*
Constant	6.67	136.99	13.08
	(9.62)*	(4.32)*	(1.95)**
Female literacy	–0.04	–1.84	–0.69
	(–2.47)*	(–2.41)*	(–4.57)*
Male literacy	0.020	1.17	0.38
	(1.09)	(1.41)	(2.24)*
Female labour-force	–0.03	–0.34	–0.31
participation	(–2.82)*	(–0.65)	(–3.56)*
Urban	–0.005	–0.39	0.03
	(–0.080)	(–1.27)	(0.47)
Medical facilities	0.002	–0.29	0.08
	(0.46)	(–1.29)	(1.84)**
Poverty	5.6E–04	0.74	–0.16
	(0.06)	(1.73)**	(–1.61)
Scheduled tribe	–0.01	0.09	–0.29
	(–1.54)	(0.24)	(–3.95)*
Scheduled caste	–0.02	1.04	–0.01
	(–1.78)**	(1.63)	(–0.41)
South	–0.25	–12.29	–8.34
	(–0.77)	(–0.72)	(–4.19)*
East	–0.29	–30.04	–2.96
	(–0.92)	(–1.82)**	(–1.44)
West	–0.44	2.94	0.50
	(–1.65)**	(0.22)	(0.24)
λ	0.59	0.66	–0.41
	(4.45)*	(5.42)*	(–1.98)*
Mean squared error	0.36	18.14	3.71
Adjusted R^2	0.74	0.68	0.79
Log likelihood	–23.45	–223.23	–140.17
Sample size	51	51	51

Notes.   Asymptotic t-ratios in brackets.
  * significant at 5%
  ** significant at 10%

in the district-level regressions, and, accordingly, some variables that were statistically significant in the latter are not significant in the former (this applies, for instance, to the South 'dummy' in the mortality and fertility regressions). This is not surprising, since the region-level regressions are based on a smaller number of observations and reflect a considerable loss of information.

Aside from this, the main difference between the two sets of regressions is that, in the region-level regressions, higher female labour-force participation is associated with *lower* child mortality (both sexes combined). Although this association is not statistically significant, it suggests that the positive association between these two variables obtained in the district-level regressions may reflect a failure to adequately control for poverty in those regressions.[44]

5.2 Fertility and Gender Bias in Child Mortality

As we discussed earlier, the links between fertility and gender bias in child survival are far from clear. While some authors have argued that high fertility is typically associated with high levels of female disadvantage in survival, others have taken the opposite view.

To shed some light on this issue, we have included the total fertility rate as an *additional* regressor in the equation for female disadvantage.[45] We find that higher fertility is associated with *higher* female disadvantage in child survival, and that the association is statistically significant.[46] Thus, it appears that, after controlling for other pertinent factors, the relative survival chances of girls are lower in areas of high fertility. These results contribute to dispelling any

[44] Kishor's (1993) study, mentioned earlier, found that female labour-force participation had a positive and statistically significant effect on both female and male child mortality. In that study, too, the positive association between female labour-force participation and child mortality may reflect the lack of adequate control for poverty (the regressions presented there only include rough proxies for the 'level of development'). An additional reason may be the omission of female literacy from the analysis (bearing in mind that there is likely to be a negative correlation between female literacy and female labour-force participation).

[45] This procedure assumes, in line with the literature on the subject, that level of fertility affects the relative survival chances of girls but is not affected by it.

[46] The coefficient on the total fertility rate is 0.13, and its t-ratio is 2.04. None of the other coefficients change very much, nor are there important changes in levels of statistical significance.

fear that rapid fertility decline in India might entail some intensification of gender bias in child survival.

5.3 Interaction between Female Literacy and Medical Facilities

One way in which female literacy may help reduce child mortality is by enabling women to take better advantage of available medical facilities. If that hypothesis is correct, then we might expect female literacy and medical facilities to have synergistic effects on child mortality, in the sense that the influence of one of these two variables is stronger when the other is also at work. We test this hypothesis by including an interaction term in the regression for child mortality, as an additional right-hand side variable. This interaction term (the product of 'female literacy' and 'medical facilities') allows the effect of medical facilities to vary with the level of female literacy, and vice versa. We find the coefficient of this interaction term to be negative and statistically significant, suggesting that medical facilities and female literacy do have synergistic effects in reducing child mortality.[47]

5.4 Structural Change

Another issue of interest is the stability of the estimated relationships over time. When detailed results of the 1991 Census are available, it will be possible to carry out regression exercises similar to those presented here and to compare them with the 1981 results. Meanwhile, a tentative assessment of structural change has been attempted as follows.

We estimated an additional regression equation, with 'crude birth rate' (CBR) as the dependent variable, using 1981 district-level data. All the explanatory variables in Table 3 were retained except 'medical facilities'.[48] This equation was used to 'predict' the crude birth rate

[47] The coefficient on the interaction term is –0.011, with a t-ratio of –2.55. The statistical significance of the other variables remains unchanged.

[48] The reason for dropping this variable is that 1991 information on medical facilities is not available at the time of writing.

in 1991, using the 1991 values of the independent variables. In the absence of district-level information for 1991, this could only be done at the state level. These predicted CBRs were then compared with the actual figures derived from the 1991 Census.[49]

This comparison indicates that our regressions *under-predict* the decline of the crude birth rate between 1981 and 1991 in each of the 14 states considered (i.e. the predicted CBR is, in each case, higher than the actual CBR). The difference between predicted and actual CBR (expressed as a proportion of actual CBR) is very small in the case of Madhya Pradesh (1.1 per cent), and also relatively small (less than 10 per cent) in the case of Haryana, Rajasthan, and Uttar Pradesh, but particularly large in West Bengal (21 per cent), Punjab (24 per cent), Andhra Pradesh (25 per cent), Kerala (41 per cent), and Tamil Nadu (46 per cent). The under-prediction of CBR decline in all states suggests that structural change in the 1981–91 period has reinforced cross-sectional effects identified in this study. Further, the state-specific patterns are consistent with recent evidence of an accelerated demographic transition in south India, and of much greater inertia in the large north Indian states.[50]

5.5 Sex Ratio and Child Mortality

Finally, we examined the hypothesis that, even for given values of the explanatory variables included in this analysis, child mortality is higher in areas of higher gender inequality. The idea is that high levels of gender inequality tend to suppress the agency of women in society, one consequence of which may be higher levels of child mortality (insofar as, in India, the health of children depends a great deal on the initiative of women).

To test this hypothesis, we used the juvenile sex ratio (number of females per 1,000 males in the 0–10 year age group) as an additional right-hand side variable in the equation for child mortality.[51]

[49] The 1991 CBR estimates were calculated by Professor P.N. Mari Bhat (Population Research Centre, Dharwad). We are most grateful to him for making these unpublished estimates available to us.

[50] On this, see particularly Visaria and Visaria (1994).

[51] As with similar exercises presented in this section, the validity of this procedure requires that the added variable (in this case, the juvenile sex ratio) is not affected by the left-hand variable (in this case, the child mortality rate).

The juvenile sex ratio is interpreted here as a rough indicator of basic gender inequality.[52] Holding other factors constant, we find that child mortality is higher in districts with a lower juvenile sex ratio, and this effect is statistically significant.[53] This lends some support to the proposed hypothesis.

6. Discussion

6.1 Women's Agency and Demographic Outcomes

The findings of this study clearly demonstrate the role of women's agency and empowerment in reducing mortality, fertility, and gender inequality.

Consider, for instance, the determinants of gender bias in child mortality. It is striking that, while the variables directly relating to women's agency (specifically, the female literacy rate and female labour-force participation) have a strong and statistically significant negative impact on female disadvantage, those relating to the *general* level of economic development and modernization in the society (e.g. poverty, urbanization, male literacy, and medical facilities) do nothing to improve the relative survival chances of girls *vis-à-vis* boys. In fact, to the extent that these variables do have a statistically significant influence on female disadvantage in child survival, this influence operates in the 'wrong' direction in each case; higher levels of male literacy and urbanization, lower levels of poverty, and improved access to medical facilities are all associated with a *larger* female disadvantage (see Table 3 for details). The reason is that these variables reduce male child mortality more than female child mortality. Insofar as a positive connection exists in India between the level of development and reduced gender bias in survival, it seems to work *through* variables that are directly related to women's agency, such as female literacy and female labour-force participation.

Similarly, while indicators of development such as male literacy,

[52] The reason for using the juvenile sex ratio, rather than the sex ratio in the population as a whole, is that the latter can be quite sensitive to migration patterns at the district level (see Miller, 1981).

[53] The coefficient on the juvenile sex ratio, measured as the ratio of girls to boys in the 0–10 year age group, is –0.166, with a t-ratio of –3.23.

reduced poverty, greater urbanization, and the spread of medical facilities do have positive effects on *absolute* levels of child survival, these effects are relatively small compared with the powerful effect of female literacy. This point is illustrated in Table 6, which indicates how the predicted values of Q5 and FD respond to changes in female literacy when the other variables are kept at their mean value (responses to male literacy and poverty are also shown in the table).[54] We see that the influence of female literacy on child mortality and gender bias is quite large, especially in comparison with that of male literacy or poverty.

The same point emerges in connection with the determinants of fertility. In this case, in fact, none of the variables relating to the general level of development and modernization is statistically significant. By contrast, female literacy and labour force participation appear to be crucial determinants of the total fertility rate. As shown in Table 6, for instance, female literacy alone is a considerable force in reducing fertility. Here again, the message seems to be that some variables relating to women's agency (in this case, female literacy) often play a much more important role in demographic outcomes than do variables relating to the general level of development.

6.2   Cross-section and Time-series Analysis

As we discussed in the preceding section, our results lend little support to the notion that gender bias in India automatically declines in the process of economic development (except insofar as the latter enhances female literacy and female labour-force participation). This may seem surprising, but it is worth noting that our finding is consistent with the widely discussed phenomenon of sustained decline in India's ratio of females to males since the beginning of this century.[55]

---

[54] The simulations in Table 6 concerning the effect of changes in the level of poverty are based on equations in which the head-count ratio of poverty is used as an explanatory variable in place of the Sen index. The substitution was made because percentage changes in the head-count ratio are more straightforward to interpret. The use of the head-count ratio in place of the Sen index makes little overall difference to the estimates.

[55] On this issue, see Drèze and Sen (1995), chapter 7, and the literature cited there.

TABLE 6. *Effects of Selected Independent Variables (Female literacy, Male literacy and Poverty) on Child Mortality (Q5), Female Disadvantage (FD) and Fertility (TFR)*

Assumed level of independent variable (%)	Predicted values of Q5, FD, and TFR, when the female literacy rate takes the value indicated in the first column			Predicted values of Q5, FD, and TFR, when the male literacy rate takes the value indicated in the first column			Predicted values of Q5, FD, and TFR, when the proportion of the population below the poverty line takes the value indicated in the first column[a]		
	Q5	FD	TFR	Q5	FD	TFR	Q5	FD	TFR
10	166.4	10.7	5.38	172.9	–2.0	5.18	151.5	9.8	4.79
20	157.7	5.9	5.07	168.0	–0.1	5.13	152.7	8.5	4.85
30	149.0	1.1	4.76	163.1	1.8	5.08	153.8	7.1	4.91
40	140.2	–3.3	4.45	158.2	3.9	5.03	154.9	5.8	4.97
50	131.5	–7.1	4.15	153.3	5.9	4.98	156.0	4.4	5.03
60	122.8	–10.3	3.84	148.4	8.0	4.93	157.2	3.1	5.09
70	114.0	–12.8	3.53	143.5	10.1	4.88	158.3	1.8	5.15
80	105.3	–14.8	3.22	138.7	12.2	4.83	159.5	0.5	5.21

Note. [a] For convenience of interpretation, the 'Sen index' has been replaced here by the 'head-count ratio' (i.e. the proportion of the population below the poverty line). The figures presented in these three columns are based on the same regressions as in Table 3, with the Sen index replaced by the head-count ratio.

In 1901, the ratio of females to males in the Indian population was 972. From then on, the female–male ratio declined almost monotonically until 1991 (the last year for which census estimates are available), when it reached the lowest-ever recorded value of 927.[56] The causes of this decline are a matter of debate, and the results we presented here are of some relevance in that context. The regressions presented in Table 3 suggest that the only important force that may have worked in the direction of reducing gender bias over this period is the expansion of female literacy. Most other developments, including the expansion of per-capita income, urbanization, and male literacy, would have worked in the other direction, if our cross-section results are any guide to the corresponding effects over time.[57]

The preceding observations should not be taken to imply that economic development in India is comprehensively detrimental to the position of women in society. That statement requires at least three qualifications. First, the results suggest that gender bias is reduced by an expansion of female literacy, and that expansion is part of economic development. Even female labour-force participation can be expected to increase in the future, and that too is likely to reduce gender bias.

Second, the relationship between gender bias and the level of economic development may well be nonlinear, with the relative position of women first declining and later improving as, say, the level of per-capita income increases. Some authors have indeed stressed the plausibility of such a nonlinear relationship (see particularly Kishor, 1995). In our own work, we have found no evidence of this type of nonlinearity, but this may reflect the fact that India is still at an early stage of development. The relationship between gender bias and economic variables may well change in the future.

[56] For the latest figures on female–male ratios in India and Indian states since 1901, see Nanda (1992), 102–3.

[57] One possible qualification concerns time trends in female labour-force participation. Given the frequent changes in definition and treatment of women's work in Indian censuses, it is difficult to state with any confidence whether female labour-force participation rates in India have increased or decreased since the beginning of this century (see e.g. Duvvury, 1989, for further discussion). It is, however, unlikely that a major *increase* in female labour-force participation has taken place over that period.

Third, our investigation has been confined to one aspect of gender bias — differences in mortality rates between boys and girls. Obviously, all aspects of gender inequality need not move in the same direction, and it would be difficult to deny that *some* aspects of the condition of Indian women have improved considerably in the recent years.[58]

6.3 Demographic Change

Since population growth in India is often a subject of intense concern, it is worth reiterating that the only variables we found to have a significant effect on fertility are female literacy and female labour-force participation. In addition, of course, there is likely to be a significant causal link between mortality and fertility, with the latter going down as mortality declines. The direct promotion of child health, female literacy, and female labour-force participation are likely to be more conducive to reduced fertility than are indirect interventions based on promoting the general level of economic development.

It would, of course, be helpful to know more about the precise links between fertility and child mortality. The problem is that there are simultaneous causal links in both directions, links that are quite difficult to estimate. We made one attempt at such estimation, based on two-stage least squares estimation of the fertility equation (with child mortality as an additional right-hand side variable in the fertility regression). Identification of the effect of child mortality requires the inclusion in the model of at least one exogenous variable that influences child mortality but not fertility. 'Availability of drinking water' seemed like a plausible candidate, but tentative estimates based on using it as an instrument for child mortality gave no useful results. This is an important area of further research.

---

[58] The gender gap in literacy, for instance, has somewhat narrowed between the 1981 and 1991 censuses. Similarly, the survival advantage of women in the older age groups has noticeably increased since 1971, and the age at which that advantage begins has also come down; as a result, female life expectancy has recently overtaken male life expectancy (see Karkal, 1987; Dyson, 1988; and Rajan et al., 1992).

REFERENCES

Agarwal, Bina (1986), 'Women, Poverty and Agricultural Growth in India', *Journal of Peasant Studies*, 13 (4).
—— (1994), *A Field of One's Own: Gender and Land Rights in South Asia* (Cambridge: Cambridge University Press).
Agnihotri, Satish (1994), 'Missing Females: A Disaggregated Analysis', mimeo, University of East Anglia; forthcoming in *Economic and Political Weekly*.
Amin, S. (1990), 'The Effect of Women's Status on Sex Differentials in Infant and Child Mortality in South Asia', *Génus*, 46 (3–4).
Bardhan, Pranab (1974), 'On Life and Death Questions', *Economic and Political Weekly*, 9 (Special Number).
—— (1984), *Land, Labour and Rural Poverty* (New York: Columbia University Press).
—— (1988), 'Sex Disparity in Child Survival in Rural India', in T.N. Srinivasan and P.K. Bardhan (eds.), *Rural Poverty in South Asia* (New York: Columbia University Press).
Barro, Robert J. and Jong-Wha Lee (1993a), 'Losers and Winners in Economic Growth', Working Paper 4341, National Bureau of Economic Research.
—— (1993b), '*International Comparisons of Educational Attainment*', paper presented at a conference on 'How Do National Policies Affect Long-Run Growth?', World Bank, Washington, DC.
Basu, Alaka M. (1989), 'Is Discrimination in Food Really Necessary for Explaining Sex Differentials in Childhood Mortality?', *Population Studies*, 43 (2).
—— (1991), 'Demand and Its Sociocultural Context', in J.K. Satia and S.J. Jejeebhoy (eds.), *The Demographic Challenge: A Study of Four Large Indian States* (Bombay: Oxford University Press).
—— (1992), *Culture, the Status of Women and Demographic Behaviour* (Oxford: Clarendon Press).
—— (1993a), '*Women's Roles and the Gender Gap in Health and Survival*', mimeo, Institute of Economic Growth, Delhi.
—— (1993b), 'Fertility Decline and Increasing Gender Imbalances in India: Including the South Indian Turnaround', mimeo, Institute of Economic Growth, Delhi University.
Basu, Alaka M. and Roger Jeffery (eds.) (forthcoming), *Girl Schooling, Women's Autonomy and Fertility Change in South Asia* (New Delhi: Sage).
Becker, G. (1960), 'An Economic Analysis of Fertility', in *Demographic*

and Economic Change in Developed Countries (Princeton: Princeton University Press).

Beenstock, M. and P. Sturdy (1990), 'The Determinants of Infant Mortality in Regional India', *World Development*, 18 (3).

Behrman, J.R. and B.L. Wolfe (1984), 'More Evidence on Nutrition Demand: Income Seems Overrated and Women's Schooling Underemphasized', *Journal of Development Economics*, 14.

—— (1987), 'How Does Mother's Schooling Affect the Family's Health, Nutrition, Medical Care Usage, and Household Sanitation', *Journal of Econometrics*, 36.

Bhuiya, A. and K. Streatfield (1991), 'Mothers' Education and Survival of Female Children in a Rural Area of Bangladesh', *Population Studies*, 45 (2).

Bourne, K. and G.M. Walker (1991), 'The Differential Effect of Mothers' Education on Mortality of Boys and Girls in India', *Population Studies*, 45 (2).

Budakoti, D.K. (1988), 'Study of the Community and Community Health Work in Two Primary Health Centres in Chamoli District of Uttar Pradesh', M.Phil. Dissertation, Centre for Social Medicine and Community Health, Jawaharlal Nehru University, New Delhi.

Cain, M. (1984), *'Women's Status and Fertility in Developing Countries'*, Centre for Policy Studies, Working Paper 110, The Population Council, New York.

Caldwell, J.C. (1979), 'Education as a Factor in Mortality Decline: An Examination of Nigerian Data', *Population Studies*, 33 (3).

—— (1986), 'Routes to Low Mortality in Poor Countries', *Population and Development Review*, 12 (2).

Caldwell, J.C., P.H. Reddy, and P. Caldwell (1982), 'The Causes of Demographic Change in Rural South India: A Micro Approach', *Population and Development Review*, 8 (4).

—— (1989), *The Causes of Demographic Change* (Madison: University of Wisconsin Press).

Chen, L., E. Huq, and S. D'Souza (1981), 'Sex Bias in the Family Allocation of Food and Health Care in Rural Bangladesh', *Population and Development Review*, 7 (1).

Cleland, J. (1990), 'Maternal Education and Child Survival: Further Evidence and Explanations', in J. Caldwell et al. (eds.), *What we Know About Health Transition: The Cultural, Social and Behavioural Determinants of Health* (Canberra: Health Transition Centre, Australian National University).

Cleland, J. and J. van Ginneken (1987), 'The Effect of Maternal

Schooling on Childhood Mortality: The Search for an Explanation', paper presented at a Conference on Health Intervention and Mortality Change in Developing Countries, University of Sheffield, September.

Cleland, J. and J. van Ginneken (1988), 'Maternal Education and Child Survival in Developing Countries: The Search for Pathways of Influence', *Social Science and Medicine*, 27 (12).

Das Gupta, Monica (1987), 'Selective Discrimination against Female Children in Rural Punjab', *Population and Development Review*, 13 (1).

—— (1993), 'Fertility Decline in Punjab, India: Parallels with Historical Europe', mimeo, Center for Population and Development Studies, Harvard University.

—— (1994), 'What Motivates Fertility Decline? Lessons from a Case Study of Punjab, India', mimeo, Center for Population and Development Studies, Harvard University.

Das Gupta, Monica and P.N. Mari Bhat (1995), 'Intensified Gender Bias in India: A Consequence of Fertility Decline', Working Paper No. 95.02, Harvard Center for Population and Development Studies.

Dasgupta, Partha (1993), *An Inquiry into Well-being and Destitution* (Oxford: Clarendon Press).

Drèze, Jean and Amartya Sen (1989), *Hunger and Public Action* (Oxford: Oxford University Press).

—— (1995), *India: Economic Development and Social Opportunity* (Oxford and New Delhi: Oxford University Press).

Duvvury, Nata (1989), 'Women in Agriculture: A Review of the Indian Literature', *Economic and Political Weekly*, 28 October.

Dyson, Tim (1988), 'Excess Female Mortality in India: Uncertain Evidence on a Narrowing Differential', in K. Srinivasan and S. Mukerji (eds.), *Dynamics of Population and Family Welfare 1987* (Bombay: Himalaya).

Dyson, Tim and Mick Moore (1983), 'On Kinship Structure, Female Autonomy, and Demographic Behavior in India', *Population and Development Review*, 9 (1).

Gillespie, S.R. and G. McNeill (1992), *Food, Health and Survival in India and Developing Countries* (Delhi: Oxford University Press).

Government of India (1981), *Census of India 1981*, Series 1, Part II–B(i), Primary Census Abstract, General Population (New Delhi: Office of the Registrar General).

Government of India (1982), 'Final Population Totals', *Census of India 1981*, Series 1, Paper 1 of 1982 (New Delhi: Office of the Registrar General).

—— (1981), *Census of India 1981*, Series 1, Paper 2 of 1984 (New Delhi: Office of the Registrar General).

—— (1986), 'Study on Distribution of Infrastructural Facilities in Different Regions and Levels of Urbanization', *Census of India 1981*, Occasional Paper 1 of 1986 (New Delhi: Office of the Registrar General).

—— (1988), 'Child Mortality Estimates of India', *Census of India 1981*, Occasional Paper No. 5 of 1988 (New Delhi: Office of the Registrar General).

—— (1989), 'Child Mortality, Age at Marriage and Fertility in India', *Census of India 1981*, Occasional Paper No. 2 of 1989 (New Delhi: Office of the Registrar General).

—— (1990), *Sample Registration System: Fertility and Mortality Indicators 1988* (New Delhi: Office of the Registrar General).

—— (1993), *Sample Registration System: Fertility and Mortality Indicators 1991* (New Delhi: Office of the Registrar General).

Guio, Anne-Catherine (1994), 'Aspects du Sex Ratio en Inde', M.Sc. thesis (unpublished), Université de Namur, Belgium.

Gulati, S.C. (1992), 'Developmental Determinants of Demographic Variables in India: A District Level Analysis', *Journal of Quantitative Economics*, 8 (1).

Gupta, D.B., A. Basu, and R. Asthana (1993), 'Population Change, Women's Role and Status, and Development in India: A Review', mimeo, Institute of Economic Growth, Delhi University.

Gupta, N., P. Pal, M. Bhargava, and M. Daga (1992), 'Health of Women and Children in Rajasthan', *Economic and Political Weekly*, 17 October.

Harris, Barbara (1990), 'The Intrafamily Distribution of Hunger in South Asia', in Jean Drèze and Amartya Sen (eds.), *The Political Economy of Hunger* (Oxford: Clarendon).

Indian Council of Medical Research (1989), *Evaluation of Quality of Maternal and Child Health and Family Planning Services* (New Delhi: ICMR).

Indian Institute of Management (1985), *Study of Facility Utilization and Programme Management in Family Welfare* (Ahmedabad: Public Systems Group, Indian Institute of Management).

International Institute for Population Sciences (1994), *National Family Health Survey: India 1992–93* (Bombay: IIPS).

Iyengar, Sudarshan and Ashok Bhargava (1987), 'Primary Health Care and Family Welfare Programme in Rural Gujarat', *Economic and Political Weekly*, 4 July.

Jain, A.K. (1985), 'Determinants of Regional Variations in Infant Mortality in Rural India', *Population Studies*, 39 (3).

Jain, A.K. and M. Nag (1985), *'Female Primary Education and Fertility Reduction in India'*, Working Paper No. 114, Center for Policy Studies, Population Council, New York.

—— (1986), 'Importance of Female Primary Education for Fertility Reduction in India', *Economic and Political Weekly*, 6 September.

Jain, L.R., K. Sundaram, and S.D. Tendulkar (1988), 'Dimensions of Rural Poverty: An Inter-regional Profile', *Economic and Political Weekly*, Special Number, November.

Jeffery, P., R. Jeffery, and P. Lyon (1989), *Labour Pains and Labour Power: Women and Child-bearing in India* (London: Zed).

Jesani, Amar (1990), 'Limits of Empowerment: Women in Rural Health Care', *Economic and Political Weekly*, 19 May.

Karkal, M. (1987), 'Differentials in Mortality by Sex', *Economic and Political Weekly*, 8 August.

Karve, Irawati (1965), *Kinship Organisation in India* (Bombay: Asia Publishing House).

Khan, M.E., R. Anker, S.K. Ghosh Dastidar, and S. Bairathi (1989), 'Inequalities between Men and Women in Nutrition and Family Welfare Services: An Indepth Enquiry in an Indian Village', in J.C. Caldwell and G. Santow (eds.), *Selected Readings in the Cultural, Social and Behavioral Determinants of Health*, Health Transition Series no. 1 (Canberra: Health Transition Centre, Australian National University).

Khan, M.E., S.K. Ghosh Dastidar, and R. Singh (1986), 'Nutrition and Health Practices among the Rural Women: A Case Study of Uttar Pradesh', *Journal of Family Welfare*, 33 (1).

Khan, M.E., R.B. Gupta, C.V.S. Prasad, and S.K. Ghosh Dastidar (1988), *Performance of Health and Family Welfare Programme in India* (Bombay: Himalaya Publishing House).

Khan, M.E. and C.V.S. Prasad (1983), *Under-Utilization of Health Services in Rural India: A Comparative Study of Bihar, Gujarat and Karnataka* (Baroda: Operations Research Group).

Khan, M.E., C.V.S. Prasad, and A. Majumdar (1980), *People's Perceptions about Family Planning in India* (New Delhi: Concept).

Khan, M.E., C.V.S. Prasad, and N. Qaiser (1983), 'Reasons for Underutilization of Health Services: Case Study of a PHC in a Tribal

Area of Bihar', paper presented at the ICMR/Ford Foundation Workshop on Child Health, Nutrition and Family Planning.

Khemani, Stuti (1994), 'Neoclassical vs. Nash-bargained Model of Household Fertility: Evidence from Rural India', undergraduate thesis, Department of Economics, Mount Holyoke College, USA.

Kishor, Sunita (1993), ' "May God Give Sons to All": Gender and Child Mortality in India', *American Sociological Review*, 58 (2).

—— (1995), 'Gender Differentials in Child Mortality in India: A Review of Evidence', in M. Das Gupta, T.N. Krishnan, and Lincoln Chen (eds.) (1995), *Women's Health in India: Risk and Vulnerability* (Bombay: Oxford University Press).

Krishnaji, N. (1987), 'Poverty and Sex Ratio: Some Data and Speculations, *Economic and Political Weekly*, 6 June.

Kundu, Amitabh and Mahesh Sahu (1991), 'Variation in Sex Ratio: Development Implications', *Economic and Political Weekly*, 12 October.

Leslie, Joanne (1988), 'Women's Work and Child Nutrition in the Third World', *World Development*, 16 (11).

Leslie, J. and M. Paolisso (eds.) (1989), *Women, Work and Child Welfare in the Third World* (Boulder, CO: Westview).

Mandelbaum, David G. (1988), *Women's Seclusion and Men's Honor: Sex Roles in North India, Bangladesh and Pakistan* (Tucson: University of Arizona Press).

Miller, Barbara (1981), *The Endangered Sex* (Ithaca: Cornell University Press).

—— (1989), 'Changing Patterns of Juvenile Sex Ratios in Rural India, 1961 to 1971', *Economic and Political Weekly*, 3 June.

—— (1993), 'On Poverty, Child Survival and Gender: Models and Misperceptions', *Third World Planning Review*, 15 (3).

Minhas, B.S., L.R. Jain, and S.D. Tendulkar (1991), 'Declining Incidence of Poverty in India in the 1980s', *Economic and Political Weekly*, 6–13 July.

Mull, Dorothy (1991), 'Traditional Perceptions of Marasmus in Pakistan, *Social Science and Medicine*, 32 (2).

Murthi, Mamta, Jean Drèze, and Anne-Catherine Guio (1995), '*Mortality, Fertility and Gender Bias in India: A District Level Analysis*', Discussion Paper 61, Development Economics Research Programme, STICERD, London School of Economics.

Nag, Moni (1989), 'Political Awareness as a Factor in Accessibility of Health Services: A Case Study of Rural Kerala and West Bengal', *Economic and Political Weekly*, 25 February.

Nanda, Amulya Ratna (1992), 'Final Population Totals: Brief Analysis of Primary Census Abstract', Census of India 1991, Series 1, Paper 2 of 1992, Office of the Registrar-General, New Delhi.

Olsen, R.J. (1994), 'Fertility and the Size of the U.S. Labour Force', *Journal of Economic Literature*, 32.

Prakasamma, M. (1989), 'Analysis of Factors Influencing Performance of Auxiliary Nurse Midwives in Nizamabad District', Ph.D. thesis, Centre for Social Medicine and Community Health, Jawaharlal Nehru University, New Delhi.

Priya, Ritu (1990), 'Dubious Package Deal: Health Care in Eighth Plan', *Economic and Political Weekly*, 18 August.

Rajan, S.I., U.S. Mishra, and K. Navaneetham (1991), 'Decline in Sex Ratio: An Alternative Explanation?', *Economic and Political Weekly*, 21 December.

—— (1992), 'Decline in Sex Ratio: Alternative Explanation Revisited, *Economic and Political Weekly*, 14 November.

Raju, S. and M.K. Premi (1992), 'Decline in Sex Ratio: Alternative Explanation Re-examined', *Economic and Political Weekly*, 25 April.

Reddy, K.N. and V. Selvaraju (1993), 'Determinants of Health Status in India: An Empirical Verification', mimeo, National Institute of Public Finance and Policy, New Delhi.

Rosenzweig, Mark (1988), 'Risk, Implicit Contracts and the Family in Rural Areas of Low-income Countries', *Economic Journal*, 98.

—— (1993), 'Women, Insurance Capital, and Economic Development in Rural India', *Journal of Human Resources*, 28 (4).

Rosenzweig, Mark and T. Paul Schultz (1982), 'Market Opportunities, Genetic Endowments, and Intrafamily Resource Distribution: Child Survival in Rural India', *American Economic Review*, 72.

Rosenzweig, Mark and Oded Stark (1989), 'Consumption Smoothing, Migration, and Marriage: Evidence from Rural India', *Journal of Political Economy*, 7.

Satia, J.K. and S.J. Jejeebhoy (eds.) (1991), *The Demographic Challenge: A Study of Four Large Indian States* (Delhi: Oxford University Press).

Schultz, T. Paul (1981), *Economics of Population* (Reading, MA: Addison-Wesley).

—— (1994), 'Sources of Fertility Decline in Modern Economic Growth: Is Aggregate Evidence on Demographic Transition Credible?', mimeo, Yale University.

Sen, A.K. (1976), 'Poverty: An Ordinal Approach to Measurement', *Econometrica*, 44.

Sen, A.K. and S. Sengupta (1983), 'Malnutrition of Children and the Rural Sex Bias', *Economic and Political Weekly*, Annual Number.

Sen, Ilina (1986), 'Geography of Secular Change in Sex Ratio in 1981: How Much Room for Optimism?', *Economic and Political Weekly*, 22 March.

Shah, M.H. (1989), 'Factors Responsible for Low Performance of Family Welfare Programme', in B. Jena and R.N. Pati (eds.) (1989), *Health and Family Welfare Services in India* (New Delhi: Ashish).

Sharma, O.P. and Robert D. Retherford (1990), *'Effect of Female Literacy on Fertility in India'*, Occasional Paper No. 1 of 1990, Office of the Registrar-General, New Delhi.

Simmons, G.B., C. Smucker, S. Bernstein, and E. Jensen (1982), 'Post-Neonatal Mortality in Rural India: Implications of an Economic Model', *Demography*, 19 (3).

Sopher, David (1980a), 'The Geographical Patterning of Culture in India', in Sopher (1980b).

Sopher, David (ed.) (1980b), *An Exploration of India: Geographical Perspectives on Society and Culture* (Ithaca, NY: Cornell University Press).

Srinivas, K. (1991), 'The Demographic Scenario Revealed by the 1991 Census Figures', *Journal of Family Welfare*, 37.

Subbarao, K. and L. Raney (1994), 'Social Gains from Female Education: A Cross National Study', Discussion Paper No. 194, World Bank, Washington, DC.

Thomas, D., J. Strauss, and M.H. Henriques (1991), 'How Does Mother's Education Affect Child Height?', *Journal of Human Resources*, 26.

Tulasidhar, V.B. and J.V.M. Sarma (1993), 'Public Expenditure, Medical Care at Birth and Infant Mortality: A Comparative Study of States in India', in P. Berman and M.E. Khan (eds.) (1993), *Paying for India's Health Care* (New Delhi: Sage).

United Nations (1987), *Fertility Behaviour in the Context of Development: Evidence from the World Fertility Survey* (New York: United Nations).

—— (1993), *Women's Education and Fertility Behaviour: A Case Study of Rural Maharashtra, India* (New York: United Nations).

Venkatachalam, R. and V. Srinivasan (1993), *Female Infanticide* (New Delhi: Har-Anand).

Visaria, Pravin and Leela Visaria (1994), 'Demographic Transition: Accelerating Fertility Decline in the 1980s', *Economic and Political Weekly*, 17–24 December.

Vlassoff, Carol (1980), 'Unmarried Adolescent Females in Rural India:

A Study of the Social Impact of Education', *Journal of Marriage and the Family*, 42 (2).

Ware, H. (1984), 'Effects of Maternal Education, Women's Roles, and Child Care on Child Mortality', in W.H. Mosley and L.C. Chen (eds.), *Child Survival: Strategies for Research* (New York: Population Council).

NAME INDEX

SUBJECT INDEX

accountability 52–9, 82–9
Africa 18–19
agrarian relations
 in Kerala 280–94
 in Uttar Pradesh 37–8, 91–2,
 102–6
 in West Bengal 137–56, 196–
 200
 see also land reform
Andhra Pradesh 31, 35, 183, 191,
 238–42, 360, 378, 392
anthropometric indicators 34, 41,
 238
Assam 183, 260, 360, 375, 378

Bahrain 45
Bahujan Samaj Party 106
Banda 64
Bangla Congress 131
Bangladesh 167, 168
Bihar 42, 44, 173, 183, 187, 191,
 360, 376, 378
Botswana 18
Brahmins
 in Kerala 274–80
 in Uttar Pradesh 64, 96, 104–6,
 107
Brazil 23
Buddhism 14–15

Calcutta 131
capabilities 5–7
caste 62, 84–8, 97–102, 104–6
Chamars 84–5, 87
child labour 80–2
child mortality 39–41, 50, 61–2,
 357–97

China 10–13, 23–5
class 87–91
 and political mobilization
 130–3, 148, 161–2, 196–9
Cochin 16, 209, 252, 273, 286–7,
 300–3, 319, 321
Communist Party of India 134
Communist Party of India
 (Marxist)
 in Kerala 17, 211–12, 313–17
 in West Bengal 131–4, 138–43,
 150–6, 196–200
compulsory education 267–70
Congress Party 17, 246
couple protection rate 227–8
criminalization of politics 108
Cuba 14

decentralization 81, 98–102
democracy 5, 96–100, 155–63
 see also Panchayati Raj Institutions
demographic indicators 13, 357–97
 in Kerala 3, 7, 13, 224–33
 in South India 38–41
 in Uttar Pradesh 11,13, 38–41
 in West Bengal 184–91
 regional contrasts 38–41
demographic transition 359–60

East Asia 19–23
East India Company 209
economic growth 4–7, 19–23,
 102–9
 and demographic change 359–
 60
 in Kerala 4, 212–24